APPLYING EDUCATIONAL RESEARCH

APPLYING EDUCATIONAL RESEARCH
A PRACTICAL GUIDE FOR TEACHERS

SECOND EDITION

Walter R. Borg

Longman
New York & London

Senior Editor: Naomi Silverman
Production Editor: Halley Gatenby
Text Design: Angela Foote
Cover Design: Joseph DePinho
Text Art: J & R Services, Inc.
Production Supervisor: Judith Stern
Compositor: TC Systems
Printer and Binder: Interstate Book Manufacturers

Applying Educational Research, Second Edition

Copyright © 1987 by Longman Inc.

All rights reserved. No part of this publication may be reproduced, stored
in a retrieval system, or transmitted in any form or by any means, electronic,
mechanical, photocopying, recording, or otherwise, without the prior permission
of the publisher.

Longman Inc.
95 Church Street
White Plains, N.Y. 10601

Associated companies:
Longman Group Ltd., London
Longman Cheshire Pty., Melbourne
Longman Paul Pty., Auckland
Copp Clark Pitman, Toronto
Pitman Publishing Inc., New York

Library of Congress Cataloging-in-Publication Data

Borg, Walter R.
   Applying educational research.
   Includes bibliographical references and index.
   1. Education—Research—Handbooks, manuals, etc.
l. Title
LB1028.B59 1987   370'.7'8   86-15382
ISBN 0-582-28673-5

87 88 89 90 9 8 7 6 5 4 3

To Marie

CONTENTS

PART 2
EVALUATING RESEARCH EVIDENCE   79

CHAPTER 5
EVALUATING RESEARCH REPORTS   81

CHAPTER 6
EDUCATIONAL MEASURES   106

CHAPTER 7
STATISTICAL TOOLS: WHY DO WE USE
THEM AND WHAT DO THEY MEAN?   138

PART 3
KINDS OF EDUCATIONAL RESEARCH 151

CHAPTER 1

EDUCATIONAL RESEARCH AS A TOOL IN IMPROVING EDUCATION AND MAKING EDUCATIONAL DECISIONS

Overview

The main goal of the book, to make the reader an intelligent consumer of educational research, is discussed. To achieve this goal the learner must develop skills in locating research relevant to a given problem and must also be able to evaluate research reports and interpret research findings. The contribution of each chapter to these skills is described.

This book helps prepare the learner to make educational decisions based upon educational research literature and action research. These two approaches are compared with personal experience and expert advice, which form the basis for most educational decisions. A few key terms related to educational research are then defined, and the main types of educational research are briefly described in order to help students fit what they learn into a broad context. Finally, suggestions are made for studying this book.

Objectives

1. State the main goal of this book and describe the skills that must be mastered to achieve this goal.
2. Discuss the pros and cons of personal experience, expert advise, review of educational research literature, and action research as aids in making educational decisions.
3. Define 12 important terms used in educational research.
4. Briefly describe the main types of educational research.
5. Describe a strategy that can be used in studying this book.

The Scope of This Book

This book is written primarily for the master's degree student in education who will not write a thesis and for teachers and administrators in the public schools. Our aim is not to train you to be an educational researcher. Instead, our main goal is to help you to evaluate and interpret educational research and apply the results to educational practice. A vast body of information and ideas is contained in the educational research literature. In fact, useful information relevant to virtually any practical problem or question related to education can be found. If you can locate and interpret research information related to the educational problems that arise in your work, this information can give you new insights into your problems and can help you to make intelligent decisions.

Unfortunately, the useful information that has emerged from educational research is difficult to locate and even more difficult to interpret and relate to the practical problems that teachers and school administrators must address. Although we have little objective information about the degree to which teachers use research in decision making, what evidence exists suggests that little use is made of such data. For example, 87.5 percent of the in-service teachers surveyed by Reys and Yeager (1974) reported that they seldom or never read research articles. Shaver points out that many people ignore research results in areas such as the link of smoking to lung cancer and of the nonuse of seat belts to injury in auto accidents (Shaver, 1982). He asks why teachers should be different in their inattention to research. One answer is that because teachers belong to a profession, they should seek any relevant information that will help them advance in their profession and do their jobs better. In general, physicians do not ignore medical research, and mechanical engineers do not ignore the results of research on the properties of metals and other materials they use to design and build new machines.

Although many applied sciences such as medicine and engineering traditionally seek research evidence as a means of decision making, the tradition in education has been otherwise. Thus, if you want to benefit from the findings of educational research, you must not only go against the tide but must also develop needed skills to use research in your teaching. One skill you must master is locating sources.

In recent years the computer has been harnessed to the task of locating sources that relate to a given educational problem. The use of computer searches of educational literature has eliminated most of the drudgery involved in manual procedures that were necessary in the past. However, the computer is no more efficient than the search plan that is entered into the terminal. Thus, to use the computer effectively, you must learn how to develop a search plan and express this plan in terms that the computer can understand and respond to. In Chapters 2, 3, and 4 you will learn how to define your problem, locate relevant sources in the educational research literature, make notes on the sources you have found, and write your review.

Once you have located books, articles, and reports that relate to your problem or question, you are faced with a difficult task. You must read these sources, determine how much confidence you can place in the findings, and decide how to apply these findings to your own problem or question. Your ability to interpret educational research information is closely related to your understanding of the research process. One of the reasons that research findings have not been used more extensively in making educational decisions is that few educational practitioners know enough about the research process to interpret the typical research report. Educational researchers have reported their findings mainly for the benefit of other researchers and often have given little attention to the application of their findings to practical educational problems. The result has been a serious lack of communication between the researcher and the practitioner.

In a few educational areas teachers and researchers have already worked on the problem of using research findings and applying them to practical school problems. For example, Alan Bell (1983) describes how research on understanding mathematics can be applied to mathematics teaching.[1] Articles like this can be very useful, since they make the connection between research and practice that you, the teacher, must make for articles that report research findings but do not tell how these findings can fit into your classroom needs. Unfortunately, articles on how to use research in practice are not always available, so that in order to make the best use of research, the teacher must develop the necessary skills and knowledge to apply research to practical school problems.

Since a knowledge of the research process is needed to interpret educational research, one solution to the communication breakdown between researcher and practitioner is to help the practitioner gain the knowledge she needs.[2] For example, if a researcher selects her sample of students entirely from schools serving middle-class children, the teacher who wants to apply research results must be aware that the sample is biased in favor of middle-class students and must be able to interpret these results in terms of her own students, who may come predominantly from the working class.

But a thorough knowledge of the research process requires a great deal more work and study than most teachers have the time and interest to complete. Therefore, in this book we have tried to give you the *minimum essentials* about the educational research process that you need in order to use research to help you in making better educational decisions. This approach is, of course, a compromise. You will not learn enough about the research process to make many of the very complex and sophisticated interpretations of research findings that an experienced educational researcher could make. But, we believe we can help you build enough understanding of this process to make reasonably valid interpretations of most of the research reports you read. Chapters 5, 6, and 7 are aimed at giving you this foundation. In Chapter 5, you will learn to evaluate the introductory section of a research report and identify possible sources of bias. You will also learn how to evaluate the researcher's objectives and hypotheses and will learn something about research procedures.

All research involves measurement, and the validity of research results is determined to a great degree by the accuracy of the measures that the researcher employs. Therefore, in order to interpret educational research and apply the findings to practical school problems you must have a basic understanding of educational

1. Several articles on research use are given in the Recommended Reading for this chapter.
2. Since both men and women work as educational researchers and practitioners it is appropriate to use both male and female pronouns in this book. The author regards combinations such as he/she or him/her as cumbersome and has avoided them. He also has rejected using plurals such as "they" or "them" in places where singular pronouns are more appropriate. Therefore, when not referring to a specific person, we have decided to use female pronouns in the odd-numbered chapters and male pronouns in the even-numbered chapters.

measurement. Chapter 6 describes the use of paper-and-pencil tests, question-naires, interviews, and direct observations as measures in educational research. If you have taken a course in educational measurement, much of Chapter 6 will be a review for you. If not, Chapter 6 will give you the minimum foundation you need to understand the role of educational measures in research.

Researchers use statistics to measure relationships or differences between the groups they are studying and help draw inferences about the populations from which the researcher's subjects were drawn. Most educational researchers have had con-siderable training in statistics, and most of the research reports that you will read use statistical procedures to test the researcher's hypotheses. The problem we faced in writing Chapter 7 was to devise a way to give you enough understanding of statistics to help you interpret the findings of research reports without burdening you with the mathematics that must be learned in order to carry out a statistical analysis. Our attempted solution has been to give you a very simple introduction to some of the concepts underlying statistical theory and then list in alphabetical order a few of the widely used statistical procedures and describe each in brief, nontechnical language. The information in Chapter 7 will surely not make you into a statistician, but we hope in most cases it will give you some insight into how the researcher analyzed her results, why the selected statistical tool was used, and what the results mean. Of course, if you have a background in mathematics, you may not be satisfied with our brief treatment of statistics. In this case, we urge you to obtain and read an introduc-tory text in educational statistics. This will better prepare you to interpret the statistical information given in research articles.

Once you have gained a basic understanding of the educational research process, the next step is to read research articles and try to apply what you have learned to the evaluation and interpretation of these articles. Chapters 8, 9, and 10 are designed to introduce you to several different kinds of research and give you some practice in reviewing research reports. We have selected only articles that are good examples of educational research. Moreover, the articles deal with topics that are of interest to most teachers and report findings that can be applied in many practical educational situations.

The educational research literature contains some information that is relevant to most practical educational questions for which you may seek answers. However, you will encounter many problems where the information you find by searching the literature will not provide sufficient guidance for making a decision. For example, suppose you were assigned the task of selecting a new general science textbook for use in Grade 7 in a large school district. Of the books available, there may be one or two new ones that have not been evaluated by researchers or science specialists. If one of these new books looks promising, you may feel that you need information about the book's effectiveness before making a decision. In situations like this you may decide to carry out an action research project to get more data upon which to base your decision. Action research, although using many of the same procedures as other kinds of educational research, is simpler and easier to conduct. While most educational research seeks to discover knowledge that can be applied to a broad range of educational situations, action research aims at gathering evidence that relates to a specific local problem. Therefore, in action research the selection of an appropriate sample is less likely to be a problem, a smaller number of subjects can often be used, and only the simplest kinds of statistical analysis are needed. In effect, action research provides the teacher and administrator with a way to apply the scientific method to the solution of local educational problems. In Chapter 11 you will learn the essentials that you will need to carry out action research. This chapter describes a few of the simplest research designs and also discusses sampling, measurement, and analysis procedures that are appropriate for action research projects.

The Author's Assumptions

In this book we have tried to provide you with the *minimum* skills you will need to locate and evaluate educational research reports related to a given problem and to conduct action research. We have made certain assumptions in writing the book. Among them are the following:

1. Most readers are or will become teachers or school administrators and are not interested in becoming educational researchers.
2. Most readers will have had little or no previous instruction in research methods, educational measurement, and statistics.
3. The minimum skills needed to use educational research literature and action research as aids to decision making can be learned without extensive training in research methodology, measurement, and statistics.

To achieve our goal, we have cut away all but the bare essentials of research methods, statistics, and measurement. This means that there is virtually nothing in this book that is not important to achieving the goal of becoming an intelligent consumer of educational research literature. Thus, thorough and careful study of this book is necessary.

Ways of Making Educational Decisions

Since many teachers and administrators have been getting along in their jobs for years without ever having read the educational research literature or conducted an action research project, you may wonder why we recommend these approaches to decision making. In today's schools, most educational decisions are probably based on personal experience. Expert judgment is also widely used. Searches of the research literature and action research seem to be used much less often. Let's consider the pros and cons of these four decision-making approaches.

Most people find personal experience to be an attractive basis for making decisions. We are generally more comfortable with approaches we have tried ourselves as opposed to those that have been successful for others. Using personal experience as a basis for making decisions has the advantage of being quick and easy. When a decision must be made immediately, personal experience is often the only approach open to us. Also, many minor day-to-day educational decisions are too unimportant to justify the more rigorous and time-consuming methods such as searching the research literature or conducting an action research project. However, personal experience has several serious flaws as a basis for making important decisions. First, we accumulate personal experience in a very haphazard fashion. In educational situations, there is no reason to assume that the children we teach or the situations in which we teach them are representative. Thus, personal experience with unique groups of students may suggest problem solutions that will be totally ineffective with other groups of students. For example, in the late 1950s after the Soviet Union had launched *Sputnik* there was a great clamor to improve the American high school science curriculum. University professors in areas such as chemistry and physics developed new curriculums based on their university experience. In most high schools these curriculums failed because they were too difficult for all but the brightest students. Personal experience in university teaching had not proven to be a good basis for deciding what to include in high school science courses.

Another weakness of personal experience is that it is subject to errors in recall. Often our memory of past experience is faulty. If we are committed to a given approach or strategy, we are more likely to remember incidents when the approach was successful than those when it failed. Also, we often overlook the fact that an approach or problem solution that we have used, such as a method of dealing with pupil misbehavior, may work for some teachers and some students but not for others. Finally, decision making based upon personal experience ignores the knowledge and experience accumulated by others. A basic rule in decision making is that the more relevant information the decision maker has, the more likely she is to make a sound decision.

Expert opinion is a better basis for decision making, but it still has some serious limitations. The expert usually combines her personal experience with knowledge of some of the experience and research of others. The expert's interpretation of the work of others is almost always influenced by her own experience, and in some cases the expert only refers to the work of others when this work agrees with her own preconceived notions. In effect the expert functions as a broker between her client and other researchers and scholars who have contributed ideas and knowledge related to the problem in question. In some cases this is very helpful, since the expert is usually better able than the practitioner to weigh and interpret the relevant evidence. However, in cases where the expert is committed to a given solution or where her experience has been gained in settings that are substantially different from the local situation, her advice may not lead to a sound decision.

Once the practitioner has gained the skills necessary to read and evaluate research and professional literature, she can probably get better information by going directly to the relevant research sources, rather than seeking the help of an expert. The practitioner has the advantage of knowing the local situation better than does the expert. Also, when a teacher or administrator evaluates the research herself, she can be confident that all relevant information has been reviewed. If the practitioner conducts her search with an open mind, the danger of omitting or distorting a particular point of view is much less than if she seeks the advise of an expert. In most cases, a literature search for information related to a well-defined local problem will produce information that is more recent and more relevant than one is likely to obtain from an expert. Also, by searching the literature herself, the teacher or administrator will achieve a depth of understanding of the problem that can rarely be gained by seeking expert advice. The disadvantage of searching the literature for yourself is that a careful search involves some hard work. However, if this work produces a better solution to an important problem in your classroom, school, or district, your time has been well spent.

If a literature search does not produce a satisfactory solution to your problem, you should consider carrying out an action research project. The teacher or administrator is concerned with a specific answer to a local question and is usually not interested in generalizing the findings to broad national populations. Therefore, her action research sample need only be representative of the local population of students to whom the results will be applied. Similarly, since the practitioner is more interested in the *practical* significance of the findings rather than the *statistical* significance, most action research projects can be analyzed using the simplest statistical procedures. In fact, many action research projects need no statistical analysis at all to serve their purpose as an aid to decision making.

Action research is a far better basis for decision making than personal experience. Most of the discoveries and progress made by Western civilization during the past 200 years have been achieved by using the scientific method to attack our problems and questions. Action research employs the scientific method to attack the problems of the educational practitioner. Scientific method is a very powerful tool, which teachers and administrators should use whenever they are called upon to make important educational decisions.

Some Terms You Should Know

Before you proceed, there are a few important terms related to research that you should understand. You will probably not remember these definitions until you have encountered the terms several times in your reading. Therefore, we suggest that you review these definitions occasionally when reading later chapters. Other terms will be defined when they are first used.

Subject An individual who is studied in a research project. In educational research the subjects are usually students or teachers, but in other fields, such as experimental psychology, the subjects often are animals such as rats or pigeons. Subjects in educational research may also be called cases, clients, students, or pupils.

Variable Anything in the research situation that varies. For example, tests measure characteristics that vary from subject to subject such as IQ, reading achievement, or anxiety, all of which are called variables. Height, weight, time of day, teacher enthusiasm, study habits, algebra aptitude, light intensity, diet, ethnic background, popularity, and delinquent behavior are examples of a few of the variables that have been studied in educational research. Several kinds of variables are defined later in this list.

Dependent Variable/Independent Variable In research, the *dependent variable* is the variable that the researcher is trying to change in the research. The *independent variable* is the variable to which different subjects are exposed to different degrees or the variable on which the groups of subjects to be compared are different. It is the variable that is expected to bring about or account for a difference or a change in the dependent variable. For example, suppose that the researcher wants to study the effect of teacher praise on pupil achievement. She could select 50 teachers and randomly assign them to two groups. Teachers in the experimental group would be trained to use a large number of praise statements, while teachers in the control group would be trained to use no praise statements. After six months, pupils in all 50 classrooms would be given an achievement test to see if teacher praise affected pupil achievement. In this example, pupil achievement is the dependent variable, and teacher praise is the independent variable. Depending on the nature of the research, the independent variable may be virtually any characteristic the investigator chooses to study. Differences in the independent variable can be achieved either by selecting subjects that differ in that variable or by exposing subjects to different treatments that make them different. For example, in studies comparing the achievement of boys and girls, sex is the independent variable, and it is obviously manipulated by selection. On the other hand, teacher praise was manipulated by exposing teachers to different treatments.

Experimental Group/Control Group In educational research, subjects are often placed in experimental groups and control groups. The *experimental group* consists of subjects who are given the treatment, that is the program or experience the researcher wants to study. The *control group* consists of subjects who are not given the treatment in research. For example, a researcher who wanted to test the effects of a new drug on pain would divide her subjects into two groups, experimental and control. The experimental group would be given pills containing the drug being studied while the control group would receive either a pill made of sugar or flour (or some other substance known to have no effect on pain) or nothing. The purpose of the control group is to control for extraneous variables that could affect the subjects' response but have nothing to do with the new drug.

The purpose of the experimental group is to measure the effect of the treatment (or independent variable) upon the dependent variable. In our example, we would measure the effect of the drug upon pain reported by the subjects. In effect, we subtract the pain relief reported by the control group from the pain relief reported by the experimental group to estimate the effect of the drug. Without a control group we would be unable to estimate how much of the pain relief reported by the experimental group was due to the drug and how much was due to extraneous variables.

Population/Sample The *population* is the defined group to which the researcher plans to apply her research results. The researcher selects her *sample* from the population. For example, suppose the researcher wants to study the attitudes toward school of Chicano children in Grades 4, 5, and 6 in the public schools in Texas, Arizona, and New Mexico. All children fitting into this group would be the population. Her sample would be the children she actually selects to participate in the study, probably not more than two or three hundred out of a population of thousands.

Generalizability The degree to which we can generalize the results of a research study to the population from which the researcher's sample was drawn. If the researcher randomly selects a large sample from the population, then her results can be generalized within small limits of error to other samples drawn from the same population. However, in most educational studies random samples cannot be obtained. When samples are not random, the possibility of biases (that is, systematic differences between subjects in the sample and those in the population) may occur. These limit the confidence we have in generalizing the research results to the population.

Hypothesis When a researcher plans a research project, she usually makes a statement that describes how she expects her research to come out, that is, what differences or relationships she expects to find. This statement is called a hypothesis. The purpose of much educational research is to test the reseacher's hypothesis; that is, determine whether the expected relationship is present or absent.

Statistically Significant When the researcher analyzes the results of her research, she determines by using statistical procedures whether the difference or relationship she found is large enough to be likely to occur again if the study were repeated using other samples from the same population. If the level of significance meets or exceeds the level selected by the researcher before conducting the research, then it is concluded that the difference or relationship is statistically significant. The researcher usually selects the 0.01 or 0.05 level of significant to test her hypothesis. If either of these levels is reached the researcher may be confident that similar results would probably be obtained if the study were repeated using other samples drawn from the same population.[3]

Extraneous Variable A variable that influences the results of a research project but has nothing to do with the experimental treatment. For example, suppose we are studying the effect of high and low levels of teacher enthusiasm (the independent variable) upon pupil attention (the dependent variable). It may be that extraneous variables such as time of day and level of outside noise would have an effect on pupil attention if they were not controlled. These extraneous variables could change the apparent effects of teacher enthusiasm on pupil attention. Much of what researchers do in designing their studies is aimed at eliminating or controlling extraneous variables.

Types of Educational Research

This book will introduce you to a body of knowledge related to educational research, about which you probably have had little previous learning or experience. When confronted with a new field of learning, most students learn more effectively if they have at the start an overall framework into which they can fit what they learn. To help you place what you learn from this book into a meaningful context, we will now give you a brief overview of some of the kinds of educational research you will be studying later. Study carefully the overall picture given in the next few pages, and

---

3. This is a nontechnical definition that will be sufficient to interpret research at the level of this book.

you will find the ideas and information in the remainder of the book easier to learn and remember.

DESCRIPTIVE RESEARCH

One of the first steps in any science is to describe objectively the subjects with which the science is concerned. It is difficult to move on to the study of complex relationships unless we first collect the basic descriptive information needed to understand the nature of our subject. Education is no exception to this rule, and you will find that much educational research is aimed at describing the characteristics of students, teachers, and the educational environment. For example, it was necessary to carry out research aimed at giving us an objective description of children with Down's syndrome before we could move on to studies concerned with the most effective methods of teaching these children.

As part of your introduction to descriptive research we will give you some information about research employing questionnaires, interviews, and direct observations—all well-established ways of collecting descriptive data.

Survey Research.   Survey research typically employs questionnaires and interviews in order to determine the characteristics, opinions, attitudes, preferences, and perceptions of persons of interest to the researcher. Perhaps the best-known surveys are those carried out by the various public-opinion polls. Surveys in education can be used to explore a very wide range of topics such as the extent to which open classrooms are being used at the elementary level and the perceptions of teachers and principals about the effectiveness of such classrooms, the related work experience of high school shop teachers, the preferences of school superintendents regarding different forms of federal aid to education, procedures currently being used to help handicapped children adjust to regular classrooms, and the classroom management problems encountered by first-year elementary teachers.

Survey studies that deal with sensitive topics, such as premarital sex relations, or that attempt to elicit deeper and more complex responses than can be easily measured with questionnaires frequently employ interviews. Some survey studies employ a combination of questionnaires and interviews; the questionnaires are employed to collect basic descriptive information from a broad sample, and the interviews are used to follow up the questionnaire responses in depth for a smaller sample.

Observational Research.   Direct observation is essentially a technique for gathering data about the subjects involved in a study. Therefore, it is basically a measurement technique that can be employed in most kinds of educational research. In this book we deal with observational research under descriptive research since it is an extremely effective way of gathering many kinds of descriptive information. For example, if we are interested in studying the interactions between abused children and other children in first grade classrooms, direct systematic observation will probably provide more valid data than any other descriptive research methodology. As you can see from this example, the great advantage of the observational process is that it enables the researcher to collect direct information about human behavior that can be collected only indirectly by other measurement techniques such as paper-and-pencil tests. To give another example, we can probably learn much more about interracial attitudes by observing children of different races in their interactions with one another than we can by asking questions about racial interactions on a paper-and-pencil test.

Observational research is especially effective in situations where the researcher wishes to study specific areas of human behavior in detail. For example, the following questions are well suited for study by observational research: What specific teaching strategy is most effective to teach basic number facts to severely retarded children? How do preschool children respond to a television program that contains a high number of violent acts? What specific counseling procedures are most highly related to realistic vocational decisions by high school students?

Systematic observations as used in research, however, are far different from the casual or unsystematic observations that are a part of daily living. Observational research must be designed in such a way that observers do not have the kinds of knowledge about the subjects that are likely to bias their perceptions. Other errors in observational research that are likely to reduce its validity include using broad, general definitions of the behavior to be observed rather than narrow, specific definitions, using subjective procedures rather than objective procedures for recording the observational data, and requiring that the observer record more aspects of behavior than can be attended to effectively.

In order to collect reliable observational data, it is usually necessary to train observers in the observation process. Such training, along with information on the reliability of the observation data, is included in most good observational studies.

CAUSAL-COMPARATIVE RESEARCH

In education as well as other behavioral sciences such as psychology and sociology, we often wish to compare two groups of individuals who differ in some important characteristic in order to identify possible causes for the phenomenon in which we are interested. For example, suppose we are interested in the possible causes leading some students with high IQs to drop out of high school. Using the causal-comparative research method, we could identify two groups of individuals with high IQs, one made up of dropouts and the other consisting of students who successfully completed high school. We could then gather observational and test data on these subjects that would permit a comparison of the two groups on variables that we believe might relate to dropping out. These might include such things as home environment, peer acceptance, and self-concept. Comparing the two groups on these variables might help us identify possible causes for dropping out. This knowledge could then be used to identify potential dropouts and help them make adjustments that would reduce the likelihood that they would drop out.

You will note that causal-comparative research is very useful in studying independent variables that cannot be manipulated in an experiment such as causes of juvenile delinquency, effects of brain damage on human performance, or effects of broken homes on the social adjustment of children. However, since causal-comparative research is conducted after the fact, that is, *after* subjects have become delinquent or suffered brain damage, we can only explore *possible* causes and effects with this kind of research.

CORRELATIONAL RESEARCH

One of the goals of science is to seek relationships between variables related to the science in question. Correlational research is a useful approach to the study of relationships between educational variables. Correlational research involves the computation of one or more correlation coefficients. The *correlation coefficient* is a statistical tool that permits us to compare the scores of a group of subjects on two variables and obtain a numerical estimate of the magnitude of the relationship between these variables. Learning about such relationships helps us gain a better understanding of the variables. For example, a study could be conducted in which we would correlate the use of various study techniques by a sample of high school students with their academic achievement. The results might show that some of the study techniques are much more closely related to achievement than others. This information could then be used to develop a program to train students to use more effective study methods. It could also improve our understanding of how students learn.

An important advantage of correlational research is that by learning the relationships between a complex phenomenon such as teaching ability and simpler variables such as teacher enthusiasm, explaining skills, and use of verbal praise, we can gradually gain a better understanding of the complex phenomenon. In effect we can begin to separate teaching ability into a number of specific components. This is somewhat analogous to learning about a cake by determining what ingredients have gone into it.

Correlational research is also used to help us make predictions. For example, if we find a correlation between the grade point average (GPA) of college seniors and scores they obtained on the Scholastic Aptitude Test (SAT) taken before starting college, we can use this information to predict the grade point averages that future students are likely to earn, based upon their SAT scores. Such predictions are, of course, subject to error but in many cases are sufficiently accurate to make rough estimates of an individual's future performance.

EXPERIMENTAL AND QUASI-EXPERIMENTAL RESEARCH

When college students think of research, they usually tend to think of experiments. Most of us have read about classic experiments in the physical sciences, and many of us have repeated such experiments in high school chemistry and physics laboratories. Although education and the other behavioral sciences are far less advanced than the physical sciences, experiments can be carried out in education and have contributed significantly to the advances we have made in knowledge about such education-related areas as human learning, motivation, and effective teaching.

In the simplest form of experiment we hypothesize that a particular kind of experience, called an *experimental treatment,* will bring about changes in the behavior of the experimental group subjects, that is, those who undergo the experience. You will recall that the experimental treatment is one form of independent variable, while the specific behavior we seek to change by the experimental treatment is called the dependent variable. Other subjects serve as a control group and are not given the experimental treatment, but are measured on the dependent variable. A comparison of the performance of the experimental and control subjects on the dependent variable then permits us to estimate the effect of the experimental treatment.

For example, suppose we want to determine the effect of monetary rewards (the independent variable) upon the algebra achievement (dependent variable) of ninth-grade students who have low mathematical aptitude. To carry out an experiment we would first identify a sample of ninth-grade students with low mathematics aptitude who were scheduled to take algebra. We would randomly assign half of these students to the experimental group and half to the control group. Students in the experimental classrooms would be given monetary rewards for successfully completing homework assignments, passing tests, and giving correct answers in class. The control-group students would be given the same algebra course except that they would receive no monetary rewards. At the end of the term, all students would be given the same algebra achievement test, and scores of the experimental and control subjects would be compared to determine the effects of monetary rewards on algebra achievement.

The two essential requirements for experimental research are (1) subjects be *randomly* assigned to the experimental and control groups, and (2) the experimental group be given a treatment that is withheld from the control group.

In many of the studies carried out in schools, an experimental treatment can be employed, but the school authorities will not permit the researcher to assign students randomly to the experimental and control groups. Thus, students must be assigned to these groups on some nonrandom basis. For example, Mr. Smith's second-period class is designated the experimental group, and Mrs. Johnson's third-period class is designated the control group.

Studies that are essentially experimental in nature where it is not possible to assign subjects randomly to the experimental and control groups are called *quasi-experimental* research.

ACTION RESEARCH

Action research involves the application of the steps of the scientific method to classroom problems. Although it is similar in some respects to regular educational research, action research differs principally in the extent to which findings can be generalized beyond a local school situation. Educational research usually involves a large number of cases in order to help reduce some of the random errors that occur in small samples. It involves establishing as much control as possible, consistent with the research goals, over such variables as teaching ability, pupil IQ, and socioeconomic status. Perhaps most important, regular educational research involves more precise sampling techniques than are found in action research. Many action research projects are carried out in a single classroom by a single teacher; others are carried on by all teachers in a school or even a school district. As action research projects become more extensive, they become more similar to other types of educational research. The emphasis in action research, however, is not on obtaining generalizable scientific knowledge about educational problems, but on obtaining knowledge concerning a specific local problem.

The results of an action research project by a single teacher have important implications for this teacher, but because of the few cases, lack of control, and absence of sampling techniques, one must be very cautious in generalizing the results to other classrooms. The principal advantage of action research is that it provides the teacher or administrator in the field with objective, systematic techniques of problem solving that are far superior to an appeal to authority or reliance on personal experience, which so often guide decisions in education.

A Study Strategy

Let's briefly discuss a strategy that many students find effective for studying books of this sort:

1. Read the Overview and Objectives. Each chapter begins with a brief overview and a list of objectives. Both are intended to give you an idea of the scope of the chapter and to help you focus on the main concepts that you should learn. The objectives are stated in the same order that they are covered in the body of the chapter. You will find that some objectives are concerned with understanding important concepts—these usually require that you state the concept and describe or explain it. Other objectives call for applying what you have learned—these usually state the conditions under which you should be able to apply the concept. Both are important. It is a good idea to read the objectives slowly and think about each one after you read it. If you pause and think about each objective for 20 to 30 seconds, you will remember them much longer than if you merely read them and go on. Some students find it helpful to read the objectives two or three times, so that they have them firmly in mind before they start reading the body of the chapter.

2. Read the Body of the Chapter. As you read the chapter, try to locate the main ideas related to each objective. Use a red pen to underline main concepts. Avoid underlining too much. Most of the content explains or discusses the main ideas, or gives examples that are designed to help you place these ideas into a meaningful context. Once you understand a concept, you can state or explain it in a variety of contexts. Thus, the concept itself is all you need to remember. For most of the content you will find you can cover the important ideas by underlining 10 to 20 percent of the text.

3. Check Your Mastery. After you finish reading the chapter, go back to the objectives and see if you can state the concepts or carry out the activities as described in each objective. If you find any objectives that you have not mastered, reread the sections related to that objective that you have underlined and then check yourself again.

4. Complete the Application Problems. Most chapters have application objectives as well as concept mastery objectives. A good way to increase your skill and check your achievement of the application objectives is to complete the Application Problems given in these chapters. After you complete the application problems, check your answers against the model answers given in the back of the book.

5. Review Previous Chapters. As you progress through the book, review the objectives and the material you have underlined in previous chapters before starting to read a new chapter. You will find that each chapter builds on what you have learned in the previous chapters. If you are to become skillful in locating and interpreting educational research, you cannot afford to forget the main concepts in the early chapters when you study the later chapters.

6. Prepare for Tests. If you follow this strategy, you will find it easy to prepare for tests. Reread the objectives and underlined material once or twice and you should be ready. However, you can prepare even better if you work with a classmate as a last step in your study sequence. Go through your underlined material for the first chapter to be covered on the test and ask your classmate questions. Check her answers and add any ideas that she omitted. For the next chapter, reverse roles and have her ask questions on the concepts she has underlined. By the way, this is also a good strategy for getting to know some of your classmates.

References

BELL, A. W. (1983). The design of teaching using research on understanding. *International Reviews on Mathematical Education, 15*(2), 83–89.

REYS, R. E., & YEAGER, T. (1974). Elementary teachers and research in mathematics education. *School Science and Mathematics, 74*(5), 431–436.

SHAVER, J. (1982, November). *Making research useful to teachers.* Presented at the annual meeting of the National Council for the Social Studies, Boston, Mass.

Recommended Reading

EAKER, R. E., & HUFFMAN, J. O. (1981). *Teacher perceptions of dissemination of research on teaching findings.* East Lansing, Mich. Michigan State University, Institute for Research and Teaching. (ED 205 501)[4]

This questionnaire survey examines the perception of 105 teachers of the use of educational research findings as a resource for instructional improvement. The results generally indicate that teachers believe that research findings have practical classroom applications.

A review of the responses given to 40 questionnaire items provides some useful insights into teacher perceptions and attitudes about educational research.

GAGE, N. L. (1978). *The scientific basis of the art of teaching.* New York: Teachers College Press.

This small book is an excellent source for the teacher who wants to learn about research related to teaching. It also discusses in a very readable fashion many important research issues that give the reader perspectives into teaching research that can hardly be found elsewhere.

4. This number indicates that the reference is available in *Resources in Education (RIE)*. Most college libraries have microfiche copies of all *RIE* documents.

MAXIM, G. W. (1977). Effects of two instructional treatments on ability to interpret research. *Improving College and University Teaching, 25*(2) 108–109, 111.

This study was designed to determine the effectiveness of a structured instructional approach versus an inquiry based instructional approach in training teachers to interpret educational research findings. Both approaches were found effective with no significant difference between them in teacher learning gains. (This text employs both approaches.)

ROSNOW, R. L., & ROSENTHAL, R. *Understanding behavioral science: Research methods for research consumers.* New York: McGraw-Hill, 1984.

This small book is an excellent supplement to your text. The sections on the nature of behavioral research and the limits of behavioral research are especially recommended for the teachers who wants to gain more depth of understanding of the research process in the behavioral sciences.

SLAVIN, R. E. (1981). A case study of psychological research affecting classroom practice: Student Team Learning. *Elementary School Journal, 82*(1), 5–17.

The author describes the research foundation upon which the Student Team Learning (STL) program was based. He then reviews the development of STL and dissemination of these methods to the public schools. He discusses five conditions that must be met in order for psychologically based educational programs to be widely implemented in the schools.

This article gives the reader insight into the problems of translating research findings into classroom materials and strategies that teachers can use.

TRAVERS, R. M. W. (1983). *How research has changed American schools.* Kalamazoo, Mich.: Mythas Press.

Useful to the student who wants to gain a long-range perspective of the impact of research on American education. For the most part, the book is organized by major research areas such as the Psychology of School Subjects and by the work of important early researchers such as Judd and Thorndike. In general Travers's treatment of early research in education is the best part of the book.

ARTICLES ON RESEARCH UTILIZATION

The following articles are examples of the kind of information you can find in the educational literature to help you utilize research results in your teaching.

BELL, A. W. (1983). The design of teaching using research on understanding. *International Reviews on Mathematical Education, 15*(2), 83–89.

CAMPBELL, P. F. (1984). Using a problem-solving approach in the primary grades. *Arithmetic Teacher, 32*(4), 11–14.

DRISCOLL, M. J. (1980). *Research within reach: Elementary school mathematics.* St. Louis, Mo.: CEMREL, Inc. (ED 202 738)

GROTBERG, E. H., & FOWLER, A. (1981, April). *Users' manual for research: Translating Head Start findings into action (Expanded notebook version).* Washington, D.C.: Administration for Children, Youth, and Families. (ED 213 514).

LAY, N. (1979). Practical application of selected motor learning research. *Journal of Physical Education and Recreation, 50*(7), 78–79.

ZAMEL, V. (1976). Teaching composition in the ESL classroom: What we can learn from research in the teaching of English. *TESOL Quarterly, 10*(1), 67–76.

PART 1
SOURCES OF EDUCATIONAL INFORMATION

CHAPTER 2

LOCATING EDUCATIONAL INFORMATION

Overview

This chapter discusses the first five steps you should take in reviewing the educational literature for material related to your problem or question. These include defining your problem, reviewing secondary sources, selecting the most appropriate preliminary sources, translating your problem statement into key words, and searching the preliminary sources for relevant references. We will briefly discuss primary, secondary, and preliminary sources of information. Then we will describe in detail the four most important preliminary sources and how to use them in conducting a literature review. In searching preliminary sources, you should use three-by-five-inch cards to record bibliographic data on any references you locate that appear relevant to your problem. We will describe format and give you some guidelines for making your bibliography cards.

Objectives

1. Define preliminary, primary, and secondary source, give an example of each, and describe how each is used in a review of educational research literature.
2. Name and briefly describe four preliminary sources that are useful for locating publications related to educational problems.
3. Given a general problem statement, write a specific problem statement and make up a list of key words or terms.
4. Given a list of key words, translate the words into ERIC Descriptors and Psychological Index Terms.
5. Describe the steps to take in conducting a manual search of *Education Index, Resources in Education, Current Index to Journals in Education,* and *Psychological Abstracts.*
6. Describe the procedure for making bibliography cards and converting them to a single format.

In the behavioral sciences, including education, research rarely provides *final* answers for the questions that concern practitioners and researchers. However, educational research has generated much useful information that can *help* the teacher or administrator decide on courses of action relative to nearly any educational problem.

The research literature can tell you what is known about a given educational question, and this knowledge can be weighed and interpreted in terms of the local situation. There are two keys needed to open the door to educational research knowledge. First, you must be able to locate published evidence that is relevant to your problem. This chapter and the two following will help you develop these skills. Second, you must be able to evaluate the evidence you find and relate it to the question you seek to answer. Chapters 5, 6, and 7 will provide you with the basic tools needed for this task, while subsequent chapters will give you experience in evaluation.

Preliminary, Primary, and Secondary Sources

In order to locate and use educational research, you must be familiar with three major sources of information. Preliminary sources are used to *locate* books, articles, and other educational documents that relate to your problem. Most preliminary sources are either *indexes,* such as *Education Index,* which give the author, title, and place of publication of educational writings, or *abstracts,* such as *Psychological Abstracts,* which give a brief summary or abstract of each publication listed in addition to the bibliographical data. Preliminary sources are usually organized by subject.

Primary sources are those publications in which persons who carry out research report their findings. Primary source information is communicated directly from the researcher to the reader. Most primary sources in education are journals such as the *Journal of Experimental Education.* Each article in these journals typically reports on a different research project. However, books also frequently contain reports of original research, and they then become primary source information.

Secondary sources are publications in which the author is reporting on research that someone else carried out. The most common secondary sources in education are scholarly books and textbooks. For example, a text in educational psychology will usually pull together and discuss the results of much of the recent research in areas such as human development, reinforcement, punishment, motivation, and student achievement. The advantage of secondary sources such as textbooks is that they give the reader a quick and readable overview of research and opinion related to the educational topics covered. The disadvantage of secondary sources is that the author may not accurately report the primary source findings. Since his coverage must be brief, he will surely omit much of the information he has found, and he may select information or interpret the research findings in a way that supports his own point of view.

The person who is seeking information on a given educational problem uses the appropriate preliminary sources to locate relevant primary and secondary source references. He reads secondary sources to get a quick overview of research related to his problem and primary sources to get detailed in-depth information. Let us start by outlining the specific steps that are carried out in this process, and then we will look at each step in detail.

Steps in Reviewing Educational Literature

We will first define each step and will then discuss each in greater depth:

1. Define the Problem. Your problem description should be short, specific, and clearly written. (Chapter 2)

2. Review Secondary Sources. Reading a brief discussion of your problem area in one or two secondary sources gives you an introduction to your problem and helps you redefine it in more precise terms. (Chapter 2)

3. Select the Most Appropriate Preliminary Source(s). For most educational problems, you can identify the one or two sources that are most likely to lead you to information relevant to your problem. (Chapter 2)

4. Translate the Problem Statement into Key Words. In order to look up relevant studies in the subject index of the preliminary source(s) you select, you must make a list of key words or descriptors that fit the main concepts related to your problem. (Chapter 2)

5. Search the Preliminary Source(s). You should decide whether to conduct a manual or computer search. Then, follow a systematic search procedure, and make bibliography cards on primary source references that appear to be related to your problem. (Chapters 2 and 3)

6. Read Primary Sources. Read the primary source references related to your problem. Make note cards that outline the relevant information from the references you read. (Chapter 4)

7. Organize Notes. The findings from the studies you have reviewed should be weighed, combined, and organized to give you the best answer available to your problem. (Chapter 4)

8. Write Report. Emphasize the studies that contribute most to solving your problem. Interpret each study in terms of its relevance to your problem or to the local situation. (Chapter 4)

DEFINE THE PROBLEM

The teacher or administrator usually goes to the educational research literature in search of information that will help solve a specific educational problem. The first step in locating relevant research is to define your problem as clearly and specifically as you can. It is usually easiest to frame your problem in the form of the question you want to answer. A broad, fuzzy question such as "What does research tell us about the effectiveness of teaching methods?" is not very helpful when you start looking into the preliminary sources. Over 40,000 references published in the past 15 years have something to do with teaching methods. More specific questions related to teaching methods might be: "Does whole class instruction or individual instruction result in greater pupil achievement in primary grade classrooms?" "How effective is the skill-centered method of teaching first-grade reading?" "What teaching styles are used by peer tutors in the elementary school?" Narrow your problem scope until it covers only the specific question you seek to answer.

REVIEW SECONDARY SOURCES

Once you have stated your problem or question in specific terms, it is a good idea to check one or two secondary sources in order to get a general picture of work that has been done on your topic. This step usually requires no more than a half-day's reading, and the overview you get provides a framework that can be used in fitting your later reading of primary sources into a meaningful context. Let's review a few secondary sources that often prove to be helpful.

NSSE Yearbooks.   Each year the National Society for the Study of Education publishes two yearbooks. Each yearbook covers recent research related to a major educational topic and contains 10 to 12 chapters that deal with different aspects of that topic. Each chapter is written by a different author, usually a researcher who has done important work in the area his chapter covers. Authors typically emphasize a few important studies or theoretical papers. If a yearbook has been published in the past few years that deals with the broad area into which your problem falls, you should check the chapter titles to see if it includes a chapter that relates to your specific problem. The areas covered by recent yearbooks are:

1985   Part I—Education in School and Nonschool Settings
        Part II—Learning and Teaching the Ways of Knowing
1984   Part I—Becoming Readers in a Complex Society
        Part II—The Humanities in Precollegiate Education
1983   Part I—Individual Differences and the Common Curriculum
        Part II—Staff Development
1982   Part I—Policy Making in Education
        Part II—Education and Work
1981   Part I—Philosophy and Education
        Part II—The Social Studies
1980   Part I—Toward Adolescence: The Middle School Years
        Part II—Learning a Second Language

The society also publishes a series of volumes on *Contemporary Education Issues* that can be very helpful if a recent volume has been concerned with your problem. Recent titles in this series include: Adapting Instruction to Student Differences (1985), Colleges of Education: Perspectives on Their Future (1985), Women and Education: Equity or Equality? (1984), Curriculum Development: Problems, Processes and Programs (1984). A complete list of volumes in this series may be found at the back of the most recent *NSSE Yearbook*.

Review of Educational Research.   This journal is devoted exclusively to review of research literature in areas related to education. It is published quarterly and each issue typically contains four to seven reviews.

In addition to providing a brief discussion of research on an important educational topic, each review also includes an extensive bibliography, which may list primary source articles that are relevant to your problem. For example, a recent issue

(Summer 1984) includes a review of research on perceived problems of beginning teachers by Simon Veenman. The text of this article covers 25 pages and cites nearly 200 references.

Since the articles in a given issue of the *Review* are generally not related, the easiest way to determine whether a review has been published relating to your problem is to go to a college library and check the tables of contents for the past five years. It is always advisable to check the *Review* because if you find an article relevant to your problem, it will not only give you a good overview of related research, but will also provide a long list of primary source references, some of which you might otherwise miss.

Review of Research in Education.   This annual series started in 1973. Each volume contains chapters written by leading educational researchers that provide critical surveys of research in important problem areas. Volume 10, published in 1983, includes chapters such as "Nonverbal Communication in Teaching" and "Research on Teaching as a Linguistic Process: A State of the Art."

Encyclopedia of Educational Research, Fifth Edition.   This monumental work, published in 1982, includes the work of over 300 contributors in more than 2000 pages. The contents are organized in alphabetical order by topic. However, if your topic is not found in the alphabetical listing, it is advisable to check the 12,000 entries in the index. This is an excellent source for getting a brief review of topics related to your area of interest.

Handbook of Research on Teaching, Third Edition.   This is an excellent source for students who are interested in research in any area of teaching. The book contains 35 articles organized into five main areas: Theory and Method of Research on Teaching, the Social and Institutional Context of Teaching, Research on Teaching and Teachers, Adapting Teaching to Differences Among Learners, and Research on the Teaching of Subjects and Grade Levels. Most of the articles are written by educational researchers with extensive experience on their topics. Extensive bibliographies are provided. A subject index can be used to locate research on specific topics of interest to the reader.

Books in Print.   The secondary sources we have just discussed contain reviews of research in many educational areas. If you find a recent review in one of these sources that relates to your problem, you can get a good overall picture of important relevant research in an hour's reading.

There are, however, a great many significant educational questions that have not been dealt with recently by any of these sources. If your problem relates to one of these, your best chance of finding a discussion of recent research probably lies in checking recent scholarly books, monographs, and textbooks.

The best source for locating current scholarly books related to your problem is the most recent edition of *Subject Guide to Books in Print,* which is available in most libraries and bookstores. Start by looking up specific key terms related to your topic. For example, suppose you are interested in the academic achievement of minority children. In the 1984–1985 edition there are two recent books that appear to deal with this topic listed under Academic Achievement. Under Prediction of Scholastic Success, another relevant book is listed, and under Minority Education seven additional titles are listed. Thus, by using this source you would promptly identify ten potentially useful books, all published since 1982. A quick scanning of the tables of contents of these books would probably locate the kind of overview of your problem that you usually seek in secondary sources.

If you find no scholarly books that relate specifically to your topic, you may find reports of research in a recent textbook in areas such as educational administration, child development, or educational psychology. For example, a check of three randomly selected textbooks in educational psychology revealed that all three contained short discussions of topics such as motivation, reinforcement, sex roles, and reading instruction. Since most textbooks cover a broad subject field, coverage of specific questions is usually brief, often less than a page. On the other hand, scholarly books that you locate in *Books in Print* usually deal with a more limited topic, covering it in much greater depth.

Library Card Catalog.   The subject card catalog in a university library is another good place to look for secondary sources that relate to your problem. Most libraries purchase as many scholarly books as their budgets allow. Since much new research is conducted in education each year, it is necessary to read recent sources in order to get a picture of the current state of knowledge. Libraries generally do not purchase all the new textbooks that are published.

Preliminary Sources.   Both *Education Index* and *Psychological Abstracts*, which we will discuss later in this chapter, list new professional books in the fields of education and psychology.

SELECT THE MOST APPROPRIATE PRELIMINARY SOURCES

After you have read brief discussions of recent work related to your problem in one or two secondary sources, it is usually possible to rewrite your problem in more specific terms. Think about what you have read and how it fits into your initial problem statement. Rewrite your problem statement so that it indicates in clear and specific terms what you hope to find out by your search of the literature. Enter your revised problem statement in your *Manual Search Record Form* (see Figure 2.1).[1] (Note that in Figure 2.1 we have retained the question format recommended earlier.) You are then ready to select the preliminary sources that can help you locate the most recent and important primary source references related to your problem.

There are several preliminary sources that are useful to educators. We will em-

---

1. A blank form that you can photocopy may be found in Appendix 1.

MANUAL SEARCH RECORD FORM

Mary Alpha   *Supt Omega*   *April 30 '85*   *June 15 '85*
Your Name   Person Requesting Search   Starting Date   Due Date

Purpose of Search: *To select a new basic reading program for the District*

Preliminary Problem Definition: *Which basic reading program results in the highest level of reading achievement when used with elementary pupils similar to those in our district?*

Secondary Sources Reviewed: *Arnell, Jane & Browns, Freda a Guide to the selection and Use of Reading Instructional Materials 1989, Alexander Graham*

Preliminary Source Selected: *Education Index*

Instructions: Start with current year and work back. Enter a check mark
after you have checked a key word and made up necessary
bibliography cards. Enter an "N" if you find no relevant
references for a given key word.

Key Words, Index Terms of Descriptors (in alphabetical order)	MARCH 19 _55_	19 _83-4_	19 _82-3_	19 _81-2_	19 _80-81_	
Reading Readiness ~~*Beginning Reading*~~	✓	N	✓	✓	N	
Reading Achievement	✓	✓	✓	✓	✓	
Comprehension in Reading ~~*Reading Comp.*~~	✓	✓	✓	✓	✓	
Reading Improvement	N	N	*drop this term*			
Reading-Curriculum-Evaluation ~~*Reading Programs*~~	✓	✓	✓	N	✓	
Reading research	✓	✓	N	N	N	
Reading bibliography	N	N	N	N	N	
Reading-teaching-evaluation	✓	✓	✓	✓	✓	
Readers - evaluation	✓	✓	✓	✓	✓	
Reading - textbooks	✓	✓	N	N	✓	

Figure 2.1 Manual Search Record Form for Searching a Preliminary Source

phasize the four most important, which are *Resources in Education* (RIE), *Current Index to Journals in Education (CIJE), Education Index,* and *Psychological Abstracts.*

Resources in Education (RIE).   This reference has been published monthly by the Educational Resources Information Center (ERIC) since 1966. A nationwide network including a coordinating staff and 16 clearinghouses select, abstract, index, store, retrieve, and disseminate significant reports related to education. A typical issue contains resumes of over 1100 documents related to education. In addition to bibliographic data, abstracts are provided for most references in *RIE*. These are typically 200 words in length and provide enough information for you to judge whether the reference is "on target" for your problem. *RIE* reviews "report litera-ture," which consists of virtually all educational documents other than journals. This includes speeches given at professional meetings, final reports of federally funded research, state education department documents, school district reports, and other published and unpublished reports.[2] Other preliminary sources in education generally do not provide abstracts of report literature, and before *RIE* began, most of these sources were very difficult to locate. Many of these reports are never published in journals or other periodicals, and *RIE* is often the only means of locating them. Some reports abstracted in *RIE,* such as final reports of federally funded research pro-jects, are subsequently published in journals. However, the journal version of the report will usually give much less detail and there is often a two- to three-year lag between completion of a report and publication of the results in a journal. Therefore, *RIE* is the one preliminary source that should be searched regardless of your prob-lem or area of interest in education.

Current Index to Journals in Education (CIJE).   This reference is also published monthly as part of the ERIC system. Its primary coverage is educational journals and periodicals, which you will recall are not covered by *RIE.* The *CIJE* coverage is very thorough, providing abstracts of articles from approximately 780 publications including many foreign periodicals. Most of the sources covered are educational periodicals, but when articles relevant to education are published in other periodicals such as *Time, Nursing Outlook,* or *Personnel Journal,* these are also abstracted in *CIJE.* Many journals peripheral to education, such as the *Journal of Geography* and the *Journal of Family Therapy,* are regularly reviewed for articles related to education. For the majority of educational problems, a search of *RIE* and *CIJE* is sufficient to locate most of the relevant references. The abstracts provided in *CIJE,* although briefer than *RIE,* are still very useful in helping the reviewer decide which articles should be read.

Education Index.   Published monthly except July and August by the H.W. Wilson Company, this index primarily covers educational periodicals, yearbooks, and monographs printed in the English language. Articles from over 300 periodicals

2. Early volumes covered only research reports for projects sponsored by the U.S. Office of Education.

related to education are indexed. Coverage in *Education Index* includes only biblio-graphical data. Therefore, *CIJE* is the preferred preliminary source for searches of educational periodical literature. For exhaustive literature searches, that is, those that attempt to cover everything written about a given educational problem, *CIJE* is used for the period 1969 to date and *Education Index* is used for 1929 to 1968. However, for most education problems a search that covers that most recent 10 years is sufficient, and *CIJE* is recommended.

Psychological Abstracts. This monthly publication of the American Psycho-logical Association regularly covers over 950 journals, technical reports, mono-graphs, and other scientific documents—in fact, most of the world's literature in psychology and related disciplines. Books, secondary sources, and articles periph-eral to psychology make up about 30 percent of the sources listed. There is consider-able overlap between *CIJE* and *Psychological Abstracts*. However, for any educa-tional problem that is related to some area of psychology, such as child development, learning, counseling, or student attitudes, *Psychological Abstracts* will usually provide a more thorough coverage and more detailed abstracts than *CIJE*.

OTHER USEFUL PRELIMINARY SOURCES

These four sources have very broad coverage and are recommended for locating information related to most educational questions. However, there are several more limited preliminary sources that typically cover a single area related to education. For a thorough review, these sources should be searched when your problem fits into one of the areas covered. A search of one of these specialized preliminary sources will usually locate a few useful references that are not covered in the four broad sources referred to earlier.

Child Development Abstracts and Bibliography. Articles in this area that are drawn from about 180 periodicals in medicine, psychology, biology, sociology, and education are covered in this source. The three numbers published each year include abstracts under six major subject headings, as well as an author index and subject index. These are combined into annual volumes.

Sociological Abstracts. This source is published five times each year. Each issue contains subject, author, and source indexes in addition to abstracts that are similar in format and length to *Psychological Abstracts*. The subject index is also similar to *Psychological Abstracts,* typically listing from three to ten phrases that describe the content of the article. For example, under the broad subject heading "Attitudes/Attitudinal" in the December 1984 issue (vol. 32[5], p. 1678) here is a typical entry: "school-relevant behavior/attitude differences; residential structure; national survey, follow-up questionnaire, first year college students; 03434." Note that this example contains information on the population and methodology employed. This kind of information is often given in the subject index of *Sociological Abstracts*.

    As a rule, articles are abstracted and appear more promptly in *Psychological*

Abstracts than *Sociological Abstracts*. Thus, when searching areas covered by both, such as topics in social psychology, *Psychological Abstracts* is likely to cover a higher percentage of recent articles. However, if you are studying a research topic that cuts across both psychology and sociology, it is useful to look over the tables of contents of an issue of both abstracts and compare coverage on your topic.

Research Related to Children.   The ERIC Clearinghouse on Early childhood Education publishes these bulletins twice a year. They provide brief descriptions of research in progress and recently completed research classified into nine content areas such as "Growth and Development," "Special Groups of Children," and "Educational Factors and Services." Each bulletin contains subject, investigator, and institution indexes, in addition to the project descriptions.

Exceptional Child Education Resources (ECER).   The Council for Exceptional children has published this listing quarterly since 1969. More than 200 journals are regularly searched for material concerning exceptional children. The format is similar to that used in *Current Index to Journals in Education*. However, many journals searched for *ECER* are not covered by *CIJE*. Each issue contains subject, author, and title indexes, and the final issue each year contains indexes for the entire volume.

TRANSLATE THE PROBLEM STATEMENT INTO KEY WORDS

All preliminary sources in education include subject indexes. Thus, an important step in your literature review is to translate the statement of your problem or question that you wrote on your *Manual Search Record Form* into a set of key words or terms that you can look up in the subject index of the preliminary sources you have selected. The method of selecting key words or index terms differs slightly for the different preliminary sources. Let's see what steps we should take for each of the principal preliminary sources.

1. For all preliminary sources you start by underlining the most important words and terms in your problem statement. If your problem statement does not express your problem in clear, specific terms, you should think through your problem, read some additional secondary sources, and rewrite your problem statement before proceeding.

2. The second step for all preliminary sources is to list these underlined words in pencil in the Key Words section of your Record Form (Figure 2.1).

3. Next, list synonyms and closely related words for each important word or term you underlined in Step 1. These three steps are enough to get you started on a search of the Subject Index section of *Education Index*.

4. For *RIE* and *CIJE,* the two ERIC sources, an additional step is required. To assist the user in identifying key words or terms ERIC has published the *Thesaurus of ERIC Descriptors*. This volume, which is available in the reference section of your library, lists all terms used to classify ERIC documents by subject. For a given subject area, it will provide synonyms, narrower terms, broader terms, and related terms. For example, the general search term "dropouts" is further analyzed into such terms as "high school dropouts," "potential dropouts," "dropout identification," and "dropout teaching."

You will usually find that some of the key words you have written on your Record Form appear in the *Thesaurus* in slightly different form. For example, if you had listed "Racial relations" as a key term, you would find in the *Thesaurus* that the term "Race relations" is listed instead. In such cases, erase the word or term you have listed and enter instead the *Thesaurus* term. For many terms listed in the Thesaurus, related terms (RT) are given. If any of these related terms seem relevant to your problem, add them to the list on your Record Form. Some of the terms you listed originally may not be included in any form in the *Thesaurus*. Omit these terms from your list. Finally, you should look in the most recent monthly issue of *RIE* where you will find a list of all ERIC descriptors that have been added since the *Thesaurus* was published. Check this list and add to your *Record Form* any of the descriptors that relate to your problem. The final result of translating your original terms will be a list of ERIC descriptor terms that you can use to search the subject indexes of *RIE* and *CIJE*.

5. If you have selected *Psychological Abstracts* as a preliminary source, you use the *Thesaurus of Psychological Index Terms* to translate your original key words list into terms that are used in the Subject Index of *Psychological Abstracts*. Although this *Thesaurus* was not developed until 1973, the terms you select will, for the most part, be satisfactory for searching earlier volumes because the *Thesaurus* includes most of the 800 index terms used before 1973. The index term "Bibliography" should always be checked in *Psychological Abstracts*. Under this heading you will find a listing of bibliographies on a wide variety of subjects. If you can locate a recent bibliography in your area of interest, it will, of course, be of great help in carrying out the review of the literature.

Since the index terms listed in the *Thesaurus of ERIC Descriptors* are not identical to those listed in the *Thesaurus of Psychological Index Terms,* you will have to use different key word lists if you decide to search both these sources.

SEARCH THE PRELIMINARY SOURCES

Now that you have a set of appropriate key terms listed on your Record Form, you can start your manual search of the preliminary source itself. Here we will discuss how you proceed with each preliminary source. If you decide to conduct a computer search, the procedures are given in Chapter 3.

Searching Education Index. *Education Index* lists only the bibliographical data concerning each item. The year for *Education Index* runs from September to the following June. For the current quarter each of the monthly issues must be searched, but these monthly issues are combined quarterly, and the quarterly issues in turn are combined into a yearly volume for the immediate past year.

In searching all preliminary sources, you should start with the most recent issue and work back. The Record Form (Figure 2.1) provides a systematic procedure you can follow. To check each of your key words in a volume of *Education Index,* look up the word and read the titles of articles listed under the word. If you find a title that indicates that the article deals with some phase of your topic, copy the bibliographical data (author, title, and source of publication) onto a three-by-five-inch bibliography card (see Figure 2.2). A separate card should be used for each reference. It is often difficult to judge the contents of an article from the title, and many articles for which you prepare bibliography cards will later be found to contain nothing pertinent to your topic. In deciding whether to prepare a bibliography card and check a particular article, you should generally follow the rule that it is better to check an article that proves of no use than to overlook one that may be important. Thus, whenever in doubt, prepare a bibliography card and check the article in question.

After you read the titles given under your first key word, place a check on the Record Form, indicating that this word has been checked. Then look up the next key word in the Subject Index, and continue until you have checked all the terms you listed. Then go through the same process with the next most recent volume of *Education Index.* If, after checking several volumes of the *Education Index,* you find nothing pertinent to your topic under a given key word, this key word can be dropped and not checked in the remaining volumes.

To illustrate the process, let us now use the Record Form to search five years of *Educational Index* to gather information that will help select a new basic reading program for the elementary schools of the Middletown School District. Our specific problem can be stated in the following question: "Which basic *reading program* results in the highest level of *reading achievement* when used with *elementary* pupils similar to those in Middletown?" Our initial selection of key words includes "Beginning reading," "Reading achievement," "Reading comprehension," "Reading improvement," "Reading programs," and "Reading research." It is usually best to list your

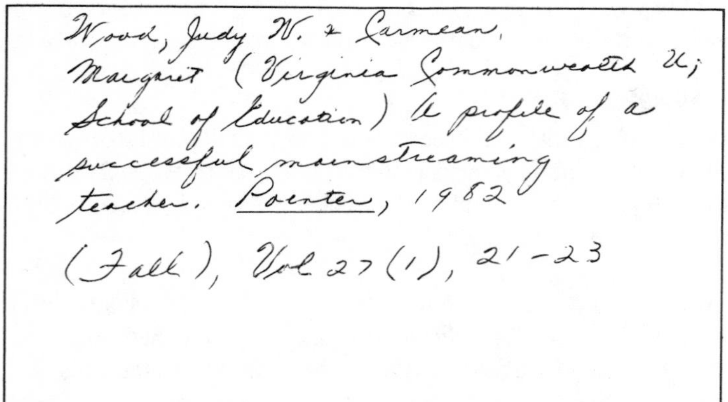
Wood, Judy W. & Carmean, Margaret (Virginia Commonwealth U; School of Education) A profile of a successful mainstreaming teacher. Pointer, 1982 (Fall), Vol 27(1), 21-23

Figure 2.2 Sample Bibliography Card in *Psychological Abstracts* Format key words first on a separate sheet of paper and then copy them onto your Record Form in alphabetical order, as we have done in Figure 2.1. It would be ideal if we could search for studies that include all three of the most important concepts in our problem statement; that is, *reading programs, reading achievement,* and *elementary.* Any study that included all three of these concepts would probably be "on target" for our problem. We will learn in the next chapter that such searches are possible using a computer, but for manual searches we can only look up one key term at a time. Thus, what we must do in our search of *Education Index* is to look up each term and then judge from the title whether a given article is related to our problem. In using the *Index,* we would usually look up our key terms in alphabetical order. In searching the March 1985 issue of *Education Index* we find nothing under "Beginning reading" except a notation, "See Reading readiness." Thus we change our first key term to "Reading readiness" and check the articles entered under that term. One pertinent article is listed, so we make up a bibliography card and then enter a check mark in the first column for "Reading readiness," indicating that we have checked this term and found one or more relevant references. Next we check "Reading improvement" but find nothing, so we enter N in the first column. Instead of "Reading comprehension," the term "Comprehension in reading" is used in *Education Index,* so we make this change in our key-word list. After checking the headings in *Education Index,* we also change "Reading programs" to "Reading-curriculum-evaluation" and add "Reading-teaching-evaluation," "Readers-evaluation," and "Reading-textbooks." You will recall that when you fail to find a given term in your preliminary source or if the term fails to produce any relevant references for two or three years, you should drop it, as we have done with "Beginning reading" and "Reading improvement." Notice that we have also added "Reading-Bibliography." It is usually a good idea to include a bibliography heading if one is found in the *Index,* because if you are fortunate enough to find a bibliography on your topic, you will locate many relevant references with little effort. Note that even though we found no relevant bibliographies in our search, we retained the term.

Five of the references located in *Education Index* in this brief search are listed below in the format used in *Education Index* to give you an idea of the kinds of articles you are likely to find on this problem:

> Informed strategies for learning: a program to improve children's reading awareness and comprehension. S. G. Paris and others. bibl *J Educ Psychol* 76: 1239-52 D '84

> Effective reading programs: a critical review of outlier studies. J. V. Hoffman and W. L. Rutherford. bibl *Read Res Q* 20: 79–92 Fall '84

> Basal reading texts: what's in them to comprehend? *Read Teach* 38: 194–5 N '84

> Main idea identification: instructional explanations in four basal reader series. V. C. Hare and B. Milligan. bibl *J Read Behav* 16 no 3: 189–204 '84

> Relationship of cognitive style and word type for beginning readers. E. Burton and R. Sinatra. bibl *Read World* 24: 65–75 0 '84

The procedure we have described would provide a fairly complete search of *Education Index,* if extended over a 10-year period. However, let us suppose that the purpose of our search were to locate very quickly a few references on the relative effectiveness of different reading programs that we could discuss in a teacher workshop. In this case we may decide to select only the two or three key terms that seem most likely to produce relevant articles and search only these in *Education Index.* For example, we may decide to search only Reading achievement, Reading-curriculum-evaluation, and Readers-evaluation.

In other words, the depth of a literature search is determined to a large degree by your purpose. For many of the day-to-day problems that arise in the public schools, sufficient information can be obtained from a brief search that covers only one preliminary source for a period of two or three years. However, if the evidence you find is to be the basis for making a major educational decision such as "Should the school district adopt an ability grouping program?" then a thorough search involving at least two preliminary sources and extending over a 10- to 15-year period is usually called for in order to obtain the information needed to make a sound decision.

Searching Psychological Abstracts.   Every issue of *Psychological Abstracts* has 16 sections, each covering a different area of psychology. In addition to abstracts, the monthly issues also include brief subject and author indexes.

The sections most pertinent to the researcher in education are: Developmental Psychology, which includes abstracts in areas such as Cognitive and Perceptual Development and Psychosocial and Personality Development; and Educational Psychology, which includes such topics as Curriculum and Programs, Teaching Methods, Academic Learning and Achievement, and Special and Remedial Education. The coverage of the 16 areas of psychology is very thorough. For example, many journals such as *Elementary School Journal, Harvard Educational Review,* and *Journal of Reading Behavior,* which are predominantly educational journals, are covered in *Psychological Abstracts.* Many foreign psychological journals are also covered.

Currently, two volumes of *Psychological Abstracts* are published each year, one including the January to June numbers and one including the July to December numbers. For each volume of abstracts, subject and author indexes are prepared in a separate volume. In using *Psychological Abstracts,* you turn first to the index volume to check your key words. The index volumes of *Psychological Abstracts* do not contain complete bibliographical data like those in *Education Index,* but list only the subject of the article in the briefest possible terms, usually about 10 to 15 words. You will find a number after each of these brief descriptions. This number refers to the number of the abstract. Write down the numbers of articles that appear to relate to your topic, and then look these up in the volume of abstracts.

Suppose that you are an elementary school principal and your school has recently started a mainstreaming program. You want to conduct a very limited search to learn more about teachers who have been successful in mainstreaming classrooms. This information can help you in teacher placement decisions and also in conducting an in-service program to prepare your teachers for their new role. You look up "Mainstreaming" in the *Psychological Abstracts* index volumes, since this seems to be the most important key term for your problem.[3] In Volume 70 (July–December index for 1983) you find the following entry:

affective and cognitive characteristics, successful mainstreaming teachers, 13665

Since this reference seems very pertinent to your problem, you would then look up 13665 in the Abstracts part of Volume 70, where you would find:

13665. Wood, Judy W. & Carmean, Margaret. (Virginia Commonwealth U, School of Education) A profile of a successful mainstreaming teacher. *Pointer,* 1982 (Fall), Vol 27(1), 21–23.-A survey completed by school administrators, regular classroom teachers, and special education teachers was used to form a profile of the affective and cognitive characteristics of the successful mainstreaming teacher. These characteristics include concern for the needs of handicapped children and sensitivity to their feelings, patience and a strong desire to help the exceptional child, concern for each child as an individual, the abilities to motivate students and to individualize instruction, and an understanding of special education and its goal of helping handicapped students reach their highest potential. These characteristics can be used as guidelines for preservice and inservice teacher training program. (8 ref)-*Journal abstract.*

Note that in addition to the bibliographical data needed to locate the original article, a brief but informative abstract is provided. These abstracts are very useful because they help you decide whether or not a given article actually pertains to your problem. This decision is much easier to make on the basis of an abstract than solely on the basis of the bibliographical data found in *Education Index*. After reading the abstract, you decide whether the article is pertinent. This abstract indicates that the article is closely related to your problem, so you would list the bibliographical data on a three-by-five-inch bibliography card (see Figure 2.2), and continue your search for additional references related to your problem.

When the research topic is exclusively educational, such as school lunch programs, little is gained by checking *Psychological Abstracts*. On the other hand, in areas relating to educational psychology, you may decide to check both *Psychological Abstracts* and one of the education sources such as *Education Index, RIE,* or *CIJE* in order to be assured of getting a full coverage of the field.

You can use the same Record Form to search *Psychological Abstracts* that you used in searching *Education Index*. You should, however, use a separate *copy* of the Record Form for each preliminary source that you search.

Searching RIE and CIJE.   Once you have selected your key descriptor terms from the *Thesaurus of ERIC Descriptors,* the procedure for searching *RIE* and *CIJE* is similar to that used in searching *Psychological Abstracts*.

In searching *RIE,* first check your descriptors in the subject index of the monthly

---

3. For a more extensive search, you would search several related terms taken from the *Thesaurus of Psychological Index Terms* such as Reading materials, Reading disabilities, and Remedial reading.

issues for the current year and then in the semiannual index volumes for previous years. When you locate a reference in the subject index that relates to your topic, copy the ED number given at the end of the bibliographical data. Then look up each ED number in the Document Resumes section, where you will find a description of the reference like the sample entry shown in Figure 2.3. Notice in this figure that the Document Resume contains a great deal of useful information in addition to the usual brief abstract.

If you wish to obtain the full document that is abstracted in the entry, you can order it through the ERIC Document Reproduction Service. A Reproduction Service

SAMPLE RESUME

ERIC Accession Number—identification number sequentially assigned to documents as they are processed.

Author(s).

Title.

Organization where document originated.

Date Published.

Contract or Grant Number.

Alternate source for obtaining document.

Language of Document—documents written entirely in English are not designated, although "English" is carried in their computerized records.

Publication Type—broad categories indicating the form or organization of the document, as contrasted to its subject matter. The category name is followed by the category code.

ERIC Document Reproduction Service (EDRS) Availability—"MF" means microfiche; "PC" means reproduced paper copy. When described as "Document Not Available from EDRS," alternate sources are cited above. Prices are subject to change; for latest price code schedule see section on "How to Order ERIC Documents," in the most recent issue of RIE.

ED 654 321   CE 123 456
Smith, John D.   Johnson, Jane
Career Planning for Women.
Central Univ., Chicago, IL.
Spons Agency—National Inst. of Education (ED), Washington, DC.
Report No. — CU-2081-S
Pub Date — May 83
Contract — NIE-C-83-0001
Note — 129p.; Paper presented at the National Conference on Career Education (3rd. Chicago, IL, May 15-17, 1983).
Available from—Campus Bookstore, 123 College Ave., Chicago, IL 60690 ($3.25).
Language—English, French
Pub Type—Speeches/Meeting Papers (150)
EDRS Price—MF01/PC06 Plus Postage.
Descriptors—Career Guidance,*Career Planning, Careers, *Demand Occupations, *Employed Women, *Employment Opportunities, Females, Labor Force, Labor Market, *Labor Needs, Occupational Aspiration, Occupations
Identifiers—Consortium of States, *National Occupational Competency Testing Institute
   Women's opportunities for employment will be directly related to their level of skill and experience and also to the labor market demands through the remainder of the decade. The number of workers needed for all major occupational categories is expected to increase by about one-fifth between 1980 and 1990, but the growth rate will vary by occupational group. Professional and technical workers are expected to have the highest predicted rate (39 percent), followed by service workers (35 percent), clerical workers (26 percent), sales workers (24 percent), craft workers and supervisors (20 percent), managers and administrators (15 percent), and operatives (11 percent). This publication contains a brief discussion and employment information concerning occupations for professional and technical workers, managers and administrators, skilled trades, sales workers, clerical workers, and service workers. In order for women to take advantage of increased labor market demands, employer attitudes toward working women need to change and women must: (1) receive better career planning and counseling, (2) change their career aspirations, and (3) fully utilize the sources of legal protection and assistance that are available to them. (SB)

Clearinghouse Accession Number.

Sponsoring Agency—agency responsible for initiating, funding, and managing the research project.

Report Number—assigned by originator.

Descriptive Note (pagination first).

Descriptors—subject terms found in the Thesaurus of ERIC Descriptors that characterize substantive content. Only the major terms, preceded by an asterisk, are printed in the subject index.

Identifiers—additional identifying terms not found in the Thesaurus. Only the major terms, preceded by an asterisk, are printed in the subject index.

Informative Abstract.

Abstractor's Initials.

Figure 2.3 Sample Entry from *RIE*, "Document Resume" Section, with Identifying Characteristics. From *Resources in Education, 20*, 2 (February 1985), viii

price code is listed in the Document Resume for each document.[4] The document can be ordered on microfiches, which are small sheets of microfilm each containing up to 60 pages of text. It can also be ordered in printed-copy form reproduced at about 70 percent of the document's original size. The advantages of microfiches are their low cost and small size. However, they require a special microfiche reader, which enlarges the image to normal page size. Nearly all libraries now have these special readers. Most university libraries also maintain a collection of ERIC microfiches, so it is not necessary to order them through the Reproduction Service unless you want a personal copy.

Like *RIE, CIJE* is published monthly and cumulated semiannually. The monthly numbers contain a Subject Index, an Author Index, and a Main Entry Section. Using the descriptors related to your topic selected from the *Thesaurus of ERIC Descriptors,* search the Subject Index, and note the EJ numbers of relevant references. Then look up these EJ numbers in the Main Entry Section, which provides approximately the same information as that in the Document Resumes in *RIE*. For example, the article by Wood and Carmean that we located in *Psychological Abstracts* is also listed in the July-to-December 1983 volume of *CIJE*. This entry is shown in Figure 2.4. Note that the abstract for this article provided in *CIJE* is much briefer than that found in *Psychological Abstracts*.

As a general rule, the abstracts given in *RIE* and *Psychological Abstracts* give more detail than those provided in *CIJE* and are therefore more useful in helping you decide which references are related to your problem. Compared with *Education Index, CIJE* has the advantages of a more comprehensive index (based on the *Thesaurus of ERIC Descriptors)*, multidisciplinary journal coverage, and abstracts for many of the articles indexed.

EJ 281 105   EC 151 832
A Profile of a Successful Mainstreaming Teacher.
Wood, Judy W.; Carmean, Margaret *Pointer*; v27 nl
p21-23 Fall 1982
Descriptors: *Cognitive Ability; *Disabilities;
  *Humanistic Education; Knowledge Level;
  *Mainstreaming; *Success; Teacher Attitudes;
  *Teacher Characteristics
Cognitive and affective characteristics of a successful mainstreaming teacher are reported from a sample of administrators, regular classroom teachers, and special educators. Among the characteristics noted are love for children and a concern for their needs, positive attitudes toward and knowledge of special education and mainstreaming. (CL)

Figure 2.4 Sample Entry from *CIJE*, "Main Entry Section" (July-December 1983), 198

---

4. The prices of *RIE* documents change from time to time. See "How to Order Eric Documents" in the latest issue of *RIE* for current prices. In 1985 articles up to 480 pages could be obtained on microfiche for 97¢. Paper copies are *much* more expensive.

For most educational topics, the most productive strategy for making a thorough search would probably be to search *RIE* and *CIJE* for the years from 1969 to date, search *RIE* and *Education Index* for the years 1966 to 1968, and then search *Education Index* from 1965 back as far as you plan to extend your review.

Preparing Bibliography Cards

During your search of the preliminary sources, you should prepare a bibliography card for each book or article that you believe might contain material pertinent to your problem. Although information included in the bibliographical data for a given citation is always about the same, these data can be recorded in many different formats. If you are writing a review-of-the-literature paper for your master's degree, you should check the rules in effect at your college concerning acceptable format for the bibliography section. Some schools permit you to use any format generally acceptable in your field of study, while other schools have a specific format that all graduate students must follow. If your school permits the use of any format acceptable in your field, the easiest approach will be for you to use the format of the preliminary source from which you expect to obtain most of your references.

Current Index to Journals in Education is often the most productive source for students working in education, and therefore its format is advantageous to use when permitted. Most of the references will come from the subject index of *CIJE,* and articles listed in this section give the bibliographical data but not the author's name. Therefore, you must get the bibliographic data from the Main Entry Section, not the Subject Index. In the Main Entry Section the title of the book or article is given before the author's name. For your bibliography card, the author's name (last name first) should be listed before the title. This change is necessary because it is much more convenient for you to maintain your card file in alphabetical order by author, and the bibliography as prepared for a thesis or term paper normally will be listed in this order. If *CIJE* format is chosen, the bibliographic data from articles found in other sources, such as *Education Index* and *Psychological Abstracts,* should be converted to the *CIJE* format. Let us compare bibliographical data for the same article as it appears in *CIJE, Education Index,* and *Psychological Abstracts.*

CURRENT INDEX TO JOURNALS IN EDUCATION

EJ 281 635   EC 151 765

The Role of New and Old Information in the Verbal Expression of Language-Disordered Children. Skarakis, Elizabeth; Greenfield, Patricia M. *Journal of Speech and Hearing Research;* v 25 n 3 p 462–67 Sep 1982 (Reprint: UMI)

EDUCATION INDEX

Skarakis, Elizabeth, and Greenfield, P. M. Role of new and old information in the verbal expression of language-disordered children. bibl J Speech & Hearing Res 25: 462–7 S '82

PSYCHOLOGICAL ABSTRACTS

8164. Skarakis, Elizabeth & Greenfield, Patricia M. (U California, Santa Barbara) The role of new and old information in the verbal expression of language-disordered children. *Journal of Speech & Hearing Research,* 1982 (Sep), Vol 25 (3), 462–467.

Although these forms are similar, it will be noted that the *Journal of Speech and Hearing Research* is abbreviated in *Education Index* and not in the other two sources and that the volume number, pages, and year are given in different format. Note also that all main words in the title are capitalized in *CIJE* while only the first word is capitalized in the other sources. *CIJE* indicates that the article is available from University Microfilms International (UMI) while the others do not provide this information. Finally, note that *Education Index* format omits "The" when this is the first word in the title. Obviously, many errors and inconsistencies can be avoided by selecting one format and converting all references to that format when making up bibliography cards.

If you are reviewing the literature in one of the areas of educational psychology, you will normally obtain the majority of your references from *Psychological Abstracts,* and in this case the *Psychological Abstracts* format may be preferred.

If your college has specified a format for the bibliography that differs from the one used by your preliminary sources, the easiest procedure is to copy the bibliographic data from the preliminary sources in whatever form it is found. Then, when checking the reference itself in order to determine whether it contains anything pertinent to your review of the literature, you can recopy the bibliographic data in the required school format on the other side of your bibliography card. You need copy this only for studies that contain pertinent information. Usually, only one out of every three or four references for which you prepare bibliography cards will contain material that you wish to use in your review of the literature.

Accuracy is extremely important in preparing bibliography cards. A mistake made in copying the bibliographic data can often cause a great deal of extra work. For example, if you incorrectly copy the name of the journal, or the date, volume number, or pages, you won't find the article when checking out the source. Then you are faced with the problem of trying to determine which portion of your bibliographic material is incorrect. Unless you take special care, it is easy to make such mistakes, and then you must usually go back to the preliminary sources in order to find the reference. As you may well have covered a number of preliminary sources, this search can take much longer than it would have taken to use more care initially. Even if you make an error in some portion of the bibliographic data that will not interfere with finding the materials, such as misspelling the author's name, the mistake is still serious because it will probably be repeated in your paper or report. Nothing reflects more unfavorably upon an individual's scholarship than frequent errors in bibliographic data.

Recommended Reading

BERRY, D. M. (1980). *A bibliographic guide to educational research (2nd ed.).* Metuchen, N.J.: Scarecrow Press.

This small book provides a great deal of information on locating sources in the field of education. The chapters are organized by type of reference, such as Books, Periodicals,

Research Studies, and Government Publications. In turn, each chapter is divided into sections. For example, the chapter on Research Studies is divided into ERIC Documents, Theses and Dissertations, and Other Research Studies. The book has author-editor, title, and subject indexes.

GOVER, H. R. (1981). *Keys to library research on the graduate level: A guide to guides.* Lanham, Md.: University Press of America.

Designed to give graduate students the skills they need to use the library resources at their disposal fully, this book covers the card catalog, basic periodicals indexes, computer-prepared indexes and abstracts, and the Library of Congress classification system.

WOODBURY, M. L. (1982). *A guide to sources of educational information (2nd ed.).* Washington, D.C.: Information Resources Press.

This comprehensive guide to virtually every type of information related to education contains detailed descriptions of more than 700 sources, plus backup chapters on how to locate and use them. Among the kinds of sources included are dictionaries, encyclopedias, bibliographies, abstracting and indexing services, instructional materials, tests and assessment instruments, and many more.

Application Problems

1. Suppose you are an elementary school principal. The superintendent is very concerned because many of the new elementary teachers in the district are having trouble with discipline and classroom management. He asks you to check the recent educational literature and try to find information on *specific* things that teachers can do in the classroom to improve classroom management and reduce discipline problems. The following activities will help you to learn how to use educational literature when faced with problems of this kind.

   a. Check the 1984–1985 *Books in Print* and list bibliographic data for one book that deals with classroom management and/or discipline published in 1984 or later.

   b. Check the *NSSE Yearbooks* from 1979 to date. Do any of these volumes deal with the problem? If so, list bibliographic data for the volume, check the chapters in the selected volume, and give the author and title of one chapter that appears to be most relevant.

   c. Check the 1979–1984 volumes of the *Review of Educational Research* (vols. 49–54). Do any of the articles in these volumes relate to classroom management or discipline? If so, list bibliographic data for relevant articles.

   d. Check the 1985 volumes of *CIJE, RIE, Education Index,* and *Psychological Abstracts* and list bibliographic data for one relevant article from *each* of these four preliminary sources.

2. Write or select five problem statements or questions related to education in areas that interest you. Following are some sample questions to help you. You may select some of your problems from this list, but be sure to write at least two problem statements or questions of your own.

   What strategies can a teacher use to improve the classroom climate in the elementary grades?

   What classroom management procedures are effective in reducing disruptive student behavior in secondary schools?

What can the teacher do to increase the amount of school time in which students are academically engaged?

What can the teacher do to manage retarded children who are placed in regular classrooms?

How can social skills be taught in elementary school?

What is the impact of teacher anxiety on the educational process?

What effect does team teaching have on science achievement at the secondary school level?

What has been the effect of special educational programs for gifted secondary school students?

Should teachers write behavioral objectives, in other words, what effect do these objectives have on student learning?

How effective is the values clarification approach in improving pupil self-concept and achievement?

How should parents be involved in the education of their gifted children?

What educational approaches have been found effective in stimulating moral development?

What factors in the school situation can increase or decrease cheating?

What are the characteristics of teachers who are successful in working with gifted children?

How can classroom rewards be used to improve pupil performance?

What effect has desegregation had on the academic achievement of black students?

What are other countries doing provide educational programs for gifted students?

How can feedback be used to improve learning in the elementary school?

How can pupils be taught self-control that will improve their classroom behavior?

What methods are effective for early identification of gifted children?

3. Review your five problems and select the one that seems most interesting, photocopy the Manual Search Record form from Appendix 1, and enter purpose and problem definition.
4. Check the table of contents of the *NSSE Yearbooks* and the *Review of Educational Research* for the most recent five years to see if an article or chapter has been written that relates to your problem statement. If you find a reference, enter bibliographic data in your copy of the Manual Search Record Form (Appendix 1).
5. Check the subject volume of *Books in Print* for the most recent year available and try to locate at least three books published since 1975 that appear to relate to the problem statement you selected. Enter bibliographic data under secondary sources in the Record Form. If you need more space, use back of form.
6. Check your library card catalog, try to locate an additional book related to the problem

you have selected, and enter bibliographic data under secondary sources in the Record Form.

7. Select one of the secondary sources you located in Steps 4, 5, and 6, read the section most relevant to your problem, and write a brief summary of what you have learned.

8. Rewrite your problem definition, based on what you have read.

9. Select the preliminary source you believe is most relevant to your problem and enter it in the Record Form.

10. Make up a list of key words related to your problem and enter it in the Record Form.

11. Check your key words in one volume of your preliminary source. Make up bibliography cards for three references that appear relevant to your problem. (If you can't find three references, check a second year of your preliminary source.) Keep these cards, as you will use them in an application problem in a later chapter.

CHAPTER 3

COMPUTER SEARCHES OF PRELIMINARY SOURCES

Overview

The use of a computer to locate relevant references in the preliminary sources offers some significant advantages over a manual search. Many university libraries have terminals and can conduct computer searches in education at a low cost. There are six major steps you must take to carry out a computer search. These include defining the problem to be searched, stating the purpose of the search, selecting a data base, selecting descriptors, planning several alternate search strategies, and conducting the search. In cases where relevant descriptors cannot be found, a proximity search can be carried out instead of a descriptor search.

Objectives

1. Briefly describe four advantages of conducting a computer search of preliminary sources in education.
2. Name and describe three data bases related to education that are available for computer searches.
3. Describe each of the six main steps you should carry out in planning and conducting a computer search of the ERIC data base.
4. Describe proximity searching and explain when it is appropriate to use this procedure.
5. Using the Computer Search Record Form, select a problem and plan a search.

The increased availability of preliminary sources such as indexes and abstracts has made the task of locating literature related to your problem or question much easier. For example, in the field of education the person searching the literature prior to 1929 would have to check the table of contents of each journal, month by month, to locate articles related to her area of interest. Even though there were fewer journals in 1929 (the 1929 volume of *Education Index* searched only 160), the task was slow and laborious. There were some broad indexes of periodical literature available, such as *Pooles Index,* but their coverage of educational literature was very sketchy so that in order to conduct a thorough search, the researcher had to consult the primary source journals themselves.

The task became much easier in 1929, the year that *Education Index* was first published. It was no longer necessary to check every journal, issue by issue, or to rely on the limited coverage of education provided by the general indexes to periodical literature. Instead the researcher looked up her topic in *Education Index,* which was arranged alphabetically by subject, and copied the bibliographical data she needed to locate the articles in the journals. There was still no easy way to locate educational documents such as papers presented at professional meetings and unpublished research reports. Most researchers simply ignored these works or checked them in a hit-or-miss way by trying to locate the programs of professional meetings or watching the newspapers for items related to education.

The problem of locating educational documents was largely solved with the start of *Research in Education* (later to become *Resources in Education*) in 1966. It was designed specifically to provide access to the thousands of important educational documents that emerge each year but are never published. Since *RIE* provides detailed abstracts and the microfiches containing the complete text of most of the documents covered are available in all major libraries in the United States, this service made readily available kinds of educational documents that were almost impossible to search systematically before 1966.

In 1969, ERIC began publishing *CIJE,* thus providing a very thorough coverage of journals related to education and providing abstracts that were lacking in *Education Index.* The development of the ERIC *Thesaurus* also made the researcher's task easier by providing a standard terminology and linking relevant terms, the descriptors, to every article cited in *RIE* and *CIJE.* Finally, the availability of the ERIC data base on computer now makes it possible to conduct a more detailed search in ten minutes than could be done manually in ten weeks.

Primary sources such as professional journals or research reports are carefully read by reviewers to prepare the entries for preliminary sources such as *RIE, CIJE,* or *Psychological Abstracts.*[1] When reading an article, the reviewer decides which descriptors apply to the article, writes a brief abstract, and prepares all information that must be included in the preliminary source. Entries like those shown in Figures 2.3 and 2.4 are the final result of this process.

Since all reviewers for a given preliminary source work from the same list of descriptors, it is possible to enter the appropriate descriptors and other information for each article into a computer. The computer can then be instructed to locate and print out information on all articles for which a given combination of descriptors is present. This is essentially what one does in carrying out a computer search of a preliminary source data base.

In this chapter we will discuss the advantages of computer searches over manual searches and give you detailed step-by-step instructions with examples, so that you can conduct an effective computer search of a preliminary source.

1. Since *Education Index* provides only bibliographic data, articles cited in this source are not reviewed and key words or descriptors are not assigned to articles. Thus, *Education Index* cannot be searched by computer.

Advantages of a Computer Search

A manual search of preliminary sources, such as we described in Chapter 2, is not too difficult if you only need a few references related to a minor problem. However, if you are planning to conduct a major review of literature to write a master's thesis or to help you make an important educational decision, you will find the manual search process time-consuming and tiresome. Under these conditions a computer search of the appropriate preliminary sources has the following important advantages:

1. *Low Cost.* An exhaustive search of the ERIC data base, which includes all references that have been listed in *RIE* and *CIJE,* can usually be carried out at a cost of $20 to $40. A comparable manual search would take from 25 to 75 hours. Less comprehensive searches, such as are usually needed for a graduate-level term paper, can usually be conducted for about $10.

2. *Speed.* If you need preliminary source information immediately, the computer will print out this information while you wait, usually in 5 or 10 minutes.

3. *Provides a Printout.* For most data bases the computer will provide a printout of either the bibliographical data plus descriptors or the complete citation as it appears in the preliminary source. This saves you the trouble of copying data onto bibliography and note cards, since you can cut out citations you want to check and paste them onto your cards. In many cases you will have to make additional notes when you read the reference to supplement the abstract obtained in the computer search, but the savings in time will still be significant.

4. *Permits Simultaneous Searching.* When doing a manual search, you can only look up one descriptor at a time in the subject index of your preliminary source. Therefore, manual searches are difficult to conduct for problems that involve several concepts that must all be present in a reference in order to fit the researcher's needs. For example, a problem such as "the effects of television violence on the aggressive behavior of preschool children" involves four major concepts: *television, violence, aggression,* and *preschool children.* It would be very time-consuming to locate references that include all four concepts using the manual search procedure. In contrast, the computer can search for references that have any combination of descriptors.

Therefore, a high percentage of the references that are listed in a computer search are likely to be "on target." This saves much reading and rejecting of nonrelevant references, which you must do when carrying out a manual search.

Where Can You Have a Computer Search Conducted?

Many universities have terminals that link them to one of the information retrieval systems such as the Lockheed *DIALOG* system or the *SDC/ORBIT* system. You should visit the reference section of your library and see if a terminal is available. If not, there are organizations that will conduct computer searches for you (Pugh, Embry, & Brandhorst, 1976). Having an on-line terminal available speeds up the computer search process and permits the researcher to check the number of relevant references and to get other information that will usually result in a better search. If an on-line terminal is not available, commercial information retrieval services provide order forms on which you can list your problem, descriptors, and other information. These forms are then mailed to the service center where the information is fed into the computer and the search is carried out. For example, Psychological Abstracts Information Service carries out searches of the *Psychological Abstracts* data base (PASAR searches). Information specialists help formulate the search plan, thus improving the chances that the search will be "on target." PASAR searches typically cost between $40 and $60. Guidelines and the PASAR Request Form may be found on the last pages of each number of *Psychological Abstracts*.

The cost of a computer search varies with the service used, the data base searched, and the length of the search. On-line computer time ranges from about $35 to $120 per hour, while the cost of printouts of the selected citations ranges from 5¢ to 35¢ for each citation. Careful planning of the search is essential in order to keep on-line computer time to a minimum. It is usually advisable to go over your search strategy with the person who operates the terminal *before* going on-line. A typical ERIC search on the Lockheed DIALOG system including a printout of 200 abstracts, which is mailed to you, will cost about $30.

In addition to ERIC, a number of other data bases provide information that can be very useful for some research problems. Review the following carefully, and decide whether any of these sources would be more useful than ERIC or should be used to supplement ERIC for your research problem.

Abstracts of Instructional and Research Materials in Vocational and Technical Education (AIM/ARM) may be used in conjunction with ERIC by researchers whose problem falls into the area of vocational and technical education. Materials are indexed using the ERIC *Thesaurus* and may be searched, as can ERIC, using the Lockheed DIALOG system. The two data bases can be searched with little additional effort on the part of the researcher. Yarborough (1975) reports little overlap between *AIM/ARM* and ERIC. For further information on *AIM/ARM,* contact the Center for Vocational Education, Ohio State University, 1960 Kenney Road, Columbus, Ohio 43210.

Exceptional Child Education Resources focus on the education of handicapped and gifted children. References are indexed using ERIC descriptors. The data base is available in the Lockheed DIALOG system. Information can be obtained from the Council for Exceptional Children, 1920 Association Drive, Reston, Virginia 22091.

Psychological Abstracts is available for computer search using the Lockheed DIALOG system in addition to the PASAR search service mentioned above. The references are indexed using the *Thesaurus of Psychological Index Terms*. Many of the descriptors in this thesaurus differ from the ERIC descriptors, so check to see which descriptors best fit your problem. If a thorough coverage is necessary, it is usually desirable to search both data bases. For further information contact the American

Psychological Association, 1200 Seventeenth Street, N.W., Washington, D.C. 20036.

Comprehensive Dissertation Index is based on material from *Dissertation Abstracts International* and *American Doctoral Dissertations.* This data base is available in the Lockheed DIALOG, SDC/ORBIT, and DATRIX II computer systems. To use the DATRIX II system, you may obtain an order form from University Microfilms, 300 North Zeeb Road, Ann Arbor, Michigan 48106 or, if immediate help is needed, phone Dissertations Hotline at (800) 521-3042. The student lists key words and other information about her topic, mails the order form, and receives a printout giving the title, author, degree date, and university for each reference. The issue and page reference in *Dissertation Abstracts International (DAI)* is also given if the dissertation has been abstracted. You may either locate the abstracts you want to read in *DAI* or have them printed out by the computer. The cost of a DATRIX II search is $15 for 150 titles plus 10¢ each for any citations over 150.

Smithsonian Science Information Exchange (SSIE) gathers information on ongoing and recently completed research projects in all fields, including about 1800 per year in the behavioral sciences. Several services are offered including research information packages on major topics, custom searches, and computer searches using the SDC/ORBIT system. All searches are based on the *Notice of Research Project,* a form that contains the project title, funding organization, performing organization, names of investigators, period covered, funding level, and a 200-word technical summary of the work to be performed. This information can be useful in avoiding duplication of research effort, learning about current work, and locating possible funding sources for similar work. For further information contact SSIE, Room 300, 1730 M Street, N.W., Washington, D.C. 20036.

Steps in Conducting an On-Line Computer Search

The following steps have been carried out using the Lockheed DIALOG system as an example. This system contains the data bases that are usually the most important for educational research problems. The same procedure can be used, with some adaptation, for conducting on-line searches with other systems. See Figure 3.1 for a convenient *Record Form* that you can use when planning a computer search. A blank copy of this form is included in the appendixes and may be photocopied.

DEFINE THE RESEARCH PROBLEM

To conduct a successful search, you must write a short but precise statement of your research problem. Most students find it easiest to state their problem in the form of the specific question that they want to answer. If your description is too general, your search will probably produce a great many items that are not closely related to your problem, and that will increase the cost. For example, suppose you are interested in the following problem: "What teaching methods can be used to improve the reading comprehension of elementary pupils who have learning disabilities?" This question describes the investigator's interest in a few words and is written in terms that will help focus the search such as *teaching methods, reading comprehension, elementary,* and *learning disabilities.* In contrast, a statement such as "What is the best way to teach elementary reading?" is not precise enough to describe the problem. If you have difficulty stating your problem in specific terms, read two or three secondary sources in order to get a quick overview of your problem area. We have entered this problem definition into the Computer Search Record Form (Figure 3.1) and will use it as an example.

STATE THE SPECIFIC PURPOSE OF THE SEARCH

Literature searches are conducted for several reasons. Here are some reasons why students, teachers, and school administrators search educational research literature:

- To learn as much as possible about a given problem prior to conducting research related to that problem.
- To update an earlier review. Computer searches can be helpful in updating a review of literature. It is not uncommon for a graduate student to take two or three years after completing the review of literature to complete her research project and write her thesis or dissertation. By this time the review will be somewhat out of date. Using the same descriptors employed in her initial search, she can update her review by instructing the computer to select only those references published since her initial computer search was conducted. If, in reviewing the literature related to a problem in your school, you locate a recent review of research in this area, you may decide to update the previous review rather than duplicate the earlier search. This can save a great deal of time. Remember, however, that any review you find is a secondary source. To check the accuracy of the reviewer, you may want to read the most important primary sources that she cites.
- To prepare a master's paper or term paper that reviews research related to a given topic.
- To assemble evidence related to a major educational question that can be used to help make an important decision. For example, should our school district adopt minimum competency examinations for high school graduation?
- To help locate or develop a new program for adoption in your school. (The example given in Figure 3.1 would fit into this category.) Another example: What research reports, publications or programs are available on drug abuse that could be incorporated into our junior high school curriculum?
- To help a teacher deal with a specific problem in her own classroom. For example, what kinds of reward and/or punishment can I use to reduce disruptive pupil behavior in my class, or what can I do to stop John from hitting the other children?
- To obtain quick information related to a local school problem. For example, the school board requests a report on ways to reduce plate waste in school cafeterias, to be presented at their next meeting.

COMPUTER SEARCH RECORD FORM

Mary Jones
_____
Your Name

Supt. Smith
_____
Person Requesting Search

Purpose of Search: *To get information for, an inservice teacher education program for elementary teachers in mainstream classroom*

Problem Definition: *What special teaching methods can be used to improve the reading comprehension of elementary pupils who have learning disabilities?*

Secondary Sources Reviewed: *Held, D, F. (1984) The Intuitive Approach to Reading and Learning Disabilities: A Practical Alternative. New York; C. C. Thomas*

Data Base to be Searched:
ERIC using the DIALOG SYSTEM

ERIC Descriptors or Psychological Index Terms:

1. *Learning disabilities* (4991)
2. *Learning problems* (1139)
3. *Reading difficulties* (939)
4. *Reading comprehension* (5062)
5. *Reading* (3227)
6. *Reading achievement* (3100)
7. *Reading skills* (5782)
8. *Remedial reading* (2115)
9. *Reading instruction* (9713)
10. *Reading programs* (3781)
11. *Teaching methods* (40486)
12. *Classroom techniques* (3481)
13. *Elementary education* (27292)
14. _____
15. _____
16. _____

Search 1: *1 and 4 and 11*

Search 2: *1 and 4 and 11 and 13*

Search 3: *(1 or 2) and (4 or 8) and (9 or 11)*

Search 4: *(1 or 2) and (4 or 8) and (9 or 11) and 13*

Search 5: *(1 or 2 or 3) and (4 or 5 or 6 or 7 or 8) and (9 or 10 or 11 or 12)*

Search 6: *(1 or 2 or 3) and (4 or 5 or 6 or 7 or 8) and (9 or 10 or 11 or 12) and 13*

Figure 3.1 Computer Search Record Form for Planning the Search of a Preliminary Source

You should think through the precise purpose of your search, since you will use different approaches for different kinds of searches. The purpose of our sample search is given in Figure 3.1.

SELECT THE DATA BASE

The next step is to select one or more data bases that are most relevant to the research problem. For most educational studies a search of the ERIC data base, which includes *RIE* and *CIJE,* will produce much of the relevant literature. For our problem on teaching reading to learning disabled children, a search of *Exceptional Child Education Resources* and *Psychological Abstracts,* both of which are also available in the DIALOG system, could be added to ERIC to give a more complete coverage. However, at this point we will limit our search to the ERIC data base.

SELECT DESCRIPTORS

Using the procedures prescribed for your data base, select the descriptors, index terms, or key words (all synonymous terms) that best describe your problem in terms that the computer will accept. Remember that the *exact* terms used in indexing the materials into the system must be used. If you spell a descriptor incorrectly or make some similar error such as adding an s, the computer will not recognize the descriptor and will report no references.

For example, using the *Thesaurus of ERIC Descriptors,* let's see how we would locate the descriptors that would fit our study of "teaching methods to improve reading comprehension of learning disabled elementary children." First we would take the four main concepts from our problem statement and put them in order of importance, that is, "Learning disabilities," "Reading comprehension," "Teaching methods," and "Elementary pupils." Although the order of the first three terms is not critical, it is necessary to identify the least important term because we may want to drop this term if our initial search produces too few references. We have decided that "Elementary pupils" is the least important term because nearly all studies of reading are carried out in the elementary grades, so we will probably get most relevant studies whether we specify elementary level or not. Also, studies not carried out in the elementary grades may still provide useful information if related to our other three main concepts.

Our next steps are: (1) Look up each of our main concepts in the ERIC *Thesaurus.* For each descriptor listed in the *Thesaurus* a considerable amount of information is provided. Study the sample *Thesaurus* entry in Figure 3.2 before proceeding. (2) Select the descriptor that most closely fits each concept. (3) Select related terms (RT) that can be used to conduct a broader search if necessary. (4) List the selected descriptors and related terms on the Record Form exactly as they appear in the *Thesaurus.* When checking the descriptors in the *Thesaurus,* you will see that the number of *CIJE* and *RIE* references having each descriptor is given. This information can be useful in helping you set up your search plans, and you may want to enter it with the descriptors for future reference. Note in Figure 3.1 that we have listed 13 descriptor terms. In addition to "Learning disabilities," we have listed two related

DESCRIPTOR

ADD DATE
date term was
added to the Thesaurus

POSTINGS NOTE
number of times term
was used in indexing
CIJE and RIE

COMPETENCY BASED EDUCATION

CIJE: 789   RIE: 2,216

Mar. 1980
GC: 330

DESCRIPTOR
GROUP CODE

SCOPE NOTE
usage definition

SN   Educational system that emphasizes the specifica-
tion, learning, and demonstration of those competencies (knowledge, skills, behaviors) that are of
central importance to a given task, activity, or
career

USED FOR

UF   Consequence Based Education
Criterion Referenced Education
Output Oriented Education
Performance Based Education (1974
   1980)
Proficiency Based Education

former descriptor used
from 1974 to 1980

NARROWER TERM

NT   Competency Based Teacher
   Education

BROADER TERM

BT   Education

RELATED TERM

RT   Academic Standards
Accountability
Back to Basics
Behavioral Objectives
Competence
Individualized Instruction
Minimum Competencies
Minimum Competency Testing
Performance
Student Certification

Figure 3.2 Sample *Thesaurus* Entry, Alphabetical Descriptor Display

terms, "Learning problems" and "Reading difficulties." Although the term Learning disabilities refers to a specific type of handicap, the two related terms may produce studies that would be useful, even if not focused on the child with a learning disability. In addition to "Reading comprehension" we have also listed "Reading achievement," "Reading skills," and "Remedial reading" plus the broad descriptor "Reading." One of the rules that persons who prepare abstracts and select descriptors for ERIC references follow is to use the most specific descriptors possible. For example, a study of Reading achievement would have this, not Reading, as a descriptor, since the former is more specific. Thus, broad descriptors such as "Reading" are used only for references in which reading is treated very broadly. We have listed four related terms, "Reading instruction," "Reading programs," and "Classroom techniques," in addition to "Teaching methods." When we look up "Elementary pupils," we find that the closest ERIC descriptor is "Elementary School students." However, ERIC requires that a "level" descriptor be given for each reference, and "Elementary education" seems to be the most appropriate for our search. This descriptor seems to fit our problem better, so it has been listed. Since this is the least important of our four concepts, no related terms were listed on our Record Form. By selecting different combinations of these descriptors, we can conduct as broad or narrow search as we wish.

Many searches are conducted as part of an exhaustive review of literature to be included as part of the student's thesis or master's paper. This kind of review is very sharply focused, since such papers usually cover a narrow problem but usually should include all relevant references for the past 10 years or longer. All relevant narrow descriptors are chosen when possible, and the computer is instructed to locate references that contain combinations of descriptors, which further narrows the search. Searches 5 or 6 (Figure 3.1) would provide an exhaustive search of the ERIC data base. Often, when a very thorough search is called for, the student may search more than one data base in order to get more complete coverage. For example, ERIC, *Psychological Abstracts,* and *Exceptional Child Education Resources* may all be searched to obtain maximum coverage on a problem in special education. In carrying out searches using all three of these data bases, we have found little overlap in the references obtained.

The computer can also be useful in helping the teacher or administrator locate references that relate to a decision that must be made or a question about which some current information is needed. Usually such searches use fewer combinations of descriptors, since an exhaustive coverage is not needed. In our example (Figure 3.1), the best approach for conducting a brief search would be Search 2, which includes only the three descriptors most on-target. A single data base is sufficient for brief searches. To avoid getting very large numbers of references, it may also be advisable to instruct the computer to select only the 10 to 30 most recent references for each descriptor or descriptor combination.

Since there is no source available that gives precise definitions of the ERIC descriptors, we have no way of knowing how a reviewer decides to use one descriptor in preference to another that is closely related. By listing a few related descriptors for each major concept as we have done above (Figure 3.1), we will find more references. Doing an exhaustive search using a large number of descriptors reduces the chance that we will miss an important reference but also means that the computer will select more references that are not closely relevant to our problem.

PLAN THE COMPUTER SEARCH

The next step is to combine the descriptors we have selected into one or more search plans. In planning your search, it is best to start with the descriptors that most closely fit the concepts related to your problem. Descriptors may be combined using *and* and *or.* As we plan alternate searches, you will see that *or* connectors tend to increase the number of references selected by the computer, since there are more references that have one descriptor *or* the other than have either by itself. But *and* connectors tend to reduce the number of selections, since only references that have all of the descriptors connected by *and* will be selected. Before planning your searches, you should also note the number of *CIJE* and *RIE* references for each descriptor. If one of your key descriptors has only been assigned to a few references, you may want to order information for all of these references. As a rule, such a descriptor should not be linked with other descriptors with an "and" connector, since doing so will probably reduce the number of references reported by the computer to near zero. For example, if we were interested in the use of Indemnity Bonds by school districts, we would find in the *Thesaurus* that the system contains only four *CIJE* and eight *RIE* references with this descriptor. However, you will note on Figure 3.1 that all the descriptors we have chosen have been used with fairly large numbers of references, so that we can safely plan searches that involve simultaneous searching of all of the concepts in our problem statement, using "and" connectors. Therefore, let us plan a search of our four most relevant descriptors connected with *and* as follows:[2]

> Learning disabilities (1) *and* Reading comprehension (4) *and* Teaching methods (11) *and* Elementary education (13). (Search 2 in Figure 3.1.)

We would expect this search to locate only a few references, but those located should be mostly on target, since all four of our most relevant descriptors are used. This is planned for our second search, because when as many as three *and* connectors are used, the search is often so narrowly focused that not enough references to meet our needs are produced.

First, we will plan to conduct a search from which we have omitted *Elementary Education*, earlier identified as our least important concept. Thus, Search 1 as planned in Figure 3.1 consists of:

> Learning disabilities *and* Reading comprehension *and* Teaching methods; or, for the computer, 1 *and* 4 *and* 11.

In our instructions to the computer we would use the "set" numbers that indicate the order in which the descriptors were entered into the computer: 1 *and* 4 *and* 11 (see Figure 3.1). This search plan tells the computer to locate only references that have all three of these descriptors, since we have connected the descriptors with *and*. This search should produce more references than Search 2 and would probably be sufficient for the purpose given on our Record Form (Figure 3.1).

If we wanted a more thorough search, we could include some of our related terms. Remember that related terms are usually joined with *or* connectors, while different concepts in our problem are joined with *and* connectors. In our third search plan we will use one related term with each of our three most important descriptors. This will give us the following, which is listed as Search 3 in Figure 3.1:

> (1 or 2) *and* (4 or 8) *and* (9 or 11).

This search plan tells the computer to locate references that have either descriptor 1 *or* 2 (that is, Learning disabilities *or* Learning difficulties) *and* either descriptor 4 *or* 8 *and* either descriptor 9 *or* 11. This will broaden the search related to our three most important concepts and would therefore be expected to produce more references than Search 1 or 2.

For Search 4 we will add our least important concept, *Elementary education*, to Search 3 with an "and" connector. This search, like Search 1, would be severely

---

2. It is important to refer frequently to Figure 3.1 while you read the following search descriptions.

restricted by using three *and* connectors, but would probably produce more references than Search 1.

(1 or 2) *and* (4 or 8) *and* (9 or 11) *and* 14.

Next, we will plan a search (Search 5) that will use all 12 descriptors related to our three main concepts. This is the kind of search a student may want to carry out for a master's paper or a superintendent might want to help her make a major school decision. Search 5 would instruct the computer to locate references containing combinations of the following descriptors:

(1 or 2 or 3) *and* (4 or 5 or 6 or 7 or 8) *and* (9 or 10 or 11 or 12).

This search would produce more references than any of our previous searches because of the use of a large number of terms related to our three main concepts that we have included. You will recall that including related terms (RT) connected with "or" increases the number of references that the computer will locate. This would be a very broad search and would probably include many references that are not closely related to our problem. It may also produce such a large number of references that it would take a great deal of time to read the abstracts and select those most relevant to our problem. The person who carries out this type of search accepts the extra work of checking a large number of abstracts in order to reduce the chances of overlooking an important reference.

If the number of references located in Search 5 were very large, we could reduce these, as we did in Search 4, by adding descriptor 13, "Elementary education." In this case (Search 6) the computer would be instructed to include descriptor 13 with an *and* connector to Search 5.

Your Record Form would now contain all the information important to planning your search. You would have stated your problem, described the purpose of the search, selected a data base, tested your descriptors, and planned several alternative searches.

CONDUCT THE SEARCH

You have now completed the planning of your search, but you have not yet spent any money or used any computer time. It is important to plan your search *very carefully* before you go on-line. You should also explain your search to the person who will operate the computer terminal, so that she will understand what you want to do and the search strategy you have selected. This person may have some valuable suggestions for conducting your search. However, be sure that you fully understand how these suggestions will change your search before agreeing to them. Once you are in communication with the computer, you must pay long distance telephone charges plus computer charges. If you have to take time to revise your search plan while on-line, the cost of your search will increase.

Once you are on-line, the first step is to enter your descriptors. Each descriptor will be given a number, and once the descriptors are all entered, you can refer to them by number, thus saving time.

The computer will then tell you how many *CIJE* and *RIE* references there are in the data base (that is, in the ERIC system) for each of your descriptors. Figure 3.3 gives this information for the 13 descriptors.[3] For example, "Learning disabilities" is Descriptor 1 (that is, the first entered). The system contained 5848 references that have "Learning disabilities" as a descriptor at the time this search was conducted. In looking over Figure 3.3, you will note that broad descriptors such as "Reading" have been applied to very large numbers of references in the ERIC system. Using broad descriptors increases the scope of your search but also may result in the computer selecting many references that will be peripheral to your problem. Notice that the computer printed a message after "Reading" in Figure 3.3 suggesting that you should use a more specific term than "Reading," if possible. Of course, in selecting our descriptors, we have chosen several specific terms related to reading. If you are conducting a sharply focused search and are not interested in references that give peripheral or background information, it is advisable to avoid broad descriptors for which many thousands of references are available.

Once our 13 descriptors have been entered, we can enter each of the six searches as planned in Figure 3.1 into the computer to determine how many references each will produce. Figure 3.3 gives the results of this step. Notice that related groups of descriptors that are connected by *or* are placed in parentheses and these related groups are connected ısing *and*. We must now decide which of these searches to use, since the computer can supply bibliographical data and abstracts for any or all the references identified in these searches. Note that Search 1, which includes the most on-target descriptors for our three main concepts, produced 42 references. Since most of these references would be relevant to our problem, this search would be sufficient for most purposes. If you did not need an exhaustive search, you could log off the computer at this point and have the data on these 42 articles mailed to you.

Search 2 combines Search 1 (set 14 on Figure 3.3) with Descriptor 13, Elementary education. Note that this search produced only 10 references, probably because we have used three *and* connectors, thus greatly restricting its scope. The amount of restriction brought about by using the third *and* connector is also seen by comparing Searches 5 and 6. For Search 6, adding the Elementary education descriptor (13) with the third *and* connector reduced the number of references from 938 to 238.

As discussed earlier, the purpose of our search determines how broad it should be. If we need only a few references to prepare a brief report for the school board, the 10 references produced by Search 2 would probably be sufficient, since they are all likely to be relevant to our problem. On the other hand, if the purpose of our search were to get information that would help us set up an in-service teacher training program, the 42 references located by Search 1 would probably be sufficient. If we want a broader coverage as a starting point for developing a district-wide or state-wide program, probably Search 3 would be our best choice, since it produced

---

3. The *Thesaurus* lists the number of references having each descriptor and is accurate at the time the *Thesaurus* was published. The computer will give you current data.

```
? S LEARNING DISABILITIES
          1 5848 LEARNING DISABILITIES {CATEGORY IN FEDERAL LEGISL
? S LEARNING PROBLEMS
          2 1238 LEARNING PROBLEMS {CATEGORY IN FEDERAL LEGISLATIO
? S READING DIFFICULTIES
          3 1198 READING DIFFICULTIES {PROBLEMS IN READING, CAUSED
? S READING COMPREHENSION
          4 5866 READING COMPREHENSION
? S READING
          5 46526 READING {{NOTE: USE A MORE SPECIFIC TERM IF POSSI
? S READING ACHIEVEMENT
          6 3414 READING ACHIEVEMENT {LEVEL OF ATTAINMENT IN ANY O
? S READING SKILLS
          7 6334 READING SKILLS {COMPLEX BEHAVIORS DEVELOPED THROU
? S REMEDIAL READING
          8 2305 REMEDIAL READING {DIAGNOSIS AND TUTORING OF STUDE
? S READING INSTRUCTION
          9 10931 READING INSTRUCTION
? S READING PROGRAMS
          10 3929 READING PROGRAMS
? S TEACHING METHODS
          11 44518 TEACHING METHODS {WAYS OF PRESENTING INSTRUCTIONA
? S CLASSROOM TECHNIQUES
          12 4356 CLASSROOM TECHNIQUES {TECHNIQUES USED IN THE CLAS
? S ELEMENTARY EDUCATION
          13 30672 ELEMENTARY EDUCATION {EDUCATION PROVIDED IN KINDE
? C1 AND 4 AND 11
          14   42 1 AND 4 AND 11
? C14 AND 13
          15   10 14 AND 13
? C{1 OR 2} AND {4 OR 8} AND {9 OR 11}
          16   172  {1 OR 2} AND {4 OR 8} AND {9 OR 11}
? C16 AND 13
          17   38 16 AND 13
? C {1 OR 2 OR 3} AND {4 OR 5 OR 6 OR 7 OR 8} AND {9 OR 10 OR 11 OR 12}
          18 938 {1 OR 2 OR 3} AND {4 OR 5 OR 6 OR 7 OR 8} AND {9 OR
               10 OR 11 OR 12}
? C18 AND 13
          19 238 18 AND 13
```

Figure 3.3 Selected Descriptors, Set Numbers, Number of References for Each Descriptor and Combination, and Six Searches

172 references. However, the introduction of related terms into Search 3 would result in a smaller percent of our references being closely related to our problem than would be the case for Searches 1 and 2. If we need a very thorough review as part of a major research funding proposal, Search 6 would probably be our best choice. This search would include many references that were only peripherally related to our problem but would give us a much broader understanding of the context into which our problem fits and would also reduce the chances of missing an important reference.

Search 5, which produced 938 references, would be inappropriate for anything other than an exhaustive search in which you must reduce the chances of missing an important source as much as possible and where you want a good coverage of peripheral material that will help you place your problem into a broad context of research and theory.

Once you have decided which of the alternate searches best meets your needs, it is often helpful to instruct the computer to print bibliographical information on 10 to 15 of the references it has located in that search. This gives you an idea of the kinds of references that have been selected. If none of the references seems to be relevant to your problem, you should log off the computer and restudy your search plans to determine whether they really fit your topic.

Reducing the Number of References in Your Search

Reading the abstracts for 938 references, deciding which ones are sufficiently relevant that you should read them, and categorizing them in some manner suitable for your problem is a tiresome task that will take the average reader from 10 to 15 hours. Two strategies that can help reduce the number of references in your search are (1) instructing the computer to print out data on recent references only, and (2) limiting the search to major descriptors.

ASKING FOR MOST RECENT REFERENCES

The computer prints out the references from the ERIC data base that are included in the search you have selected in a definite order. First, all references from *CIJE* are printed in chronological order, starting with the most recent. Then *RIE* references are printed, again in chronological order. Thus, you can reduce the total number of references printed out by requesting a limited number from *RIE* and *CIJE*. For example, if we wanted only the 50 most recent articles from the 172 located in Search 3 (Figure 3.2), we would first ask the computer how many EJ's (references from *CIJE*) and how many ED's (references from *RIE*) were included in the 172. We could then ask the computer to print 25 citations from each source.

Another technique that can be used, if only recent references are wanted, is to put a "date command" into the computer. If a date command "1980–1985" is entered, then only references published during those years will be included in your search. Date commands are also useful when you want to study literature from specific years. For example, suppose you were conducting a historical study designed to compare the content of articles dealing with school segregation at five-year intervals starting in 1968. Using date commands, you could limit your search to articles published in 1968, 1973, 1978, and 1983 having the descriptor "School segregation."

LIMITING YOUR SEARCH TO MAJOR DESCRIPTORS

Have you wondered where the information comes from that is entered into the computer for each reference in the ERIC system? This information is prepared at one of the ERIC clearinghouses by an abstractor. The abstractor reads the article or document, writes the abstract, and decides what descriptors to assign to the article. Descriptors are selected to identify the subject content, age and educational level dealt with, research methodology employed, tests used, as well as other information. The descriptors selected are classified as Major Descriptors and Minor Descriptors. Up to six Major Descriptors are assigned each document, in order to cover its main focus. Minor Descriptors are used to indicate less important aspects of the subject covered, as well as to describe nonsubject features such as educational level and research methods.

An effective way to reduce the number of references that will be produced by a given search is to tell the computer to select only articles for which your key descriptors have been classified as major descriptors. You do this by entering each descriptor followed by "/DE* or MAJ." For example, instead of entering only "Learning disabilities" (Figure 3.3), we would enter "Learning disabilities/DE* or MAJ." When Search 3 (Figure 3.1) is conducted with major descriptors only, the number of references drops from 172 to 31. This is a greater reduction than is usually found—the usual being about a 50 percent drop when search is limited to major descriptors. Although we would lose some interesting references peripheral to our problem by limiting our search to major descriptors, we would lose only a few closely on target.

Proximity Searching

Proximity searching is a procedure for searching the citations entered in the data base for specific words or phrases. This technique is very useful when you want to search a very narrow and sharply defined topic or when there are no descriptor terms that really fit.

Proximity searching may be carried out with any of the DIALOG data bases although the coverage may differ from one data base to another. The search may be carried out for single words, phrases, or for two or more words that appear in close proximity in the material searched. These words do not have to be descriptor terms; any combination of words can be used. For ERIC, the material searched for each reference includes the title, descriptions, identifiers, and abstract. For example, suppose the researcher were interested in studies dealing with the use of forced busing to achieve school desegregation. We find that "forced busing" is not a descriptor although there are some ERIC descriptors that relate to this topic, such as "Busing" (657 references), "Bus transportation" (737 references), "School buses"

(235 references), which could be combined with "School desegregation" (3564 references) or "School segregation" (482). Using these descriptors would probably produce most references related to forced busing but would also require review of hundreds of citations in order to find those that were relevant. For example, a search of "Busing and School desegregation" in the ERIC data base produced 468 references. A search of "Busing or Bus transportation or School buses" and "School desegregation or School segregation" would produce hundreds more.

The researcher will obtain much more sharply focused citations by carrying out a proximity search using the words "forced busing." In conducting a proximity search, different instructions can be given to the computer, so that different criteria will be met before a citation containing "forced busing" is selected. These instructions are called "proximity operators," the most common of which are "W," "N," "F," and "C." If the W limiter is used, one of the selected words (busing) must directly follow the other (forced) in order for the reference to be selected. If the N limiter is used, the words "forced busing" must be adjacent but can be in either order. It would not be used in this case, since there is little likelihood that any references would use the term "busing forced." If the F limiter is used, both words must appear in the same field (for example, both words must be somewhere in the title). If the C limiter is used, the selected words need only appear someplace in the citation. Thus, different proximity operators can be used to broaden or narrow the search as desired.

When we searched "Forced (W) busing," we located 18 references. A search of "Forced (F) busing" produced 24 citations, while "Forced (C) busing" produced 25 citations. These few citations were all on target, thus saving much of the labor that would have been required if a search involving the five relevant descriptors named above had been conducted.

For most educational topics a search of relevant descriptors is the best choice. The proximity search, however, is a very useful tool when a problem arises that its special characteristics can help solve.

Getting the References

After you have decided which search to use, you have several options with respect to the kind of information you can ask the computer to give you and how you will receive this information. To receive the information, you can either instruct the computer to print out data on the selected references immediately while you are on-line, or to print the information after you go off-line and mail the printout to you. If you need the information immediately or your search includes 20 or fewer references, it is preferable to select the first option. However, for searches involving a large number of references, it is much cheaper to have the printout mailed to you. You will usually receive it in about a week.

The computer can supply information to you at the following three levels of detail:

1. The first option provides you with the title and accession number (for ERIC either the EJ or ED number). If your funds are limited and your search involves 20 references or fewer, you may choose to select this option. The title is often useful in helping you decide whether you should read an article but is much less useful than an abstract. In some cases the title tells you almost nothing. For example, in our search for references related to teaching reading to learning disabled elementary students the titles located included "A Corner on Reading," "The Reluctant Reader," and "Case Studies in Reading." For most searches this is a poor option, since the extra time taken to look up irrelevant references is worth more than the small saving in search costs.

2. The second option includes complete bibliographic data, the EJ or ED number, and a list of descriptors that apply to the reference. For example:

> EJ188759   EC111239
>   Learning Word Meanings: A Comparison of Instructional Procedures
>   Pany, Darlene; Jenkins, Joseph R.
>   Learning Disability Quarterly, 1, 2, 21-32 Spr 78
>   Language: English
>   Descriptors: *Learning Disabilities/ *Teaching Methods/ *Reading
> Comprehension/ *Word Recognition/ Reading Instruction/ Reading Skills/
> Vocabulary Skills/ Word Study Skills/ Elementary Education/ Exceptional Child
> Research

This option, which gives the descriptors plus the bibliographical data, gives you a little better basis for judging the content of the article. Also, if you want to read the article, you can go directly to the journal, instead of first looking it up in *CIJE* for the bibliographical data. At present, the cost of having the printout mailed to you for this level is 5¢ per reference.

3. The third option includes all the data from the second option plus an abstract if one has been prepared. Here is an example from another computer search we conducted that was concerned with teacher use of educational research.

> ED246023   SP024890
>   On Getting from Here (Research) to There (Practice).
>   Fenstermacher, Gary D.
>   Mar 1984 7p.; In: Egbert, Robert L., Ed., and Kluender, Mary M.,
> Ed. Using Research to Improve Teacher Education: The Nebraska
> Consortium. Teacher Monograph No. 1. (SP 024 888), p22-27.
>   EDRS Price - MF01/PC01 Plus Postage
>   Language: English
>   Document Type: POSITION PAPER (120)
>   Geographic Source: U.S.; Virginia
>   Journal Announcement: RIENDOV84
>   Target Audience: Teachers; Practitioners
>   There is no easy way to get from research on teaching to teaching practice;
> moreover, trying to make teaching practices directly out of research can have
> destructive effects for teaching. Research can be extremely beneficial when
> results are linked with teachers' goals, and when teachers are aware that a
> specific occasion is appropriate for realization of the goal. This awareness enables
> them to engage in actions appropriate to fulfilling the goal. Research results can
> be brought to bear on teaching practices through careful, considered incorpora-
> tion into the practical arguments in the minds of teachers. If research is pre-

sented to teachers in a manner that shows regard for their prior beliefs and experience, teachers will be encouraged to consider the research and its impact on practice. (CJB)

    Descriptors: *Adoption (Ideas); Behavior Change; Educational Research; Elementary School Teachers; Elementary Secondary Education; *Research Utilization; Secondary School Teachers; *Teacher Attitudes; *Teacher Behavior; *Teacher Improvement

    Identifiers: *Research Practice Relationship

At present the cost of having abstracts of your search sent to you is 10¢ per abstract. This is generally the best option because the abstracts usually tell you enough so that you can decide whether you should look up and read the original reference, thus saving you the trouble of locating and scanning irrelevant articles.

CHECKING YOUR PRINTOUT

When you receive your computer printout of abstracts, the first step is to read all abstracts and code them in terms of their relevance to your problem. The purpose of the code system is to help you decide which references to read first. Some codes also identify the aspect of your problem that a given reference relates to, thus helping sort your note cards by topic or subtopic before you start reading. Any code that meets your needs is satisfactory; here is the one that we use:

    ++_____a very important and relevant reference
    +_____relevant reference, should be read
    √_____check this reference, it may be relevant
    o_____not relevant, do not check

After you have read the abstracts and coded each reference, cut out all references you plan to read or check and paste each on a five-by-eight-inch note card. Start your reading with the most recent of your most important articles (i.e., ++). After reading and making whatever supplementary notes are needed for all of your ++ references, read your + references and finally look up your √ references, scan them, and read and make notes on those that prove to be relevant. You will find many helpful suggestions on how to read and take notes on primary source references in the next chapter.

Developing Search Skills

You should not expect your first attempt at computer searching to be a complete success. Most people have to plan and carry out three or four searches before they are sufficiently familiar with the *Thesaurus* and the search process to use the system fully. Therefore, it is advisable to conduct a few small-scale searches on topics needed for term papers or topics related to specific classroom problems that interest you. Such searches, if well planned, will usually cost less than $10 and will give you much valuable experience. Once you have had this practice at using the system, you can plan major searches with more confidence.

EJ282648 EC152054

Peer Tutors Help Autistic Students Enter the Mainstream.

Campbell, Ann: And Others

Teaching Exceptional Children. v15 n2 p64–69 Win   1983

Available from: Reprint: UMI

Language: English

Document Type: JOURNAL ARTICLE (080): PROJECT DESCRIPTION (141)

A peer tutoring program in which tutors were taught behavioral techniques as well as background information through a broad game format was successful in promoting integration of a class of autistic adolescents in a middle school. Peer tutors helped to promote positive attitudes among students and teachers.

(CL)

Descriptors: *Attitude Change: *Autism: Behavior Modification; Middle

Schools; *Peer Influence; *Peer Teaching; Program Descriptions; Student

Attitudes; Teacher Attitudes

EJ274446 EC151160

Peer Tutors Help Autistic Students Enter the Mainstream.

Campbell, Ann; And Others

Teaching Exceptional Children. v15 n2 p64–69 Win   1983

Available from: Reprint: UMI

Language: English

Document Type: JOURNAL ARTICLE (080); PROJECT DESCRIPTION

(141)

The peer tutoring program was initiated at the Belle Vue (Florida) Middle School as an effective way of bringing autistic students into contact with the mainstream. (SW)

Descriptors: *Autism; Mainstreaming; Middle Schools; *Peer Relationship;

*Peer Teaching; Program Descriptions

Figure 3.4 Two Citations of the Same Article, from the ERIC System

THE SYSTEM IS NOT PERFECT

It is not uncommon for researchers to be suspicious of computer searches because they have carried out a search in which references that they knew were relevant to their topic did not appear. The usual reason is the researcher's failure to use a sufficient number of related terms with "or" connecters.

However, the article may also have failed to show up because of an error in assigning descriptors. Keep in mind the process employed in preparing abstracts and selecting descriptors for a given article. The article is assigned to one of the ERIC clearinghouses, and someone who is presumably knowledgeable about the subject reads the article, prepares the abstract (in most cases), and selects the descriptors.[4] Unfortunately, both the preparation of the abstract and decision as to which descriptors are relevant are quite subjective. Therefore, if the same article were assigned for review to a half dozen different persons, it is unlikely that any two would include the same material in their abstract or would list exactly the same descriptors. This subjectivity is clearly illustrated by the two *CIJE* printouts from the ERIC system shown in Figure 3.4. If you will look carefully at these two references, it is clear that they are two different reviews of the same article. However, if you read the two abstracts, you will see that they have little in common. A look at the descriptors is even more surprising. The first review lists nine descriptors, while the second review lists only six. Note furthermore that only four of the descriptors, "Autism," "Middle schools," "Peer teaching," and "Program descriptions" are common to the two reviews. This clearly illustrates the fallibility of this system. This kind of error, however, is rare and should not stop you from using computer searching, since, although the system is far from perfect, it is still much faster and better than manual searching.

References

PUGH, E., EMBRY, J. D., & BRANDHORST, W. T. (1976, June). *Survey of ERIC data base search services.* Washington, D.C.: National Institute of Education, Educational Resources Information Center.

YARBOROUGH, J. (1975, September). *How to prepare a computer search of ERIC: A non-technical approach.* Stanford, Calif.: ERIC Clearinghouse on Information Resources (ED 110 096).

Recommended Reading

PUGH, E., EMBRY, J. D., & BRANDHORST, W. T. (1976, June). *Survey of ERIC data base search services.* Washington, D.C.: National Institute of Education, Educational Resources Information Center.

This booklet lists organizations that maintain the ERIC data base and describes the data bases available from each organization. The final section lists geographically over 200 local organizations that can provide computer searches. This section contains virtually all information the student needs to locate services available in his area, including such information as the address and telephone number, data bases available from each organization, cost per search, and so on.

YARBOROUGH, J. (1975, September). *How to prepare a computer search of ERIC: A non-technical approach.* Stanford, Calif.: ERIC Clearinghouse on Information Resources (ED 110 096).

This booklet provides a brief description of the ERIC system, describes data bases of interest to educators, and gives the reader a step-by-step process for preparing an ERIC computer search. Also included is a glossary of terms used in information retrieval systems and an annotated bibliography.

---

4. Since clearinghouses often use college students to do the actual reading and abstracting, this presumption of knowledgeability is sometimes false.

Application Problems

1. Check your university library to answer the following questions:
    a. Is the *Thesaurus of ERIC Descriptors* available?
    b. Is the *Thesaurus of Psychological Index Terms* available?
    c. Does your university have a terminal for conducting computer searches? If not, list the location of the closest terminal. _____

   _____

    d. If your university has a terminal, check which of the following data bases are available:

   _____(1) ERIC _____(2) *Psychological Abstracts* _____(3) *AIM/ARM*
   _____(4) Exceptional Child _____(5) *Comprehensive Dissertation Index*
   _____(6) *SSIE*.

   Check your university's list of data bases and list any others that might be useful. _____

   _____

2. Suppose you are planning to set up a program of individualized instruction in your elementary school for children with learning disabilities and want to locate research related to this topic. Carry out the following steps.
    a. Photocopy the Computer Search Record Form (Appendix 1).
    b. Enter the Purpose of Search and the Program Definition.
    c. Check the 1984–1985 Subject Index of *Books in Print* for books related to this problem and list two under Secondary Sources.
    d. Write *Psychological Abstracts* under data base to be searched.
    e. Underline key words in Problem Definition.
    f. Look up key words in the *Thesaurus of Psychological Index Terms* and enter these words (or synonyms from the *Thesaurus*). Which is least important of your key terms?
    g. Enter broader, narrower, or related terms that might be useful in case you decide to conduct a broad search.
    h. Make out three possible searches and enter in Record Form: A brief search, using key terms only, a broader search with two "or" connectors, and an exhaustive search.
3. Make a photocopy of the Computer Search Record Form (Appendix 1).
    a. Select one of the problem statements or questions you wrote for Application Problem 1 in Chapter 2 and write it in the Problem Definition section of the record form.
    b. Underline the key words in your problem definition and, using the ERIC *Thesaurus*, list one descriptor and two related terms for each key word. Enter these descriptors in your record form.
    c. Plan the following complete searches, and for each write down the search plan on your record form including descriptor numbers, "and" connectors, and "or" connectors as they would be entered into the computer.
        (1) A search that would be likely to produce a few references that are closely related to your problem or question, using not more than two "and" connectors.
        (2) A search that would be likely to produce a large number of references, many of which are not closely on target.

CHAPTER 4

PRIMARY SOURCES IN EDUCATION

Overview

After completing your search of preliminary sources, it is time to locate, read, and note the references that this search identified. Most will be primary source references. This chapter describes the four main types of primary sources: professional journals, reports, scholarly books, and dissertations. You will learn how to locate these references in the library and from other sources, how to check them with a minimum of effort, and how to take the notes you will need in preparing your report. Finally, you will learn how to organize your notes and use them in writing the report.

Objectives

1. Name and briefly describe the four major types of primary source references.
2. Discuss the advantages of reports over professional journals.
3. Describe *Dissertation Abstracts International*.
4. Describe how you can obtain references not available in your local library.
5. Describe the recommended strategy for reading and making notes on research articles, theoretical articles, and longer references such as reports, books, or dissertations.
6. Explain how your note cards can be classified to facilitate writing your report.
7. Describe what should be covered in each of the main sections of your report.
8. State 11 rules that you should follow in writing the body of your report.

Types of Primary Sources

The end product of your search of the preliminary sources in your field will be a set of bibliography cards, which may also include brief abstracts if you have conducted a computer search. The next step in carrying out your review is to start checking the references you have located, reading them, and making notes on any information that is relevant to your problem.

However, before we discuss ways to obtain the references you need and give you a few hints on how to read them and take notes, let's look briefly at the kinds of publications in which most primary source information is reported. In the next few pages we will describe four types of primary source publications: professional journals, reports, scholarly books and monographs, and dissertations.

PROFESSIONAL JOURNALS

There are a great many journals that are devoted in varying degrees to publishing reports of research in education and related behavioral sciences. Some of these are general, publishing articles on a wide range of educational topics. Others are limited to a single area such as teacher education, mathematics education, or learning disabilities.

The *American Educational Research Journal* is a good example of the general journals, publishing what it describes as "original reports of empirical and theoretical studies in education." Published quarterly, a typical issue contains four to eight articles averaging about 10 pages in length, plus several book reviews.

The *Journal of Teacher Education* is an example of a single-area journal. Published bimonthly, each issue deals with some specific aspect of teacher education such as in-service education, or educating handicapped children. Each number includes up to a dozen short articles, averaging about four pages each. Only a few are original reports of research; most report opinions or experiences of persons involved in teacher education.

Both general and single-area journals vary greatly in the types of articles they publish. Some emphasize reports of original research studies, while others emphasize theory or opinion articles or articles describing new programs or the experiences of the authors. All make a contribution to our knowledge and understanding of educational problems. However, you must be sensitive to the kind of article you are reading, since each contributes differently to an understanding of your problem. We will discuss this further in the section on note taking.

REPORTS

Many of the important research findings and theoretical papers in education are first published as reports. Virtually all funding agencies require final reports on any projects they support. In addition to reports on research projects a variety of reports are published by state and federal agencies, professional associations, and local school districts. Reports come from many sources and range from reports of small-scale projects conducted in a single school to national policy statements made by presidential task forces. Most of these reports are abstracted in the Documents Resume section of *Resources in Education,* and unless published elsewhere, microfiche copies are distributed by ERIC to most college and university libraries. *Resources in Education* includes a wide variety of different kinds of reports such as papers read at professional meetings, reports from local, state, regional, and federal education agencies, documents prepared by universities and colleges, and conference proceedings.

Many important educational documents, such as the findings of presidential task forces or the conclusions emerging from major national conferences, are published only as reports. The ERIC microfiche file also includes many papers that report on important new research or discuss new programs or theoretical positions.

Reports have some advantages over professional journals as sources of new ideas and research findings in education. The most important advantage is that reports are usually available with much less delay than information published in journals. When a researcher finishes a federally funded project, he must submit a final report within a short time limit, and copies of this report are sent to ERIC for inclusion in *RIE*. If he also decides to publish his findings in a professional journal, he must rewrite his report, submit it to a journal, and typically wait about two years before it is published. Reports also have the advantage of giving more detailed information, since they are not subject to the severe space limitations that journals impose on the author. Finally, reports are easily accessible from the ERIC microfiche file, and since most are not copyrighted, may be copied without restrictions.

SCHOLARLY BOOKS AND MONOGRAPHS

Research or theoretical works of major importance, although often starting as reports, are sometimes further developed and expanded into scholarly books or monographs. Some such works are published by commercial publishers, but many are published by university presses, since the sales potential for most is small. *The Invisible Children* by Ray Rist (1978) is a good example of a scholarly book that reports important research insights having national implications. Rist reports in great depth on the experiences of a group of black children who were bused to an upper-middle-class white elementary school in Portland, Oregon. Both his research methods and his findings would be of value to any elementary teacher or administrator interested in school integration.

DISSERTATIONS

Most doctoral dissertations in education report on original research and therefore are primary source documents. In searching educational topics in preliminary sources such as *Psychological Abstracts,* you will find many references listed from *Dissertation Abstracts International (DAI).* This is a monthly compilation of abstracts of doctoral dissertations submitted by more than 375 cooperating institutions in the United States and Canada. It has been published in various forms since 1938, when it first appeared as *Microfilm Abstracts.* There are two sections: Section A contains dissertations in the humanities and social sciences including education; Section B covers the sciences (including psychology) and engineering. The abstracts within each issue of Section A are organized into 32 major content areas, one of which is Education. There are 37 subtopics such as "Adult," "Art," "Higher," "Preschool," and "Teacher training" under the Education content area. Students interested in checking dissertations in one of these broad areas of education should check the table of contents to locate pages containing relevant abstracts.

Each monthly issue also contains a *Keyword Title Index* in which the bibliographic entries are classified and arranged alphabetically by important key words contained in the title. To search a specific topic, check the Keyword Title Index to locate relevant abstracts. For example, a student interested in the social development of preschool children could check "Social," "Development," and "Preschool" in the Keyword Title Index, read the titles listed under each key word, and copy the page numbers for abstracts related to his topic. He would then read each of the selected abstracts.

Abstracts in education vary in length up to a full page and usually give a good coverage of the essentials of the dissertation. Thus, you can nearly always decide from reading the abstract whether a given dissertation is sufficiently relevant to your problem to justify reading the entire paper.

It is also possible to conduct a computer search through the *Dissertation Abstracts International.* To conduct a search, you first enter the key words from your problem statement. For older dissertations the computer searches the title for these words and terms. However, for recent dissertations the computer searches the entire citation including the abstract for the terms you have selected.

Data bases such as ERIC use a controlled vocabulary. In other words, the terms given in *Thesaurus of ERIC Descriptions,* and only those terms, are used to classify the references contained in the data base. The *Comprehensive Dissertation Index* data base does not use a controlled vocabulary, and therefore it is impossible to predict what key words have been used to classify a given dissertation. Thus, a search of this data base is somewhat more hit-or-miss than ERIC. To get a complete search, it is necessary to introduce a large number of synonymous terms in hopes that one of the terms entered will be in the title. Essentially, a search of the *Comprehensive Dissertation Index* is a proximity search. For example if you were interested in dissertations dealing with learning disabilities, you would enter "Learning (W) Disabilities" and would retrieve data on dissertations with this term in the title. You should remember, however, that for dissertations published since 1980, terms can be searched for in the entire record, including the abstract. Abstracts entered into the system since 1980 can also be printed on-line by the terminal in your library. However, it is almost as fast and somewhat less expensive to have the computer print a briefer format such as bibliographic data and then look up the abstracts in your library's copy of *Dissertation Abstracts International.* You can also conduct simultaneous searches of the key concepts in your problem statement using "and" and "or" connectors in the same way they are used in computer searches of ERIC. For example, we entered Searches 1 and 2 from our search plan concerned with improving the reading comprehension of elementary pupils with learning disabilities (see Figure 3.1). Search 1 produced no dissertations, and Search 2 produced only three. This illustrates the need for using a large number of related terms in order to get sufficient coverage of this data base.

Any dissertation covered in *Dissertation Abstracts International* may be purchased from University Microfilms International on either microfilm or xerox, and the order number is given at the end of the abstract. The cost of a microfilm copy is currently $16, while a xerox copy may be obtained for $25.50. Interlibrary loan is another option for obtaining a dissertation you need for your literature search. However, many universities will not loan dissertations, and most are rather slow in mailing them. Often the cost of borrowing a dissertation through interlibrary loan is greater than the cost of buying the microfilm.

Dissertation Abstracts International can be considered a preliminary source, since it helps the reader locate dissertations, that is, primary source documents. However, *DAI* is also a primary source, since the abstracts are written by the authors of the dissertations.

Obtaining Primary Sources

USING THE LIBRARY

The majority of your references will probably be in professional journals, because this is the principal outlet for reporting primary source research. In using the library to obtain these materials, a great deal of time may be wasted. You should, therefore, examine the layout of the library and talk with the reference librarian to determine what method of obtaining your materials will require the least amount of time. In a library where periodicals in a given field are all shelved in a central location and where study space is available in the stacks, it is usually desirable to work in the stacks. Some libraries, however, do not permit students to enter the stacks, and some, because of space limitations, have journals shelved in such a way that they are difficult to find and cannot be used in the immediate area where they are shelved. In this case you can usually save time by making out call slips for about 10 periodicals. While waiting for the library clerk to return with these periodicals, you can make out call slips for your next 10 references. The clerk can then look for the second 10 references while you are scanning and making notes on whatever you received from the first 10 call slips. Because a certain percentage of the references that you want will be lost, checked out, or in the bindery, it is always advisable to submit call slips for 10 or more at a time. Spending a few minutes to determine the most efficient way of obtaining references in your college library will, in the long run, save a great deal of time and effort.

OBTAINING MATERIALS NOT LOCALLY AVAILABLE

You will almost certainly find that some of the materials you wish to examine are not available in your college library. There are several ways to obtain these materials, and you should not give up merely because a source is not available locally. For articles published in professional journals, the quickest and easiest way to obtain those not locally available is to write directly to the author and ask for a reprint of the article. Most authors receive reprints of their articles and usually are willing to send a reprint to anyone requesting it. Reprints thus received become your personal property and should be kept in your file, so that you may recheck the article if necessary.

The main problem encountered in writing for reprints is obtaining the address of the author. If you located the article in *Psychological Abstracts* or *RIE,* the address is usually given. This information, however, is not available in *Education Index* or *CIJE*. A great many authors may be located by checking the various professional directories that are available, such as *Who's Who in American Education, Biographical Directory of the American Psychological Association,* and *American Educational Research Association Biographical Membership Directory*. The reference librarian can usually suggest other directories if an individual is not listed in any of these. If your library does not have a membership directory that you need, check with faculty members who are likely to belong to the organization.

If you cannot obtain a reprint of the article from the author, the next step is to see if the needed journal is available in other libraries in the vicinity. In large population centers where several colleges or universities are located within a small geographical area, you can usually find the materials you need at one of the available libraries. In areas where there are no other libraries, it is usually possible to obtain needed materials through interlibrary loan. Check the policies of your local library regarding interlibrary loan. Many libraries place restrictions upon graduate students in the use of this service because it is rather expensive.

You may sometimes obtain microfilm or photocopies of references not locally available. The librarian in your local library will locate needed materials and arrange for their reproduction, but you must usually pay the cost of reproduction and shipping. This cost varies considerably, usually from 15¢ to 35¢ per page, so it is often practical for short articles but expensive for books or lengthy documents. Reproduction of copyrighted material is restricted, so you should check the current regulations with your librarian. As a rule, however, you may make a single copy of most reference material for private study or research without violating the copyright laws. If a needed reference appears to be of major importance to your problem, you should obtain it by some means. The satisfaction of knowing you have done a thorough and scholarly review of the literature will more than compensate for the expense.

Reading and Note Taking

RESEARCH ARTICLES AND REPORTS

You will recall that after completing your search of preliminary sources, it was recommended that you code the references located to indicate their importance to your problem. You should then start your review by checking the most recent of the most important studies. The reason for starting with the most recent studies is that they have the earlier research as a foundation and thus are likely to be more valuable. By reading the most important articles first, you quickly build up a reasonably deep understanding of your problem. You can then profit more from the subsequent study of articles that are only peripherally related to your topic, since after gaining this insight, it is much easier to fit these less important studies into the overall picture.

When you finally open the journal to an article you wish to check, first read the abstract. Most research articles start with a brief abstract or end with a summary. By reading this, you can usually determine whether the article contains any information that would justify reading it in its entirety. After reading the abstract or summary, if you decide the article is sufficiently pertinent to your problem, first check the accuracy of the data on your bibliography card, because the source where you obtained these data could have been in error. Then record the same bibliographic data, or an abbreviated form that tells enough to identify the source, on the top of a five-by-eight-inch note card. Then you are ready to take notes on the article as you read it. If you have conducted a computer search, the brief computer printout for the article or report should be pasted on the five-by-eight-inch card. There is usually enough space on the back of the card for any additional notes.

In writing a research article, the author attempts to present the essential material in as brief a form as possible. You will find that the average research article is only five or six pages long and thus takes little time to read. Reports, scholarly books, and dissertations are usually much longer than articles published in journals. For these longer references, scan the entire document and then read carefully only those parts that are directly relevant to your problem. Tables are usually provided that summarize the results of the research. A brief review of these tables usually tells enough to decide whether you should study the reference in greater depth.

You will also find that the majority of research articles and reports follow a standard pattern that further reduces the time needed to review them. This format usually includes (1) an abstract, (2) a brief introduction that states the problem and cites important previous research, (3) a statement of the objectives or hypotheses to be tested, (4) a description of the research procedures including subjects, measures, and research design, (5) a report of the findings, (6) a summary (if no abstract is given), and (7) a discussion and conclusions section.

In taking notes you should be brief and should abbreviate whenever possible to save space. However, you should not omit anything that you feel might be needed later in the preparation of your report, since rereading the article will waste time. A brief outline of the reference using short sentences or phrases with headings for the problem, hypotheses, procedure, findings, and conclusions will usually be sufficient.[1] The problem can usually be stated in a single sentence. In the introductory section of the report you will often find brief descriptions of previous research. If any of the work described is related to your problem, copy the bibliographic data onto bibliography cards, code their probable level of importance, and check these references when time permits. The hypotheses or objectives are usually brief and should be copied verbatim onto your note card. Under "Procedures" you should usually describe the research method used (experimental, survey, correlational, or whatever). You should also briefly describe the research subjects, giving their number and indicating how they were selected. Measures used in the study, such as questionnaires, standardized tests, or observation forms should also be described. The findings will usually refer back to the hypotheses or objectives. Major findings should be listed briefly along with their level of statistical significance. Often the findings are summarized in a table. A copy of the table may be made and pasted onto your note card.

It is also desirable to record your own evaluation of the study and to note how it may relate to your problem while the article is still fresh in your mind. It is advisable to make note of any promising or unusual techniques employed in the study, new measures that may be of use, interesting theoretical points, and any apparent problems or weaknesses that make the results questionable or limit their application to your problem. (See Figure 4.1 for a sample note card.)

Being able to evaluate a research article or report critically is important because you will often find several studies in the literature that test similar hypotheses but yield different results. Unless you can make a critical comparison of these studies, it

---

1. An evaluation form such as that given in Appendix 1 can also be used for recording your notes. Such a form is especially useful when you are learning the evaluation process, but after you have reviewed a few articles and have learned the process, you will probably prefer note cards.

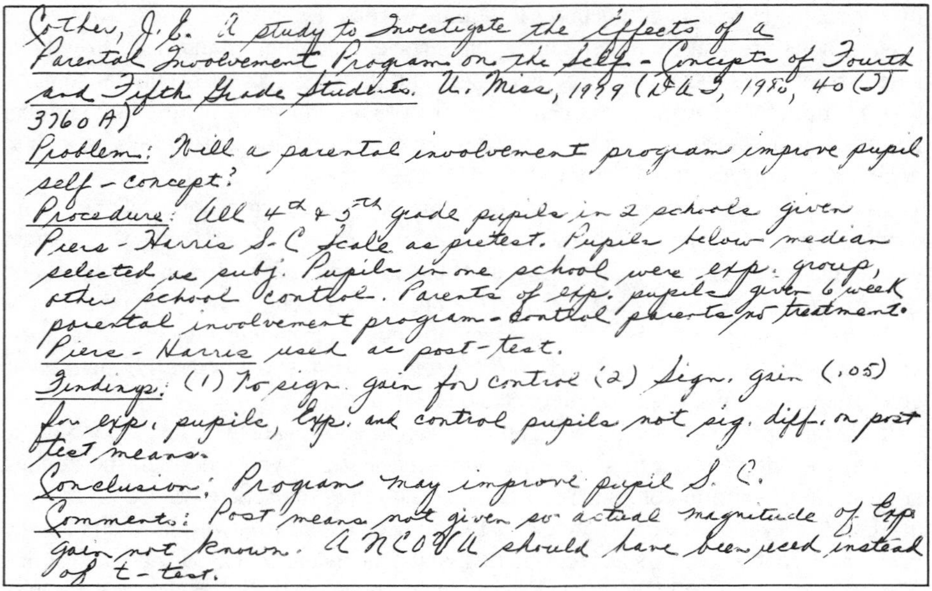
Cother, J.E. A Study to Investigate the Effects of a Parental Involvement Program on the Self-Concepts of Fourth and Fifth Grade Students. U. Miss, 1979 (DAI, 1980, 40(7) 3760 A)
Problem: Will a parental involvement program improve pupil self-concept?
Procedure: All 4th & 5th grade pupils in 2 schools given Piers-Harris S-C Scale as pretest. Pupils below median selected as subj. Pupils in one school were exp. group, other school control. Parents of exp. pupils given 6 week parental involvement program - control parents no treatment. Piers-Harris used as post-test.
Findings: (1) No sign. gain for control (2) Sign. gain (.05) for exp. pupils, Exp. and control pupils not sig. diff. on post test means.
Conclusion: Program may improve pupil S.C.
Comments: Post means not given so actual magnitude of Exp gain not known. ANCOVA should have been used instead of t-test.

Figure 4.1 Sample Note Card

is difficult to determine which of the conflicting results is more likely to be correct. Critical evaluation also helps you decide how relevant the findings are to the problem that exists in your own school or district. Chapters 5, 6, and 7 present a detailed discussion of methods for critically evaluating research articles and give you the basic information you will need to make an evaluation.

THEORETICAL AND OPINION ARTICLES

In education many of the articles that you encounter will not be reports of research projects but will present a theory, describe a program, or state the experiences or opinions of the author concerning some educational topic. Such articles do not follow the research article format and usually do not contain a summary. When checking a theoretical or opinion article, first scan the article to get some idea of its content. One method of scanning is to read only the first sentence in each paragraph. After scanning, decide whether the article contains material of importance, in which case you should read the entire article. Notes on a theoretical or opinion article can usually be prepared most quickly using a sentence outline approach.

Research reports are usually of more value than opinion articles because they provide evidence that relates to your problem. Such evidence must be given more weight in seeking an answer or solution to your problem than is given to opinion articles or articles that describe the experience of others but report no research evidence. However, theoretical and opinion articles are often very helpful in giving you insights and stimulating ideas that can help you deal with your problem more effectively. Thus, all types of professional literature can contribute to a better under-standing of your problem and the development of possible answers or solutions.

QUOTATIONS

As you read, be alert for quotations that might be useful in preparing the review of the literature for your report. If you find material that you may wish to quote, copy it very carefully onto the note card, enclosed in quotation marks, and record the page number from which the quote was taken. Most systems of referencing require that the page number be given for direct quotations, and this also facilitates checking the quotation if necessary.

Students often use far too many quotations in their reviews. A good rule to follow is to copy for possible quotation only materials that are stated very skillfully, or in very concise terms, or are typical and clear reflections of a particular point of view that you wish to illustrate in your paper. After copying a quotation, recheck to be sure that you have copied it exactly. Inaccurate quotations are a serious reflection on the scholarship of the writer, and it is almost certain that some of the quotations will be checked for accuracy by faculty members who read the paper.

CLASSIFYING ARTICLES YOU READ

In reading articles for your review of the literature, you should keep constantly in mind the purpose of your review and should attempt to relate the material you read to your problem. Do not restrict yourself to the narrow study of only that research that is very closely related to your problem. Very often studies that are only partially related to your problem will give you new viewpoints and acquaint you with new ideas that can be profitably applied to your problem.

In doing your review of the literature, you usually find that the articles you read can be classified into several categories. For example, in the field of ability grouping, the author found some articles that compared the achievement of students in ability-grouping and random-grouping systems, some articles that made comparisons of sociometric scores and social status measures between the two systems, some that discussed methods of grouping, and so on. In carrying out your review, you should be alert for such natural subdivisions because they form a basis for classifying your note cards and organizing your report.

A CODING SYSTEM

As a pattern for your review emerges, you should develop a system of coding that will permit you to indicate what type of material is contained on a given note card. The coding system adopted will be different for each literature review. An example of a coding system used by the author in a review of the literature in ability grouping may be helpful to you in developing your own coding. These codes are generally placed in the upper right hand corner of the note card.

S   Studies dealing with social interaction
A   Studies describing grouping systems and their relationship to student achievement

G   Studies discussing problems involved in grouping, such as individual variability
    and so forth
B   Studies relating grouping to behavior problems
P   Studies relating grouping to personality adjustment, personality variables, and
    self-concept

Using such a code is helpful in several ways. It makes you actively aware of the
major areas of concentration in your topic. It makes it possible to check your notes
on a specific portion of the literature quickly, and it makes the job of writing your
review of the literature much easier. The more extensive studies, of course, may
contain material relating to two or three subtopics. These are recorded on your note
card by indicating all the codes for subtopics covered in the article.

Writing the Report

Whether you have carried out your literature review to help solve a local school
problem or to meet a requirement for your degree, some sort of a report of your
findings will probably be needed. The function of the report usually is to pull together
relevant information from all of the studies you have reviewed to give the reader an
overall picture of the state of knowledge about the problem you have attacked.

Reports of literature you have reviewed should usually contain the following sections:

Introduction and description of the problem or question you are seeking to
    answer.
The *body* of the paper, which discusses the relevant research you have re-
    viewed in a systematic and objective fashion.
Discussion, in which you pull together the main outcomes of your review and
    present a composite picture of the state of knowledge related to your
    problem.
Conclusions and recommendations, in which you draw conclusions based on the
    state of knowledge and recommend one or more courses of action that appear
    to be promising solutions to your problem.
References, which should include complete bibliographical data for all sources
    you have cited.

Let us now discuss these sections in more detail.

THE INTRODUCTION

Your introductory section should describe your problem and explain why you con-
ducted the literature search. Such questions as: What is the scope of the review?
Why is this problem important? What prompted you to investigate the problem, and
How can the results be applied? are often discussed in the introductory section.

THE BODY OF YOUR REPORT

The best way to organize a report is by the major subtopics that relate to your problem. If you coded your note cards by subtopic as suggested above, sort the cards into piles. Then decide the order in which the various subtopics should be discussed in your report. For most problems the best order for discussing the subtopics is obvious, while for others the order is not critical. Place your piles of note cards in whatever order you have decided to follow in your report.

Now, read the note cards in your first pile. Check your coding to be sure the cards belong in this pile. Also, decide tentatively on the order you will follow in discussing the various studies in your first pile. If several minor studies have reported similar results, these should usually be discussed together. By reporting closely related studies together or in close proximity, you can emphasize areas of difference and/or agreement that would be of interest to the reader. Repeat this process until the cards in each of your piles are arranged in the approximate order that you plan to deal with them in your report.

Many major studies you have reviewed are likely to contain findings that are related to several of your subtopics. These cards should be placed with the first subtopic in which the findings will be discussed and then moved to later subtopics as your writing progresses.

You now have all of your information in the order that it will be discussed in your report. However, before you actually start writing, it is a good idea to reread the note cards in your first pile once or twice in order to get this information firmly in mind. This review does not take very long and makes the actual writing much easier.

Now, with the first pile of note cards in front of you, you are ready to start writing the body of your report, in which you will review the articles and reports that you have read and noted. In writing, you will usually pick up your first note card, review it briefly, decide whether to treat it alone or with others, write what you want to say about it, include your citation to indicate where the information came from, and then go on to the next card. Here are a few important rules you should keep in mind when writing the body of your review.

1. Discuss major studies in detail, but devote very little space to minor studies. This seems obvious, but it is distressing to see how many reports give the same three or four sentences to each study regardless of its importance.

2. If you have located several minor studies having similar results or similar weaknesses, discuss all of them together. One approach is to discuss the best study in the set in some depth and then dispose of the others with a single sentence such as: "Several other small scale studies, involving fewer than twenty subjects, have reported similar results (Adams, 1976; Black, 1976; Carter, 1977; Davis, 1979; Edward, 1980)."[2] Another example: "Several one-year studies reported better

---

2. These citations are given using the author-date method recommended by the American Psychological Association. Before writing your report, find out what citation system is favored by your school district or university and use that system.

achievement for students in ability-grouped classrooms (Frank, 1969; Grey & Brown, 1973; Redd & Green, 1980). However, because of their short duration, all of these studies were probably subject to Hawthorne Effect."

3. Do not fall into a set pattern in discussing the studies in your report. Some writers invariably start their discussion of each study with the author's name. For example, consecutive paragraphs may start: Jane found that . . . , Smith studied . . . , Brown reported that. . . .

4. Avoid repeating the same words in discussing each research report. This is difficult, but you should do your best. For example, instead of using the word "study" repeatedly you can use other words such as "experiment," "project," "investigation," "research," and so forth.

5. Use short, simple sentences when possible. Long, complex sentences may confuse the reader.

6. Avoid jargon, little-used words, and pedantic expressions. The purpose of your report is to communicate, not to impress the reader with your vocabulary.

7. Use frequent subheadings in your report to help the reader follow your sequence of thought more easily. Also, if you cannot find subheadings that fit your content or if they do not seem to follow from one to another, your paper is probably not well organized.

8. Use direct quotations only when they convey an idea especially well or when you want to make sure the reader realizes that you are stating someone else's position, which is not necessarily your own. Most neophytes use far too many quotations. This tends to interfere with the flow of your paper and make it difficult to read.

9. Include transition sentences to connect the main ideas or subtopics covered in your paper. The reader should feel that each of your sections proceeds logically from what has come before it.

10. The body of your paper should report what you have found in objective, unbiased language. You can make your own viewpoints and preferences known in the "discussion" or "conclusions" sections that follow.

11. Describe the methods used and discuss the limitations of important studies, so that the reader has enough information to weigh the results and draw his own conclusions.

THE DISCUSSION SECTION

In this section you should pull together all of the findings relevant to your problem and give the reader a systematic composite of the state of knowledge. There are several methods that can be used to pull together research findings. These range from simple counts of the numbers of studies reporting positive and negative findings such as used by Rosenshine (1971) to sophisticated systems that weigh the findings of relevant studies on the basis of important design variables such as the meta-analysis procedure developed by Glass, McGaw, and Smith (1981).

For students who are just learning to interpret educational research literature, some simple tabulation system is probably the best place to start. For example, in combining the research on a question such as "What is the relationship between class size and achievement?" the reviewer could look at three levels of findings. First, the number of studies reporting nonsignificant results favoring large classes could be compared with the number favoring small classes. Second, the same comparison could be made between studies reporting significant results. Finally, the results of the 10 studies that are evaluated as being the best by the reviewer could be considered. If desired, these three levels could then be combined by giving a weight of $+1$ to nonsignificant findings, $+5$ to significant findings, and $+10$ to significant findings from major studies that favor small classes. Weights of -1, -5, and -10 would be assigned to comparable studies that favor large classes.[3] The composite score for all studies would then provide a rough estimate of whether the evidence favored small or large classes. A much more sophisticated analysis of research on this question has been conducted by Glass and Smith (1978). This paper is a good model for students who are interested in the problem of combining research evidence.

CONCLUSIONS AND RECOMMENDATIONS SECTION

Based upon your discussion of the research findings, you should briefly state your conclusions and make recommendations for future courses of action. Any conclusions and recommendations you make should be firmly supported by the evidence you have assembled in the body of your paper. Avoid overconcluding or advocating a course of action not supported by the evidence. Remember, research evidence is a much better basis for decision making than personal experience. Thus, it is rather foolish to go to the effort of reviewing the evidence and then allow your personal experience to outweigh this evidence in arriving at your conclusions and recommendations.

REFERENCES

All the references that you have cited should be included in this section. Complete bibliographic data should be given for each reference. There are a great many acceptable formats for listing your references. Check with your university or school district to see if there is a preferred format. If not, the format recommended by the American Psychological Association (1983) is easy to use and should be considered.

Regardless of what format you select, it is very important to be consistent. Since you will locate your references in several preliminary sources, you will probably record them on your bibliography cards in several different formats. Be sure to convert all of these to a single format before having your reference list typed, and check it carefully for accuracy and consistency after it is typed.

References

AMERICAN PSYCHOLOGICAL ASSOCIATION. (1983). *Publication manual of the American Psychological Association* (3rd ed.). Washington, D.C.: American Psychological Association.

3. This weighting is purely arbitrary and used for illustration only. A description of two methods of combining research data is given in Chapter 5.

GLASS, G. V., McGAW, B., & SMITH, M. L. (1981). *Meta-analysis in social research.* Beverly Hills, Calif.: Sage.

GLASS, G. V., & SMITH, M. L. (1978). *Meta-analysis of research on the relationship of class-size and achievement.* Boulder, Colo.: University of Colorado Laboratory of Educational Research.

RIST, R. C. (1978). *The invisible children: School integration in American society.* Cambridge, Mass.: Harvard University Press.

ROSENSHINE, B. (1971). *Teaching behaviors and student achievement.* London: National Foundation for Educational Research in England and Wales.

Recommended Reading

CUMMINS, M. H., & SLADE, C. (1979). *Writing the research paper: A guide and sourcebook.* Boston: Houghton Mifflin.

This is a detailed guide that can be very useful to the student who wants to upgrade his skills in writing research papers. The book deals with material selection, use of the library, writing the rough draft, and writing the final draft. Seventeen samples of writing drawn from a variety of content areas are also included.

JOLLEY, J. M., MURRAY, J. D., & KELLER, P. A. (1984). *How to write psychology papers.* Sarasota, Fla.: Professional Resources Exchange.

This readable handbook gives practical guidelines for preparing term papers and research reports. The use of the library is also discussed briefly. Although focused primarily on psychology, most of the content is also applicable to writing papers in education. A sample term paper and research report are given in the appendices.

WILSON, J. A. R. (1976). *Research guide in education.* Morristown, N.J.: General Learning Press.

This guide is divided into three sections. The first gives a brief overview of education as a discipline. The second describes procedures the student can use to define his topic and locate information, and the third discusses the actual process of writing a paper.

Application Problems

1. Check all articles in volume 52 (1983–1984) of the *Journal of Experimental Education* and then:
   a. Locate an article that would be useful to a high school principal who is considering setting up remedial math classes for low achievers, which may lead to poor self-concept and attitude toward school.
   b. Locate a study concerned with teaching aids to improve the handwriting of first-grade pupils and list bibliographical data.
2. Locate a dissertation in the April 1985 issue of Section A of *Dissertation Abstracts International* that is concerned with the following problem: A junior high school teacher discovers as a result of the district testing program that most of the students in her seventh-grade homeroom have low self-concepts as compared with national norms. She wants to find out if there are any programs available that are designed to improve the self-concept of junior high school students.
   a. List the bibliographical data for the dissertation
   b. Briefly describe how you found this reference
   c. Write a brief review of the abstract on five-by-eight-inch note card following the format recommended in Chapter 4.

3. Locate in your library and list the titles of two journals that specialize in each of the following areas:
   a. Adult education
   b. Teaching biology
   c. Educational administration
   d. Special education
   e. Reading
4. Check the most recent issue of *Resources in Education,* locate an example of each of the following types of reports, list bibliographical data and ED number, locate the microfiche for one of these references in your library's microfiche file, scan the reference, and prepare a five-by-eight-inch note card.
   a. Paper presented at a professional meeting
   b. Report by a professional association
   c. Conference or committee report
5. List three of your main interests in education. Try to find a journal that emphasizes each of these areas and list the titles. Check recent issues of each journal until you locate an article that is closely related to your interests. Make up a bibliography card for this article.

PART 2

EVALUATING RESEARCH EVIDENCE

CHAPTER **5**

EVALUATING RESEARCH REPORTS

Overview

This chapter introduces you to some of the procedures you should use in evaluating a research report. Four questions are given, which should be considered in checking the introductory section of a report for possible bias. The importance of good hypotheses or objectives is discussed, null and directional hypotheses are compared, and four criteria for a good hypothesis are stated. We then consider the function of sampling in research, describe four kinds of samples, and discuss some of the problems involved in using volunteer samples. The evaluation of educational measures is then introduced, and the meaning of validity and reliability is discussed. Finally, procedures for combining the results of related studies into an overall picture, such as meta-analysis, are described, and a sample meta-analysis article is provided. Many of the topics introduced in this chapter will be discussed at greater length in later chapters.

Objectives

1. Given an introductory section of a research report, the learner will identify factors that might indicate investigator bias.
2. Describe three indicators of possible bias that are often found in the introductory section of a research report.
3. Given a statement of a research problem, the learner will write a null hypothesis, a directional hypothesis, and an objective.
4. Explain the conditions under which a directional hypothesis may be used.
5. Discuss the pros and cons of using null hypotheses versus directional hypotheses.
6. Describe four criteria that can be used to evaluate a hypothesis.
7. Given a description of a population, describe how a simple random sample, a systematic sample, a stratified sample, and a cluster sample would be selected.
8. Describe the problems involved in using volunteer samples and explain why most educational researchers use volunteers.
9. Define population validity and explain how it is estimated and how it relates to applying research results to other groups drawn from the target population.
10. Briefly define reliability and validity of educational measures.
11. Explain how the teacher or administrator judges the degree to which research results can be applied to the local schools.
12. Describe two methods of combining research data to obtain a composite of information related to a given problem or question.

In Chapter 4 you learned that in addition to an abstract or summary the typical research report includes:

1. An *introduction,* which states the problem and cites important previous research. In this section the author also justifies or discusses the importance of the problem and sometimes tries to fit it into a theoretical context.

2. A statement of the *objectives* to be achieved or the *hypotheses* to be tested. In many articles this is included in the introduction. We will consider it separately because of its importance.

3. A description of the *research procedures* including the sample of subjects, measures used, and research design.

4. A report of the *findings.*

5. A *discussion* of the findings and statement of conclusions.

Nearly all research reports follow this format. This makes it easier for the person reading the article to locate quickly those aspects of the report that are most relevant to her needs or problem. It also leads to brevity, which is very important for journal articles, since space in journals is very limited. Unfortunately, this format tends to inhibit creative writing and may lead to rather tiresome reading. In evaluating a research report, there are specific things that the reviewer should look for in each of the parts listed above. We will now discuss each part and suggest what you should look for in making your evaluation. At this point, although you have been introduced to some of the basics, your knowledge of research methods is very limited and your evaluation of a research report is likely to overlook many important strengths and weaknesses. However, this chapter will focus your attention on some of the important aspects of evaluation. As you progress through this text, your evaluations will become increasingly sophisticated. The Research Report Evaluation Form found in Appendix 1 will also help remind you of things you should look for. Study this form for a few minutes before proceeding.

The Introductory Section

This is perhaps the best place in the research report to learn something about the researcher. Who is she and what are her affiliations? Why did she do the research? Why does she think it is important? Does she seem to know about other related research? Does she seem committed to a particular point of view? These questions are important in evaluating the research report. For example, the language used by the investigator can reflect biases that can lead to distortions in the way the research is conducted and reported.

Whenever the researcher has reasons for wanting her research to support a particular viewpoint, the likelihood of bias is greatly increased. Occasionally the individual will be so emotionally involved with her topic that she deliberately slants her findings or even structures her design to produce a predetermined result (e.g.,

Evans, 1976). Such cases of deliberate bias are often easy to detect because the same emotional involvement that motivates the individual to bias her work is usually reflected in the language of her research report. Studies that are introduced with slanted remarks such as "this study was conducted to prove" must be considered suspect. The scientist does not carry out her work to prove a point but to get an answer.

The use of emotionally charged words or intemperate language in the introduction is the most obvious indicator of a biased viewpoint. For example, in reviewing the literature concerned with ability grouping, the author found several articles that referred to ability grouping as "segregation." Inasmuch as this word has strong negative emotional associations for most of us, its use in this context suggests bias. One is not surprised to find that an article entitled "Must We Segregate?" (Tonsor, 1953) is strongly biased against ability grouping.

The investigator's professional affiliation should also be noted, since it may predispose her toward a particular point of view. For example, a comparison of racial attitudes of children in private and public schools in the South might be biased if conducted by an official in the NAACP. A person's affiliations do not necessarily indicate that she is biased, but those that suggest possible bias should serve as a signal to be alert for other indications of bias.

If you are doing a reasonably thorough review of the research literature related to a particular question, you will soon notice that a few key studies are cited in most of the subsequent research reports. If most of these important studies are not reviewed in a research report you are evaluating, it could indicate that the researcher has not done a thorough review of previous work. This could be an indication of careless work. If important studies that disagree with the author's findings are omitted, it suggests bias, and perhaps an effort to "sell you a bill of goods."

Since most research journals allow the author little space for reviewing previous research, you should not expect detailed reviews. However, the 5 to 10 most relevant previous studies should be cited, if only briefly. Research reports not appearing in journals (such as reports listed in *RIE*) usually provide much more detailed reviews, since they are not subject to space limitations.

In summary, look for evidence related to the following questions when reading the introductory section of a research report:

1. Does the phraseology suggest that the researcher is inclined to favor one side of the question?

2. Is emotional or intemperate language of either a favorable or unfavorable nature employed?

3. Does the researcher hold a theoretical position or have a stake in a particular point of view? Does she belong to a group (racial, vocational, religious, political, ethnic, or other) that would predispose her in a given direction about the subject of her research?

4. Does the review of previous research cite most of the important studies? Has the researcher omitted studies that appear to be in conflict with her viewpoint?

The Objectives and/or Hypotheses

WHAT ARE HYPOTHESES?

In our day-to-day activities we are often faced with problems for which we must gather information and seek answers. In order to focus our information gathering, we try to identify possible solutions or explanations to our problem and then gather the information needed to see if a given explanation is correct. These "educated guesses" about possible differences, relationships, or causes are called *hypotheses*.

This simple process that we use to attack our day-to-day problems is similar to the approach an investigator may use to investigate a problem in educational research. First, the investigator hypothesizes a relationship between two or more variables, or a difference between two or more treatments. She then collects evidence related to her hypothesis and examines the evidence to decide whether or not to reject the hypothesis. For example, a teacher may have noted that one of her first-grade pupils appears to be making no progress in reading. A review of previous research in this area may suggest several possible causes for this problem. These possible causes may be stated as hypotheses. The teacher may then plan and carry out a program aimed at testing each hypothesis by manipulating the possible cause and then checking the child's progress in reading.

A research report should include a clear statement of the research objectives and/or the hypotheses that the investigation proposes to test. In planning a research project, one of the first things the researcher does is formulate her objectives and/or hypotheses. These in turn guide much of her thinking in planning the rest of the research project. Thus, if the objectives or hypotheses are unclear or are stated in broad general terms, the reviewer can assume that the project is probably poorly planned and executed.

DIRECTIONAL AND NULL HYPOTHESES

Hypotheses may be stated in two forms, directional and null. The *directional hypothesis* states a relationship between the variables being studied or a difference between experimental treatments that the researcher expects to emerge. For example, the following are directional hypotheses:

1. Pupils of low ability in ability-grouped classrooms will receive more favorable scores on a measure of inferiority feelings than pupils of low ability in random-grouped classroom.

2. There is a positive relationship between the number of older siblings and the social maturity scores of six-year-old children.

3. Children who attend preschool will make greater gains in first-grade reading achievement than comparable children who do not attend preschool.

In contrast to the directional hypothesis, the *null hypothesis* states that no relationship exists between the variables studied or no difference will be found between the experimental treatments. For example, in null form, the first of the aforementioned hypotheses could be stated: "There will be no difference between the scores on a measure of inferiority feelings of low-ability pupils in ability-grouped classrooms and low-ability pupils in random-grouped classrooms." The null hypothesis does not necessarily reflect the scientist's expectations but is preferred by many researchers because this form can be used in nearly any study that explores a difference or relationship. Also, the null hypothesis is better suited to the statistical tools that are used to analyze research evidence.

Directional hypotheses, however, are equally acceptable when the researcher can cite either theory or previous research to support the view that if *any* difference or relationship is found, it can *only* be in the hypothesized direction. When you review a study in which directional hypotheses are used you should look carefully at the reasons or evidence the author gives to support her use of directional hypotheses. Some researchers use directional hypotheses without justification, since it is easier to obtain statistically significant results when directional hypotheses are used. In such cases the reviewer should discount any results that are significant only by a small margin.

CRITERIA FOR GOOD HYPOTHESES

In reviewing a research report you should apply the following four criteria when you evaluate the hypotheses:

1. The hypothesis should state an expected relationship or difference between two or more variables. For example, in correlational studies, that is, those in which data on two or more variables are collected on the same individuals and correlations are computed, a directional hypothesis might state: "There is a positive relationship between peer-group acceptance and attitude toward school of sixth-grade boys."

In experimental studies, where an experimental treatment such as a new reading program is administered to one group of subjects but not to another group, differences between the treatments are usually hypothesized. For example, a null hypothesis for an experimental study might state: "There will be no difference in the reading achievement of first-grade pupils trained with Experimental Program A and comparable pupils trained with Conventional Program B."

2. The hypothesis should be grounded in theory or previous research. The researcher should state definite reasons based on either theory or evidence for considering the hypothesis worthy of testing. After completing the review of the literature, the research worker will have detailed knowledge of previous work relating to her research project. In many cases she will find conflicting research results, so that her hypothesis cannot agree with all available information. Although not part of the hypothesis itself, an important requirement for sound hypotheses is that the researcher state her reasons for formulating her hypothesis and show that the hypothesis does not conflict with the preponderance of previously reported evidence.

In addition to agreeing with knowledge already established within the field, hypotheses should be formulated in accordance with theories in education, psychology, or other behavioral sciences. When this is possible, the results of the research will contribute to the testing of the theory in question. In many areas of education so little research has been done that reasonably conclusive information is not available. In this case educational theory may form the only basis for the researcher's hypotheses.

Occasionally, we find a study in education that has used the "shotgun approach." In this approach the research worker administers all the measures she can think of to her subjects in the hope that something she tries will yield useful results. This approach should be avoided because it uses measures for which no hypotheses have been developed. Many dangers are involved in applying such research results to educational practice. When we do not have some understanding of why a particular relationship exists, there is always a danger that factors are operating that may be detrimental to the educational program.

3. A hypothesis should be testable. Hypotheses are generally stated so as to indicate an expected difference or an expected relationship between the measures used in the research. The relationships or differences that are stated in the hypotheses should be such that measurement of the variables involved can be made and necessary statistical comparisons carried out in order to determine whether the hypothesis as stated is or is not supported by the research. The researcher should not state any hypothesis that she does not have reason to believe can be tested or evaluated by some objective means.

4. The hypothesis should be as brief as possible consistent with clarity. In stating hypotheses the simplest and most concise statement of the relationship expected is generally the best. Brief, clear hypotheses are easier for the reader to understand and also easier for the research worker to test.

OBJECTIVES

In some research carried out in education, especially descriptive studies, it is appropriate for the research worker to list objectives rather than hypotheses. For example, a survey aimed at determining the extent of differences in the salaries of university professors in different fields of learning could test a hypothesis such as "There will be no difference between the mean salaries of faculty members of comparable ranks in different areas of learning."

In a study of this sort, however, it is probably more desirable merely to state objectives of the study such as: "The objectives of this research are: (1) to study the salaries paid professors of comparable academic ranks in different fields of learning, and (2) if differences are found to exist, to attempt to identify the factors that appear to contribute to the observed differences." Like hypotheses, objectives should be clear and concise. They should state as specifically as possible what the investigator wants to achieve as a result of her study. Objectives are often stated as questions.

This format is useful, since it focuses upon the specific questions that the investigator hopes to answer.

The Research Procedures

SAMPLING

Most educational research involves studying the behavior of human subjects. It is very rare for the investigator to study all individuals who would be appropriate subjects for a given research project. For example, let us suppose that a researcher wishes to study the effect of a new reading program on the reading comprehension of visually impaired children in first-grade classrooms. Since it would be impossible for the investigator to carry out the new reading program for the entire population, that is, visually impaired children in all first-grade classrooms, the usual procedure is to select a sample from the population to be studied and to carry out the research on that sample. The purpose of such research is to draw conclusions about the effect of the new program on the population by studying a sample of subjects who represent the population. The investigator can select such a sample in several ways. The size of the sample and the procedure used in selecting it determine the degree of confidence with which the researcher can apply the research findings to the population.

You can probably see that no sample is likely to be exactly like the population from which it is drawn. For example, if you randomly selected three male students from each class in a large high school and measured their height, it is very unlikely that the average height of this sample would be identical to the average height of all male students in the school. The difference is due to a *random error,* that is, even though your selection was random, you happened to select a larger proportion of tall (or short) students than existed in the entire student body. Such random errors become smaller as we select a larger random sample. We can estimate the probable size of random errors by statistics.

If instead of randomly selecting your sample you asked each teacher to send three boys to be measured, the teachers might pick students who could most easily make up the lost class time—the brighter ones. Since there is a relationship between intelligence and physical size, a *systematic error* or *bias* would occur. Systematic errors tend to be in a given direction and cannot be estimated statistically. These errors are therefore more serious, since they can distort the research findings and lead to false conclusions.

Kinds of Sampling. *Simple random sampling* is usually considered the best approach, but this procedure cannot be used in most educational research. In *simple random sampling,* all the individuals in the defined population have an equal and independent chance of being selected as a member of the sample. By "independent" we mean that the selection of one individual does not affect in any way the selection of any other individual.

The usual way to select a random sample is to assign a number to each person in the population and use a table of random numbers to select the sample. A table of random numbers lists thousands of numbers in random order. To use it you randomly select a starting point and then list as many numbers as you need for your sample. You then refer to your numbered population list and select the individuals whose numbers you have taken from the table.

The main purpose for using random sampling techniques is that random samples yield research data that can be generalized to a larger population within margins of error that can be determined statistically.

Systematic sampling, like simple random sampling, is used to obtain a sample from the defined population. This technique can be used if all members in the defined population have already been placed on a list such as a membership directory or a school census. Suppose the researcher wants to select a sample of 100 pupils from a census list of 1000 pupils. To use systematic sampling, the researcher first divides the population by the number needed for the sample ($1000 \div 100 = 10$). Then the researcher selects at random a number smaller than the number arrived at by the division (in this example, a number smaller than 10). Then, starting with that number (e.g., 8), she selects every 10th name from a list of the population, thus selecting pupils 8, 18, 28, 38, and so on for a total of 100.

Systematic sampling is a slightly easier procedure to use than simple random sampling. It differs from simple random sampling in that each member of the population is not chosen independently. Once the first member has been selected, all the other members of the sample are automatically determined. Systematic sampling can be used instead of simple random sampling if one is certain that the population list is not in some systematic order. For example, suppose that a school census list is arranged by classroom, with pupils within each classroom listed in alphabetical order. If we selected every 23rd name, we might get nothing but children whose names start with *W, X, Y,* or *Z.* Since some ethnic groups have a disproportionate number of last names starting with these letters, our systematic sample may have more students from these groups and fewer than normal from other groups. This would, of course, lead to a biased sample, that is, one that is not representative of the population from which the sample was drawn.

Stratified sampling is a device to assure that certain population elements are represented. In many educational studies, it is desirable to select a sample in such a way that the research worker is assured that certain subgroups will be represented in the sample in proportion to their numbers in the population itself. Such samples are usually referred to as stratified samples. Let us say, for example, that we wish to conduct a study to see if there are significant differences on Thematic Apperception Test aggression scores of pupils at different ability levels selected from ability-grouped sixth-grade classrooms. Under ability grouping systems, pupils are classified into three levels on the basis of general intelligence or past achievement scores and placed in classrooms accordingly. In this case, if we were to define the population as all sixth-grade pupils in the district and then select a random sample, our random sample may not include a sufficient number of cases from one of the three ability levels. In this research we must also consider the possibility that girls will react differently in terms of aggression scores than boys. In order to avoid samples that do not include a sufficient number of pupils of each sex at each ability level, a stratified sample can be selected. All sixth-grade pupils in the district would be divided into one of the following six groups: superior boys, superior girls, average boys, average girls, slow boys, and slow girls. Subsamples of the desired size would then be selected at random from each of the six groups.

In *cluster sampling* the unit of sampling is not the individual but rather a naturally occurring group of individuals. Cluster sampling is used when it is more feasible or convenient to select *groups of individuals* than it is to select individuals from a defined population. This situation occurs when it is either impractical or impossible to obtain a list of all members of the accessible population or when it is difficult to break up established groups in order to collect data from a few selected group members.

Cluster sampling is often used in educational research with the classroom as the unit of sampling. Suppose that one wishes to administer a study methods question-naire to a random sample of 300 pupils from a population defined as all sixth graders in four school districts. Let us say that the population includes a total of 1250 sixth graders in 50 classrooms, with an average of 25 pupils in each classroom. One approach would be to draw a simple random sample of 300 individuals using a census list of all 1250 pupils. In cluster sampling, though, one would draw a random sample of 12 classrooms from a census list of all 50 classrooms. Then one would administer the questionnaire to every pupil in each of the 12 classrooms. Teachers and adminis-trators usually prefer using entire classrooms, since this approach is less disruptive to the school routine than random sampling in which a few students would probably be selected from each class.

Volunteer Samples.   Random sampling of broad populations is possible for survey research in which slight demands are made on the subjects. For example, most public opinion polls can obtain random samples, since they typically ask only a few questions and take only a few minutes of the respondent's time. Demands on the subject are much greater in most educational research; consequently, even if the researcher selects a random sample, she can rarely get cooperation from all the subjects selected. When some subjects refuse to participate in a study, the remaining subjects no longer constitute a random sample because persons who agree to partici-pate are likely to be different from those who do not.

Furthermore, legal and ethical constraints on the researcher require her to obtain informed consent from human subjects (or their parents in the case of minors) before involving them in a research project. As a result, nearly all educational research is conducted with volunteer samples. The main difficulty in applying the results of a study that has used a volunteer sample is that some *systematic error* or *bias* may exist that makes the members of the sample different from the population from which the sample was drawn. Studies have shown that volunteers tend to be different from nonvolunteers in many ways. For example, studies have found that volunteers tend to be better educated, of higher social class, and more intelligent than nonvolunteers

(Rosenthal & Rosnow, 1975). You can often estimate the amount of sampling bias by checking to see what percent of the persons approached agreed to participate. The higher this percentage, the less bias is likely to occur. Skillful researchers work closely with school personnel, fully explain their research, solicit their ideas and suggestions, and provide benefits to those who participate in the research. These actions tend to increase the percentage of volunteers and thus reduce bias.

Population Validity. In evaluating a research report, one aspect of the study that must be considered is its *population validity*. Population validity is the degree to which the sample of subjects in the study are representative of the population from which they were selected. To establish population validity the researcher must show that the sample she has selected is similar to the *accessible population,* which is the population from which she drew her sample. She must also show that the accessible population is similar to the *target population,* which is the population to which the researcher wants to generalize or apply her research findings. For example, if you were interested in the sexual stereotypes among high school seniors, the *target population* could be defined as all seniors in U.S. public and private high schools. This is, of course, a very broad population, and it would be very difficult and expensive to draw a national sample from this population and use the selected individuals in your research. Instead of sampling this broad target population, let us suppose that it were necessary, because of limited funds, to draw your sample entirely from the Denver public high schools. Then the Denver seniors would be the *accessible population.* It may be that the accessible population (Denver public school seniors) is different in certain ways (such as IQ, reading level, or ethnic composition) from the target population (all U.S. seniors). To the degree that such differences exist, the research findings based on a Denver sample might not apply to the target population. Thus, to establish population validity, the researcher must show similarities between the sample, the accessible population, and the target population on variables that appear related to the researcher's problem. Using our example of sexual stereotypes, the researcher suspects that different racial groups, because of cultural differences, are likely to perceive the roles of women differently. Thus, if the researcher can demonstrate that her sample, the accessible population, and the target population all have about the same proportion of blacks, whites, Hispanics, and other racial groups, then this evidence helps establish the population validity of her study.

Evidence on population validity is difficult to obtain, mainly because there is little data available on the characteristics of broad national populations. However, sources such as census data, statistical abstracts published by the U.S. Department of Education, and national norms reported by publishers of standardized tests provide information that can help establish population validity. The characteristics of students in local school districts that often make up the accessible population are often easier to obtain, since the typical school district gathers a good deal of test and demographic data about its students.

Relevance to Local Groups.   The person conducting a critical evaluation of a research report should give close attention to the accessible population and the sample that was used in the study. However, even more important than population validity in many cases is the degree to which subjects in the research sample are similar to the students in your school or classroom to whom you want to apply the research findings. The results of any research project are most valid for subjects who actually participated in the project. However, these results should also be valid for other groups that are very similar, that is, persons drawn from the same defined population as the research sample. As the similarity between the research sample and the group in which we are interested decreases, there is an increased chance that the research results will not apply. For example, suppose a teacher works in an upper-middle-class suburban school in California. Results from a study of the reading problems of inner-city black children in Philadelphia would have to be applied very cautiously and may not be relevant because of the differences between her class and the research sample. On the other hand, some of the Philadelphia findings might apply to her class if the reading problems identified were not related to race, socio-economic status, or geographic area.

Therefore, the teacher or school administrator who is seeking research data to help deal with a local problem must not only consider carefully how the research sample is different from local students, but how these differences might affect the relevance of the research results.

This is a difficult task for several reasons. First, the researcher often tells the reader very little about the sample and the accessible population from which it was drawn. Second, local teachers or administrators often have only limited knowledge about the characteristics of children in their own school or district. Third, it is difficult to decide what differences between the research sample and the local population are really critical or important with respect to the specific findings to be applied.

Often, if the research appears to offer a promising solution to your problem, the best approach is to try out the course of action suggested by the research findings and see how well it works with local students. This involves using *action research,* which we will discuss in Chapter 11.

EVALUATING MEASURES USED IN RESEARCH

All research involves measurement, and the results of a research project can be no better than the measures that were used to obtain these results. Therefore, an important part of evaluating a research report is to evaluate the measures used in the research. In this section we will briefly summarize the most important things to consider when you are evaluating an educational measure. Then, in the next chapter we will discuss educational measurement in greater depth. This will give you some of the basic information you need to make intelligent evaluations of educational measures. A thorough check of all tests and measurement techniques reported in all studies that are of major importance; that is, any study that has yielded findings that mended. You should make such a check, however, of the measures used in any studies that are of major importance; that is, any study that has yielded findings that make an important contribution to the topic or question being reviewed should be thoroughly checked. If standard measures are cited with which you are not familiar, you should study a specimen set, consult the *Mental Measurements Yearbooks,* and check other sources of information to be discussed in Chapter 6.[1] If the measure used is new or has been developed for the research being evaluated, obtain a copy and weigh the measure carefully against your knowledge of test development techniques and the theoretical constructs upon which the measure is based.

There are three questions that you should keep in mind when reading the description of the measures used in a research project:

1. What evidence of validity is available? The general definition of validity is the degree to which a test or other measurement tool measures what it claims to measure. There are four different kinds of validity, each of which is important in certain kinds of research. For example, content validity is important in studies of school achievement, since it is concerned with the degree to which the achievement test used in a study is related to the curriculum taught in the study. An achievement test that asks many questions about content that students have not been taught and few about content they have been taught has low center validity and thus will not accurately measure what students have learned. You will learn more about validity of tests in Chapter 6.

Researchers should report evidence of validity for measures they use in their research, and this evidence should be studied carefully because interpretation of the research results hinges on the validity of the measures upon which these results are based. Since validity evidence is difficult to obtain, the absence of extensive validity data in a new measure does not mean the measure lacks validity, but it definitely limits the interpretations that can be made. Many teachers and school administrators accept standardized educational measures at face value and assume that these measures are valid, although little evidence is put forth by the test publisher to support this assumption. In the case of research that uses measures of dubious validity it is generally safer to consider the results reported to be tentative at best.

2. What evidence of reliability is available? Reliability refers to the consistency of a measure. In other words, reliability evidence gives us information about the degree to which a measure will yield similar results for the same subjects at different times or under different conditions. For example, one kind of reliability is called test-retest reliability. To determine test-retest reliability (also called the coefficient of stability), the test developer administers her measure to a large sample of appropriate individuals. She then waits for a period of time and administers the measure to the same subjects again. Finally, she determines the degree to which the first set of scores relates to the second set of scores. This relationship, usually expressed as a correla-

---

1. Specimen sets are available for many published measures. Typically they contain a copy of the test, answer key, test manual, and technical reports on that test.

tion coefficient, gives us an estimate of the stability of the test scores over time.[2] For a test that is highly reliable, individuals tested will obtain very similar scores on both administrations of the measure. As these scores become less similar, the reliability of the measure becomes lower. You will learn more about test reliability in Chapter 6.

The author of a research article should always report the kind of reliability that has been established for each of her measures and the reliability coefficients that have been obtained. In reviewing the article, these should both be checked. Reliability evidence is much easier to obtain than validity evidence. Thus, when no reliability coefficients are reported, we can usually conclude either that the study was not carefully conducted or that the investigator failed to report reliability because it was low.

Since tests having very low reliability make large errors of measurement, they often obscure differences or relationships that would be revealed by the use of more reliable instruments. Thus, the student should consider carefully the possible effects of low reliability upon the reported results of studies she evaluates and should not reject a promising idea or approach because of negative findings based on unreliable measures.

3. Is the measure appropriate for the sample? In evaluating the research of others, you should remember that even a well-standardized and generally accepted measure will have little value if administered to an inappropriate sample. A typical mistake made by inexperienced researchers is to use a measure that is more appropriate for some subsamples of the research group than others, therefore biasing results in favor of the subsamples whose previous learning or background gives them an advantage on the measure. Occasionally tests are employed that are either too easy or too difficult for the majority of the sample measured. For example, a study of achievement of children at different ability levels will have little meaning if the test used has too low a ceiling, thus limiting the level of achievement that a superior student can display.

Some measures are inappropriate because of cultural bias, that is, they contain questions that are easier for persons from one culture than persons from other cultures. Cultural bias is difficult to estimate. However, if you are interested in applying research findings to an important local problem or question, it is usually desirable to examine a copy of the measures for possible cultural bias and also see what other reviewers have to say about this question.

EVALUATING RESEARCH FINDINGS AND CONCLUSIONS

The main purpose of reading research articles is to learn about the research findings, determine how these relate to the problem you are studying, and decide how much confidence you can place in these findings. Evaluating research results is a complex

---

2. *Correlation* is a statistical technique for measuring the degree of relationship between two sets of scores. A correlation coefficient of zero indicates no relationship while a coefficient of 1.00 indicates a perfect relationship. Correlation is discussed in Chapter 7.

process. The more you know about such topics as research design, experimenter bias, sampling, education measurement, and statistics, the more sophisticated your evaluation will be. However, a person who is primarily concerned with using research results to help solve practical problems and make sound decisions usually has neither the time or the desire to become an expert in areas like research design and statistics. Thus, in this book we propose to give you the minimum essentials you will need to use educational research intelligently, without trying to make you into a sophisticated researcher. This means you will not be able to evaluate the more subtle aspects of educational research without additional training (Borg & Gall, 1983). You will, however, be able to evaluate most of the research reports you read, recognize their main limitations, and decide how the results relate to the students in your school, or to the problem or question for which you need an answer.

Different kinds of research tend to be susceptible to different kinds of errors, biases, and limitations. Thus, we will postpone our discussion of the specific problems of interpreting and evaluating research results until Chapters 8–10 when we review articles that are examples of the major kinds of educational research.

COMBINING RESEARCH FINDINGS

Teachers usually conduct research reviews in order to get an answer or locate possible solutions to a specific educational question or problem. Typically, several studies will be found that relate to the problem at hand. In order to get a clear picture of the overall state of knowledge related to your problem, you must use some procedure for combining the research findings. We will briefly review two techniques that can be used.

Vote Counting.   The easiest but also the least accurate procedure for combining the evidence from a set of related studies is a simple tally. In this method all studies are placed in categories based on the significance and direction of the results. For example, using a four-category system, a study producing significant positive results (i.e., in the hypothesized direction) is coded + +. Positive results that fail to reach significance are coded +, negative nonsignificant results are coded −, and negative significant results are coded − −. The reviewer then adds up the number of studies in each category to get an overall picture of the research evidence. A number of variations of the vote-counting approach have been used. In the most common of these, nonsignificant results, regardless of direction, are coded "0," while significant results are coded + or −. For an example of the vote counting method see Rosenshine's (1971) small classic, which reviews the relationships between specific teaching behaviors and student achievement. His findings, although now 15 years old, still provide some useful insights for the classroom teacher. The vote counting method is discussed in Cooper (1984) and Glass et al. (1981).[3]

Meta-analysis.   The term *meta-analysis* has come to be applied to a variety of quantitative procedures that have evolved over the past 30 years (Rosenthal, 1984) for combining and comparing research results. The most widely used procedure was

3. See Recommended Reading.

developed by Glass (1976). His method, in essence, involves translating the findings of a set of related studies into "effect sizes." In its simplest form the effect size is computed by taking the difference between the effect of the experimental treatment and the control treatment on the dependent variable and dividing this difference by the standard deviation of the dependent variable for the control group. By calculating an effect size for every relevant study in your review, you are translating the various results into a comparable unit of measure (i.e., the difference or "effect" in standard deviation units), which can then be averaged in order to give you a composite quantitative estimate of the results of the studies you have reviewed. Although meta-analysis has been criticized on several grounds, it is probably the best method we now have available (Educational Research Service, 1980; Glass et al., 1981; Rosenthal, 1984).

Since all studies do not report the necessary means and standard deviations, Glass and his associates (1981) have developed procedures for estimating the effect size from virtually any statistical data reported in the studies being analyzed. They also provide several examples of meta-analysis which will help you understand the procedure and appreciate its value.

In recent years a great many meta-analyses of educational literature using the Glass procedures have been conducted. These have made a very important contribution to our understanding of the state of knowledge about many key educational questions. You are urged to use this procedure if called upon to conduct a review of research.

We have included a brief meta-analysis recently published by Holmes and Matthews (1984). This article will not only give you a better understanding of the meta-analysis process; it will also give you a clear picture of the research related to an important question in education.

Sample Meta-Analysis Article:
"THE EFFECTS OF NONPROMOTION ON ELEMENTARY AND JUNIOR HIGH SCHOOL PUPILS: A META-ANALYSIS"

C. Thomas Holmes and Kenneth M. Matthews
UNIVERSITY OF GEORGIA

Abstract
In this study data from all studies identified as meeting the selection criteria were mathematically integrated to determine the effect of grade-level retention on ele-

Holmes, C. T., Matthews, K. M., "The Effects of Nonpromotion on Elementary and Junior High School Pupils: A Meta-Analysis." *Review of Educational Research*, Summer, 1984, pp. 225–236. Copyright 1984, American Educational Research Association, Washington, D.C. Reprinted by permission of the author and the American Educational Research Association.

mentary and/or junior high school pupils. When each effect size calculated was treated equally, a grand mean effect size of −.37 was obtained indicating that, on the average, promoted children scored .37 standard deviation units higher than retained children on the various outcome measures. When the effect sizes within each study were first averaged so that each study could be given equal weight, a grand mean of −.34 was obtained. By using the effect sizes from only those studies in which the promoted and nonpromoted pupils had been matched, a grand mean of −.38 was calculated. The high degree of consistency in these measures lends credibility to the validity of these findings.

In addition to the grand means, effects sizes were calculated on various dependent variable measures, including academic achievement (further subdivided into various areas), personal adjustment (which included self-concept, social adjustment, and emotional adjustment), and attitude toward school, behavior, and attendance. In all cases, the outcomes for promoted pupils were more positive than for retained pupils.

By the end of the Civil War, schools in most urban communities had organized their pupils into grades with goals expressed for each level. During the next 70 years the schools in rural areas followed suit. "This . . . graded system permitted teachers to concentrate their talents and training on pupils of relatively similar chronological age, maturity, and experience levels" (Knezevich, 1975, p. 378). It was with this organization of the school into grade levels that the issue of which students to retain first arose.

The question of whether to retain low-achieving and/or socially immature pupils in elementary grades has been a persistent concern of school administrators. As far back as the turn of the century, William H. Maxwell, superintendent of schools of New York City, called attention to the problem of nonpromotion in the public schools (Caswell, 1933). Leonard P. Ayres (1909) reported the first comprehensive study of pupil progress with his book *Laggards in Our Schools*. Since then hundreds of articles have been written presenting cases for or against nonpromotion, and many studies have been conducted in attempts to clarify this issue. These studies have reported inconsistent findings and conclusions.

The debate has continued over the last 80 years and promises, after a recent lull, to appear once again at the forefront with the increasing emphasis on competency-based education. The rate of nonpromotion had declined over the last few decades, but is now on the increase. Hubbell (1981) found that the number of children retained in the

124 schools she surveyed in California had risen steadily each year over the last 5 years. Greensville County (Virginia) Schools retained 1,300 of their 3,750 students as a result of a move to base promotion exclusively on student mastery of skills (Owens & Ranick, 1977). Approximately half of the first, second, and third graders in the Washington, D.C., school system failed to meet the new math and reading standards in each of the last 2 years and therefore were retained in grade (CBS, 1981). With this reassessment of retention policies by school districts, a look at the existing research seems appropriate.

After reviewing the research on promotion/retention for the Philadelphia School District, Reiter (1973) concluded that the research tells us that "how the pupil is promoted or retained is more important than whether he is" (p. 20). He reported that the research indicated that nonpromotion and social promotion have negative effects. However, Hess (1978) concluded that the available research "produces a varied range of conclusions" (p. 155).

The Best of ERIC (1979) reported that Jackson (1975) had provided the only critical review of the research on grade retention. After concluding that the available research was generally of poor quality and contained major flaws, he stated that it provided only mixed results. In conclusion Jackson wrote, "Thus those educators who retain pupils in a grade do so without valid research evidence that such treatment will provide greater benefits to students with academic or adjustment difficulties than will promotion to the next grade" (p. 627).

McAfee (1981) agreed with Jackson's assessment of the quality of existing research. However, he dismissed the possibilities of more research employing an experimental design as follows:

> To determine whether or not retention is beneficial, all would agree that implementation of experimental designs would best allow us to answer the question. Unfortunately, it seems that most school districts will be unwilling to adopt such a strategy because of the political ramifications. (p. 22)

It is hoped that the decisions of school officials not to randomly select students for retention are not based solely on political considerations but also on possible consequences to the children in their care.

Holmes (1983) found eight reports of studies in which retained pupils had been matched on the basis of achievement test scores with promoted counterparts. All eight studies used standardized achievement test scores as measurements of the dependent variable achievement. After analyzing the studies, Holmes concluded,

> If, as is often the purported case today, retention of pupils is accomplished with the intention of improving the academic achievement in the basic skills of these pupils, the research does not seem to support this practice. It seems that retained pupils fall behind during the year that they are retained and spend the rest of their academic careers in vain attempt to catch up. (p. 4)

Jackson (1975) stated that studies comparing groups of regularly promoted students with those retained under normal school policies were biased in favor of promotion. He arrived at this conclusion by assuming that the fact that the promoted students were promoted indicated that they were doing better than those who were retained. Although undoubtedly this was sometimes true, it has not always been ignored in the research design. When retained groups are selected from

schools with more stringent retention policies than the policies in the schools from which the control groups were selected, his assumption need not hold. With some studies selecting control groups from age peers and some from grade peers (the latter may be biased in favor of retention), some selecting control groups from within the same school and some from without, and one of the studies employing an experimental design, some of the research biases may be compensated for in a meta-analysis.

Cognizant of the danger of a possible bias, as well as knowing the current concerns educators have about this issue, a meta-analysis of the existing research was undertaken.

Methods

Light and Smith (1971) concluded that "progress will only come when we are able to pool, in a systematic manner, the original data from . . . studies" (p. 443). Glass and Smith (1976) pioneered one such technique of integration. It was decided that this technique, meta-analysis, was suitable for examining the effects of non-promotion on elementary and junior high school pupils.

Meta-analysis, as defined by Glass (1978), is based on the concept of effect size. In this study, effect size was defined as the difference between the mean of the retained group and the mean of the promoted group, divided by the standard deviation of the promoted group. This procedure results in a measure of the difference between the two groups expressed in quantitative units which are additive across studies.

Sources of Data

A systematic search of the literature was conducted to identify studies that were potentially relevant. In the initial phase, *Current Index to Journals in Education* (ERIC), *Research in Education* (ERIC), and *Dissertation Abstracts International* were computer-searched. In addition, a manual search was conducted of *Education Index* and *Master's Thesis in Education*. In the second phase, each report located in phase one was consulted, when possible, for additional citations. The search produced a bibliography of approximately

650 entries. (The complete bibliography is available on request from the authors.)

The following selection criteria were used to reduce the completed bibliography to the list of 44 studies included in the meta-analysis (see Appendix). To have been included in the final list, the reported study must have (a) presented the results of original research of the effects on pupils of retention in the elementary or junior high school grades, (b) contained sufficient data to allow for the calculation or estimation of an effect size (see Holmes, 1984), and (c) compared a group of retained pupils with a group of promoted pupils. The 44 studies consisted of 18 published studies, 14 dissertations, and 12 master's theses.

A total of 11,132 pupils were included in these 44 investigations. There were 4,208 nonpromoted pupils, with 6,924 regularly promoted pupils serving as controls. As few as 30 and as many as 1,929 pupils were involved in individual studies.

Chronological and Geographical Distribution

Figure 1 shows the chronological distribution of the studies included in the meta-analysis. The earliest publication date among the studies is 1929. The most recent is 1981, with most studies conducted between 1960 and 1975.

To determine whether changes in society and/or the educational setting make it more appropriate to set a specified time range for the inclusion of studies, a Pearson product-moment correlation was computed between the year the study was reported and the mean effect size (*ES*) for the study. A correlation coefficient near zero would suggest that changes taking place over time have no systematic effect on the magnitude of the effect size and would support the decision to include all studies. Because the coefficient obtained was $-.07$, all studies were included in the meta-analysis.

All but two of the studies identified the state in which the study was conducted. Two others were carried out in public schools in Canada. The remaining 40 studies were conducted in 26 different states (see Figure 2), The location of the two studies that were not identified could be placed in a particular region of the United States: One was undertaken in the northeastern United States, and the other was conducted in the southeastern United States. Geographically the studies were well distributed over the continental United States

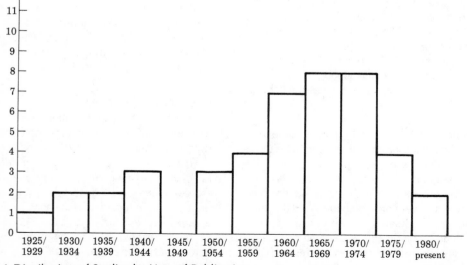

Figure 1 Distribution of Studies by Year of Publication

Figure 2 Geographic Distribution of the Studies

with the exception of the Mountain States' not being represented.

Results

In all, 575 individual effect sizes were calculated. This represents a mean of 13 effect sizes per study. However, as many as 160 effect sizes and as few as 1 effect size were obtained from individual studies. As indicated in Table I, the mean *ES* obtained from averaging the 575 effect sizes was −.37. This value indicates that on the average, the groups of nonpromoted pupils scored .37 standard deviation units lower on the various outcome measures than did the promoted group. It is statistically unlikely that a mean *ES* as large as .37 would be found if the literature showed no overall effect of nonpromotion, $t(574) = 10.28$, $p<.001$.

The overall effect size includes *ES*s that were calculated with data measuring several dependent variables and represents the overall effect of nonpromotion on pupils retained in elementary or junior high school grades. These 575 *ES*s were then grouped into five major areas of dependent variables: (a) academic achievement, (b) personal adjustment, (c) self-concept, (d) attitude toward school, and (e) attendance. The first two areas were further subdivided.

Because some of the studies yielded many effect sizes and others produced only one, a decision was made to reexamine the data to see if any one study had produced substantial distortions in the mean effect sizes.

All individual effect sizes obtained from a single study that measured the same general area were averaged, and then the mean of the averages was taken. In this way, all studies that measured an effect contributed equally to the grand mean effect size. As can be seen in Table 1, most of the differences obtained from the original calculations were small. Nine of the 15 mean effect sizes calculated were within .04 standard deviation units of the original calculations. However, a noticeable difference was observed in the self-concept mean effect size, as the difference between the promoted and nonpromoted groups almost vanished, going from −.19 to −.02 standard deviations.

Academic Achievement

The effect of nonpromotion on pupil's academic achievement was measured in 31 of the 44 studies. From those studies, 367 effect sizes were calculated. When the mean of these 367 *ES*s was calculated, a value of −.44 was obtained, indicating that the promoted group on the average had achieved .44 standard deviation units higher

Table 1 Mean effect sizes overall and by area

	ESs	Studies	$ES(SE_{\bar{x}})$	ES (by study mean)
Overall effect size	575	44	−.37(.036)****	−.34
Academic achievement	367	31	−.44(.035)****	−.43
Language arts	85	14	−.40(.063)****	−.54
Reading	75	24	−.48(.060)****	−.50
Mathematics	77	20	−.33(.116)***	−.45
Work study skills	32	1	−.41(.102)****	−.41
Social studies	7	3	−.35(.159)*	−.37
Grade point average	4	3	−.58(.394)	−.78
Personal adjustment	142	21	−.27(.050)****	−.38
Social adjustment	60	13	−.27(.074)****	−.24
Emotional adjustment	9	5	−.37(.239)*	−.20
Behavior	13	7	−.31(.103)**	−.35
Self-concept	34	9	−.19(.083)**	−.02
Attitude toward school	26	8	−.16(.042)****	−.17
Attendance	6	4	−.12(.051)*	−.14
Mode of publication[a]				
Journal	98	13	−.29(.041)	
Master's thesis	121	15	−.35(.051)	
Dissertation	346	15	−.35(.038)	
Monograph	10	1	−.42(.078)	
Grade at retention				
1	49	9	−.26(.082)****	
2	4	1	−.64(.119)**	
3	134	5	−.41(.080)****	
4	78	5	−.36(.056)****	
5	52	3	−.16(.075)**	
6	50	2	−.42(.072)****	
Equal time in school	279		−.46(.044)****	
Achievement	209	14	−.53(.050)****	
Personal adjustment	62	7	−.33(.091)****	
Self-concept	5	2	.48(.225)*	
Attitude	2	1	−.08(.020)	
Attendance	1	2	−.21(.060)	
After equal grade	181		−.28(.045)****	
Achievement	135	13	−.21(.049)***	
Personal adjustment	13	3	−.78(.299)**	
Self-concept	19	2	−.48(.075)****	
Attitude	14	3	−.25(.041)****	
Attendance	—	—	—	
ES calculations/estimations				
From definition	179	23	−.37(.066)	
Est. from dependent t	211	5	−.42(.039)	
Est. from F	38	5	−.46(.061)	
Est. from X^2	31	4	−.38(.039)	
Est. from independent t	34	3	−.10(.056)	
Est. from proportions	66	4	−.07(.022)	
Est. from other	16	4	−.20(.042)	

[a] Not significantly different from one another.
*$p < .10$ that $ES = 0$.
**$p < .05$.
***$p < .01$.
****$p < .001$.

than the retained group, $t(366) = 12.57$, $p<.001$. Each of the subareas produced negative mean effect size values, indicating that nonpromotion had a negative effect on the pupils (language arts, $-.40$, $t[84] = 6.35$, $p<.001$; reading, $-.48$, $t[74] = 8.00$, $p<.001$; mathematics, $-.33$, $t[76] = 2.84$, $p<.01$; work study skills, $-.41$, $t[31] = 4.02$, $p<.001$; social studies, $-.35$, $t[6] = 2.20$, $p<.10$; grade point average, $-.58$, $t[3] = 1.47$, ns).

Personal Adjustment

Of the 575 individual effect sizes calculated, 142 were measures of what has been labeled personal adjustment variables. These 142 effect sizes were obtained from 21 studies and yielded a mean ES of $-.27$. Following retention, the retained students scored an average of .27 standard deviation units below that of promoted students in measures of personal adjustment, $t(141) = 5.40$, $p<.001$. Three subareas were identified: (a) social adjustment, (b) emotional adjustment, and (c) behavior. Once again all subareas produced nega-

tive effect sizes (social adjustment, $-.27$, $t[59] = 3.65$, $p<.001$; emotional adjustment, $-.37$, $t[8] = 1.55$, $p<.10$; behavior, $-.31$, $t[12] = 3.01$, $p<.05$).

Self-Concept

Nine studies measured the effect of retention on the self-concepts of pupils who had been retained in either elementary or junior high school. With data from these studies, 34 effect sizes were calculated. These 34 ESs produced a mean of $-.19$. On self-concept measures, the promoted pupils outscored the retained pupils by .19 standard deviation units, $t(33) = 2.29$, $p<.05$.

Attitude toward School

Eight studies measured pupil attitudes toward school. These studies yielded 26 effect sizes with a mean ES of $-.16$, $t(25) = 3.81$, $p<.001$. Although this does not indicate large differences in attitudes toward school between the groups, the difference that was measured indicated that re-

Table 2   Studies with matched subjects

Study	IQ	Achievement test	SES	Sex	Grades	Other	ES
				Matched on			
1	x		x	x		x	$-.23$
2	x		x	x			$-.39$
3	x			x		x	$-.96$
4				x	x	x	$-.66$
5		x					$-.39$
6	x	x	x	x		x	$-.63$
7	x	x				x	$-.06$
8		x		x		x	$-.40$
9	x			x		x	$+.20$
10	x			x		x	$-.41$
11		x				x	$-.05$
12		x					$-.04$
13		x		x			$-.42$
14	x	x		x		x	$-.48$
15	x	x				x	$-.65$
16	x			x		x	$-.59$
17	x						$-.51$
18	x	x		x		x	$-.16$
						Mean ES	$-.38$

tained students held school in less favor than the promoted students.

Research Bias

As indicated in Table 1, the findings are remarkably consistent when the data are examined from several research perspectives. Of particular concern was the possibility that significantly different findings would result when the retained and promoted subjects were matched on various relevant criteria. Eighteen of the 44 studies had matched subjects. All but one of these had included IQ and/or achievement test scores as matching criteria. Table 2 indicates the criteria used in the 18 studies with matched subjects. A mean effect size was calculated with these studies to see if matching the groups produced different results from the overall effect sizes previously calculated. A grand mean *ES* of −.38 was obtained,

which is very similar to the −.37 and the −.34 shown in Table 1. The high degree of consistency between these measures supports the conclusion that differences in the designs of the studies resulted in no significant amount of bias in the results.

Conclusion

Those who continue to retain pupils at grade level do so despite cumulative research evidence showing that the potential for negative effects consistently outweighs positive outcomes. Because this cumulative research evidence consistently points to negative effects of nonpromotion, the burden of proof legitimately falls on proponents of retention plans to show there is compelling logic indicating success of their plans when so many other plans have failed.[4]

4. The appendix and reference list have been omitted to save space.

References

BORG, W. R., & GALL, M. D. (1983). *Educational research: An introduction* (4th ed.). White Plains, N.Y.: Longman.

COOPER, H. M. (1984). *The integrative research review.* Beverly Hills, Calif.: Sage.

EDUCATIONAL RESEARCH SERVICE. (1980). Class size research: A critique of recent meta-analysis. *Phi Delta Kappan, 61,* 239–241.

EVANS, P. (1976). The Burt affair: Sleuthing in science. *APA Monitor,* no. 12, pp. 1, 4.

GLASS, G. V., McGAW, B., & SMITH, M. E. (1981). *Meta-analysis in social research.* Beverly Hills, Calif.: Sage.

ROSENTHAL, R. (1984). *Meta-analytic procedures for social research.* Beverly Hills, Calif.: Sage.

ROSENTHAL, R., & ROSNOW, F. L. (1975). *The volunteer subject.* New York: Wiley.

TONSOR, C. A. (1953). Must we segregate? *National Association of Secondary School Principals' Bulletin, 37,* 75–77.

Recommended Reading

BORG, W. R., & GALL, M. D. (1983). *Educational research: An introduction (4th ed.).* White Plains, N.Y.: Longman.

    This text will be useful for the student who requires more information on critical evaluation, sampling, and measurement.

COOPER, H. M. (1984). *The integrative research review.* Beverly Hills, Calif.: Sage.

This book emphasizes the importance of using rigorous methodology in reviewing and integrating previous research findings. Each stage of the research review process is discussed in depth. Careful study of this reference is recommended to anyone planning to do a review of educational research literature.

EDUCATIONAL RESEARCH SERVICE. (1980). Class size research: A critique of recent meta-analyses. *Phi Delta Kappan, 61,* 239–241.

This article provides a number of criticisms of the meta-analysis process. A reply by Glass is published in the same issue (p. 242–244).

GLASS, G. V., McGAW, B., & SMITH, M. E. (1981). *Meta-analysis in social research.* Beverly Hills, Calif.: Sage.

This is the current key source for Glass's meta-analysis procedures. The book discusses the problems of integrating research data and shows how meta-analysis addresses these problems and gives many specific examples of how the procedures can be applied. The authors also answer the main criticisms of the meta-analyses procedure that have been made in recent years.

JACKSON, G. B. (1975). The research evidence on the effects of grade retention. *Review of Educational Research, 45,* 613–635.

In most areas of educational research, the majority of studies located by the reviewer are likely to have significant deficiencies in research design. The task of pulling together a large amount of flawed evidence and obtaining an accurate composite picture of the state of knowledge is difficult. This article provides the student with an excellent model that can be followed in pulling together her own review of research relevant to her problem.

MILLMAN, J., & CORWAN, D. B. (1974). *Appraising educational research: A case study approach.* Englewood Cliffs, N.J.: Prentice-Hall.

This book contains nine educational research articles covering a variety of educational topics and research procedures. Special notes and a detailed critique are provided for each article. The critiques were developed and modified on the basis of comments supplied by over 800 students and provide an excellent model for students who are studying the critical review process.

ROSENSHINE, B. (1971). *Teaching behaviours and student achievement.* London: National Foundation for Educational Research in England and Wales.

Provides a good example of how research evidence can be combined to provide practical guidance on ways that specific kinds of teaching behavior such as praise, clarity, and enthusiasm can influence student achievement. Although this book was published 15 years ago, much of the evidence presented is still useful to the teacher or school administrator.

ROSENTHAL, R. (1984). *Meta-analytic procedures for social research.* Beverly Hills, Calif.: Sage.

This book describes a variety of meta-analysis approaches and compares their use and the results obtained. Illustrations of the different procedures are given. The final chapter deals with the evaluation of meta-analysis procedures and results and is especially recommended to students who plan to use one of these techniques.

ROSENTHAL, R., & ROSNOW, F. L. (1975). *The volunteer subject.* New York: Wiley.

Since it is very difficult to obtain nonvolunteers for most research, it is important for behavioral scientists to understand volunteer subjects and use them effectively. This book builds upon the extensive research of the authors but also pulls together other important research on the volunteer subject. Topics covered include characteristics of the volunteer, suggestions for reducing volunteer bias, and implications for interpreting research findings.

Application Problems

1. Review the following introductory section of a research article and identify possible indications of investigator bias.

TEAM TEACHING IS THE ANSWER

BY R. B. SMITH

Two years ago the author recommended that the freshman psychology course at Catatonic State University be taught using the team teaching approach. Each faculty member in the department selected the topics in which he had the greatest expertise and developed lessons in these topics. We felt that this approach had many advantages to the timeworn lecture approach that students find so dull in which one instructor is responsible for the entire course, including areas in which he has had little background. The purpose of this study was to demonstrate objectively that the team teaching approach produced better achievement and better attitudes among freshman students than a conventional lecture approach carried out by a single instructor.

2. Write a null hypothesis and a directional hypothesis to fit the following problem statement: A serious problem in teaching high school social studies is that achievement tests have shown that although students seem to master facts about the democratic system, the majority cannot explain the principles underlying the system. The problem to be investigated in this research is to determine whether the students of teachers who use a high frequency of analysis, synthesis, and evaluation questions in social studies discussions will display higher levels of achievement on a test of social studies concepts than the students of teachers who use a high frequency of fact questions.

3. Evaluate the following "hypothesis" using the criteria given in this chapter:

Two experiments were undertaken. The first investigates the use of video feedback in changing specific teacher behavior, and the second deals with the effect of modified teacher behavior on pupil performance.[5]

4. The district reading supervisor wants to study student attitudes toward reading in a large urban school district in hopes that this survey will produce information that can be used to modify the school's reading program. She has decided to select her sample from all sixth-grade pupils listed on the district roster. This roster lists pupils alphabetically by classroom for each of the district's 200 elementary schools. Forty of these schools (having 3520 sixth-grade pupils) are classified as serving predominantly upper-middle-class neighborhoods. A total of 54 schools (4968 pupils) serve lower-middle-class neighborhoods, 62 schools (6211 pupils) serve working-class-neighborhoods, and 44 (4507 pupils) are inner-city schools serving mainly welfare families. There are a total of 800 sixth-grade classrooms, containing an average of 24 pupils. Total district enrollment in Grade 6 is 19,206. Describe the steps you would take:

    a. To select a simple random sample of 1000 from this population.

    b. To select a systematic sample of 1000.

---

5. P. J. Dawson, K. E. Dawson, S. R. Forness. (1975). Effect of video feedback on teacher behavior. *Journal of Educational Research, 68*(5), 197–201.

    c. To select a sample of 1000 pupils stratified on the basis of socioeconomic status of the schools.

    d. To select a cluster sample of about 1000 pupils.

5. In Problem 4, what is the accessible population? To what target populations might the results be generalized?

6. Evaluate one of the Chapter 5 articles from Appendix 2.

CHAPTER 6

EDUCATIONAL MEASURES

Overview

Since no research is better than the measures used in it, the person who wants to evaluate and apply educational research findings must have a basic knowledge of educational measurement. This chapter aims at providing this basic knowledge. The use of paper-and-pencil tests, questionnaires, interviews, and direct observation to collect educational data is described. Important characteristics of educational measures such as objectivity, validity, and reliability are discussed. Then a number of important sources of information on educational measures are briefly reviewed.

Objectives

1. Describe the advantages and limitations of group-administered paper-and-pencil tests.
2. Discuss questions that the reviewer should consider in evaluating a questionnaire study.
3. Describe advantages and limitations of the interview as a measurement procedure in educational research.
4. Describe three types of interviews and give an example of an educational study where each would be appropriate.
5. Discuss questions that the reviewer should consider in evaluating studies that use interviews.
6. Discuss questions the reviewer should consider in evaluating studies that use direct observation.
7. Define "low-inference" and "high-inference" variables and give an example of each.
8. Briefly describe the procedure usually used to train observers.
9. Define test objectivity and describe factors that influence it.
10. Define five kinds of test validity, and describe the conditions under which they are used.
11. Define four kinds of test reliability, compare them, and describe the conditions under which they are used.
12. Explain three sources of error that can lead to spurious increases in reliability coefficients, and describe a method of determining reliability that controls for these errors.
13. Name and describe six sources of information that can help you locate and evaluate educational tests.

All scientific research involves measurement, and progress in any science is limited by the accuracy and sophistication of the measures that have been developed. In the physical sciences, measurement has become very accurate and sophisticated. But in education, we are concerned with the most complex of all scientific subjects, the human being. As a result our measures are much less accurate and sophisticated than those that have been developed in the more mature sciences. In some areas of human performance such as strength, manual dexterity, and visual acuity our measures are quite precise and reliable. In others, such as achievement, our measures are moderately accurate. But when we attempt to measure such complex human characteristics as personality, our measures are crude and subject to large measurement errors.

The research findings of any study are no more accurate than the measures on which these findings are based. For this reason, the person who is interested in applying educational research results to practical problems must know something about educational measurement and must know how to evaluate the measures used in a research project. This chapter is designed to give you the minimum tools you will need to make such evaluations. If you want to know more about educational measurement, consult one of the books listed at the end of the chapter.

Kinds of Measures
Used in Educational Research

In the behavioral sciences and education we are interested in a very large number of human phenomena, which must be measured if they are to be studied. As a result, researchers in these areas have developed a variety of different procedures for measuring human characteristics and behavior. We will now review briefly four widely used measurement procedures used in educational research: paper-and-pencil tests, questionnaires, interviews, and direct observations. The chapter will give most attention to paper-and-pencil tests.

PAPER-AND-PENCIL TESTS

There are literally thousands of paper-and-pencil tests available that purport to measure variables ranging from the academic aptitude of preschoolers to the yarn dexterity of textile workers. Tests are probably used in more educational research projects than all other kinds of measure combined. They have a number of important advantages. First, they are generally cheaper than other forms of measurement. Also, because of their huge number and variety, a researcher can usually find one or two paper-and-pencil tests that claim to measure virtually any human characteristic or behavior. They are also generally easier to use and require less time than other forms of measurement.

You should, however, also be aware of some of the limitations of paper-and-pencil tests. First, the subject must be able to read and write in order to respond to most of these tests. Differences in reading ability can seriously distort the scores of many students on tests that measure variables having nothing to do with reading. For example, since most achievement tests are timed, a slow reader may complete fewer items and obtain a lower score on a science achievement test than a fast reader, even though the slow reader knows more science. Thus, in evaluating a research project that has employed paper-and-pencil tests, you should check the steps that were taken to eliminate reading ability as a factor. Steps often taken include: (1) reading all test items aloud to subjects, (2) checking the test for reading difficulty, and (3) giving help to poor readers such as reading and explaining difficult words.

Another limitation of most paper-and-pencil tests is that they rely on self-report, that is, the student tells you what he thinks, feels, does, or knows. This is not a serious problem in areas such as achievement but can lead to many misleading answers on tests in areas such as racial attitudes, personality, or vocational interests. In attitude measurement, for example, the individual may wish to hide his true attitude in order to get a more socially acceptable score. Some tests in areas such as personality and attitudes attempt to disguise their purpose in order to reduce this problem. However, for most paper-and-pencil tests, the purpose of the test is clear to the subject, and when it is, faking or distortion of an individual's score is always possible.

A third limitation that can be serious for group-administered tests is that it is difficult for the tester to determine the physical and mental state of the persons being tested. If a child is ill, tired, or emotionally upset, he is likely to perform below his capacity on a paper-and-pencil test. This can distort the research findings and can also lead the teacher to make bad decisions about such children. Individually administered tests are much less susceptible to this problem.

For some variables, even though paper-and-pencil tests are available, more accurate measurement is possible using other techniques. It is usually possible to get more thoughtful and complete responses to an interview than can be obtained from a paper-and-pencil measure such as a study habits test. Direct observation of the person is another technique that usually provides better evidence about his behavior than will a paper-and-pencil test. For example, observation of aggressive behavior in the classroom will usually provide better information on levels of aggression than a test that asks pupils what aggressive behavior they indulge in. Similarly, we can learn more about a student's counseling skills by watching him conduct a counseling session than we can by giving him a multiple-choice test about counseling. Later in this chapter we will discuss further how the tests used in a research project can be evaluated.

QUESTIONNAIRES

The questionnaire is similar to the paper-and-pencil test. In fact there are no characteristics that invariably differentiate between a test and a questionnaire. A test *usually* contains a set of items related to a single variable such as vocabulary or arithmetic achievement that have correct and incorrect answers and produce a score that indicates the individual's level of performance on that variable. In contrast, the questionnaire *usually* contains questions aimed at getting specific information on a variety of topics. There are no right or wrong answers to these questions, and no total score is computed by combining the questionnaire responses. Questions may be of either the closed form, in which the question permits only certain responses (such as a multiple-choice question), or the open form, in which the subject makes any response he wishes in his own words (such as an essay question). Which form will be used is determined by the objective of the particular question. Generally, though, it is desirable to design the questions in closed form so that quantification and analysis of the results may be carried out efficiently. In many cases the results for each questionnaire item are analyzed and reported separately by the investigator, since each item deals with a different topic.

In evaluating a questionnaire study, the reviewer should consider the following questions:

1. Was the questionnaire pretested? It is impossible to predict how questionnaire items will be interpreted by respondents unless the researcher tries out the questionnaire and analyzes the responses of a small sample of subjects before starting his main study. This pretest should include a sample drawn from the same population that will be sampled in the main study. The results are used to refine the questionnaire and locate potential problems in interpretation or analysis of the results. If such a pretest is carried out, it suggests that a careful study has been done.

2. Did the questionnaire include any leading questions? A copy of the questionnaire is usually included in the research report and should be carefully checked by the reviewer for leading questions. It has been found that the way a question is stated has a great deal to do with the answers obtained. If a question is framed in such a way that the subject is given hints as to the kind of response that is expected, there is some tendency to give the researcher what he wants. This tendency is especially strong when the letter of transmittal that accompanies the questionnaire has been signed by someone that the subject is eager to please. Results obtained from leading questions are almost surely biased and should be ignored by the reviewer.

3. Were any psychologically threatening questions included in the questionnaire? In constructing questionnaire items, it is important to avoid questions that may in some way be psychologically threatening to the person answering. For example, a questionnaire sent to school principals concerning the morale of teachers at their schools would be threatening to some principals because low morale suggests that the principal is failing in part of his job. When he receives a questionnaire containing threatening items, a person usually does not return it. If he does return it, little confidence can be placed in the accuracy of his reply because of his ego involvement in the situation.

In reading the questionnaire, the reviewer should try to put himself in the position of the respondent and then try to judge whether any of the questions might be threatening to him. Responses to such items should be given little credence.

4. Were the subjects who received the questionnaire likely to have the information requested? The most obvious consideration involved in selection of subjects for a questionnaire study is to get people who will be able to supply the information the researcher wants. Very often the group who will have the data wanted is immediately apparent. But in some cases, if the researcher does not have a thorough knowledge of the situation involved, he may send the questionnaire to a group of persons who do not have the desired information. For example, a graduate student seeking data on school financial policies sent questionnaires to principals of a large number of elementary schools. Many of the questionnaires returned were incomplete, and few specific facts of the sort wanted were obtained. This study failed because the trend in recent years has been for the superintendent and his staff to handle most matters concerning school finance. Inasmuch as the principals who received the questionnaire had little specific knowledge concerning this topic, they were unable to supply the information requested on the questionnaire.

5. What percentage of subjects responded to the questionnaire? The most difficult problem in conducting a questionnaire study is to get a sufficient percentage of responses. If this percentage is low, below 70 percent for example, one can place little confidence in the results reported, unless evidence is presented to show that the respondents are representative of the population from which they were drawn. In many cases, the persons who respond to a questionnaire are different from the persons who do not. Therefore, their answers will not accurately represent the results that would have been obtained if everyone in the sample had responded.

6. What steps were taken to contact nonrespondents, and how many ultimately responded? In a well-conducted questionnaire study the researcher should conduct at least two followups of nonrespondents in order to get a higher percentage of responses. He should also compare the answers of persons who responded initially with those who responded only after follow-up contacts were made. This comparison helps the reviewer estimate what the pattern of responses would have been if all subjects had responded. It also provides some idea of how respondents and nonrespondents differ in their responses to each question. If followups and the comparisons are not made, the reviewer should place less confidence in the results that are reported.

THE INTERVIEW

The interview is a form of measurement that is very widely used in descriptive research, such as surveys, but can also be used to collect a variety of educational data in other types of research. This method is unique in that it involves the collection of data through direct verbal interaction between individuals. This direct interaction is the source of both the main advantages and disadvantages of the interview as a research technique. Perhaps its principal advantage is its adaptability. The well-trained interviewer can make full use of the responses of the subject to alter the interview situation. As contrasted with the questionnaire, which provides no immediate feedback, the interview permits the research worker to follow up leads that show up during the interview and thus obtain more data and greater clarity. The interview situation usually permits much greater depth than other methods of collecting research data. A serious criticism of questionnaire studies is that they are often shallow, that is, they fail to dig deeply enough to provide a true picture of the respondents' opinions and feelings. In contrast, the experienced interviewer, by careful motivation of the subject and maintenance of rapport, can obtain information that the subject would probably not reveal under any other circumstances. Sensitive information that may be difficult to obtain except by interview usually concerns negative aspects of the self or negative feelings toward others. Respondents are not likely to reveal this type of information about themselves on a questionnaire and will only reveal it in an interview situation if they have been made to feel at ease by a skillful interviewer.

Although it has a number of important advantages over other data-collection tools in certain situations, the interview does have definite limitations as a research tool. Most important, the very adaptibility gained by the interpersonal situation leads to subjectivity and possible bias. The interactions between the respondent and the interviewer are subject to bias from many sources. Eagerness of the respondent to please the interviewer, a vague antagonism that sometimes arises between interviewer and respondent, or the tendency of the interviewer to seek out answers that support his preconceived notions are but a few of the factors that may contribute to biasing of data obtained from the interview.

Many factors that lead to distorted responses are classified as *response effects* by survey researchers. *Response effect* is concerned with the tendency of the respondent to give inaccurate or incorrect responses or more precisely is the difference between the answer given by the respondent and the true answer. For example, a respondent, if asked his annual income, may give an incorrect reply for any of a great many reasons. He may forget some sources of income such as stock dividends, he may be ashamed of or wish to hide some income such as money won gambling, he may want to impress the interviewer and therefore exaggerate his income, and so on.

In addition to response effect, another disadvantage of the interview as a research tool is that it is a costly and time-consuming technique to use and therefore limits the number of subjects who can be included in the research being collected.

In evaluating educational studies that use interviews to collect data, you should be alert to information related to the following questions:

1. How well were the interviewers trained? The level of training required for interviewers is directly related to the nature of the information being collected. In studies where the interviewer must draw inferences or make judgments, or collect personal or sensitive data, the interviewer needs extensive training to be effective. Information on the training of interviewers should be contained in the reports of research where interviews were employed.

2. How was information recorded? Tape recordings provide the most accurate method of collecting information from interviews. When the interviewer takes notes instead of recording the interview, he may miss or overlook important information. Also, since the interviewer who takes notes decides what will be recorded, his notes may be biased. For example, he may write information that agrees with his preconceived ideas or beliefs and omit information that disagrees with these beliefs.

3. How much judgment was called for? Interviews fall into three main types:

structured, semistructured, and unstructured. In structured interviews, the interviewer asks specific questions from an interview guide and does not deviate from these questions. In an unstructured interview, the interviewer does not employ a detailed interview guide but has a general plan and usually asks questions or makes comments intended to lead the respondent toward giving data to meet the interviewer's objectives. Unstructured interviews are generally called for in situations where the type of information sought is difficult for the subject to express or is psychologically distressing to the individual. Because of the threatening nature of topics usually covered by unstructured interviews, this procedure must constantly be adapted to the respondent and is highly subjective and time-consuming. Unstructured interviews obviously call for a great deal of judgment on the part of the interviewer as to what he should ask, what responses should be pursued further, and what should be recorded. As the amount of interviewer judgment goes up, the objectivity and precision of the data collected tend to decrease.

Most interviews used in educational research are semistructured. The interviewer follows a guide that lists questions covering all essential information needed by the researcher. However, he also has the option to follow up any answers in an effort to get more information or clarify the respondent's replies.

4. Were the interview procedures tried out before the study began? Although the interview can provide valuable data, you must remember that it is a highly subjective technique. When used in research, all possible controls and safeguards must be employed if we expect to obtain reasonably objective and unbiased data. A careful pilot study is the best insurance against bias and flaws in design. After the interview guide has been developed, a pilot study should be conducted to evaluate and improve the guide and the interview procedure and help the interviewer develop experience in using the procedure before any research data for the main study are collected. Such pilot studies should be described in the research report. Conducting a pilot study indicates to the reviewer that the project has been carefully carried out.

5. Were leading questions asked? A factor that often biases the results of interview studies is the use of leading questions by the interviewer. A leading question is any question whose phrasing leads the respondent to consider one reply more desirable than another. Let us say, for example, that we were interviewing a random sampling of voters concerning their attitudes toward federal aid to education. After establishing whether the respondent is familiar with the issue of federal aid to education, a reasonable question might be, "What is your opinion of federal aid to education?" A question that could be classified as moderately leading might be, "Do you favor federal aid to education?" This question is a little easier for the respondent to answer in the affirmative than the negative. A more serious attempt to lead the respondent would result in a question such as "In view of the dangers of federal control, do you feel that federal aid to education is advisable?" Here the respondent is strongly motivated to give an unfavorable response to federal aid. Questions can be slanted even further by the use of emotionally toned words to which the individual is inclined to react for or against with little thought for the basic issue involved. Such a question might be, "Do you favor federal aid to education as a means of providing each child with an equal educational opportunity?" In this case the concept of "an equal educational opportunity" is likely to elicit favorable replies.

In reports of interview studies an interview guide or list of the questions asked should be included. The reviewer should study these questions for possible signs of bias.

6. *How much did the interviewer know about the research?* Ideally, the interviewer should know as little as possible about the research for which he is collecting data. Obviously, he can infer a great deal from the questions on the interview guide, but he should not be told anything about the hypotheses or research design. Such information permits bias that could not occur if the interviewer had no access to the information.

For example, suppose a clinical researcher wants to study the effectiveness of two different approaches designed to improve the marital adjustment of young couples. He selects 30 young couples who are having serious marital problems and randomly divides them into two groups. He then gives one group a program of counseling designed to improve their overall personal adjustment. The other group receives a program in which they identify specific conflict situations and then role-play until they arrive at mutually acceptable solutions. Three months after the completion of the programs, the researcher trains an interviewer who will interview each couple to determine the marital adjustment problems they have had during the past month, collect data on the seriousness of these problems, find out if the problems have been resolved, and if so, how.

It is clearly impossible to keep the interviewer from knowing that the study has something to do with marital adjustment. However, he should not be told anything about the treatments and of course should not know which couples were given each treatment. If he has this information bias can easily occur. In the aforementioned example, if he considers counseling to be the better approach, he may consciously or unconsciously record information that supports his bias and overlook information that disagrees with his bias. Or he may be more cordial in his relationship with the couples who received counseling. Or he may frame some of his questions to these couples in ways that will tend to increase positive responses.

In summary, the interview is an excellent technique for gathering certain kinds of research information. However, because of its subjectivity and the face-to-face situation in which interviews are conducted, there are many potential sources of bias and distortion. Thus, in reviewing studies in which interviews have been used, you should carefully consider evidence related to the six questions we have discussed.

DIRECT OBSERVATION

In recent years educational researchers have increasingly turned to direct observation in the classroom as a method of collecting data. In most studies the observer is trained to record the occurrences of specific behavior. For example, in a study completed by the author (Borg & Ascione, 1979), observers were trained to record the frequency of four kinds of teacher praise in elementary classrooms. Use of praise was then related to pupil variables such as work involvement and disruptive behavior. Praise in this study would be classified as *low-inference* behavior. This means that since the observer counts the frequency of specific, clearly defined kinds of praise that he has been trained to recognize, he is not called open to interpret or draw inferences from what he observes. This approach usually produces very reliable and valid measures of the variables being observed.

On the other hand, if the observer is given a general definition of praise and is asked to rate the teacher on a scale from one to ten on his use of praise, then praise becomes a *high-inference* behavior, because the observer must translate his general impression into a single judgment. This process calls for a high level of inference or judgment on the part of the observer and introduces possible sources of error and bias that are not present when observing low-inference behavior. Data on teacher use of praise collected by a trained observer is likely to be much more valid than data collected by interviewing the teacher or having him fill out a questionnaire.

Early observational studies often used untrained observers, such as principals, and asked for general ratings rather than the recording of specific frequencies. Sometimes, the researcher would ask the principal to rate all teachers in his school on such general variables as dedication or warmth without giving him precise definitions of the variables. Such high-inference ratings are usually invalid for several reasons. First different principals will define or interpret these abstract variables differently. Second, such ratings permit bias, such as is the case when the principal's general opinion of the teacher influences his ratings of specific teacher performance. Third, since some principals visit classrooms much more often than others, some ratings are likely to be much more valid than others. When a reviewer encounters a study that uses untrained observers to rate the subjects on abstract high-inference variables, he can have little confidence in the validity of the results.

In evaluating the use of observational procedures in an educational study, the reviewer should consider the following questions:

1. Were high-inference or low-inference behaviors observed? Although some high-inference behavior such as teacher enthusiasm can be observed reliably, low-inference behaviors are preferable in most research. An important advantage of low-inference variables is that studies using such variables are usually easier to translate into practice. For example, a study that recommends that teacher's use verbal praise whenever a child gives a correct response during a discussion lesson is easier for the teacher to adopt than a study that indicates that teachers should be warmer or more enthusiastic.

2. Were observers trained to identify the variables to be observed? The researcher should describe the kind and duration of training given the observers. Most observer training programs approximate the following sequence:
1. The observer studies definitions and examples of the behaviors to be observed.
2. The observer studies the observation form to be used.
3. All observers watch the kind of activity they are being trained to observe (such as

time on task in a first-grade classroom) and independently record what they see on the observation form. Activities observed are usually recorded on video or audiotape by the researcher, so that they can be replayed.

4. The recording of the activity is replayed. The correct scoring and differences between observers are discussed.

5. Steps 3 and 4 are repeated until the observers independently obtain very similar scores on the observed behaviors.

3. What was the interobserver reliability? Reliability indicates the level of agreement between the observations of independent observers. This can be determined by computing a correlation coefficient between the scores of different observers or by determining the percentage of events observed in which the two observers agreed. If observers have been adequately trained, the percentage of agreement is usually above 85 percent or the correlation coefficient is above .75.

4. How long was the observation? Observations aim at obtaining a representative sample of the behavior of the individuals being observed. If the observation time is too short, such a sample is not obtained. In that case another short observation of the same subjects could produce markedly different scores. There are no set rules on how long observations should be, since this depends on many factors such as the nature of specific behaviors, the circumstances under which the behavior can occur, and its frequency of occurrence. For example, if you are observing a classroom behavior that occurs very frequently and can occur in a variety of situations, such as the number of times the teacher repeats her questions during recitation, a one-hour observation may be sufficient to obtain a reliable score. But, if you are measuring low-frequency behavior such as fighting among pupils, a much longer period of observation would be needed. As reviewer you must consider the entire observational situation and estimate whether the length of the observation used by the researcher was sufficient.

5. How conspicuous was the observer? Ideally, the observer should be stationed behind a one-way screen and his presence should not be known to the subjects being observed. In practice, this is rarely possible, and as a result the presence of the observer is likely to have some impact on the persons being observed. For example, an observer entering a classroom for the first time probably will arouse the curiosity of the students and possibly the teacher. The resulting inattentiveness of the students to the teacher may not reflect their usual behavior and thus may provide nonrepresentative observational data. To reduce this effect the observer should not record any observational data for at least the first five or ten minutes that he is in the classroom. It may be necessary in some cases for the observer to make several visits to the classroom before students take him for granted and behave as if he were not present.

As a rule, the observer should be as unobtrusive as possible. He should not comment or participate in any way in the ongoing activity, nor should he make nonverbal responses to the situation such as laughing or shaking his head.

The researcher should describe the observational situation, and the reviewer should estimate possible effects of the presence of the observer. Since research articles are often brief, sufficient information may not be given for the reviewer to answer this question, but in any case the reviewer should keep this problem in mind.

The four basic kinds of measures that we have discussed—paper-and-pencil tests, questionnaires, interviews, and direct observation—are found in a great many different forms. When you encounter a measurement procedure that you do not know how to evaluate, you should consult references on educational or psychological measurement such as those listed at the end of this chapter.

Characteristics of Educational Measures

All educational measures have important characteristics that must be considered when a measure is being evaluated. The most important characteristics are objectivity, reliability, and validity, and we will discuss these at some length, with special attention to their relevance to paper-and-pencil tests. Many of the characteristics of tests require statistical analysis and are called *test statistics*. See Table 6.1 for a brief summary of the most frequently used test statistics.

OBJECTIVITY

The objectivity of a measure depends on the degree to which it may be influenced or distorted by the beliefs or biases of the individuals who administer or score it. The degree of objectivity of paper-and-pencil tests can usually be determined by carefully studying the administration and scoring procedures to see where judgment is called for or bias may occur. Short response tests using multiple-choice, true-false, and similar items were developed to try to overcome the lack of objectivity of essay tests

Table 6.1   Table of test statistics

Statistic	Purpose
Validity coefficient	Used to describe the strength of relationship between test scores and scores on a criterion measure
Standard error of estimate	Used to describe the margin of error to be expected in an individual's predicted score on a criterion measure based on his test score
Reliability coefficient	Used to describe the item consistency or stability of a test
Item-validity coefficient	Used to describe the strength of relationship between item scores and scores on a criterion measure
Index of discrimination	Used to describe the validity of a test in terms of the persons in contrasting groups who pass each item
Item-reliability coefficient	Used to describe the strength of relationship between an item score and total test score
Index of item difficulty	Used to describe the percentage of persons who correctly answer a particular test item

Source: From W. R. Borg and M. G. Gall, *Educational Research: An Introduction* (4th ed.), © 1983, p. 371. Reprinted by permission of Longman Inc., White Plains, N.Y.

that in the past were virtually the only kind of test used in education. Research showed that when different teachers scored the same essay tests, they often awarded substantially different grades. Since these early studies new procedures have been developed that greatly increase the objectivity of essay tests. However, short response tests are generally more objective than essay tests, even if we employ the best procedures for scoring the latter.

Most standardized tests, such as the achievement tests that are used so widely in the public schools, are highly objective. The person giving the test reads instructions verbatim from the test manual. The manual also contains information on time allowed to complete the test, how to respond to pupil questions, and other topics related to test administration. Scoring of such measures is also highly objective. If followed carefully, the scoring procedure, which consists of checking answers against a scoring key, eliminates virtually any chance or bias. Many standardized short response measures can be scored by machine, which provides maximum objectivity.

When the administrator is given more latitude in administering a test or when scoring the test requires making decisions or judgments, objectivity is reduced. However, there are many tests in which a degree of objectivity is sacrificed in order to achieve other purposes of the measure. For example, in the Thematic Apperception Test (TAT) the subject is shown a series of pictures and is asked to tell a story related to each picture. Such tests, called *projective techniques,* are based on the theory that when presented with an amorphous stimulus and freedom of response, the subject's response will reveal his inner thoughts, fantasies, and structuring of reality. Obviously, since each individual's stories on the TAT will be different, much judgment is called for in scoring and interpreting the measure. This clearly permits biased scoring and reduces objectivity. Projective measures usually require extensive training and experience to administer, score, and intepret. Thus, in evaluating research in which such measures are employed, the reviewer must give special attention to the qualifications of the researcher and the steps taken in the research to reduce the chances of bias. Probably the most effective strategy to reduce bias is to have the tests administered and scored by persons who know nothing about the research being conducted. This is a desirable precaution in any study but is especially important when measures are used that are low in objectivity.

VALIDITY

A major task of the researcher is to locate tests that provide consistent scores and measure the variables that are to be explored in the research. The degree to which a test actually measures the variables it claims to measure is called *validity.* Different kinds of test validity are relevant to different types of measures and different testing situations. When a new measure is developed, the developer attempts to establish the validity of his measure. A researcher should always check the validity evidence available on measures he employs and describe this evidence in his research report. In turn, when you review a research report, you should take note of the validity evidence presented. Since measures with low validity are only measuring to a limited degree what they claim to measure and may well be measuring some other undefined variable, you can have little confidence in the results of studies that use such measures.

The five kinds of test validity that you should understand in order to interpret and use educational research findings are: content validity, predictive validity, concurrent validity, construct validity, and face validity.

Content Validity.   *Content validity* is the degree to which items on a test represent the content that the test is designed to measure. Content validity should not be confused with face validity, which is concerned with the degree to which the test *appears* to measure what it purports to measure and is usually based on a subjective appraisal of what the test measures. For example, if a test purports to measure reading achievement and if the items appear to deal with relevant content in this area, the test can be said to have face validity. In contrast to face validity, which is a subjective judgment that the test appears to cover relevant content, content validity is determined by systematically comparing the test content with the course content. This means that a given achievement test may have high content validity for the tenth-grade social studies course in High School A and low content validity for the course as taught in High School B, if the two schools have curriculum guides and use textbooks that cover markedly different content.

Content validity is important primarily in achievement testing and various tests of skill and proficiency, such as occupational skill tests. For example, a test of achievement in ninth-grade mathematics will have high content validity if the items covered on the test are representative, in type and proportion, of the content presented in the course. If test items cover topics not taught in the course, ignore certain important concepts, and unduly emphasize others as compared with their treatment in the course, the content validity will be lower. Unlike some types of validity, the degree of content validity is not expressed in numerical terms as a correlation coefficient (sometimes called a validity coefficient). Instead, content validity is usually estimated by an objective comparison of the test items with curriculum content and/or textbook content. Often the test manual will describe the techniques used to arrive at the test content. The usual procedure is for the test developer to select several of the most widely used textbooks in the given subject and then carefully analyze each book to determine the concepts covered and the proportion of the total book devoted to each. He then develops his test so that the concepts covered and proportion of items on each concept is as similar as possible to the coverage in the textbooks. A table may be given in the test manual to demonstrate the content validity, that is, the degree of similarity. The researcher should select a test that is very similar to the textbook or course of study he plans to use in his research and should report evidence related to content validity.

Content validity is particularly important in selecting tests to use in experiments involving the effect of different instructional methods or programs on achievement. For example, if a school district wants to determine which of two seventh-grade general science programs results in the greater student achievement, it is essential that the achievement test selected be equally appropriate for both programs. If the test fits the content of Program A better than the content of Program B, then Program A students may score higher even though Program B is superior. In cases where two programs to be evaluated do not cover exactly the same content, the researcher can select a test that fits both programs reasonably well and then score only test items that deal with concepts covered in both programs.

Predictive Validity.   *Predictive validity* is the degree to which the predictions made by a test are confirmed by the later behavior of the subjects. Much educational research is concerned with the prediction of success in various activities. The usual method of determining predictive validity is to administer the test, wait until the behavior that the test attempts to predict has occurred, and then measure the relationship between the occurrence of the behavior and the scores of the subjects on the test. Let us take an algebra aptitude test as an example. Suppose that such a test were designed to be administered near the end of the eighth grade to predict the students' future success in ninth-grade algebra. At the end of the ninth grade, the test scores would be correlated with a measure of algebra achievement, such as grades in the algebra class or an algebra achievement test. In this case the algebra grades or the achievement test scores would be called *criterion measures*. The correlation between the algebra aptitude test and the algebra achievement test provides us a measure of the predictive validity (sometimes called *criterion-related validity*) of the aptitude test, that is, the degree to which its prediction of the students' success in algebra was borne out by their later performance.

Many research projects are aimed at predicting some future performance, and such projects provide evidence on the predictive validity of the measures that are used. The results of such projects are often useful to the school administrator who wants to predict some future student behavior. For example, in military schools predictive validity studies are conducted to develop measures that can be used to predict an individual's probability of success in programs such as pilot training. Once the validity study is finished, the administrator can use the results to set up minimum test scores for future acceptance into the program. Such minimums keep students out of the program who have very little chance of success, thus sparing them the frustration that attends failure and also reducing the cost of conducting the program.

Concurrent Validity   A second type of criterion-related validity is called *concurrent validity*. The concurrent validity of a test is determined by relating the test scores of a group of subjects to a criterion measure administered at the same time or within a short interval of time. To distinguish between concurrent and predictive validity, we determine whether the criterion measure was administered at the same time as the standardized test (concurrent) or later, usually after a period of several months or more (predictive). Concurrent validity studies are often carried out in an effort to locate simple, easy to use measures that can be used in place of complex and expensive criterion measures. For example, if a paper-and-pencil test can be used instead of an interview with a clinical psychologist to provide a preliminary diagnosis of a client's adjustment problem, the use of the test can save considerable cost. To determine the concurrent validity of such a test, a sample of persons seeking clinical help would be given both the test and the clinical interview within a short period of time. The relationship between the test diagnosis and the clinician's diagnosis would then be compared, probably using a correlation coefficient, to determine the concurrent validity of the test. In this case, the clinician's diagnosis would be the criterion measure, that is, the standard against which the test was evaluated.

In evaluating a test's concurrent or predictive validity, it is important to assess the adequacy of the criterion. Occasionally a test will be validated against another test rather than against a meaningful real-life criterion. It is of little value to know that one test of anxiety, for example, correlated highly with a criterion test of anxiety, unless the criterion test itself has been demonstrated to have significant construct or predictive validity. If the criterion is valid, so presumably is the other test that correlates highly with it.

Construct Validity.   *Construct validity* is the extent to which a particular test can be shown to measure a hypothetical construct. Psychological concepts—such as intelligence, anxiety, creativity—are considered hypothetical constructs because they are not directly observable but rather are inferred on the basis of their observable effects on behavior. In order to gather evidence on construct validity, the test developer often starts by setting up hypotheses about the characteristics of persons who would obtain high scores on the measure as opposed to those who would obtain low scores. Suppose, for example, that a test developer publishes a test that he claims is a measure of anxiety. How can one determine whether the test does in fact measure the construct of anxiety? One approach might be to determine whether the test differentiates between psychiatric and normal groups, since theorists have hypothesized that anxiety plays a substantial role in psychopathology. If the test does in fact differentiate the two groups, then we have some evidence that it measures the construct of anxiety.

When one is mainly interested in applying research evidence to practical educational problems, construct validity is often less important than predictive, concurrent, or content validity.

Face Validity.   As mentioned earlier, *face validity* is concerned with the degree to which a test *appears* to measure what it purports to measure, while the other forms of test validity *provide evidence* that the test measures what it purports to measure. Thus, although face validity is basically different from the other forms of test validity, it is still an important feature of any test intended for practical use because most people react more favorably to tests having high face validity. Nevo (1985) suggests that tests having high face validity are more likely to:
- Bring about higher levels of cooperation and motivation while subjects are taking the test.
- Reduce feeling of dissatisfaction or injustice among low scorers.
- Help convince potential users (e.g., teachers and school administrators) to implement the test.

- Improve public relations, since laymen can more easily see the relationship between the test and the performance or characteristic it purportedly measures.

For example, face validity is low for many personality measures. Such measures often contain items that validly differentiate between normal and maladjusted groups but do not *appear* to be related in any way to the maladjustment in question. Persons tested with such measures often reject the results or refuse to cooperate because they cannot perceive any relationship between the test and the maladjustment. Thus, face validity can be an important consideration in selecting tests for use in situations where subject acceptance is essential. However, a test can *appear* to be valid when evidence for the other kinds of test validity indicates it is not. Therefore, you should never forget that face validity can only supplement information about predictive, concurrent, construct, or content validity of a test and can *never take the place of such information.*

In many cases, a single individual (such as the school principal) makes subjective judgments about the face validity of a test being considered for use in the public schools. Face validity can be better estimated by obtaining objective ratings of face validity from a sample of individuals who are drawn from the population that normally would take the test. The composite of these ratings will provide a much more reliable estimate of face validity than a single subjective judgment. For example, suppose we want to estimate the face validity of a test of social adjustment for high school students. A sample of students could be asked: "How relevant are the items on this test to your level of social adjustment? Rate each item on the following five-point scale."

5—extremely relevant
4—very relevant
3—somewhat relevant
2—not very relevant
1—irrelevant

A mean score could then be computed to estimate the face validity of each item. These item means could in turn be combined to give an estimate of the face validity of the entire test.

TEST RELIABILITY

Reliability, as applied to educational measurement, may be defined as the degree to which test scores are free from measurement errors. Reliability is usually concerned with the level of internal consistency of the measure, or its stability over time. There are several methods of estimating reliability, most of which call for computing a correlation coefficient between two sets of similar measurements. Suppose we wish to measure students' knowledge of physics. A physics achievement test consisting of one multiple-choice item would be highly unreliable. Some students may know quite a bit about physics but may not happen to know the answer to this particular test item; in contrast, some students whose overall achievement level in physics is low may happen to know or may guess the correct answer. Also, if we selected a different item, the results would probably be much different. Thus, a one-item test is suscep-tible to many chance factors and therefore is not a "reliable" estimate of the student's level of achievement in physics.

However, as the number of items on the test increases, we are sampling more and more of the concepts of physics and the test becomes increasingly reliable. These kinds of chance factors have less likelihood of occurring as the test length increases. Therefore, test length is an important element in determining test reliability.

Reliability is an extremely important characteristic of educational measures. It is much easier to establish the reliability of a test than to establish its validity. There-fore, if no specific information on reliability is provided in a research report, the reviewer may safely assume that the reliability of the test is low.

A point to watch for in evaluating test reliability is that many tests yield a number of subscores in addition to a total score. This is the case for some intelligence and achievement tests that provide subscores in order to give a profile of the student's performance in the various areas making up the test. However, reliability is often reported only for the total score. In this case, the subscores must be used cautiously unless reliability data are available for them. When such data are not available, the reviewer will have difficulty making an intelligent appraisal of the worth of the sub-scores. He may be sure that all or most of these subscores will have lower reliability coefficients than the total test reliability. The reliability coefficients of the subscores, however, may differ considerably, with some being as reliable as the total test and others being of such low reliability that they can contribute very little to the research findings.

The reliability of educational measures is usually expressed as a coefficient that indicates the degree of relationship between two sets of scores obtained from the same subjects under different conditions. Reliability coefficients range from 0, which indicates no reliability, to 1.00, which indicates perfect reliability. The closer the reliability coefficient is to 1.00, the more the test is a measure of true differences

Table 6.2   Range and median values of reliabilities reported for various types of measures

Type of test	Number of reliabilities	Value of reported reliabilities		
		Low	Median	High
Achievement batteries	32	.66	.92	.98
Scholastic ability	63	.56	.90	.97
Aptitude batteries	22	.26	.88	.96
Objective personality	35	.46	.85	.97
Interest inventories	13	.42	.84	.93
Attitude scales	18	.47	.79	.98

Source: From G. C. Helmstadter, *Principles of Psychological Measurement,* © 1964, p. 85. Reprinted by permission of Prentice-Hall, Englewood Cliffs, New Jersey.

between different persons in the characteristic or variable that it measures. The person's score on a test is a combination of his true score and an error. As reliability increases, the size of this error decreases, resulting in a more accurate score. Also when a test is highly reliable, we can be confident that if the subjects were re-measured, most would obtain closely comparable scores. A helpful list of representative reliabilities of standardized tests is provided in Table 6.2. Note that the typical reliability level varies with the type of characteristic being measured. The reliability coefficient also reflects the degree to which a given test score is likely to be in error. In fact, the standard error of measurement, which is a statistical technique used to estimate the probable error in a test score, is closely related to reliability.

Reliability coefficients can be obtained by several different methods. Different methods produce coefficients that are roughly comparable. A description of the four most commonly used kinds of reliability follows.

Subdivided Test or Split-Half Reliability.   This type of reliability, which is also called the *coefficient of internal consistency,* is based upon estimates of the internal consistency of the test. The most widely used method of estimating internal consistency is through the split-half correlation. To determine the subdivided test reliability, the test for which reliability is to be calculated is administered to an appropriate sample. It is then split into two subtests, usually by placing all odd-numbered items in one subtest and all even-numbered items in another subtest. The scores of the two subtests are then computed for each individual, and these two sets of scores are correlated. The correlation obtained, however, represents the reliability coefficient of only half the test, and since reliability is related to the length of the test, a statistical correction must be applied in order to obtain the reliability of the entire test.

Method of Rational Equivalence.   The *method of rational equivalence,* which also provides an estimate of internal consistency, is the only widely used technique of calculating reliability that does not require the calculation of a correlation coefficient. This method gets at the internal consistency of the test through an analysis of the individual test items. It requires only a single administration of the test. A number of formulas have been developed to calculate reliability using this method. These are generally referred to as the Kuder-Richardson formulas, after the authors of an article in which these formulas were first discussed (1939). The formulas in this article are numbered, and the two most widely used are numbers 20 and 21. Formula 20 is considered by many specialists in educational and psychological measurement to be the most satisfactory method of determining test reliability. This formula is being used to an increasing degree to determine the reliability of standardized tests. Formula 21, a simplified approximation of Formula 20, is of value primarily because it provides a very easy method of determining a reliability coefficient. The use of Formula 21 requires much less time than other methods for estimating test reliability. It is highly appropriate for use in teacher-made tests and short experimental tests being developed by a research worker. One desirable aspect of the Kuder-

Richardson formulas is that they generally yield a lower reliability coefficient than would be obtained by using the other methods described. Thus, they can be thought of as providing a minimum estimate of the reliability of a test.

Alternate-Form Reliability.   This method of calculating reliability may be used whenever two or more parallel forms of a test are available. This method is also called the *coefficient of equivalence* and is computed by administering two parallel forms of the test to the same group of individuals and then correlating the scores obtained on the two forms in order to yield a reliability coefficient. The two forms of the test may be administered at a single sitting, or an interval may be scheduled between the two administrations. Some interval between the administration of the forms is usually desirable, especially if the alternate forms are nearly identical, as is the case with some achievement measures. This interval tends to reduce practice effects that may be an important factor if the two forms of the test are administered at the same sitting. Since many standardized tests are quite long, it is also undesirable to administer two forms at a single sitting, since the subjects may do more poorly on the second form because of fatigue. Administering the two forms at different times results in some differences in both the setting and in the state of mind of the individuals who are tested. Therefore, the reliability obtained is usually lower, but reflects better the testing situation that exists in most research projects. At the present time, alternate-form reliability is the most commonly used estimate of reliability for standardized tests. It is very widely used with standardized achievement and intelligence tests.

Test-Retest Reliability.   This form of reliability is useful when alternate forms of the test are not available or not possible to construct. To calculate the *test-retest reliability,* also called the *coefficient of stability,* the measure is administered to a sample of individuals, and then after a delay the same measure is again administered to the same sample. Scores obtained from the two administrations are then correlated in order to determine the test-retest reliability. The most critical problem in calculating this form of reliability is to determine the correct delay between the two administrations of the measure. If the retest is administered too quickly after the initial test, students will recall their responses to many of the items, which will tend to produce a spuriously high reliability coefficient. On the other hand, if the retesting is delayed too long, there is a good possibility that the student's ability to answer some items will change. For example, the student may pass through a period of development or learning and thus be better prepared to answer questions on the retest. These changes in students' ability to answer the test questions will lead to underestimating the reliability.

A COMPARISON OF THE METHODS OF ESTIMATING RELIABILITY

Although the different methods of estimating reliability usually produce similar results, there are some differences because different methods take into account different sources of error. Reliability coefficients based on one administration of the test, or on administration of different forms of the test at a single sitting, exclude two sources of error that are present in many research situations where a single administration of the measure is not possible. Thus administration in a single sitting results in higher reliability coefficients than will be found in practice. First, individuals differ from day to day on many subtle variables such as mood, level of fatigue, and attitude toward the test. Second, in spite of the researcher's efforts to maintain standard conditions, when tests are given on different occasions, many small variations are likely to occur in the testing situation. For example, the administrator may read the instructions more rapidly, a light may burn out in the test room, or the school band may march past the classroom window.

Computation of test-retest reliability, in which subjects are administered the same test on two different occasions, fails to reflect a different source of error because the subjects are exposed to the same items on both occasions. The items on a particular test constitute only a small sample of all items that could be written in the area that the test covers. The specific items on a single test are likely to discriminate in favor of some students and against others. This error will be reflected if the split-half or alternate-form reliability is computed, since the two sets of scores that are correlated are based on different samples of items. However, when the test-retest method is used, this source of error is not taken into account, and thus spuriously higher reliability coefficients may be obtained.

Only when different forms of the test are administered with a time interval are all three of these sources of error taken into account. Thus, the alternate-form method with a time interval provides a more conservative estimate of reliability and one that reflects conditions in most educational research projects. Since reliability data are fairly easy to collect, many standardized tests report reliability coefficients obtained from several different methods. In this case, the reviewer should decide which type of reliability is most important for the study being reviewed and should base his evaluation on this type.

Sources of Information about Measures

In some cases a reviewer who is interested in using research findings to help solve a practical educational problem will find a study that is very relevant but which does not provide sufficient information about the measures that were used. When a relevant study is located, the teacher or administrator may also want to check the results by administering the measures in the local schools before introducing the recommended change on a large scale.

For these and other related problems it is very helpful to know about available sources of information on educational measures and how to use these sources. In reviewing articles that are not highly relevant to the reviewer's problem, the reviewer usually relies upon the information given in the research report itself, since a thorough evaluation of an educational measure requires considerable time and effort. This effort, however, is justified if the reviewer plans to use the research in which the measure in question was employed as a basis for making an important decision.

The purpose of this section is to provide you with a brief description of the main sources of information about educational measures that are available.

THE MENTAL MEASUREMENTS YEARBOOKS (MMYB)

A very important source of information on standardized tests is the *Mental Measurements Yearbooks*. The most recent of the series is the *Ninth Mental Measurements Yearbook* published in 1985. This is a completely new work that supplements the earlier editions. The "Tests and Reviews" section of the current edition lists 1409 tests. There are 1266 critical test reviews and approximately 20,000 references on the construction, use, and limitations of the specific tests included in this edition. For example, a teacher who plans to develop his own instrument can find many useful sources.

The reviewer can use the *Mental Measurements Yearbooks* to obtain specific information about tests used in research projects he is evaluating. They can also be used to locate and compare tests that are available in a particular field and can help the teacher or school administrator decide which test is most appropriate for his or her school.

In using the yearbooks to evaluate a specific test, the reviewer looks up the test in the Index of Titles. The entry number of the test is given after the title. The reviewer turns to this number in the Tests and Reviews section where he will find a brief description of the test including the age range for which test is appropriate, year the test was published, the variables measured by the test, the cost of the test, the manual and other materials, the name of the author, the publisher, and other useful information. For most of the tests covered, references are given that the reviewer can check to learn more about the test. Critical reviews written by experts in the field are also provided for many of the tests. These reviews are especially valuable to the person who has limited training in educational measurement.

If as a teacher or administrator you want to select a test in a given area from several that are available, first refer to the Classified Index of Tests. Here the tests are classified under a number of broad categories such as Achievement Batteries, Character and Personality, Foreign Language, and Intelligence. Under each category is a list of the pertinent tests available in the area of interest. Upon locating tests that interest you in the classified index, note the entry numbers of these tests, check each number in the Tests and Reviews section of the book, and read the reviews to help decide which test best meets your needs. A Score Index is also provided, which lists all the scores in alphabetical order for all tests included in the *Ninth MMYB*. However, a check of some items in the Classified Index and Score Index indicates discrepancies. Thus, *both* indexes should be searched. The greatest strength of the *Ninth Mental Measurements Yearbook* is the evaluative information given in the test reviews. Its greatest limitations are that it includes only commercially published tests, thus overlooking many useful measures that are not commercially published; the Classified Index categories are too broad; and the indexes are not adequately cross referenced.

ETS TEST COLLECTION BIBLIOGRAPHIES

If you fail to locate the measures you need in the *Ninth Mental Measurements Yearbook,* the next step is to search the *Test Collection Bibliographies* published by the Educational Testing Service (ETS). There are over 200 of these bibliographies currently in print. They constitute by far the most comprehensive compilation of tests available, including over 11,000 measures. These bibliographies cover both published and unpublished tests and are frequently updated, thus overcoming a limitation of other published sources such as *Mental Measurements Yearbooks,* which are updated at infrequent intervals. However, the bibliographies provide much less information on the tests listed than do the yearbooks. The information usually given includes the name of the test, author, date published, age or grade levels for which test is appropriate, name and address of publisher, and a brief description of the variables the test is designed to measure. For experimental measures having no commercial publisher, the author frequently is listed as publisher. Many such measures, which are not available from commercial publishers, can be obtained from ETS on microfiche for individual measures or in sets of 50 measures. Many universities have purchased these sets, so you should check with the reference librarians of institutions in your area before purchasing microfiches.

In order to use these bibliographies to locate the measures you need, you should use the following procedure:

1. Check the list of *Test Collection Bibliographies* available from ETS and decide which ones are most likely to list tests that cover the variables you want to measure.

2. See if the *Test Collection Bibliographies* you need are available in any of the reference libraries in your vicinity. University departments of psychology and testing-counseling centers may also have these on file. If not locally available, order the bibliographies you need from ETS Test Collection, Educational Testing Service, Princeton, NJ 08541.

3. Read the selected bibliographies and identify measures that fit your needs.

4. Obtain single copies of the measures you have identified from ETS or the test publishers.

You will now be ready to evaluate the measures you have obtained and make your final selection.

TESTS—A COMPREHENSIVE REFERENCE FOR ASSESSMENTS IN PSYCHOLOGY, EDUCATION, AND BUSINESS

This reference (Sweetland & Keyser, 1983), provides information on more than 3,000 tests. The information on each test includes a statement of the purpose of the test, a description of the test, administration time, grade range, scoring information, cost, and publisher. Tests are listed under three major headings, Psychology, Education, and Business and Industry. Each of the sections is in turn divided into several specific subsections. For example, subsections under Education include such areas as Academic Subjects, Achievement and Aptitude, Intelligence, Reading, and Special Education.

An additional volume by the same editors entitled *Tests—Supplement* was published in 1984 and contains information on an additional 500 tests, most published since 1980.

To use these references to locate tests in a given area, check the table of contents and locate the relevant subsection. Then turn to this subsection and scan the information given. For example, if you were looking for measures designed to identify first-grade children with learning disabilities you would check "Learning disabilities" in the table of contents of the two volumes. Tests in this area are described on pages 546 to 555 in the original volume and pages 147 to 151 of the Supplement. You could then identify specific measures that would meet your needs by scanning the information provided on these pages.

These volumes are an excellent source for *locating* tests relevant to your needs. They are not useful in *evaluating* tests, since no information on reliability, validity, or norms is included.

TEST CRITIQUES

This three-volume work by Keyser and Sweetland (1985), the editors who developed *Tests* and *Tests—Supplement,* contains critiques of tests selected by specialists in the given areas, and therefore the more widely used measures are usually reviewed. Each review includes five sections: an Introduction, which contains a detailed description of the measures as well as useful background material; a Practical Application/Uses section, which provides information on administration, scoring, and interpretation; a section on Technical Aspects, which is concerned primarily with reliability and validity; an overall Critique, which is very useful in helping the potential user evaluate the test; and a brief list of References dealing with the measure and related topics. On average, seven to eight pages are devoted to each measure, and a great deal of information is provided. The three volumes currently available cover over 300 measures, and subsequent volumes are planned at six- to nine-month intervals. In using these volumes, the best approach is to check the most recent volume, since it contains cumulative indexes that cover all volumes. If you are looking for evaluation data on a test located elsewhere, use the Index of Test Titles. If you are trying to locate tests in a particular subject area, use the Subject Index.

These volumes, along with the *Ninth Mental Measurements Yearbook* are the best sources of evaluation information on available tests. The main advantage of *Test Critiques* is the thoroughness of the information provided for each measure. Its main limitation is the small number of measures covered thus far. As new volumes become available, this limitation will be largely overcome.

There are several other references that can assist you in locating and evaluating tests. Most of these are over 10 years old. However, many of the tests they cover are still in use. Descriptions of a few of these references follow.

EVALUATING CLASSROOM INSTRUCTION— A SOURCEBOOK OF INSTRUMENTS

This reference gives a comprehensive coverage of instruments used in teacher behavior research from 1954 through 1975. In the selection of measures, the following criteria were employed:

1. Relate to a major area in teacher research.
2. Apply to the classroom setting.
3. Available to researchers from commercial publishers or public sources.
4. Measure operationally defined constructs related to specific teacher or pupil variables.
5. Used in classroom research.

   Measures are classified into nine categories according to who supplies information about whom. Categories include, for example, measures "about the teacher from the pupil" and measures "about the pupil from an observer." This classification system is very helpful to the teacher or administrator who is looking for a particular type of measure. For each measure, all the information normally used by a reviewer to make an evaluation is given, such as a description of the measure, data on validity and reliability, data on administration and scoring, and so on. Author and title indexes are provided, which can be used to locate a specific measure that you wish to evaluate.

TESTS AND MEASUREMENTS IN CHILD DEVELOPMENT— HANDBOOKS I AND II

These handbooks cover over 1200 unpublished measures, that is, measures not listed in the *Mental Measurements Yearbooks*. The authors searched 148 journals for the period 1956 through 1965 for Handbook I and 1966 through 1974 for Handbook II to locate measures that can be administered to subjects from birth to age 18. Measures are classified into 11 major categories, such as Cognitive, Personality and Emotional, Attitudes and Interests, and Self-Concept. The information that the teacher or administrator normally needs to identify measures that may meet their needs is provided, including age range, variables measures, information on where the measure can be obtained, a description of the measure, data on reliability and validity, and a list of references that deal specifically with development or use of the measure. Author and title indexes can be used when the reviewer is seeking information on a specific measure he has already identified. This is a useful source of information on unpublished measures, although it should be supplemented by checking some of the more recent references such as *Test Critiques*.

THE TEST DEVELOPER

The best source of recent information on a test is often the test developer. Since there is a considerable lag between the completion of research and its publication, the developer will often have information on the test that has not yet been printed.

Also, the developer is likely to know of other researchers who have recently used the measure. This approach is especially useful in getting the latest data on recently developed tests. There may be very little published data on validity and other important characteristics of such measures but much unpublished data. Thus, it is advisable to write the test developer requesting any information that has not appeared in print. If you explain the purposes for which you want to use the test, the test developer will probably be cooperative. Current addresses for persons who have developed tests can often be found in the latest volumes of *The Consolidated Roster for Psychology* or the *Membership Directory* of the American Educational Research Association.

THE TEST MANUAL

Once you have identified tests you want to evaluate, it is often desirable to purchase specimen sets for these tests. The specimen set will typically include sample test copies, keys, and a test manual.

For published standardized tests, when the test is developed, a test manual is also prepared. These manuals are available from the test publishers. Manuals are usually not available for measures that have been developed for research purposes. The test manual provides much of the information that is needed to evaluate a standardized test. Among the questions that the manual usually helps to answer are: What validity data are available? What types of validity have been studied? What reliability data are available? For what types of subjects is the test appropriate? What conditions of administration are necessary to use the test? Is special training needed to administer the test or interpret the results? Is a shorter form of the test available that will yield substantially the same results? A limitation of the test manual is that since it is written by the test developers, it is likely to be biased. Thus, the test manual should not be your sole source of information about the test.

THE TEST ITSELF

One of the most important sources of information is a copy of the test in which you are interested, particularly if you are concerned about content validity or the appropriateness of the test for your students. For example, the test manual may claim that a particular test is appropriate for students in the fifth grade. Your examination of a copy of the test may reveal that the reading level is beyond that of the fifth graders whom you are planning to test. Or suppose that your school district wants to conduct an evaluation of two methods for teaching reading. In selecting a test of reading achievement to evaluate the effectiveness of the two methods, you may find that the test manual and other sources such as the *Ninth Mental Measurements Yearbook* do not provide enough information about the reading content covered by the test. To determine whether the reading content covered by the test is representative of that included in your training materials, your best source of information will be a copy of the test itself.

The sources we have described earlier in this chapter make it easy to locate the publisher of virtually any test you want to evaluate. The *Ninth Mental Measurements*

Yearbook gives the addresses of publishers of standardized tests. *Tests and Measurements in Child Development* tells where you can obtain the 1200 unpublished measures these handbooks review. For all tests included in the *ETS Test Collection Bibliographies* information is provided on where the test may be obtained. In fact, all of the sources reviewed in this chapter can help you determine where you can obtain copies of tests you want to examine.

Many additional sources of information on tests are listed in the Books and Reviews section of the *Ninth Mental Measurements Yearbook*. The reviewer can also check *Books in Print* for sources of test information that have been published since this book.

Remember that when you review a research report that provides important evidence related to a major decision you must make, you should learn as much as you can about the measures upon which the research evidence was based. It is generally agreed that the more knowledge you bring to the decision-making process, the more likely you are to make a sound decision.

Computer Searches for Test Information[1]

We have several excellent sources such as the *ETS Test Collection Bibliographies* that can help us locate tests we need. However, up-to-date information on validity and reliability and other evidence such as critical reviews that can help us evaluate the tests we have identified is more difficult to obtain. Many of the best sources such as *Tests and Measurements in Child Development* are somewhat out-of-date, while others such as *Test Critiques,* although recent, cover relatively few measures.

In many cases, the best way to locate up-to-date information such as validity and reliability data is to conduct a computer search. Several different computer search options are available.

PROXIMITY SEARCH

Perhaps the best choice is to conduct a proximity search, using the name of the test with (W) limiters. For example, a proximity search of ERIC for the term "Graduate (W) Record (W) Examination" located 106 references.[2] Since this examination is usually referred to as the "GRE," we also searched that term and located 136 references. There were 178 references that used either or both terms some place in the citation. To eliminate references that would not help in evaluating the GRE, we next searched:

> (Graduate (W) Record (W) Examination or GRE) and (Test Reviews or Test Reliability or Test Validity).

1. You may want to review Chapter 3 before reading this section.
2. We selected this test for our example because it is widely used for admission to graduate programs and many graduate students have taken it.

This search produced 34 references. A check of the abstracts of these references indicated that most would be useful to a student who wanted to evaluate the GRE.

There are, of course, other descriptors in the *Thesaurus of ERIC Descriptors* that can be searched along with the test name if you are interested in only certain kinds of information. For example, the descriptor "Foreign students" could be added to the above search if you were interested only in the validity and reliability of the GRE when administered to foreign students.

SEARCH OF IDENTIFIERS

Another computer search option is to use the name of the test as an identifier. In the ERIC system "Identifiers" are key words or concepts that are not descriptors but supplement the descriptors in order to add depth to the search. Identifiers are used to enter into the citation such information as geographical locations, personal names, and test names. Thus, if you are interested in a specific test, you can ask the computer to locate references that have the test name as an identifier. Again using the GRE as an example, we entered:

Graduate (W) Record (W) Examinations/ID.

This search produced 143 references. Note that we used the plural, "Examinations," in this search. There is a tendency for reviewers to enter identifiers as plural, probably because most descriptors in the ERIC *Thesaurus* are plural. Only three references were found that had the singular, that is, "Graduate (W) Record (W) Examination," as an identifier.

When we searched "(Graduate (W) Record (W) Examinations) and (Test validity or Test reliability or Test reviews)," we found 44 references. Many of these duplicated the 34 references we located using a proximity search. Most would be useful to an investigator who was interested in evaluating the GRE.

SEARCHING PsycINFO

If you are interested in getting up-to-date information on a well-known standardized test such as the Graduate Record Examination, the Stanford Achievement Test, or the California Test of Personality, PsycINFO can be useful. The names of many widely used tests are included as index terms in the *Thesaurus of Psychological Index Terms*. Thus you could conduct the following search to locate data to help evaluate the GRE:

Graduate Record Examination and (Test Reliability or Test Validity)[3]

A proximity search of PsycINFO can also be conducted, using essentially the same procedures described for the ERIC data base. If you plan to include Index Terms such as Test validity in your PsycINFO search, be sure to check the *Thesaurus,* since PsycINFO index terms sometimes differ from ERIC descriptors.

3. "Test Reviews," which we used in the ERIC searches, is not an index term in PsycINFO.

MENTAL MEASUREMENTS YEARBOOK DATABASE

This data base contains all the information covered in the *Ninth Mental Measurements Yearbook* (*MMYB*) plus updates on some of the measures that will be included in the *Tenth Mental Measurements Yearbook* when it is published, plus reviews and other information on some new tests published after the *Ninth MMYB*. If a test you wish to evaluate is covered in this data base, the updated reviews and other information may be useful. However, since the *Ninth MMYB* was published late in 1985, it will be sufficiently up-to-date for most purposes.

References

BORG, W. R., & ASCIONE, F. R. (1979). Changing on-task, off-task, and disruptive pupil behavior in elementary mainstreaming classrooms. *Journal of Educational Research, 72*(5), 243–252.

KEYSER, D. J., & SWEETLAND, R. C. (1985). *Test critiques,* 3 vols. Kansas City, Mo.: Test Corporation of America.

NEVO, B. (1985). Face validity revisited. *Journal of Educational Measurement, 22*(4), 287–293.

RICHARDSON, M. W., & KUDER, G. F. (1939). The calculation of test reliability coefficients based upon the method of rational equivalence. *Journal of Educational Psychology, 30,* 681–687.

SWEETLAND, R. C., & KEYSER, D. J. (1983). *Tests: A comprehensive reference for assessments in psychology, education, and business.* Kansas City, Mo.: Test Corporation of America.

Recommended Reading

The following books provide a good coverage of educational and psychological measurement and are recommended for students who want to build a stronger background in this area.

NOVICK, M. R., ET AL. (1985). *Standards for educational and psychological testing.* Washington, D.C.: American Psychological Association.

    This long-awaited volume was prepared by a committee of measurement experts representing the three most important national organizations that are directly concerned with testing standards. Several sections of this book are especially useful for educators who must select and use tests and interpret test results. These include the sections on validity, reliability, educational, and psychological testing in the schools and testing people who have handicapping conditions.

MEASUREMENT INFORMATION

These are introductory texts that will provide a good foundation in educational measurement.

SAX, G. (1980). *Principles of educational psychological measurement and evaluation* (2nd ed.). Belmont, Calif.: Wadsworth Publishing Co.

THORNDIKE, R. L., & HAGEN, E. P. (1977). *Measurement and evaluation in psychology and education* (4th ed.). New York: Wiley.

TESTS

The following are additional references that will help you locate tests in your area of interest and evaluative data on tests. However, the sources discussed in the body of Chapter 6 are usually more useful than those listed below.

ANTTONEN, J. (1980). *An annotated bibliography of practical tests for young children* (3rd rev. ed.). Harrisburg, Pa.: State Department of Education (see ERIC Microfiche ED 198 162).

This bibliography covers 109 tests for children aged two to six. Tests related to most of the areas covered in early childhood programs are included. The measures listed do not require subjective judgment in scoring or specialized training for administration.

LAKE, D. G., MILES, M. G., & EARLE, R. B., JR. (1973). *Measuring human behavior*. New York: Teachers College Press.

This reference contains two parts. The first contains information and critiques on 84 measures, most of which are still in general use. The coverage of each measure is quite thorough, including a description of the test as well as information on the variables measured, administration and scoring, development, a critique, and a list of relevant references. The second part lists and describes 20 other compendia of test information, which the reader can use to locate additional measures and critical reviews.

LEVY, P., & GOLDSTEIN, H. (1984). *Tests in education: A book of critical reviews*. New York: Academic Press.

The measures reviewed in this reference are for the most part British in origin, although a few measures developed in the United States are reviewed. Perhaps the book is most useful to American users in cases in which a suitable measure cannot be located in the American sources such as the *Ninth Mental Measurements Yearbook*. The test reviews are organized into seven broad content areas. Each review provides a great deal of useful information. All in all, this is an excellent source of information on British measures.

REDICK, R. L. (1975, October). A compilation of measurement devices compendia. *Measurement and Evaluation in Guidance, 8*(3), 193–202.

This article describes 30 sources of information on measurement devices in the behavioral sciences. Bibliographic data and a brief description are given for each compendium. Most of the sources described are old, being published between 1967 and 1975. However, since many tests currently in use were developed more than 100 years ago, reviews and evaluations from these sources can still be useful.

The following references on observation, interviews, and questionnaires will provide some additional information for students with a special interest in these areas. Other relevant references are found in Chapter 8. Also a check of *Books in Print* will usually uncover the most recent sources.

OBSERVATION

BORICH, G. D., & MADDEN, S. K. (1977). *Evaluating classroom instruction: A sourcebook of instruments*. Reading, Mass.: Addison-Wesley.

This book reviews a large number of instruments that can be used to evaluate teacher and pupil behavior. Many are observation forms. Most of the information that a researcher needs to select an instrument is provided.

BRANDT, R. M. (1972). *Studying behavior in natural settings*. New York: Holt, Rinehart and Winston.

Provides a detailed treatment of naturalistic research with emphasis upon observational procedures. Several naturalistic studies are described; about half are in the field of education and the rest are from other disciplines such as sociology, social psychology, and anthropology.

HERBERT, J., & ALTRIDGE, C. (1975). A guide for developers and users of observation systems and manuals. *American Educational Research Journal, 12*(1), 1–20.

The authors have developed 33 criteria that can be used to evaluate observation instruments. These criteria are useful to the researcher who wishes to select an instrument from those available as well as providing guidelines for the researcher who plans to develop his own instrument. Each criterion is discussed, and many examples are given.

INTERVIEWS

FOWLER, F. J., JR. (1984). *Survey research methods.* Beverly Hills, Calif.: Sage.

Gives a brief coverage of survey research methodology, including chapters on sampling, data collection, and analysis. Contains useful chapters on both questionnaires and interview procedures.

GORDEN, R. L. (1975). *Interviewing strategy, techniques and factors* (rev. ed.). Homewood, Ill.: Dorsey Press.

A detailed treatment of interviewing is presented, including such topics as locating, and contacting respondents, selecting interviewers, taking notes, planning the interview, arranging topics, and dealing with resistance. The interview is also compared with other data-gathering procedures such as observation and use of questionnaires.

STEWART, C. J., & CASK, W. B. (1974). *Interviewing: Principles and practices.* Dubuque, Iowa: William C. Brown.

A readable coverage of the broad field of interviews. Includes sections on most of the major kinds of interviews including employment, appraisal, and counseling. The chapters on communication, questions, and informational interviewing provide a good introduction for the student who is interested in the interview process.

QUESTIONNAIRES

BERDIE, D. R., & ANDERSON, J. F. (1974). *Questionnaires: Design and use.* Metuchen, N.J.: Scarecrow Press.

This short book is filled with useful information on designing and carrying out a questionnaire study. The sections on item construction and procedures to stimulate responses are especially valuable. The appendixes contain four sample questionnaires, follow-up letters, and a case history of a questionnaire study. Finally, an extensive annotated bibliography is provided that includes most important references on questionnaires published over the past 30 years.

BRADBURN, N. M., SUDMAN, S., ET AL. (1979). *Improving interview method and questionnaire design.* San Francisco: Jossey-Bass.

This text describes a series of methodological studies dealing with problems frequently encountered in survey research. Among the topics studied are threatening questions, interviewer expectations, respondent anxiety, and consequences of informed consent.

FINK, A., & KOSECOFF, J. (1985). *How to conduct surveys.* Beverly Hills, Calif.: Sage.

A very practical guide to the conduct of survey research. The chapters on writing survey items and organizing the questionnaire are especially relevant to Chapter 6.

Application Problems

1. Review the following questionnaire items taken from a questionnaire to be sent to a sample of high school teachers and indicate those that are nonbiased (N), leading (L), or psychologically threatening (T).

   _____ **a.** In what college did you complete your teacher training?

   _____ **b.** Have you found that much of what you learned in teacher training cannot be applied in your classroom?

   _____ **c.** How successful are you in maintaining order in your classroom?

2. A researcher develops a program designed to increase teacher empathy with minority group children. Sixty teachers volunteer to take his program for which they will receive credit at the local university. He randomly assigns the 60 teachers to two groups of 30 and trains one group in his program. He then interviews all 60 teachers to determine if the teachers who completed his program have more empathy with minority children. Is there a possibility of bias in this study? If so, explain.

3. Which of the following interview approaches is likely to produce the most reliable information about the teacher's use of thought questions? Why?

   a. Observer A observes in each classroom one hour per day for five days. At the end of each hour he checks the teacher's performance on the following scale; and at the end of the week he averages the scale scores for each teacher for the five days.

      _____ **(1)** Uses a large number of thought questions.

      _____ **(2)** Uses more thought questions then the average teacher.

      _____ **(3)** Uses an average number of thought questions.

      _____ **(4)** Uses fewer thought questions then the average teacher.

      _____ **(5)** Uses no thought questions.

   b. Observer B uses a checklist that defines thought and fact questions and gives examples. He observes in each classroom one hour per day for four days. Each time the teacher asks a question, Observer B tallys it as either a thought question or a fact question. At the end of four days he computes for each teacher:

      _____ **(1)** The average number of thought questions per hour.

      _____ **(2)** The average number of fact questions per hour.

      _____ **(3)** The proportion of thought questions, that is, number of thought questions to total number of questions.

4. Suppose you are given the task of selecting a new social studies achievement test for use in Grades 4 through 6 in your school district. All teachers in the district follow the state curriculum guide in social studies and use the same social studies textbook.

   a. Name two sources you could use to *locate* standardized social studies achievement tests.

   b. Name two sources you could use in searching for *evaluative* data on the tests you have located.

   c. What kind of validity would be most important in selecting a test?

   d. How would you determine this validity for your school district?

5. Locate the following in the *Ninth Mental Measurements Yearbook:*

   a. A test that could be used to measure reading proficiency of college students in Greek.

   b. A test to measure the aptitude for computer programming of persons in computer training programs.

6. Locate the following in *Tests and Measurements in Child Development: Handbook II.*

   a. A test to measure the attitudes of elementary school teachers toward pupils, in other words, what kind of pupils does the teacher prefer?

   b. A measure of the attitudes of parents toward child rearing that would help identify parents who reject their children.

CHAPTER **7**

STATISTICAL TOOLS: WHY DO WE USE THEM AND WHAT DO THEY MEAN?

Overview

A minimum knowledge of statistics is needed to interpret research reports. This chapter is designed to give you this knowledge in nontechnical terms. Basic concepts such as statistical significance and the normal curve are discussed. A few of the most commonly used statistical procedures are then listed in alphabetical order and defined, so that you can easily look them up when reviewing a research report.

Objectives

1. Describe why researchers study samples instead of populations.
2. Explain the meaning of statistical significance.
3. Describe the normal probability curve and explain how it relates to chance events, errors, and statistical significance.
4. State a major advantage of parametric statistics; of nonparametric statistics.
5. Given a research report, identify whether an appropriate statistical tool has been used, and if not select a tool that would be appropriate.

Most educators in the field such as teachers and school administrators have little desire or interest in learning very much about statistics. This is understandable, since it is a difficult subject and one they rarely have occasion to use in their day-to-day work. Similarly, students in teacher education programs or those in nonthesis master's degree programs have little interest in conducting research and thus feel little need for training in statistics. However, all these groups can improve their educational practices if they learn to apply research findings. This poses a dilemma, since some knowledge of statistics is needed in order to use research, that is, to apply research findings to problems and decisions in the public schools.

The purpose of this chapter is to give you the minimum statistical information you will need to understand why we use statistics and to be able to interpret research findings that are based on statistical analysis. We have tried very hard to make this chapter nontechnical and readable. You will find no formulas, nor will you be asked to make any statistical computations. When a technically correct description of a statistical tool required a long and complex explanation, we decided instead upon an approximately correct description that could be written in simple, nontechnical terms.

Why Use Statistics?

In educational research it is almost never possible to study an entire population, such as all first-grade pupils in American public schools. In some cases, it might be possible to study all subjects in a more narrow population such as all elementary school principals in Pennsylvania. However, even a study of a narrow population is likely to be very costly. Actually, we can learn nearly as much about a population by studying a sample of that population, and by studying a sample the cost and effort needed to conduct the research is likely to be much less. Therefore, the goal of most research is to select a sample that appears to be representative of the population, study that sample and then apply the results to the population.

Estimating Errors

However, we know that any sample we select is likely to be different in some respects from the entire population because of sampling errors. One of the main purposes of statistics is to help us estimate the probable size of those sampling errors. The advantage of studying a random sample of the population is that our statistical procedures are usually based upon the assumption that we have a random sample. Thus, if we have a random sample we can accurately estimate the probable size of our sampling errors. In most educational research we are unable to study random samples. It is important, therefore, that our samples be reasonably representative of the population, or any findings that emerge from studying the sample may be grossly in error when applied to the population.

Most educational researchers select as representative a sample as they can, being especially careful to avoid any obvious biases, and then use the statistical tools designed for studying random samples. In reviewing a research report, you should carefully study any evidence that the researcher provides that shows the relationship between her sample and the population to which her results are generalized.

Statistical Significance

When we say that a difference obtained in a study is statistically significant, we mean that we have used statistics to estimate the error likely to occur, and the difference we have found is larger than can be accounted for by this error. We divide the difference we have obtained by the estimated error to obtain the *critical ratio,* which we can then look up in a table to determine the level of statistical significance of the difference. Most researchers use either the .05 or .01 level as the point at which they will reject their null hypothesis. (You may recall that the null hypothesis states that no difference or relationship will be found.) When we reject this hypothesis, we are saying that our results probably reflect a real difference or relationship. In effect, when the researcher selects the .05 level for rejection of the null hypothesis, she is saying that if the probability of obtaining these results by chance is .05 (i.e., 5 percent) or less, she will accept the results as representing a true difference or relationship in the population from which her samples were drawn.

Aside from the sampling procedure, the main factor that determines the size of the sampling error is the number of subjects. Given the same sampling procedure, a large sample is more likely to be representative of the population than a small one.

Researchers have found that as the sample gets larger, differences between the sample and the population will tend to "randomize out." For example, suppose you want to determine the average height of adult males in a large city. You could station yourself on a busy street corner and measure the height of the first 20 adult males who passed. However, with this small a sample, if one seven-foot basketball player happened to pass, his height would have a considerable effect on the average. On the other hand, if you measured the first 2000 males who passed, the extreme heights of a few individuals would have little effect on the average. Also, because there are as many very short males as there are very tall males in the general population, when you measure a large sample, there is a good chance that the extreme cases will tend to balance or "randomize out." Therefore, all formulas used to estimate sampling errors include "N," the statistical symbol for the number of subjects in the sample.

Sampling errors are random and largely due to chance. In contrast, sampling *bias* is a systematic difference between the sample selected and the population. For example, if we selected a street corner where a large number of very tall or very short males regularly passed, such as the corner next to the Jockey Club, this would introduce a bias into our sample that would not be corrected by increasing sample size. Therefore, when the researcher cannot select a random sample, she should be alert to possible sources of bias and avoid them in selecting her sample.

Practical Significance

A difference is said to be of practical significance when it is large enough to have important implications for educational practice. Many researchers confuse statistical significance with practical significance and make recommendations for practice that are not justified by the evidence. Suppose, for example, that a large-scale study comparing two different first-grade reading programs (Programs A and B) is conducted. This study shows that there is a statistically significant difference in the mean reading comprehension scores of children who study under the two programs, favoring Program A. Based on this result, the researcher might recommend that the school district adopt Program A for first-grade reading instruction. However, when we compare the mean reading comprehension scores of the two groups of children, we find that those taking Program A have a mean score of 126.43 on the comprehension test, while Program B pupils have a mean of 124.51. A check of the test shows that on average, Program A children got two more answers correct on the 200-item comprehension test than Program B children. A difference of this magnitude has little

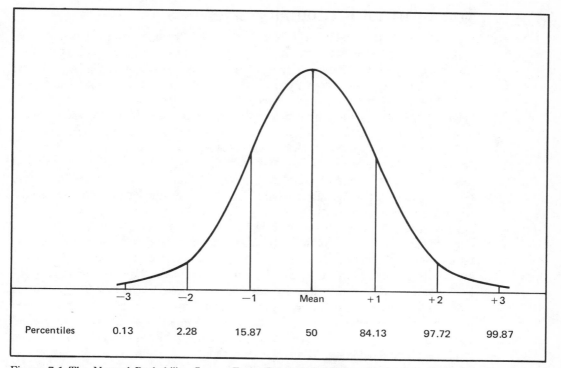

| Percentiles | 0.13 | 2.28 | 15.87 | 50 | 84.13 | 97.72 | 99.87 |

Figure 7.1 The Normal Probability Curve. From *Educational Research: An Introduction,* 3rd edition by Walter R. Borg and Meredith D. Gall. Copyright © 1979 by Longman Inc. Reprinted by permission of Longman Inc., White Plains, N.Y.

practical significance and has produced a statistically significant result only because it was a large-scale study that involved large numbers of children taking each program. Remember that as the size of the sample increases, the sampling errors become smaller, thus requiring a smaller difference to achieve statistical significance.

There are no statistical formulas to estimate the level of practical significance. However, an often used rule of thumb is to divide the difference between means on the dependent variable by the standard deviation of the measure. If the result is .50 or larger the difference is considered to have practical significance.[1] In our example, if the standard deviation of the reading comprehension test were 16.8, dividing the mean difference (126.43 − 124.51) by this standard deviation would give a result of .114, which is far short of our criterion of .50. To meet our criterion for practical significance, the difference between the Program A and B means comprehension test scores would have to be at least 8.4.

1. Some researchers use .33 rather than .50 as a criterion. Remember, however, that the rule of thumb you use is arbitrary and you should carefully examine the evidence for each individual study before making a judgment on the practical significance of the findings.

The Normal Probability Curve

Many of the characteristics of human subjects that we measure in educational research, such as IQ, anxiety, height, and manual dexterity, are normally distributed. This means that if you administer one of these measures to a large unbiased sample and plot their scores on a graph, you will obtain a bell-shaped curve similar to Figure 7.1. The baseline of this curve indicates the scores on the variable measured, and the height of the curve at any point indicates the number of subjects who obtained a given score. This type of graph is called a *frequency polygon,* or *frequency curve.* The area under the normal probability curve (i.e., between the curve and the baseline) between any two points on the baseline is the same for all true normal curves and indicates the percentage of subjects who would obtain scores between these two points. Statistics texts usually include a "Table of Areas under the Normal Curve," which can be used to estimate how many subjects can be expected to score between any two points. Note that the curve is highest at the mean and drops off rapidly as we move toward the two tails of the distribution, that is, farther from the mean. For IQ, for example, this indicates that most persons have scores close to the mean, that is, around 100 IQ, and as we get farther from the mean, fewer and fewer persons obtain scores at a given level. Given an IQ test with a standard deviation of 16 IQ points, a table of areas under the normal curve tells us that if we test a random sample of 1000 persons from the general population, about 683 will obtain scores between 84 and 116, a range of 32 points, or two standard deviations. In contrast only 157 persons will obtain scores between 116 and 148 even though this is also a 32-point range, and only two would obtain scores above 148.

Errors that result from sampling, inaccuracies of measuring instruments—in fact, most errors that we are concerned with in educational research—are also normal. That is, if you plotted the errors on a graph, they would form a curve similar to Figure 7.1. In comparing the mean scores of two different groups to determine if they are significantly different, we are, in effect, comparing the normal error curves for the two means. These error curves represent the distribution of means we would obtain if we tested many samples draw from each of the two populations we want to compare. For example, if we are comparing the manual dexterity scores of 100 black with 100 white 12-year-old boys, the means we obtain are partly an indication of the difference between the two populations and partly due to the unique characteristics of the samples we selected. If we selected 1000 different samples of 100 boys from each of these two populations and computed a mean manual dexterity score for each sample, we would probably find that each sample, because of its unique characteristics (which are sampling errors) had a different mean. If we then made graphs showing the distributions of mean scores for the 1000 black samples and the 1000 white samples, these graphs would be similar to the normal curves shown in Figure 7.2. If the tails of the two distributions overlap very little as in Figure 7.2a, Mean A would be significantly larger than Mean B. On the other hand, if the two distributions overlap considerably, as in Figure 7.2b, Mean C would not be significantly different from Mean D. Although researchers do not actually draw these error curves and compare them, the statistical procedures used to determine if two means are significantly different are designed to make this comparison.

Notice that in Figure 7.2(a) we are comparing the high tail of Error Curve B with the low tail of Error Curve A. In some studies where we are confident that if a difference exists, it must favor a given group we use a *one-tailed test of significance,* which means we will compare the high tail of one error curve with the low tail of the other. When we use a directional hypothesis, we also use a one-tailed test of significance.[2]

However, in our manual dexterity example, we do not know which group will obtain the higher mean score. Thus, we may be comparing the high tail of Error Curve B with the low tail of Curve A. Or, if Group B has the higher mean, the groups would be reversed and we would be comparing the high tail of Curve A with the low tail of Curve B. In cases where we do not know which group will have the higher mean, we use a *two-tailed test of significance.* This test of significance is used in conjunction with the null hypothesis.

There is some advantage to the researcher in using a one-tailed test of significance, since it is easier to obtain a significant difference with this test. However, the one-tailed test can only be used when theory and/or previous research indicates that the difference between means can only go in one direction. That is, if a difference is found, it must be in favor of one group and not the other. As a reviewer you should carefully check studies in which the one-tailed test has been used to be sure that the researcher was justified in using it. If the one-tailed test was used erroneously, you can conclude that the results are less significant than reported.

Most chance events when plotted on a frequency polygon also are distributed along a curve that approximates the normal curve. Suppose you flip 10 pennies and record the number of heads and tails (for example, 6 heads and 4 tails) and repeat flipping this set of 10 coins and recording the outcome 1000 times. You could then graph the number of times you got 10 heads and no tails, 9 heads and 1 tail, 8 heads and 2 tails, and so on to no heads and 10 tails. You would obtain a curve similar to Figure 7.1, with many sets of flips containing 5 heads and 5 tails but very few containing no heads and 10 tails.

Why do many human characteristics, plus statistical errors, plus purely chance events such as coin flipping, all seem to approximate a normal probability curve when plotted on a graph? Probably because all of these things in the final analysis are determined by chance. For example, your height is probably determined by a chance combination of genes combined with chance variations in environmental factors such as food, climate, and exercise.

In summary, we study samples in educational research because it is rarely possible to study entire populations. Random samples are preferable because persons in a random sample are chosen purely by chance. This means that any errors made in

2. You may want to review the section on null and directional hypotheses in Chapter 5 before reading further.

random sampling will be chance errors. Chance errors, like most chance events, are normally distributed and we can estimate the probable size of these errors using statistical tools. By comparing the estimated error with the relationship or difference found in a research project, we can estimate the probability that the difference we obtained could have occurred by chance. If that probability is very low, and most researchers select 1 percent or 5 percent as the cutoff, then the researcher rejects the null hypothesis. This means that he concludes that his results probably represent a real difference or relationship, rather than a chance difference resulting from measurement and/or sampling errors.

In educational research we rarely study random samples and thus cannot be sure that our error estimates are correct. To compensate for sampling errors that may be larger than we would obtain if we used random sampling, we can increase the size of our sample and use a more rigorous probability level to reject the null hypothesis, such as .01 instead of .05. When nonrandom samples are studied, the researcher should also describe her sample in as much detail as she can and present any evidence available to show similarity between her sample and the population. This

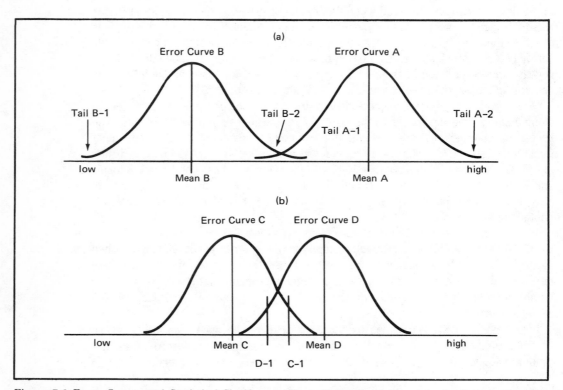

Figure 7.2 Error Curves and Statistical Significance. From *Educational Research: An Introduction,* 3rd edition by Walter R. Borg and Meredith D. Gall. Copyright © 1979 by Longman Inc. Reprinted by permission of Longman Inc., White Plains, N.Y.

helps the reader judge the degree to which the sample is likely to represent the population.

Statistical Tools

Statistical tools can be classified as *descriptive* or *inferential*. Descriptive statistical tools such as the mean, median, and standard deviation are used to describe a group of subjects. Inferential statistical tools are used to draw inferences concerning the relationships and differences found in a research project. A wide variety of statistical tools can be used to draw inferences. Some, called *parametric statistics*, make various assumptions about the characteristics of the population from which a sample has been selected. Others, called *nonparametric statistics*, make few if any assumptions about the characteristics of the population. Parametric statistics have the advantage of being more powerful than nonparametric statistics. This means they are more likely to reveal a true difference or relationship if one exists. The disadvantage of parametric statistics is that the educational researcher is often unable to meet the assumptions on which they are based. If these assumptions are not met, the parametric procedures can produce inaccurate or misleading results. However, for most of the parametric tools the assumptions must be grossly violated before any serious inaccuracy occurs. Thus, most researchers use parametric statistics because of their greater power.

The advantage of the nonparametric tools is that they are safer to use in cases where the assumptions of the appropriate parametric statistic cannot be met. Many researchers consider that use of nonparametric statistics is better scientific procedure when there is any doubt about meeting the assumptions of parametric statistics. In most cases the results are essentially the same whether the researcher uses parametric or nonparametric statistics. The exception is that results that *just reach* statistical significance using parametric statistics will not be significant if nonparametric statistics are used, because of the difference in power.

In this book we cannot teach you to make a sophisticated evaluation of the statistical procedures used in a research project, since such an evaluation requires a thorough knowledge of statistics. We can, however, give you an introduction to statistics so that when you read the results section of a research report, you will understand why certain statistical techniques were used and know what sort of information they provide.

This section lists the most commonly used statistical procedures in alphabetical order. We recommend that you read the descriptions and ask your instructor for any additional information or explanation you may need. Then, when you are reading a research report that uses one of these procedures, review the description given below. You should also review the definitions of research terms given in Chapter 1 before reading the following descriptions.

Analysis of Variance (ANOVA) When a measure such as an achievement test is administered to two or more groups in a research project, it is likely that every subject will receive a different score. In other words, the scores vary. Part of this variance is due to individual differences among subjects, such as that some students achieve more than others. In most research projects, part of the variance is due to the fact that different groups of subjects in the study are exposed to different treatments. For example, students in a group that receives peer tutoring will probably achieve more than those in a group that does not. Also, since none of our measures are perfect, some of the variance in test scores is due to error. ANOVA permits us to compare the variance due to these and other causes and determine which variances are statistically significant, that is, larger than we would expect by chance. These tests of statistical significance are called *F-tests* (see below).

Analysis of Covariance (ANCOVA) This variation of ANOVA is used when groups are administered a pretest related to the dependent variable and are found to be different on this pretest. The ANCOVA process makes an adjustment to the posttest (dependent variable) mean scores for each group to compensate for the pretest differences. If the pretest measures a variable that is closely related to the dependent variable, then this adjustment results in more accurate comparisons, since it compensates for initial group differences. The amount of adjustment to the posttest means is determined by the differences between groups on the pretest and the degree of relationship between the pretest (called the covariate) and the posttest (called the dependent variable). Several covariates can be used in a single ANCOVA.

Chi-square Test (χ^2) This is a statistical technique used to compare categorical data. For example, socioeconomic data are often reported in categories such as upper-class, middle-class, and lower-class. Using chi-square, you could determine if the number of blacks at each social class level differs significantly from a distribution based on theory. More often, however, chi-square is used to compare the distribution of individuals from two or more different groups on categorical variables such as social class. An investigator could compare social class distributions of samples of blacks and Hispanics to see if they are significantly different. Chi-square produces a numerical value, which is then looked up in a table to see if it is statistically significant. Chi-square can also be used to get a measure of relationship between two sets of categorical data called the *contingency coefficient,* which is similar to other correlation coefficients.

Correlation Coefficient Correlation is a statistical technique for determining the relationship between two sets of scores that have been obtained from the same group of subjects. The technique produces a correlation coefficient that is a numerical indication of the degree of relationship. Correlation coefficients range from -1.00 through 0 to $+1.00$. A -1.00 coefficient indicates a perfect negative relationship, for example, that the person receiving the highest score on Test A would receive the lowest score on Test B, and so on. A zero coefficient (0.00) indicates no relationship between scores on the two measures, while a $+1.00$ coefficient indicates a perfect positive relationship. In practice, perfect correlations virtually never occur. However, some correlations, such as reliability coefficients of standardized achievement tests, often range from .90 to .98. There are many different methods of computing correlation coefficients; but the coefficients produced by all of these methods mean approximately the same thing.

F-test (F) This test is used in ANOVA and ANCOVA to determine if one variance is significantly larger than another. After the F is computed, it is checked in a table to determine if it is statistically significant. When only two groups are being compared, the F-test is sufficient to tell us whether the groups are significantly different. But when a study includes three or more groups of subjects, the F-test does not tell us which pairs of groups are significantly different. In this case an additional step is required to make these multiple comparisons.

Mean (M or $\overline{X}$) The mean or arithmetic average for a set of scores is obtained by adding all scores and then dividing by the number of scores. The mean is called a *measure of central tendency* because it provides a single number that represents all of the scores in the set. It is also a descriptive statistic, since it can be used to describe a group. For example, if you are working with a group of retarded children who have a mean IQ of 50, this single number provides a rough description of the group in terms of scholastic aptitude. In many research projects the mean scores of different groups are compared on the dependent variable to learn whether the treatment given one group is more effective than the treatment given another group. Mean scores are reported in nearly all educational research reports. You will recall that the mean is essential to estimating the practical significance of the findings of studies that compare the performance of two or more groups of subjects.

Multiple Regression Analysis Regression analysis predicts an unknown performance (such as college GPA) using a known performance (such as high school GPA) and the correlation between the two. In simple regression, one predictor variable is used to predict one criterion variable. Multiple regression analysis is employed to predict performance on one criterion variable from the individual's performance on several predictor variables. The advantage of multiple regression analysis is that it permits the researcher to explore simultaneously the relationships of several independent (predictor) variables to a dependent (criterion) variable.

Standard Deviation (SD, σ, or s are all used as symbols) If we administer a measure to a class of 30 children, their scores will vary. Many of the scores will be near the mean but a few will be much higher or lower. It is often useful to be able to use a single number to indicate the amount of variability in a set of test scores. The standard deviation provides a way of estimating the variability in a set of test scores and representing this variability with a single number. The standard deviation is called a descriptive statistic because it can be used to describe the amount of variability in a set of scores.

t-test (t) This is a parametric statistical test designed to determine if the mean scores of two groups are significantly different. The test produces a value for t, which is then checked in a table to determine the level of significance. One form of this test (called the independent means t-test) can be used to compare the mean score of two independent groups. For example, the mean scores of two different samples of first-grade students who are exposed to different methods of teaching reading and are then given the same reading achievement test could be compared on reading achievement using a t-test. Another form of the t-test (called the correlated means t-test) can be used to compare the mean scores of the same students on the same measure given before and after treatment in order to determine if a significant gain occurred.

Recommended Reading

BORG, W. R., & GALL, M. D. (1983). *Educational research: An introduction* (4th ed.). White Plains, N.Y.: Longman.

This text contains a nontechnical discussion of statistics (Chapter 12) that provides more detail and theoretical foundation for the student who wants to develop a better understanding of this field.

McCALL, R. B. (1980). *Fundamental statistics for psychology* (3rd ed.). New York: Harcourt Brace Jovanovich.

A good text in elementary statistics, this book relates statistics to research methods and gives many examples. It will help the student develop a better understanding of the theoretical foundations of statistics and also provides many computational examples.

BRUNING, J. L., & KINTZ, B. L. (1977). *Computational handbook of statistics* (2nd ed.). Glenview, Ill.: Scott, Foresman.

This book provides easy-to-follow computational procedures for most of the statistical techniques presented in this chapter. It is an excellent resource for the practicing researcher.

HAYS, W. L. (1981). *Statistics* (3rd ed.). New York: Holt, Rinehart & Winston.

This book is for the student who wishes a deeper understanding of the theoretical and mathematical bases of statistics. It is a fine reference book, having a well-organized, comprehensive table of contents covering the major topics in statistics: sets, probability theory, descriptive statistics, hypothesis testing, chi-square, analysis of variance, correlation, and nonparametric statistics.

KERLINGER, F. N. (1973). *Foundations of behavioral research* (2nd ed.). New York: Holt, Rinehart & Winston.

This text will be useful to the student seeking a more extensive discussion of the topics in research design and statistical analysis covered here. The author's writing style is quite readable, and many examples are provided. Since the logic of research design and statistical analysis is fairly complicated, the student will profit by reading several sources including this one. The use of statistics in educational research is presented particularly well.

SHAVER, J. P. (1985). Chance and nonsense. *Phi Delta Kappan,* Part 1:*67*(1) 57–60; Part 2:*67*(2) 138–141.

This is an interesting and easily understood series of two articles written as a conversation between two teachers. Such concepts as statistical significance, practical significance, statistical power, and effect size are discussed in the context of one teacher's thesis study. Strongly recommended for students who do not understand these concepts.

Application Problems

For each of the following abstracts look up the statistical tool used by the researcher (in italics) and decide whether this tool was appropriate.

1. A teacher carries out a single group study to determine the effects of a multiracial team procedure on the racial attitudes of her 30 third-grade children. First she administers a racial attitude scale, then she sets up multiracial student teams and works with them for six months, then she administers another form of the same attitude scale to her students. She then computes the mean score for the pretreatment attitude scale and the posttreatment attitude scale and compares the two means using the *independent means t-test*.

2. A teacher wants to study the relationship between sex and mathematics achievement in the four sixth-grade classes in her school. She administers the mathematics section of the California Achievement Test Battery to all students ($N = 116$) and then computes a *biserial correlation* using sex as one variable and mathematics achievement scores as the other variable. She obtains a correlation of .42. (See Chapter 9.)

3. A researcher wants to determine the effects of a new reading program on the reading achievement of black, white, and Hispanic first graders. She randomly selects 100 children from each of the three racial groups from first-grade classrooms in a large urban school district. All children are given the Analysis of Reading Skills at the start of the first grade. A comparison of mean scores of the three racial groups on this test indicates that the three groups are significantly different in reading readiness. Then all 300 children are given reading instruction using the new reading program. At the end of the first grade, all 300 children are administered the reading test from the Metropolitan Achievement Tests. The researcher compares the mean scores of the three racial groups on the Metropolitan reading test using *analysis of variance (ANOVA)*.

PART 3

KINDS OF EDUCATIONAL RESEARCH

CHAPTER **8**

DESCRIPTIVE AND CAUSAL-COMPARATIVE RESEARCH

Overview

The role of descriptive research in education is discussed. Two forms of descriptive research, survey and observational, are described. An informative descriptive study dealing with student use of class time is then reprinted along with comments by the researchers and a critical review by the author. Next, the causal-comparative research method is described and contrasted with experimental research. An important study that provides a good example of causal comparative research is then reprinted and reviewed.

Objectives

1. Briefly differentiate between descriptive, correlational, and experimental research.
2. Describe the two kinds of descriptive research and give an example of an educational study of each type.
3. Explain three situations in which self-report evidence is likely to be distorted.
4. State a major advantage of direct observation as a means of gathering descriptive information.
5. Describe three errors in observational research that are likely to reduce the validity of the research results.
6. Describe the steps in the causal comparative method and give an example of a study in which causal comparative methods but not experimental methods could be used.
7. Explain why the selection of comparable groups is important in causal-comparative research.

Chapters 8 through 11 are designed to introduce you to the main types of educational research. To help you understand each research method, we will first give a brief description, which will tell you the kinds of problems the method can be used to study, the way data are usually collected, and the usual steps taken in carrying out the research. Then we will suggest things you should look for in evaluating studies that have used this research method.

Next, we have included articles from recent journals to give you examples of each type of research. Bibliographical data of other articles that illustrate the different research methods are listed in Appendix 2, organized by chapter. These articles have been carefully selected to provide good examples of one of the research methods described in the chapter. All have direct relevance to classroom teaching. To give you a better insight into the researcher as a person, we have asked the authors of the articles reprinted in the text to tell you some of the experiences they had in carrying out the research. These brief author commentaries immediately precede each article.

As you read each article, you may want to evaluate the research, using the form given in Appendix 1. The evaluation form is designed to focus your attention on important aspects of the articles you evaluate. After you have evaluated a few articles, you will no longer need the form. Refer back to chapters 5 through 7 as you evaluate each article. This will give you a good review of these chapters and help you see how you can apply what you have learned to the evaluation of actual research articles.

Immediately after each article in the text you will find a brief critical review. Since all the articles are examples of good research, the critical reviews usually cover factors you should consider in interpreting the results and discuss changes that could have strengthened the research. These reviews also point out examples of some of the concepts given in the rest of the chapter.

In doing educational research, the investigator is often confronted with many practical constraints such as a small budget, limited number of subjects available, and limited cooperation from the participating schools. Therefore, virtually no research is conducted in the best way possible. The limitations we will discuss in our reviews do not imply that the studies are weak, but are given so that you can weigh these limitations and decide how they might affect your interpretation of the results.

You may want to check your evaluation of each article against the critical review to see if you have detected the main limitations of the research.

Descriptive Research

Most scientific research can be placed in one of three broad categories. The first, descriptive research, is aimed at describing the characteristics of subjects of the science. The second, correlational, explores relationships between variables. The third, experimental, manipulates one or more variables and measures the effect of these manipulations on another set of variables.

Much of the early work in a new science is descriptive, since it is necessary to know something about the characteristics of our subjects before trying to study more complex research questions. Human beings, the usual subjects in educational research, are much more complex organisms than the subjects studied in other sciences. Also, education and the related behavioral sciences such as psychology and sociology are much newer and less advanced than natural sciences such as biology or physical sciences such as chemistry. Because of these limitations, descriptive research is important in education. There is still a great deal that we do not know about the students and teachers who are the usual subjects of educational research.

In education, most descriptive research can be roughly classified as either survey research or observational research.

SURVEY RESEARCH

Survey research typically employs questionnaires and interviews in order to determine the opinions, attitudes, preferences, and perceptions of persons of interest to the researcher. Perhaps the best-known surveys are those carried out by the various public-opinion polls. Surveys in education can be used to explore a very wide range of topics such as the extent to which open classrooms are being used at the elementary level and the perceptions of teachers and principals about the effectiveness of such classrooms, the related work experience of high school shop teachers, the preference of school superintendents regarding different forms of federal aid to education, procedures currently being used to help handicapped children adjust to regular classrooms, and problems encountered by first-year elementary teachers.

Survey studies that deal with sensitive topics, such as premarital sex relations, or that attempt to elicit deeper responses that cannot be easily measured with questionnaires frequently employ interviews. Some survey studies employ a combination of questionnaires and interviews; the questionnaires are employed to collect basic descriptive information from a broad sample, and the interviews are used to follow up the questionnaire responses in depth for a smaller sample. You will recall from Chapter 6 that both questionnaires and interviews are subject to bias because the way a question is asked can influence the responses. For example, leading questions or questions that give the respondent a clue as to what answer is desirable will yield biased responses.

In evaluating survey research, pay special attention to the specific questions asked and to the procedure that was used to select the sample. For example, if a survey designed to predict the outcome of a school bond election draws its sample from the telephone directory, the resulting sample may be biased because many welfare recipients do not have telephones and many upper-class persons have unlisted numbers that do not appear in the directory. Many such sampling biases are quite subtle but can result in erroneous and misleading conclusions.

It is also possible to describe the characteristics of a sample of individuals by making observations. The term "observation" in this sense refers to any objective procedure for recording the characteristics or behavior of your subjects. In many descriptive studies in education, tests are administered to the subjects. These tests are considered to be a form of observation since they provide information about the characteristics or behavior of the subjects. Suppose, for example, you were interested in doing a descriptive study of the personality characteristics of successful high school counselors. You would first establish a method for selecting successful counselors, such as obtaining ratings by high school students who had been counseled. Once you had selected your sample of successful counselors you could collect descriptive personality data on them in several ways such as:

1. Administer a battery of personality tests.
2. Administer an adjective checklist to close associates of each counselor to obtain a measure of personality variables.

3. Make direct observations of each counselor and record behavior that seemed to indicate certain personality characteristics such as assertiveness, anxiety, and self-reliance.

Regardless of your method of observation, the end result of your study might be a set of characteristics that successful high school counselors tend to have in common.

The procedures used to analyze descriptive research data are usually simple and easily understood (see Table 8.1). Measures of central tendency and variability are generally used. Percentages are also employed to summarize descriptive data. Suppose, for example, you had carried out a study of the characteristics of bilingual students in Grades 4, 5, and 6 whose achievement was in the top 15 percent on a standardized achievement test. Your data could include questionnaires answered by teachers and parents and interviews with the students themselves. Questions would focus on characteristics such as study habits, socioeconomic status, attitudes toward school, and parental support that you hypothesized to be related to the school success for this group. Student responses would be reported for overall scores in areas such as study habits, which would be based on several questions, as well as responses of the group to single items such as "How many hours did you spend on homework during the past week?"

Measures of variability often help the researcher estimate which characteristics are typical of the group being studied. For example, if nearly all the high-achieving bilingual students came from the middle class, variability would be low and the

Table 8.1   Statistical techniques often used to analyze descriptive research data

Procedure	Purpose
Mean (M or $\bar{X}$)	Gives an indication of the central tendency of the group on the score in question. Equals the sum of the scores divided by N. Means are reported in virtually all descriptive studies.
Median (*Med*)	Also indicates central tendency. Used when extreme scores are present that would distort the mean. The median is the middle score in the score distribution.
Mode	Also indicates central tendency. Equals the most frequently obtained score. This is a crude measure, seldom used.
Standard Deviation (*SD*)	Most widely used measure of the variability of the group. A large *SD* indicates a heterogeneous group. Based on the sum of the squares of the deviations of scores from the mean.
Average Deviation (*AD*)	Also measures variability. Equals the sum of the deviations of scores from the mean, divided by N. Used when extreme scores would unduly influence *SD*. Seldom used.
Quartile Deviation (*Q*)	Used in conjunction with the median, when a simple estimate of variability is sufficient. Equals the difference between score at Q_3 (75th percentile) and score at Q_1 (25th percentile), divided by 2.
Percentage (*P*)	Often used to report the group's responses to multiple-choice questionnaire items.

investigator might conclude that middle-class socioeconomic status is characteristic of this group. On the other hand, if these students came from all classes in about the same proportion that the classes were represented in the bilingual population, then variability would be high and social class would not appear to be a factor related to high achievement.

Often correlational analysis, which we will discuss in Chapter 9, can be used to get additional insights into descriptive research data. In the above example a correlation between social class and achievement level of a broad sample of bilingual students could be computed to estimate the relationship between the two variables.

Since a questionnaire can be regarded as an "observation," you can see that only a rough distinction can be made between survey and observation. Surveys typically employ questionnaires and interviews while other forms of descriptive research usually employ tests or direct observation.

Much descriptive research is based upon self-report evidence. That is, the subject tells you about himself. This is the case for questionnaires, interviews, and most paper-and-pencil tests. A serious potential weakness of self-report measures is that the subject may tell you only what he wants you to know. Thus, such evidence may be distorted or subject to omissions. When evaluating research based upon self-report evidence, be sure to recognize this danger and be alert to any aspects of the study that might lead individuals to provide inaccurate information. Even if the subject wants to give accurate information, he may lack the insight to do so. For example, research has shown that self-ratings on many variables differ considerably from ratings of the individual by others. If the study is in any way threatening to the subject, if he feels that honest answers can harm him, or if the questions call for a level of insight that the subject may not possess, you can assume that many subjects will lie or give inaccurate answers. You can also assume that self-report data on topics such as homosexuality, cheating on income taxes, promiscuity, or poor job performance will probably be distorted unless good rapport is established between subjects and researchers and the subjects are convinced that the investigator has used a foolproof system to ensure the confidentiality of their responses.

DIRECT OBSERVATION

Because of the weaknesses of self-report evidence, educational researchers have made increased use of direct observation of the subject's behavior using trained observers. You will recall that you were introduced to direct observation as a measurement procedure in Chapter 6.

Direct observation is essentially a technique for gathering data about the subjects involved in a study. Therefore, it is a basic measurement technique that can be employed in most kinds of educational research. In this book we deal with observation under descriptive research because it is an extremely important means of collecting descriptive data and because the techniques involved in using observers are sufficiently different from other measurement techniques, so that observational research can be considered a separate research discipline. The great advantage of the observational process is that it enables the researcher to collect direct information about human behavior that can be collected only indirectly by measurement techniques such as paper-and-pencil tests. For example, we can probably learn much more about interracial attitudes by observing children of different races in their interactions with one another than we can by asking questions about racial interactions on a paper-and-pencil test. Direct observation is especially effective in situations where the researcher wishes to study specific aspects of human behavior in detail. For example, the following questions are well suited for study by observation: What specific teaching strategies are most effective to teach basic number facts to severely retarded children? How do preschool children respond to a television program that contains a large number of violent acts? What specific counseling procedures are most highly related to realistic vocational decisions by high school students?

In reviewing studies that employ direct observation, you should pay particular attention to the specifics of the observational process. Great care must be taken in observational studies to eliminate observer bias. For example, if observers are involved in a descriptive study of the social behavior of mentally retarded children, they may tend to see a higher level of social behavior in children who they know have higher IQs. The solution to this problem, of course, is to design observational research in such a way that observers do not have the kinds of knowledge about the subjects that are likely to bias their perceptions. Other errors in observational research that are likely to reduce its validity include using broad, general definitions of the behavior to be observed rather than narrow, specific definitions, using subjective procedures such as rating the subject's performance from poor to excellent rather than objective procedures such as counting the number of times a specific behavior occurs, and requiring that the observer record more aspects of behavior than can be attended to effectively.

In order to collect reliable observational data, it is usually necessary to train observers in the observational process. Such training, along with information on the reliability of the observational data, is included in most good observational studies, and you should look for it when you review research reports. A typical sequence for training observers is given in Chapter 6.

You are now ready to relate some of what you have learned to the evaluation of an actual research report. First you will read the researchers' commentary. This is included to give you some insight into the researchers, their reasons for doing the study, some of the problems they encountered, and their perceptions of how the study contributes to our knowledge. All commentaries will not cover all of these topics. However, the commentary gives the researchers a chance to tell you things about the study that are not usually included in research journals. It also permits the researchers to communicate with you on a more informal, person-to-person basis than is possible in the journals.

Next you will read the article itself. As you read, apply what you have learned in the earlier chapters to help you evaluate the article. You may find it helpful to fill out a copy of the Research Report Evaluation Form (Appendix 1) as you read the article.

Finally, you should read the critical review and see whether you have identified some of the same points that are discussed in the review. Keep the following in mind when you read the critical reviews:

1. All articles selected for this text are examples of *good educational research* that has clear and useful implications for the classroom teacher and/or the school administrator.

2. No one has ever conducted a perfect research study in education. All studies include some aspects that could have been done better. In most cases the researchers are aware of these, but because of factors such as limited funds, need to get cooperation of participating teachers, or time limitations they have to make compromises in order to be able to carry out the research.

3. Because of the severe space limitations in professional journals, the researcher must make his report as brief as possible consistent with clarity. This means that much information is omitted from the typical research article that would answer many of the questions that arise in the mind of the reviewer. In your role as an educator, if you locate a research article that is of critical importance to a decision you must make, you can usually get additional information about the research by writing the researchers who conducted the study.

4. The fact that most studies have limitations does not mean that they are without value. Even a poor study can make a valuable contribution to knowledge if the reader keeps in mind the study's limitations when interpreting the results. Of course, the better the study is designed and carried out, the fewer limitations we must consider and the more confidence we can have in the results.

5. A major purpose of this book is to make you an intelligent consumer of educational research. The best way to do this is to provide studies for you to read and evaluate and give you critical reviews, so that you can compare your evaluations with those of an experienced researcher. Even more valuable will be the feedback you will receive from your instructor and classmates when the articles are discussed.

The first seven chapters have given you the basic knowledge you need to start reviewing educational research. You will find additional information and ideas in the commentaries and critical reviews. We believe that linking these ideas to the actual articles that serve as examples will make it easier for you to understand and remember.

Sample Descriptive Study:
"TIME USE AND ACTIVITIES
IN JUNIOR HIGH CLASSES"

Abstract[1]

This paper describes time use in different activities in junior high school and examines relationships between class time use and student achievement, behavior, and

1. The abstract from the article is reprinted here in order to provide a context in which the researcher's comments can be related.

attitude. A total of 102 English and mathematics classes were observed about 9 hours each. Data included descriptive narratives, time logs, student engagement ratings, and observer ratings of student and teacher behavior. Results showed much variation in the way individual junior high school teachers use class time, within a limited number of activity structures. Significant relationships were found between time use and class achievement and attitude in mathematics classes, but not in English classes.

The Researcher's Comments[2]

This research report illustrates how a large data base can sometimes be used to provide answers to questions *other* than the main questions a study was designed to answer. I did this analysis when some of my colleagues and I at the Research and Development Center for Teacher Education were conducting a series of studies of classroom management. The main focus of these investigations (which eventually included two large descriptive studies and two large field experiments) was on how teachers managed their classrooms and kept students engaged in activities.

To be sure that we captured information about all aspects of classroom management, we observed each class frequently and collected a variety of qualitative and quantitative data: narrative records of events, counts of students who were off task, logs of class time and activities, and a number of ratings of student and teacher behavior. Because we were interested in assessing connections between teachers' management behaviors, student engagement and learning, achievement measures were also obtained for all students. A result of all of this data collection was that we created a rich data base for exploring some potentially important questions about teaching, in addition to the questions we set out to answer about classroom management at the beginning of the school year.

How teachers in this study of junior high classrooms allocated time among different types of class activities and how these decisions affected student learning and behavior were two questions that, as a former secondary teacher and curriculum developer, I thought important. I reasoned that findings in this area could lead to recommendations that teachers could use directly in their own instructional planning. Also, there were results from previous research that suggested that class time use was worth looking into more closely. These are reviewed in our article. Whereas most of the previous time research had focused on elementary classrooms or on junior high mathematics, the study we did during the 1978–1979 school year provided information about a large number of classes—102— in two content areas, English and mathematics. I decided to conduct an analysis of the junior high data to find out what I could about patterns of time use and how they relate to student behavior and achievement in the two content areas.

Problems in Designing the Analysis

One of the important strengths of our large-scale study was the large amount of descriptive data we collected on each class. Each class was observed about 14 times, beginning the first week of school. For this study of time use, I decided to focus only on class meetings after the third week of school when "normal" classroom routines were established. This

---

2. This commentary was written by Dr. Julie P. Sanford.

left us with eight or nine one-hour observations of each class, which amounted to some 70 to 90 pages of typewritten narratives, stacks of time logs and student engagement counts, and a large number of ratings of teacher and student behavior for each class.

As in any study that includes large amounts of descriptive data, in planning our analysis, we had to balance our desire for descriptive detail (that would give us accurate pictures of real events in classrooms) with our need for manageable data amenable to analysis by computer. Therefore, for the main part of the time use study, we reduced our qualitative information to nine categories of activities and three aggregate categories. We tried to choose categories that captured activities we saw in all or most classes and that related to categories others had used in studying classrooms. However, the process of categorizing the data and analyzing it quantitatively brought limitations. Numbers indicating mean minutes of class time spent in whole-class instruction or seatwork tell us very little about the *nature* of instruction or learning experiences students received. In English classes, particularly, whole-class instruction included a wide spectrum of activities, topics, and tasks. We found that two classes having similar time use profiles might differ greatly as to the nature of activities in which students engaged. It's likely that this fact contributed to the lack of clear findings for correlations between time use variables and student behavior and achievement in English classes, as we discuss in the article. At any rate, making sense of our quantitative results required returning to the raw data. In this case, having classroom narratives as well as coded data was critical.

In the mathematics classes, there appeared to be greater uniformity of topics and instructional strategies within time use categories, and the findings we obtained in mathematics classes were more clear. The implication that a significant amount of class time in mathematics should be devoted to active instruction is, I think, important and well supported.

Followup on the Time Use Question

As I mentioned above, the junior high management study was one of a series. Some time after I did the time use article, we conducted a large field experiment in junior high and middle schools to test findings of the earlier descriptive study. This time 61 teachers participated and more content areas—science, English, mathematics, social studies, and a sprinkling of others—were examined. We collected a variety of quantitative and qualitative data, as we had in the earlier study. Using the new data, I returned to the time use question as a small part of a special study I did of management and organization in 26 science classrooms (Sanford, 1984). For that study, student achievement measures were not available, but I examined relationships between student on-task and disruptive behaviors and proportion of class time spent in such activity categories as content presentation or discussion, seatwork, small group work, testing, transitions, and aggregate categories such as whole-class active instruction. I wanted to find out if there were systematic differences in how more and less effective managers used class time. I found that science classes varied widely with regard to proportion of class time in different kinds of activities, but these differences were not related to management success. After that study I concluded that proportion of class time in different categories of activities is probably not a productive way to look at most secondary classrooms, and that total active instructional time is a less important variable than appropriateness, pacing, and accountability of instructional activities and student engagement rates. The better classroom managers in that sample of science teachers had a lot of work for students to do in class, and students were held accountable for their work.

These tentative conclusions about research in secondary instruction were supported by new work we were beginning at that time in our research program. The new work, led by Walter Doyle, relied on qualitative analysis of academic work and instruction in a smaller number of secondary classes (Doyle et al., 1985; Sanford, 1985). In recent years others in the research community have also undertaken careful analyses of case studies of classroom instruction, rather than attempting large-scale studies. I think this shift has resulted in some better understanding of the hows and whys of instructional effects in secondary and elementary schools, but each type of approach to studying instruction has limitations, and I hope we will continue to see a variety of research approaches funded and used.

References

DOYLE, W., SANFORD, J. P., SCHMIDT FRENCH, B. S., EMMER, E. T., & CLEMENTS, B. S. (1985). *Patterns of academic work in junior high school science, English, and mathematics classes: A final report* (R&D Rep. 6090). Austin: Research and Development Center for Teacher Education, University of Texas at Austin.

SANFORD, J. P. (1984). Management and organization in science classrooms. *Journal of Research in Science Teaching, 21*(6), 575–587.

SANFORD, J. P. (1985). *Comprehension-level tasks in secondary classrooms* (R&D Rep. 6199). Austin: Research and Development Center for Teacher Education, University of Texas at Austin.

TIME USE AND ACTIVITIES IN JUNIOR HIGH CLASSES

Julie P. Sanford
THE UNIVERSITY OF TEXAS AT AUSTIN

Carolyn M. Evertson
INSTRUCTIONAL SYSTEMS, INC.

Studies of class time use have drawn on a number of very different measures, including individual student time on task, days or hours of instruction, student task engagement rates, and classroom organization or allocation of time. Among measures, individual students' time on task or engaged time has often proven to be the strongest predictor of achievement gains, but some mea-

Sanford, Julie P., and Evertson, Carolyn M., "Time Use and Activities in Junior High Classes." *Journal of Educational Research,* 1983, pp. 140–147. Copyright 1983, Heldref Publications, Washington, D.C. Reprinted by permission.

sures of time allocated to instruction have also been shown to be significantly and positively related to achievement (Borg, 1980; Frederick & Walberg, 1980). In the Beginning Teacher Evaluation Study (BTES), for example, allocated time, based primarily on teachers' logs of instructional time, was significantly related to achievement in five content areas in reading and mathematics, accounting for from 2% to 24% of residual variance on the posttest (Borg, 1980). These and other findings suggest that allocated time can be a powerful tool for teachers and administrators in increasing student achievement. One reason it has potential is that allocation of time to different activities, unlike student-engaged time, can be controlled directly by the teacher. Class time spent in different activities is a variable that teachers themselves can assess and manipulate in planning for instruction.

This study looks at one aspect of class time use—class time observed in different categories of activities—and relationships between time use and student achievement, attitude, and behavior in junior high classes. Two major questions are addressed: 1) How was class time used in the 102 classes in our sample, and to what extent did patterns of time use vary across classes, teachers, and subject areas? 2) What is the relationship between how class time is spent and class mean achievement gains, student ratings of the teacher, and student behavior, as defined by on-task rates, off-task, unsanctioned rates, and observer ratings of disruptive behavior in the class?

The activity categories used in the study provide some qualitative distinctions among class activities, a distinction lacking in other studies of allocated time. For example, academic activities are categorized as whole-class instruction (teacher-led discussion, presentation, review, or recitation), seatwork (individual student tasks), or small-group instruction. Previous research leads us to expect different effects for these activities. In the Beginning Teacher Evaluation Study, McDonald (Note 1) reported that in fifth grade classrooms student engagement during whole-class presentation/recitation was more closely linked than engagement during seatwork to achievement in reading and mathematics. Evertson, Emmer, and Brophy (1980) reported that in the Texas Junior High School Study (TJHSS) a subsample of more-effective mathematics teachers used about half of each class period for lecture and discussion and less than half for seatwork. Less-effective teachers used about one-fourth of the period for lecture and discussion and more than one-half for seatwork. At the secondary level in remedial reading, Stallings (Note 2) found that time-on-task effects were greatest when only engagement in interactive instruction (as opposed to seatwork) was considered. However Rosenshine (Note 3) cited conflicting results for seatwork versus verbal interaction and called for more research on student

time use in different contexts. Good (Note 4) has pointed out that there is relatively little information describing secondary school processes.

The purpose of the present analysis, then, is to provide more descriptive information about how class time is used in junior high schools, to assess the extent to which data from the Junior High Organization Study (JHCOS) support previous research findings about the productivity of whole-class instruction time (as opposed to seatwork), and to further explore relationships between activity patterns and achievement, student ratings of the teacher, and student behavior in two diverse subject areas, mathematics and English.

Methods

The sample used in this analysis consisted of 102 classes, 52 math and 50 English, taught by 51 teachers (two classes per teacher). Teachers were participants in the Junior High School Classroom Organization Study, a year-long study of classroom management in 11 junior high schools in a large southwestern city (Evertson, Emmer, & Clements, Note 5). Data from classroom observations made between the third week of classes and the end of the year were used for the present study, resulting in eight or nine 1-hour observations of each class in the sample. Observation data included descriptive narratives of instructional and behavioral events, logs of class time use, student engagement rates, and observer ratings of specific teacher and student behaviors.

Three measures of student behavior were included: off task, unsanctioned; on task; and disruptive behavior. Off task, unsanctioned, and on task were student engagement rates derived from counts of students made every 15 minutes during observations. Students were coded as off task, unsanctioned when they were not engaging in assigned or expected tasks or were engaging in behavior contrary to class rules or procedures. Off-task, unsanctioned behavior could be disruptive or not at all disruptive. Students were coded as on task when they were engaged or involved in assignments or expected tasks, *either academic or procedural*. A class on-task average provides a measure of student cooperation and involvement in class activities. It is not equivalent to measures of academic time on task or academic learning time. A third measure, disruptive behavior, was rated on a 1-5 point scale by the observer immediately after observation of the class. A disruptive event was one that interfered with the attention or work involvement of three or more students or the teacher.

Entering achievement levels of classes were assessed by school district-administered California Achievement Tests (CAT) in mathematics and reading. Pupil achievement was assessed in May using instruments designed to reflect instructional content in the school district. Student ratings of the teacher made in May were used as a measure of student attitudes toward the teacher and class.

Using class narratives and time logs, minutes of time spent in observed class meetings were recorded for nine categories of activities. Subsequently some categories were aggregated to produce three additional activity categories. The categories were defined as follows:

Administrative and procedural routines. This category was used whenever most of the students were involved in administrative or procedural activities such as roll call, announcements, opening or closing (nonacademic) routines, discussion of grades, distribution of graded papers, discussion of schedules for assignments. If directions for seatwork or homework took more than 3 minutes and did not include content development, the time was noted in this category.

Transitions. Transitions were intervals between activities, when the majority of the class were involved in getting their supplies, passing in their papers, or otherwise getting ready for another activity.

Grading. When most of the students were involved in grading an assignment in class, this category was used. Grading or checking was considered a procedural activity, not academic. It was used when the apparent main purpose of the activity was to check answers and compute a grade on an assignment, not to review or clarify content. (When review of content was included in a grading or checking activity, the time segment was coded as whole-class instruction). Students checked their own papers or exchanged them.

Whole-class instruction. This category was used for whole-class teacher presentation of content, lecture, demonstration, or explanation, whole-class discussion, recitation, or review, or any combination of the preceding activities. Review of a homework or seatwork assignment or a graded test accompanied by teacher explanation or student recitation was included in whole-class instruction. When directions for completing an assignment included explanation of the content they were included in this category.

Seatwork. This category was used when most of the students were working on individual tasks, either the same task or different tasks, at their own pace. Short teacher interruptions of seatwork to explain or clarify directions were left in seatwork time unless they lasted more than 1 minute. Directions for seatwork were included in seatwork unless they lasted more than 3 minutes. (If they lasted more than 3 minutes and reviewed the content they were counted as whole-class instruction; if they lasted longer than 3 minutes but did not include content, they were categorized as procedural routine.)

Tests. Any activity described by the teacher as a test or diagnostic assessment was categorized here. Students worked alone, for a grade or a score, with minimal teacher assistance.

Dead time. This category was used when the majority of the students in the class had no assignment; they were simply waiting for the end of the period or for the beginning of a new activity. The teacher had not provided or suggested any academic activities for students, and no activities were dictated by classroom routine.

Small-group instruction. This category was used whenever the teacher was working with a small group of students for an extended period of time (more than 1 minute). Although the majority of students in the class may have been engaged in seatwork or procedural activities, the small group category took priority over all others.

Other. Any time use not included in the preceding categories was categorized other.

All nonacademic activities. This was a composite category including administrative routines and procedures, transitions, grading, and dead time.

Total minutes. This was simply the total minutes of class time, from the beginning of class, usually marked by the ringing of the tardy bell, to the dismissal of the class by the teacher.

Total academic time. This was a composite category that included whole-class instruction, seatwork, tests, and small-group work. It included all of the class time that had an academic focus.

Results and Discussion

Mean raw minutes of class time in each category and descriptive statistics for the 12 categories of time use were computed separately for 52 mathematics classes (26 teachers) and 50 English classes (25 teachers). Intraclass correlations between the classes taught by the same teachers indicated high levels of stability between class sections, with Pearson *r*'s ranging from .64 to .99 (*p* < .01) for most categories. Time-use categories showing the most variance between sections for a teacher were total class time, administrative and procedural time, and, for mathematics classes, grading and other. Total class time and administrative and procedural time were affected by school schedules and routines (such as announcements); when one of a teacher's two class sections was longer than the other, the difference in time was usually taken up by administrative matters. For the most part, teachers' real class time use was consistent across class sections; therefore, the teacher was used as the unit of analysis for descriptive analysis of time use and for analysis of relationships between class time use and student behavior and

outcomes. (The category other was not used in any analyses.) Pearson correlations were computed between time-use categories and teacher means on student off-task, unsanctioned behavior, student on-task behavior, observer ratings of disruptive behavior, student ratings of the teacher, and achievement residuals.

Activities in Mathematics Classes

Mean minutes of class time in different activities in mathematics classes are shown in Table 1. These data are based on eight observations each of 52 classes taught by 26 teachers, data aggregated by teachers. Table 1 provides some rough answers to the question, "How is class time used in junior high mathematics classes?" (at least in our sample from 11 schools in a single large school district). First, the standard deviations and range of teacher means for different categories of time use in Table 1 indicate that classes varied greatly in amount of time allocated to whole-class instruction or seatwork, amount of time spent in a variety of nonacademic activities, and total nonacademic or academic time. Classes were fairly uniform in length, about 55 minutes long. On the average, more time was spent in seatwork than in any other category (mean of 19.81 minutes per class), followed by whole-class instruction (mean of 15.33 minutes). An average of 14.42 minutes was taken up by nonacademic or noninstructional activities—administrative chores, transitions, dead time, and grading.

Table 1. Time use in mathematics classes

Activity or time-use category	Mean raw minutes per class meeting	SD	Range in teacher means
Administrative/procedural routine	3.76	2.24	.38– 9.16
Transitions	4.83	2.44	1.06–10.54
Grading	4.12	2.50	.25–10.06
Whole-class instruction	15.33	6.94	6.34–33.37
Seatwork	19.81	7.37	8.13–35.25
Tests	2.90	3.39	0.00–10.53
Dead time	1.71	1.65	0.00– 6.31
Small-group instruction	1.18	5.46	0.00–28.47
All nonacademic activities	14.42	3.88	6.50–21.85
Total minutes	54.29	2.00	50.59–59.06
Total academic time	39.23	4.00	31.66–46.73

Within several activity categories, however, great variation was seen across teachers. Table 2 shows contrasting time-use profiles for four teachers. Teacher A averaged only 6.34 minutes of whole-class instruction per class, based on 16 observations divided between two different class sections. Students in Teacher A's classes (and students in classes of five other teachers in the sample) spent half or more of the available class time in seatwork, and less than 10 minutes in whole-class instruction. In contrast, Teacher B used more time in whole-class instruction (average 33.25 minutes) than in seatwork. This pattern was also characteristic of six other teachers who averaged at least 20 minutes a day in whole-class instruction. Teacher C was the only mathematics teacher in our sample to use small-group instruction regularly. Four others used it rarely. Teacher D's classes spent large amounts of time in nonacademic activities, an average of 21.85 minutes per class. Narratives of these classes showed frequent procedural or behavioral discussions, long transitions between activities, and higher-than-average dead time.

A common activity sequence in mathematics classes consisted of warm-ups, followed by checking, whole-class instruction in the form of content development or review, and seatwork assignment. ("Warm-ups" were short review assignments that students routinely completed during the first 5 minutes of class, usually while the teacher checked roll and handled other adminis-trative duties.) This basic sequence was by no means the only pattern of activities, however. A few teachers frequently used more than one cycle of whole-class instruction and seatwork per class meeting. In these classes the schedule might look like this: warm-up or grading homework, teacher presentation (content development), seatwork practice, checking and discussion, seatwork (begin homework).

Activities in English Classes

Based on the descriptive statistics for time-use categories shown in Table 3, allocation of class time in 50 English classes taught by 25 teachers appeared to be similar to patterns in mathematics classes. Examination of sequences and specific activities showed important differences, however. As in mathematics classes, more class time was spent in student seatwork (mean minutes per class 19.67) than in any other category. Whole-class instruction averaged 15.57 minutes, with a wide range of teacher means. One teacher averaged only 4.75 minutes of whole-class instruction per class meeting across 16 observations of two classes. Another averaged about 29 minutes per class meeting. Ten teachers used small-group instruction to some extent, but few used it much, and grouping was almost entirely limited to spelling content. Average time spent in nonacademic activities was 13.48 minutes, and total academic time averaged 39.39 minutes, very similar to that in mathematics classes.

Table 2.   Comparison of mean minutes of class time use for selected mathematics teachers[a]

	Teacher A	Teacher B	Teacher C	Teacher D	Category mean 26 teachers
Whole-class instruction	6.34	33.25	10.00	15.54	15.33
Seatwork	29.56	8.13	8.13	17.69	19.81
Small-group instruction	0.00	0.00	28.47	0.00	1.18
Grading	3.66	3.56	3.27	4.85	4.12
Dead time	.31	0.00	0.07	2.31	1.71
All nonacademic activities	9.84	7.63	9.53	21.85	14.42
Total class time	53.37	53.81	56.27	55.08	54.29
Mean class achievement residual	−.4223	.9786	.0674	−.0787	−.0035
Mean class student off task, unsanctioned	.05	.01	.05	.11	.10

[a] Based on eight observations of two class sections per teacher.

Table 3. Time use in English classes

Activity or time-use category	Mean raw minutes per class meeting	SD	Range in teacher means
Administrative/procedural routine	5.77	2.50	1.00–11.00
Transitions	3.77	1.42	1.88– 7.73
Grading	2.54	2.54	0.00–10.45
Whole-class instruction	15.57	6.02	4.75–28.50
Seatwork	19.61	5.15	10.71–28.79
Tests	3.02	2.59	0.00– 8.38
Dead time	1.40	1.38	0.00– 5.38
Small-group instruction	1.19	2.32	0.00– 8.86
All nonacademic activities	13.48	3.83	4.93–21.73
Total minutes	53.89	2.26	49.19–57.92
Total academic time	39.39	5.51	25.55–52.22

Within these categories of activities, however, English classes showed more variation than did mathematics classes. It was not possible, for example, to identify a "typical" sequence of activities, because activity sequences varied according to different topics within the curriculum: spelling, composition, grammar, reading, poetry, and mythology. Despite district-wide curriculum requirements, teachers varied in their allotment of class time to different topics and in their choice of instructional activities to teach different topics. One pattern of time use that distinguished some teachers, however, was the number of *different* activities usually undertaken in a single class period. In these classes, for example, students and teacher might often spend entire periods in reading aloud and discussing a story or play, or students might work on grammar assignments at their desks for most of the period, after a very short introduction by the teacher. Classes of 11 teachers were usually characterized by relatively long unbroken periods of class time devoted to only one or two main activities each class. Classes of 10 others usually contained at least three activity segments other than administrative routine. For example, these classes might consist of the following sequences: a) administrative routine, b) content development (grammar review), c) grammar seatwork, d) checking, e) discussion of related grammar topic; or a) seatwork (composition journal), b) spelling quiz, c) content development of a new grammar topic, d) seatwork. Classes of four other teachers did not fall into consistent patterns

of activity with regard to number of activities or segments.

Analysis of classroom narratives showed that often English classes having similar time-use profiles differed greatly in the nature of activities students were engaged in. Classes having similar time-use averages frequently contrasted greatly when compared on pacing of activities, activity-segment length or sequence, and the extent to which students were held accountable for participating in activities. Even for a single type of instructional activity in English classes, such variation was found from class to class that few assumptions could be made about the extent or nature of instruction taking place. For example, one common whole-class instructional activity, reading of a story or play aloud, might in one class be used as a vehicle for instruction by the teacher on vocabulary, logic, reading comprehension, and composition stretegies, whereas in another the same activity might function as a time filler with little teacher input or monitoring.

Time Use, Student Behavior, and Student Outcomes in Mathematics Classes

Correlations between class mean time use in different categories and class means of three student-behavior measures, student ratings of the teacher, and mean class achievement residuals for mathematics classes are shown in Table 4. No significant relationships were found between mean time

Table 4.   Pearson correlations between time spent in activity categories and class means for student behavior and outcomes in mathematics classes ($N = 26$ teachers, 2 classes each)

| Activity/time-use category | Class means for student behavior measures[a] | | | Class means for student ratings of teacher | Class mean achievement residuals |
	Off task, unsanctioned	On task	Disruptions		
Administrative/ procedural routine	−.1111	.0816	−.2250	−.1690	−.0037
Transitions	.3321	−.4353*	.4756*	−.0996	−.2638
Grading	.1488	.0114	.0361	−.0638	.0163
Whole-class instruction	−.0533	.1545	−.2059	.1837	.4252*
Seatwork	.1654	−.1706	.2619	−.1052	−.4160*
Tests	−.3927*	.2728	−.3925*	−.1972	.1384
Dead time	.2739	−.5412*	.3899*	−.1514	−.0904
Small-group work	−.1643	.2610	−.1318	.2553	.0587
Nonacademic time	.3568	−.4491*	.3581	−.2656	−.1954
Total academic time	−.3445	.5411*	−.3870*	.3068	.1688

* $p < .05$

[a] Across all activities in 16 observations per teacher.

use and student ratings of the teacher. Significant relationships between student behavior and class time use were found for amount of class time spent in transitions, dead time, total nonacademic activity, testing, and total academic time. These correlations suggested better student behavior and less classroom disruption in classes with more total academic time (either whole-class instruction or seatwork), more testing, and less time spent in transitions, dead time, and total nonacademic activity. Magnitude of significant Pearson r's ranged from .39 to .54. There are two different, although not mutually exclusive, interpretations for these findings: students cooperate and behave better in classes in which teachers plan sufficient work and organize to "protect" time for academic instruction; high rates of disruptive student behavior and lack of student cooperation contribute to longer transitions and more dead time, thereby cutting into time available for instruction. In addition, in classes that spend more time in testing, there is less off-task or disruptive behavior.

Relationships between mean time use and mean class achievement gains were different from relationships for student behavior. Here, neither total academic time nor the amount of time taken up by procedures, transitions, dead time, grading, or other nonacademic activities were related to achievement. Instead, *how* instructional time was used appeared to make a difference: higher mean class achievement gains were related to more time spent in whole-class instruction ($r = .4252$) and less time spent in seatwork ($r = −.4160$). Not enough of the teachers in our sample used small-group instruction for us to make any conclusions about that activity.

These significant correlations for achievement gains in mathematics confirm previous research suggesting that more-effective junior high school mathematics teachers use more available class time in content development activities than do less-effective teachers (Evertson, Emmer, & Brophy, 1980). The fact that time-use patterns with regard to whole-class instruction and seatwork were not related to class behavior means suggests that in mathematics classes effective classroom management and effective use of instructional time may be two relatively independent factors affecting student achievement gains. This inference is supported by findings reported by Emmer (Note 6) working with the JHCOS data base. He identified groups of effective and less-effective classroom managers (without using class achievement as a criteria) and found no difference in time-use patterns between the two groups. However, among the subject of eight teachers identified as effective managers, use of class time in content development versus seatwork appeared to be related to class mean achievement gains. Results for mathematics activities in the present analysis also are compatible with reported findings for the productivity of student-engaged time in class presentations/recitations compared to engagement in seatwork in the BTES fifth grade classes (Borg, 1980; McDonald, Note 1).

Given the relative uniformity of curriculum content and teaching method in mathematics instruction, it may be that in classes in which teachers use much of the available time leading whole-class instructional activities, more of the content in the textbook is covered, and this fact results in higher achievement gain scores for the class. Good, Grouws, and Beckerman (Note 7) have reported that a faster pace in covering mathematics content is related to higher class achievement. In the present study, however, we have no information about content covered in the different classes. An alternative hypothesis would be that more whole-class instruction time allows more thorough discussion and more practice of content, rather than coverage of more topics or text pages.

Time Use, Student Behavior, and Student Outcomes in English Classes

Relationships between class time use in English classes and student-behavior variables, student ratings of the teacher, and class mean achievement residuals bore no resemblance to correlations obtained for mathematics classes. Table 5 shows that no significant correlations were obtained between time-use categories and class mean achievement residuals or class mean student ratings of the teacher. Results obtained for the student-behavior variables were not very consistent across the three kinds of measures. More time in seatwork was associated with less off-task, unsanctioned behavior ($r = -.4936$). Significant

Table 5. Pearson correlations between time spent in activity categories and class means for student behavior and outcomes in English classes ($N = 25$ teachers, 2 classes each)

| Activity/time-use category | Class means for student behavior measures[a] | | | Class means for student ratings of teacher | Class mean achievement residuals |
	Off task, unsanc-tioned	On task	Disruptions		
Administrative/ procedural routine	−.1298	.2336	.0884	−.2730	.1074
Transitions	.0507	−.2945	.2059	.0915	−.3032
Grading	−.0926	.0423	.2627	−.0390	.2614
Whole-class instruction	.4119*	−.1919	−.0408	−.2689	.1562
Seatwork	−.4936*	.3295	−.3751	.3693	.1253
Tests	.3237	−.1821	.1673	−.3008	.1166
Dead time	.2510	−.6691*	.3759	−.0481	−.1304
Small-group work	−.3310	.3826*	−.2953	.3286	−.0561
Nonacademic time	−.0373	−.1691	.4443*	−.1879	−.0845
Total academic time	.0024	.1732	−.4406*	.0476	.0851

* $p < .05$

[a] Across all activities in 16 observations per teacher.

relationships were not found with on-task or disruptive behavior, although there were strong trends in the expected directions. More time spent in whole-class instruction showed significant positive correlations ($r = .4119$) with off-task, unsanctioned behavior, but no significant correlations (or trends) with either of the other two measures of student behavior. Higher ratings of class disruption were also associated with larger amounts of nonacademic time ($r = .4443$), and smaller amounts of total academic time ($r = -.4406$). Small-group work was related to higher task engagement ($r = .3826$) and correlations obtained for this activity format and the other two student-behavior measures were weak, but in a direction supporting the on-task trend. In general, student behavior appeared to be somewhat better in classes in which larger amounts of time were spent in seatwork with some time in small-group instruction.

Lack of achievement results and the inconsistent behavior results obtained in the English classes in the JHCOS sample suggest that, assuming it makes some difference what kinds of activities students in secondary English classes engage in, the activity categories used in our analysis failed to describe some salient dimensions of activities. Examination of class-activity profiles and narrative class records for each of the 25 teachers showed great variation in the nature of tasks that fell into the whole-class instruction category, and compared to mathematics classes, the seatwork category as well. For example, all of the following English class activities were included in the whole-class instruction category: class recitation on grammar topics, teacher lecture on mythology, students reading a story or play aloud (with varying amounts of attention or guidance by the teacher), discussion of a story or play or poem, teacher reading a poem aloud to the class, students watching a film or listening to a record, teacher presentation on composition skills, dictionary drill, recitation over spelling or vocabulary lessons, and so on. Such variety in instructional approaches and content among classes makes unlikely a high degree of congruence between what was taught in many classes and what was included in the end-of-year achievement gains in the present analysis, as it did in earlier process-product study (Evertson, Anderson, & Brophy, 1978).

Summary and Implications

Despite the surface uniformity and apparent rigidity of secondary-school compared to elementary-school classrooms, comparison of classes on average amount of class time spent in whole-class instruction, seatwork, transitions, all nonacademic activity, testing, and other time-use categories shows differences in the way teachers use class time. For mathematics instruction, results of this study combined with previous research suggest some uniformity of instructional approaches and content focus within the activity categories used in this study. Compared to English classes, there is less variation in curriculum materials and greater consensus on curriculum goals and appropriate instructional techniques in mathematics. It is therefore possible to identify classroom-activity variables that contribute to mathematics learning. Results of the present analysis lend support to previous findings about the importance of content-development time and suggest that use of class time may be a significant dimension of effective mathematics teaching, apart from classroom management.

Differences between results for time use in mathematics and English classes in this study illustrate the importance of considering the subject-matter context in studying effective teaching in secondary schools. In English classes, there were less clear patterns of association among class time use, class achievement gains, and student behavior than in mathematics classes, and more variation in the content of instructional activities. Results for student behavior in English classes suggested better student behavior was associated with classes where more class time was spent in individual student work, not whole-class instruction; however, results were not consistent for the three different student-behavior variables. At any rate, the absence of any results for achievement in English classes provides us with no suggestions about effective time-use patterns, other than suggestions from qualitative data that highlight the importance of appropriate pacing, variety, and accountability.

Establishing links between classroom activities and learning outcomes in secondary English classes will require, first, better identification and measurement of learning goals and, second, analysis of classroom activities and academic tasks (including those done *outside* of class) in more detail than that produced by simple categorization of classroom activity format and academic/nonacademic focus. Doyle (Note 8) has suggested several dimensions that could prove productive in future studies: the relationship of classroom activities to academic task demands, the signal systems or action supports within lessons (see also Kounin & Doyle, 1975; Gump, Note 9), information-processing demands or other action requirements on students, organizational complexity, and pace of content coverage. Doyle's recommendations, and the results of this present analysis suggest the importance of considering classroom management variables, instructional variables, and curriculum variables simultaneously in research in secondary classrooms. One way to accommodate many of these recommendations would be to narrow the focus of studies to the teaching of specific topics or types of academic tasks within a curriculum area. A series of such studies focusing on teaching of different types of topics and learning goals might enable researchers to build up a knowledge base about instruction in secondary schools that goes beyond the generic skills that have been suggested by research to date.

Reference Notes

1. McDonald, F. J. *Research on teaching and its implications for policy making: Report on Phase II of the Beginning Teacher Evaluation Study*. Princeton, New Jersey: Educational Testing Service, 1975.

2. Stallings, J. S. *Allocated academic learning time revisited, or beyond time on task*. Paper presented at the annual meeting of the American Educational Research Association, Boston, April, 1980.

3. Rosenshine, B. V. *Academic engaged time, content covered, and direct instruction*. Paper presented at the annual meeting of the American Educational Research Association, New York, April, 1977.

4. Good, T. *Classroom research: What we know and what we need to know*. Austin: Research and Development Center for Teacher Education, The University of Texas at Austin, 1982.

5. Evertson, C., Emmer, E., & Clements, B. *Report of the methodology, rationale, and instrumentation of the Junior High Classroom Organization Study* (R&D Rep. No. 6100). Austin: Research and Development Center for Teacher Education, The University of Texas at Austin, 1980.

6. Emmer, E. *Effective classroom management in junior high school mathematics classrooms* (R&D Rep. No. 6111). Austin: Research and Development Center for Teacher Education, The University of Texas at Austin, 1981.

7. Good, T. L., Grouws, D. A., & Beckerman, T. M. *Curriculum pacing: Some empirical data in mathematics*. University of Missouri, Columbia.

8. Doyle, W. *How do teaching effects occur?* (R&D Rep. No. 4101). Austin: Research and Development Center for Teacher Education, The University of Texas at Austin.

9. Gump, P. V. *Classroom action structure and pupil on task behavior (a situational side of discipline)*. Paper presented at the annual meeting of the American Educational Research Association, Los Angeles, 1981.

References

BORG, W. R. Time and school learning. In C. Denham and A. Lieberman (Eds.), *Time to learn*. Washington, D.C.: National Institute of Education, 1980.

EVERTSON, C., ANDERSON, L., & BROPHY, J. *Texas Junior High School Study: Final report of process-outcome relationships* (R&D Rep. No. 4061). Austin: Research and Development Center for Teacher Education, The University of Texas at Austin, 1978. (ERIC Document Reproduction Service No. ED 173 744)

EVERTSON, C., EMMER, E., & BROPHY, J. Predictors of effective teaching in junior high school mathematics classrooms. *Journal of Research in Mathematics Education*, 1980, *11*(3), 167–178.

FREDERICK, C. W., & WALBERG, H. J. Learning as a function of time. *Journal of Educational Research*, 1980, *73*, 183–194.

KOUNIN, J., & DOYLE, W. Degree of continuity of a lesson's signal system and the task involvement of children. *Journal of Educational Psychology*, 1975, *67*(2), 159–164.

Critical Review

This is primarily a descriptive study using direct observation to determine how class time is used in junior high school classrooms. As is often the case with descriptive studies in education, some analysis of relationships has also been carried out. This tends to give us a deeper understanding of the descriptive findings. The study can thus be regarded as a combination of descriptive and correlational methodologies.

You will note that instead of formulating hypotheses, the authors have stated their two major concerns in the form of questions. Descriptive studies typically do not test hypotheses but instead state specific objectives or raise questions that the research will attempt to answer. These focus the attention of the reviewer on the goals of the project and should be kept in mind as you read the article.

METHODS

The authors have omitted much information about the sample and measures that would have helped in reviewing this study, probably because of space limitations. Information comparing the participating teachers to national teacher samples on such variables as sex, years of experience, college training, and other variables would have been helpful. Such information helps readers judge whether the participating teachers were reasonably representative of the target population and also permits them to judge whether the sample is comparable to junior high school mathematics and English teachers in their own schools. Data on possible sampling biases, that is, systematic differences between the participating teachers and other teachers in the population would also help the reader draw conclusions on the degree to which the findings could be generalized to other teacher groups. For example, if the teachers in the study had been selected by their principals, they might not be comparable to a group selected because of their willingness to volunteer or to a group selected at random. Since all teachers were drawn from a single large city, other sampling biases might be due to such variables as the district hiring practices and state certification requirements. These could have resulted in these teachers being considerably different from those found in other districts or other states.

Although the absence of data describing the teacher sample makes generalization of the results more difficult, these results can still provide valuable insights for teachers and administrators. In all likelihood groups of math and English teachers in U.S. public junior high schools have a great deal in common such as similarities in their educational background, interests, and values regardless of where they teach.

MEASURES

Obviously, in an observational study, the reliability of the observational data is very important to your appraisal of the study. You will recall from Chapter 6 that several questions about the observation process should be considered in evaluating observational research. This study addresses most of these questions. For example, most of the observational variables, such as the classification of student behavior and the categories of class activities, were "low inference" and involved counting and measures of time rather than qualitative ratings. Similarly, the amount of observation, eight to nine hours per class, would appear to be adequate for the kind of data being collected.

On the other hand it would have been desirable for the researchers to have provided information on the procedures used to train observers. This omission, when coupled with the absence of data on interobserver reliability, makes it difficult for the reviewer to estimate the quality of the observational data. It seems likely that the data were reliable, since otherwise the correlations between observational data obtained in different classes taught by the same teacher would have been much lower than reported.

The authors also failed to provide sufficient information on the achievement and attitude measures used in the study. Although information about widely used standardized achievement tests such as the CAT is not essential, more information on the end-of-year achievement measures and the student ratings would have helped greatly in interpreting the results of this important study.

RESULTS

The results and discussion sections of this article are clear and complete, suggesting that the authors may have cut their methods section to the minimum in order to devote more space to the results. The study gives us a clear picture in Tables 1 and 3 of how class time was used in these mathematics and English classrooms. Appropriate and easy-to-understand statistical tools were used. However, readers would have gained some additional insights from the correlational data if multiple regression analyses had been conducted. These would have revealed the combined influence of the different classroom activities upon student achievement and behavior.

All teachers could profit from a thoughtful study of the data given in this study. Table 2 and the ranges given in Tables 1 and 3, for example, show the great variability in use of class time from teacher to teacher that has also emerged in previous research. Consider also that some math teachers devoted less than 32 minutes of the 55-minute period to academic work. Others (or perhaps the same ones) spent nearly 20 percent of the class period in transitions (that is, moving from one topic to another). Contrast Teachers A and B in Table 2 and decide how you would explain the large achievement differences. What do these differences suggest to you about effective math teaching?

Note that total academic time on average was only 72 percent of available class time for the math classes and 73 percent for the English classes. This also agrees generally with earlier research. Does this mean that the average teacher is wasting nearly 30 percent of the class time? What would be the optimum time to devote to academics in a 55-minute period? Could teachers be trained to increase the amount of academic time in a typical class period? One recent study suggests that in-service teacher training can bring about significant increases in the time students devote to their schoolwork, as well as reduce nonacademic time and disruptive pupil behavior (Borg & Ascione, 1982).

Relationships that emerged from the correlational part of this study, especially in mathematics, also merit close attention by teachers. Clearly the way teachers use class time is significantly related to both achievement and student behavior.

The differences between the correlational results in math and English support a finding that has emerged from other recent studies, namely that there is no single best way to teach. Different subjects and different student levels call for different methods. Thus, the task of being an effective teacher is much more complex and will require much more study than many researchers had previously thought. This study also shows that subjects such as English involve a great variety of different learning activities as compared to more structured subjects such as mathematics. Therefore, finding the teaching variables that relate to better student achievement and behavior in subjects like English is likely to be more difficult.

One possible reason for the less clear-cut findings in English may have been that eight hours of observation per class is not a large enough sample of teacher behavior in subjects in which teachers use such a large variety of activities. Remember that although achievement data were based on nearly an entire school year, data on classroom activities and student behavior were based on only 8 class periods of observation for each class, or 16 per teacher. Since at junior high school level classes meet for about 180 periods during a school year, the researchers were correlating class activity data from about 4.5 percent of the class periods with the achievement gains students made during all 180 of the class periods. Student behavior data were also based upon 8 periods or about 4.5 percent of the total school year.

Since Sanford and Evertson have done an excellent job of reporting and interpreting their findings, there is no need for further discussion in this review. It should be pointed out that this study provides not only useful information about math and English teaching, but it also raises many interesting questions that are well worth some careful thought.

Causal-Comparative Research

In many research projects the investigator would like to examine the possible effects of variables that are difficult or impossible to manipulate experimentally. For example, let us suppose that a researcher wanted to study the effects of damage in a certain region of the brain on the problem-solving performance of young adults. An experimental study, which could be carried out with lower animals such as rats, would involve first selecting a sample of rats and measuring their problem-solving performance in activities such as running mazes. The next step would require that the rats be randomly divided into two groups. An operation could then be performed on the brains of one group of rats in order to destroy tissue in the region of the brain under investigation. Then the investigator could compare the two groups of rats on changes in their problem-solving performance. The difficulty with studies of this type is that one must be very careful in generalizing results obtained from studies of rats to human populations.

For ethical reasons an experimental study obviously cannot be carried out on human subjects, since it would involve inflicting brain damage. However, *causal-comparative research* procedures can be used to study this kind of problem in human subjects. To carry out a causal-comparative study, the investigator would first search hospital records for human adults who had been involved in accidents that resulted in destruction of brain tissue in the region under study. Having located a sample of such individuals, the investigator would then obtain a comparable sample of adults who had not suffered brain damage. The comparability of these two samples could be established by variables such as intelligence or achievement test scores obtained on the participating individuals before the accidents occurred. At this point the researcher would have two samples of young adults who were comparable before accidents had occurred to the brain-damaged groups. The investigator could then administer problem-solving measures to both groups in order to identify possible effects of the brain damage. In reviewing causal comparative studies you should evaluate carefully the comparability of the two groups. Closely comparable groups (except on the variable being studied) are essential to effective use of this method. If the groups are not closely comparable, the results can be the result of group differences rather than to the variable being studied. For example, some causal comparative studies of smokers and nonsmokers selected their nonsmokers from rural areas while selecting the smokers from large cities. In this case, the findings, such as higher lung cancer rates, could be due to smoking but could also be due to the higher level of air pollution found in large cities.

Examples of other problems amenable to causal-comparative research are: (1) a study of the personality characteristics of delinquent and nondelinquent adolescent boys; (2) a study of the physical development of bottle-fed versus breast-fed infants; (3) a comparison of the overt aggressive behavior of adolescent boys who view less than one hour of television per day with those who view more than four hours per day; or (4) a comparison of the academic performance of sixth-grade students who have had nutritionally deficient diets with similar students who have had nutritionally adequate diets over the previous three years.

You will note that in all these examples the causal-comparative type of research permits us to study the possible effects of variables that are difficult or impossible to manipulate experimentally with human subjects. The causal-comparative method is valuable in identifying *possible* causes or effects, but results of such studies cannot provide incontrovertible evidence that one of the variables studied actually caused the other.

Considering one of the examples listed above, if we found that delinquent boys had much higher levels of aggression than comparable nondelinquent boys, it could be that the level of aggression caused the delinquency. It is also possible, however, that participation in delinquent behavior caused the higher level of aggression. Finally, it is possible that some third variable such as a highly frustrating or unstable home environment caused both the delinquent behavior and the aggression. As you can see from this example, although causal-comparative research can identify *possible* causes, it is necessary to carry out experimental research in order to establish conclusive evidence of cause-and-effect relationship. Therefore, the two types of research frequently go hand in hand. Causal-comparative studies use human subjects in identifying possible causes, and these are then checked out with experimental studies that may use higher animals for subjects if human subjects cannot be employed.

There are, however, conditions under which the evidence from causal-comparative research can produce cause-and-effect findings that can be accepted with nearly the same level of confidence as experimental findings. These are:

1. When the sequence of events is such that although Variable A could cause Variable B, it is impossible for Variable B to have caused Variable A. For example, in the aforementioned studies of cigarette smoking, since the smoking occurs *before* the lung cancer, it is impossible that lung cancer could cause smoking. Thus, we can conclude that *if a causal relationship exists,* it can only occur in one direction.

2. When many causal-comparative studies have been conducted by different researchers working with different samples in different settings and when consistent results emerge from these studies. Again, this is the case with causal comparative research on smoking and lung cancer. When the combined evidence from these studies is considered, the probability that these results could occur if smoking does not cause lung cancer is so slight that most scientists who have worked in the area have accepted the combined results as tantamount to conclusive proof.

Let us now review a causal comparative study. This research is especially interesting because it deals with teacher burnout, a phenomenon that has become increasingly important in recent years and one that concerns most people in education.

Sample Causal-Comparative Study: "BURNOUT IN TEACHERS OF RETARDED AND NONRETARDED CHILDREN"

Abstract[3]

A three-part self-report questionnaire, which incorporated portions of the Maslach Burnout Inventory, was used to assess the degree of burnout among 111 instructors of moderately retarded children, 133 teachers of mildly retarded students and 218 regular educators. Contrary to expectations, teachers of nonretarded students reported significantly fewer and weaker feelings of success and competence accompanied by more frequent and stronger impersonal attitudes toward their students. Demographic variables were found to be significant but weak predictors of teacher burnout. The teachers also reported a low incidence of chronic or serious health problems. Comparisons were presented between regular and special educators in addition to suggestions for stress reduction.

---

3. The abstract from the article is reprinted here in order to provide a context in which the researcher's comments can be related.

The Researcher's Comments[4]

Background

The study described herein is based on a thesis conducted by the first author for her Master of Education degree at Bowling Green State University. Her project was supervised by the second author.

The topic that Mrs. Beck selected reflected an area of interest in the educational community that had just begun to attract the attention of researchers. A plethora of investigations and articles on occupational stress and teacher burnout began to emerge in the mid to late 1970s and early 1980s although job stress in teachers can trace its roots to surveys conducted in the early 1930s. Despite this, the educational literature at the time this study was proposed (fall 1980) revealed few investigations addressing stress encountered by teachers of atypical children. In fact, there were no reported research studies comparing or contrasting special and regular educators' perception of teacher stress.

The focus on teachers of mentally retarded children mirrored the teaching experiences of both of the investigators. During our work as public school teachers we saw many of our colleagues leave the special education classroom; some even deserted the profession. Indeed, the first author initially left the classroom experiencing the typical feelings of the teacher burnout syndrome identified by various researchers. It appeared to us that the characteristic complaints related to teacher stress and burnout, such as a lack of perceived success, performance of custodial tasks, and excessive paperwork, were more pronounced among teachers who instructed children of low intellectual ability. Hence, we sought to determine if teachers of mentally retarded children perceived a greater degree of job stress than did teachers of nonretarded youngsters. Three questions were specifically investigated:

1. Is there a significant difference in the degree of burnout among teachers of mildly retarded, moderately retarded, and nonretarded children?
2. Will the degree of burnout significantly increase as the student's level of intellectual ability decreases?
3. Can demographic variables be employed as predictors of teacher burnout?

Experiences

Most student-generated research is conducted on a shoe-string budget, and the present project was no exception. Approximately $1000 in expenses was incurred by the first author for such items as printing, postage, typing, and the like. The absence of financial support, even if it's minimal, can impact on how a study is conducted. For example, we would have preferred a larger return, but extensive follow-up mailings are expensive both in terms of postage and the use of commercially printed questionnaires. Consideration was also given to including a quarter or half dollar with the questionnaire, so that teachers could enjoy a soft drink or a cup of coffee while they completed the survey instrument. Such a strategy has been shown to increase response rate. Yet, with an initial sample of approximately 1000 teachers, the cost was prohibitive. On a more positive note, we were

---

4. This commentary was written by Professor Richard Gargiulo.

very fortunate in having free access to university computers, which greatly lessened out-of-pocket expenses.

Teachers are overwhelmed by paperwork, and questionnaires from ivory-tower individuals are usually not received with enthusiasm. Great care was taken, therefore, when constructing the cover letter to explain the purpose of the study, how individual responses would be used, and the guarantee of anonymity. Furthermore, the questionnaire was piloted on several occasions to ascertain how long it would take for the average respondent to complete (15 minutes). This information was also shared in the cover letter.

Aftermath

This study generated a significant number of national and international requests from fellow researchers and students for reprints and/or additional information. In many instances, the study was to be replicated using a different sample of special educators (such as teachers of learning disabled, gifted children) or for assessing burnout in teachers who lived and taught in large metropolitan areas. Results of this investigation were also shared with Christina Maslach of the University of California at Berkeley, who with Susan Jackson developed the Maslach Burnout Inventory.

Mrs. Beck uses information gained from the study regularly in her present position as a teacher supervisor. This study will also serve as the foundation for the first author's dissertation research. Additionally, the study has expanded her interest in stress to include that experienced by special education students as well as the application of stress-control techniques and relaxation strategies to pain control.

Implications in Future Directions

Several suggestions for practice and questions for future researchers were generated by our work. Although significant differences were observed among the respondents, all teachers could benefit from the implementation of stress-reduction techniques, particularly peer support groups. Administrators, for instance, may wish to develop a "buddy system" wherein experienced teachers are assigned to first- and second-year teachers in an attempt to help them "learn the ropes" and the subtleties of their jobs. Teachers-in-training should also be informed of the various types of stressors they are likely to encounter in their daily classroom routines.

The present study represents one of the early attempts to compare regular and special educators' perceptions of job stress, and thus raises a few questions.

1. Would similar findings occur when assessing teachers who work with children with other types of exceptionalities, such as hearing impairment or emotional disturbance?
2. Although the sample of elementary and secondary educators was approximately equivalent (48.5 percent versus 51.5 percent), do teachers at these grade levels experience burnout differently?
3. What effect do differences and similarities between the home and work environments have on the manifestation of teacher burnout?
4. Which types of strategies and interventions are most effective for reducing stress and thus avoiding teacher burnout?
5. Which job stressors are most likely to exacerbate teacher burnout?

Continued research into teacher stress and burnout is necessary as the profession moves toward change and the predicted teacher shortage. Such investigations offer implications in the discussion of such concepts as merit pay and career ladders.

The topic of stress in the classroom and teacher burnout could easily serve as the foundation for a lifetime of fruitful research endeavors and may be one of the few areas of educational research that directly impacts on the teacher and subsequently the individual learner.

BURNOUT IN TEACHERS OF RETARDED AND NONRETARDED CHILDREN

Cynthia L. Beck
BOWLING GREEN STATE UNIVERSITY

Richard M. Gargiulo
UNIVERSITY OF ALABAMA, BIRMINGHAM

Job stress has been researched in a variety of career situations (Collins, 1977; Mattingly, 1977; Pines & Kafry, 1978), including education (Dunham, 1976). Kyriacou and Sutcliffe (1978) defined teacher stress as a negative response (e.g., anger) accompanied by potential pathogenic physiological changes. Teacher stress has been attributed to the routine of the school day and the amount of time spent in noninstructional activities (Lieberman & Miller, 1978), the size of the school (Hinton, 1974), low salaries (Rudd & Wiseman, 1962), discipline problems (Lowenstein, 1975), and mixed ability grouping (Kelly, 1974). Continual exposure to stressful situations seriously depletes the teacher's emotional and physical resources, thus leaving the individual unable to cope successfully with further stress.

When frustration, tension, or anxiety persist or increase, stress develops into a syndrome labeled "burnout" (Freudenberger, 1975). Burnout has been described as physical and emotional exhaustion resulting from excessive demands on en-

Beck, Cynthia L., and Gargiulo, Richard M., "Burnout in Teachers of Retarded and Nonretarded Children." *Journal of Educational Research*, 1983, pp. 169–173. Copyright 1983, Heldref Publications, Washington, D.C. Reprinted by permission.

ergy, strength, or resources (Freudenberger, 1977) and "as a painful and personally destructive response to excessive stress" (Mattingly, 1977, p. 127).

Researchers have identified several factors that contribute to the burnout syndrome. Of importance to teachers, particularly special educators, are performance of custodial and managerial tasks (Mattingly, 1977), excessive amounts of direct contact with children (Maslach & Pines, 1977), a perceived lack of job success (Proctor, 1979), program structure, and work overload (Weiskopf, 1980). Youngs (1978) further speculated that a lack of opportunity for interpersonal relationships with adults and other teachers may contribute to teacher burnout. It would appear, therefore, that special educators teach in environments that make them highly susceptible to burnout (DeShong, 1981; Weiskopf, 1980).

Furthermore, recent state and federal mandates (Public Law 94-142) have placed additional time-consuming responsibilities on special education teachers (e.g., IEP conferences, annual reviews), and they have contributed to the possibility of role ambiguity and conflict with other educators (Anderson, 1976). Likewise, with the influx of exceptional students into regular classrooms, teachers of nonhandicapped children often incur new and additional duties for which they either have limited or no formal training. In an attempt to provide the required services to special children, work overload is nearly inevitable (Weiskopf, 1980).

Additionally, teachers educating handicapped children in settings other than the public schools often perform many custodial tasks. Due to the students' lower abilities, these teachers also experience minimal and infrequent pupil progress. These circumstances could easily generate stress and eventual burnout.

Burnout, however, affects not only the teacher but ultimately the student. Teachers under stress are concerned with survival and these concerns take precedence over instructional activities (Fuller, 1969; Weiskopf, 1980). Burned out teachers contribute little to the students' academic growth and many pupils may suffer a lower self-esteem as a result of the teacher's hypercritical and uncaring behavior (Partin & Gargiulo, 1980).

Although teacher burnout has been extensively researched, there are apparently no reported investigations comparing regular and special educators' perceptions of teacher stress. For purposes of this investigation, special educators were defined as teachers of mildly (educable) and moderately (trainable) retarded children. Thus, the intent of this study was to determine whether there was a significant difference in self-perceived stress among teachers of mildly retarded, moderately retarded, and nonretarded children. It was hypothesized that the degree of teacher burnout would significantly increase as the students' level of intellectual functioning decreased.

Method

Nine hundred ninety-seven full-time educators from 16 rural northern Ohio counties constituted the original subject pool. This group comprised teachers of moderately retarded (IQ = 36–51), mildly retarded (IQ = 52–67), and nonretarded children. All teacher assignments were identified from professional staff directories. Due to the small number of instructors of moderately retarded children in each county, the total population of these teachers was included in this investi-

gation (N = 184). A sample equivalent to 50% of the total number of teachers of mildly retarded students in each of the 16 counties surveyed were selected by means of a table of random numbers (N = 279). Educators of nonretarded children composed the third group of respondents. These teachers were also randomly selected using a table of random numbers. However, due to cost limitations, only 7% of the population of teachers of nonretarded children from each county were assessed (N = 534). Teachers of remedial reading, home economics, physical education, etc. were not included in the study. This selection process resulted in 184 instructors of moderately retarded children, 279 teachers of mildly retarded students and 534 regular educators, for a total of 997 teachers.

Instrument

To assess teacher burnout, a three-part self-report questionnaire was constructed. Part I contained eight questions covering respondents' demographic characteristics and occupational responsibilities; i.e., the teachers were asked to estimate the percentage of time devoted to instructional activities, professional development, noninstructional tasks, and contact with parents and other staff.

The second part of the survey incorporated 25 statements from the Maslach Burnout Inventory (Maslach, 1981), which has been used to investigate burnout in a variety of situations with different professional populations (Maslach, 1976; Maslach & Jackson, 1981). The MBI statements, which describe feelings or attitudes, were designed to measure two variables, the extent of burnout symptoms and the attitudes of human service professionals toward their clients. Each statement was rated by the teachers on two dimensions, frequency and intensity. A two-dimensional rating system was employed in an effort to allow the respondents an opportunity to provide differentiated responses. The frequency scale for each of the 25 items was labeled at each point ranging from 1 ("a few times a year or less") to 6 ("every day"). The intensity scale ranged from 1 ("very mild, barely noticeable") to 7 ("major, very strong''). The teachers were instructed to circle the number that best described themselves or, if the feeling described in the statement was absent, to mark a box labeled ''never.''

The 25 statements were further divided into three regular subscales, Emotional Exhaustion, Depersonalization, and Personal Accomplishment, and one optional subscale, Personal Involvement. The Emotional Exhaustion subscale consisted of nine items that described feelings of being overextended and exhausted by one's work. The Depersonalization subscale incorporated five items describing impersonal attitudes and responses toward one's students. The eight components of the Personal Accomplishment subscale described feelings of competence and success in one's work. The optional Personal Involvement subscale consisted of three items that assessed the teachers' empathic involvement with their students.

The Maslach Burnout Inventory manifested an internal consistency of .76 (frequency) and .81 (intensity) based on Cronbach's coefficient alpha. Internal consistency reliability coefficients for the subscales were .89 (frequency) and .87 (intensity) for Emotional Exhaustion, .76 (frequency) and .75 (intensity) for Depersonalization, and .77 (frequency) and .76 (intensity) for Personal Accomplishment. Split-half reliability for the MBI has been reported as .74 and .81 on the frequency and intensity dimensions respectively.

Concurrent validity was determined in the following manner: first, by correlating subscale scores with independent behaviorial ratings completed by subjects' spouses and coworkers, and second, by correlating subscale scores with scores on the Job Diagnostic Survey (Hackman & Oldham, 1975). Significant correlations for each of these methods ranged from .20 to .48 on the Emotional Exhaustion subscale, from .32 to .57 for the Depersonalization measure, and from .25 to .27 on the Personal Accomplishment subscale. Reliability and validity data were not provided for the optional Personal Involvement subscale. For more detailed reliability and validity information see Maslach and Jackson (1981).

Part III of the survey assessed the incidence of 10 stress-related physical symptoms. Respondents were instructed to rate the symptoms according to a five-point Likert-type scale: 1) never a problem, 2) seldom a problem, 3) sometimes a problem, 4) often a problem, and 5) a continual problem. The symptoms were: high blood pressure, heart disease, tension or migraine headaches, ulcers, sleeplessness, colitis, grinding teeth, excessive fatigue, appetite loss, and irritability.

Procedure

Surveys were individually mailed to each of the 997 teachers at their respective schools. Each survey contained a letter of explanation and a return envelope coded to identify the respondent's county of employment. A second mailing was conducted and only responses received within three weeks of the second mailing were included. A total of 462 appropriately completed questionnaires were obtained (46.3%); teachers of moderately retarded students returned 111 questionnaires (60.3%), 133 surveys were received from teachers of mildly retarded individuals (47.7%), and 218 teachers of nonretarded children reported their perceptions of teacher burnout (40.8%). Table 1 presents demographic information for all 462 respondents.

Scoring was accomplished by visual inspection of the teachers' responses. The total raw scores for each teacher on both the frequency and intensity dimensions of the four subscales were used to generate group means. High scores on the Emotional Exhaustion, Depersonalization, and Personal Involvement subscales reflected high degrees of burnout. However, since low scores on the frequency and intensity dimensions of the Personal Accomplishment subscale corresponded with a high degree of burnout, raw scores on both dimensions were inverted. This scoring procedure allowed all four subscales to be interpreted in the same manner, i.e., high scores were indicative of a high degree of burnout and conversely, low scores reflected a lower degree of burnout.

Results

To assess whether significant differences existed among the three groups of teachers on the Maslach Burnout Inventory, a one-way multivari-

Table 1.   Respondent demographic data

	N	%
Sex		
Male	144	31.2
Female	318	68.8
Age		
20–24	41	8.9
25–29	121	26.2
30–39	179	38.1
40–49	59	12.8
50 and over	65	14.1
Marital status		
Married	321	69.5
Unmarried	141	30.5
Level of education		
Bachelor's degree	166	35.9
Bachelor's degree + 15 hours	186	40.3
Master's degree	70	15.2
Master's degree + 15 hours	36	7.8
Specialist degree	4	.9
Years of teaching experience		
0–2	52	11.3
3–5	95	20.6
6–8	94	20.3
9–11	73	15.8
12 or more	148	32.0
Grade level assignment		
Preschool-Grade 6	224	48.5
Grades 7–12	238	51.5

ate analysis of variance was conducted (Barr, Goodnight, Sall, & Helwig, 1979). This procedure indicated that significant differences were evident, $F(16,902) = 3.38$, $p < .0001$. Follow-up univariate analyses revealed significant differences on both the frequency and intensity dimensions of the Depersonalization subscale—$F(2,459) = 8.99$, $p < .0001$, and $F(2,459) = 12.54$, $p < .0001$, respectively. Likewise, significant differences were also observed on both levels of the Personal Accomplishment subscale—$F(2,459) = 7.48$, $p < .0006$, and $F(2,459) = 3.42$, $p < .03$, respectively. Significant differences however, were absent on the Emotional Exhaustion and Personal Involvement subscales. Table 2 presents the means and standard deviations for each group of respondents on both the frequency and intensity dimensions of the four MBI subscales.

Post-hoc analyses using a Scheffé procedure (Nie, Hull, Jenkins, Steinbrenner, & Bert, 1975), $p < .05$, indicated that on both the frequency and intensity dimensions of the Depersonalization subscale, teachers of moderately retarded children scored significantly lower than the other two groups of educators. This finding suggested that these teachers experienced both fewer and weaker impersonal attitudes toward their stu-

Table 2.   Mean scores on the Maslach Burnout Inventory for teachers of retarded and nonretarded children

	Teachers		
Subscales	Mildly retarded	Moderately retarded	Nonretarded
Emotional exhaustion			
Frequency	22.39 (10.36)	22.85 (9.47)	23.06 (10.30)
Intensity	30.36 (12.34)	31.42 (11.85)	31.07 (12.11)
Depersonalization			
Frequency	7.34 (5.99)	5.32 (4.68)	8.07 (5.72)
Intensity	9.92 (7.75)	6.76 (5.84)	10.89 (7.33)
Personal accomplishment			
Frequency	18.57 (6.35)	18.13 (5.33)	20.58 (6.50)
Intensity	23.93 (7.13)	23.05 (6.48)	25.06 (6.73)
Personal involvement			
Frequency	8.65 (3.31)	8.53 (3.21)	8.89 (3.22)
Intensity	10.74 (3.54)	10.04 (4.01)	10.44 (3.33)

Note: Standard deviations are given in parentheses. N per group equals 133 mentally retarded, 111 moderately retarded, and 218 teachers of nonretarded children.

dents. Teachers of moderately retarded individuals also scored significantly lower than teachers of nonretarded children on both levels of the Personal Accomplishment subscale. This evidence demonstrated that instructors of moderately retarded children reported more frequent and stronger feelings of success and competence. Likewise, in comparison to teachers of nonretarded pupils, educators of mildly retarded learners scored significantly lower on the frequency dimension of the Personal Accomplishment subscale, thus implying that these special educators also experienced more frequent feelings of success.

An additional analysis was performed to determine if the demographic variables identified in Part I of the questionnaire contributed to the prediction of teacher burnout. The results of a stepwise multiple regression procedure (Nie et al., 1975) indicated that the predictor variables of age, sex, marital status, degree level, years of teaching experience, and grade level (e.g., primary) were significantly related to the MBI subscale scores. The magnitude of these correlations however, was weak and in no instance accounted for more than 11% of the variance.

The teachers reported a low incidence of chronic or serious health problems (e.g., high blood pressure) on Part III of the questionnaire. The most frequently mentioned physical symptoms with a rank of three or higher were sleeplessness ($N = 166$, 35.9%), headaches ($N = 217$, 47%), fatigue ($N = 220$, 47.6%) and constant irritability ($N = 225$, 48.7%). Other stress-related symptoms were reported by approximately 11% ($N = 49$) of the respondents. These included muscle spasms, nervousness, gastro-intestinal disorders, backaches, excessive drinking, overeating, frequent colds, fingernail biting, and facial tics.

Last, almost 72% ($N = 331$) of the teachers reported spending at least 50% of their time occupied with instructional activities, whereas nearly 22% ($N = 102$) reported that at least 20% of their time was devoted to noninstructional tasks such as writing individualized education plans, completing school forms, and grading papers. Slightly more than 75% of the respondents ($N = 348$) reported spending 5% or less of their working time in professional development activities, while

83.5% ($N = 386$) of the teachers devoted less than 10% of their time to contacts with parents and colleagues.

Discussion

The results of this investigation indicated significant differences in the degree of burnout experienced by the three groups of teachers. These differences were observed across both the frequency and intensity dimensions of the Depersonalization and Personal Accomplishment subscales. Contrary to expectations, in each of these instances teachers of mentally retarded students score significantly lower, suggesting that special educators experienced not only fewer but weaker symptoms of burnout.

One possible explanation for this observation is differences in personality typologies between the two groups of teachers. Lofquist and Dawis (1969) speculated that stress is dependent not only on environmental stressors but the reaction of the individual to stress. Thus, while a variety of stressful situations exist in a teaching environment these sources cannot be viewed in isolation but only in relation to the teacher's capabilities, personality, and perceptions. The absence of any indicative relationship between the demographic characteristics and burnout scores would seem to suggest the presence of another, perhaps intrinsic variable, not identified in this investigation. One could speculate that, as a group, special educators may be less susceptible to the effects of stress due to common personality traits that originally attracted them to a career in special education. Holland's (1972) occupational classification of regular and special educators would seem to support this position.

The results could also be attributed to a cultural attitude that imparts superhuman qualities and abilities to teachers of the mentally retarded (DeShong, 1981). DeShong speculated that special education teachers may accept this cultural view and experience guilt if this expectation is not upheld. Thus, the special educators may have responded in a socially acceptable albeit less than candid manner.

Differences in burnout between regular and special education teachers could further be due to the number of pupils for which a teacher is responsible. State-mandated enrollment ceilings restrict the number of students in special education classrooms while regular educators have historically served larger numbers of children. In addition, the use of paraprofessional aides in special education classrooms further reduces the teacher-pupil ratio. Therefore, the variety of stressors may be reduced as a result of fewer students even though special educators are confronted with more frequent stressful situations due to the inherent characteristics of their teaching environment (Weiskopf, 1980).

Stress is apparently an unavoidable consequence of the teaching profession. Hence, there have been numerous attempts to inform educators of ways to reduce stress and avoid burnout. Various authors have suggested participation in physical exercise (DeShong, 1981), recreational activities and hobbies (Miller, 1979), or meditation (Gray, 1979). The most frequently suggested method for reducing stress however, is the development of peer support groups whereby individuals meet regularly to encourage each other and identify alternative solutions to professional problems (Collins, 1977; Kahn, 1978; Miller, 1979; Weiskopf, 1980). Yet, Lieberman and Miller (1978), among others, lamented the absence of these requisite support systems and further described the working environment of teachers as isolated from peer support. It would appear therefore, that the public schools and their administrative staffs have a responsibility to encourage and assist in the formation of support groups.

The teachers who participated in this investigation were selected from rural environments and represented only one area of exceptionality. Future studies should address these limitations with an additional focus on whether teacher burnout is related to specific personality characteristics.

References

ANDERSON, R. Role and the teacher of educable mentally retarded elementary children. *Journal of Special Education,* 1976, *10,* 383–391.

BARR, A., GOODNIGHT, J., SALL, J., & HELWIG, J. *Statistical analysis system.* Raleigh, N.C.: SAS Institute, 1979, pp. 245–263.

COLLINS, G. Burn-out: The hazard of professional people-helpers. *Christianity Today,* 1977, *21,* 12–14.

DESHONG, B. *The special educator: Stress and survival.* Rockville, Md.: Aspen Systems Corporation, 1981.

DUNHAM, J. Stress situations and responses. In T. Casey (Ed.), *Stress in schools.* Hemel Hempstead, England: National Association of Schoolmasters, 1976.

FREUDENBERGER, H. The staff-burnout syndrome in alternative institutions. *Psychotherapy: Theory, Research and Practice,* 1975, *12,* 73–83.

FREUDENBERGER, H. Burn-out: Occupational hazard of the child care worker. *Child Care Quarterly,* 1977, *6,* 90–99.

FULLER, F. Concerns of teachers: A developmental conceptualization. *American Educational Research Journal,* 1969, *6,* 207–226.

GRAY, L. Slow down: You move too fast. *Teacher,* 1979, *96,* 52–53.

HACKMAN, J., & OLDHAM, G. Development of the job diagnostic survey. *Journal of Applied Psychology,* 1975, *60,* 159–170.

HINTON, M. Teaching in large schools. *Headmasters' Association Review,* 1974, *72,* 122–128.

HOLLAND, J. *The self-directed search, A guide to educational and vocational planning.* Palo Alto: Consulting Psychologists Press, 1972.

KAHN, R. Job burnout: Prevention and remedies. *Public Welfare,* 1978, *36,* 60–63.

KELLY, A. *Teaching mixed ability classes.* London: Harper & Row, 1974.

KYRIACOU, C., & SUTCLIFFE, J. Teacher stress: Prevalence, sources, and symptoms. *British Journal of Educational Psychology,* 1978, *48,* 159–167.

LIEBERMAN, A., & MILLER, L. The social realities of teaching. *Teachers College Record,* 1978, *80,* 54–68.

LOFQUIST, L., & DAWIS, R. *Adjustment of work.* New York: Appleton-Century-Crofts, 1969.

LOWENSTEIN, L. *Violent and disruptive behavior in schools.* Hemel Hempstead, England: National Association of Schoolmasters, 1975.

MASLACH, C. Burned-out. *Human Behavior,* 1976, *5,* 16–22.

MASLACH, C. *Maslach burnout inventory.* Palo Alto: Consulting Psychologists Press, 1981.

MASLACH, C., & JACKSON, S. The measurement of experienced burnout. *Journal of Occupational Behavior*, 1981, *2*, 99–113.

MASLACH, C., & PINES, A. The burn-out syndrome in the day care setting. *Child Care Quarterly*, 1977, *6*, 100–113.

MATTINGLY, M. Sources of stress and burn-out in professional child care work. *Child Care Quarterly*, 1977, *6*, 127–137.

MILLER, W. *Dealing with stress: A challenge for educators*. Bloomington, Ind.: Phi Delta Kappa Educational Foundation, 1979.

NIE, N., HULL, H., JENKINS, J., STEINBRENNER, K., & BERT, D. *Statistical package for the social sciences* (2nd ed.). New York: McGraw-Hill, 1975.

PARTIN, R., & GARGIULO, R. Burned out teachers have no class! Prescriptions for teacher educators. *College Student Journal*, 1980, *14*, 365–368.

PINES, A., & KAFRY, D. Occupational tedium in the social services. *Social Work*, 1978, *28*, 499–507.

PROCTOR, R. How to survive in today's stressful jobs. *Parade Magazine*, June 17, 1979, pp. 4–5.

RUDD, W., & WISEMAN, S. Sources of dissatisfaction among a group of teachers. *British Journal of Educational Psychology*, 1962, *32*, 275–291.

WEISKOPF, P. Burnout among teachers of exceptional children. *Exceptional Children*, 1980, *47*, 18–23.

YOUNGS, B. Anxiety and stress—How they affect teachers, teaching. *NASSP Bulletin*, 1978, *62*, 78–83.

Critical Review

This article provides an excellent example of the use of the questionnaire in survey research. However, since the responses of three types of teachers are compared, this study also illustrates the causal-comparative research method. The key feature of the study that makes it a causal-comparative design is the selection of teachers who are already teaching either moderately retarded, mildly retarded, or nonretarded children. In order to be an experimental study, it would have been necessary to start with beginning teachers and randomly assign them to teaching one of the three types of children and then wait until burnout symptoms began to show up before measuring the amount of teacher burnout. You can see that this experimental study simply could not be carried out, since (1) the teachers would not agree to being randomly assigned, (2) teachers of retarded children receive different training than teachers of nonretarded children, and (3) the researcher would probably have to wait several years for any significant amount of burnout to occur. Thus, this study illustrates one of the main advantages of causal-comparative design, namely that this design can be used in many studies where experimental research is impossible for practical or ethical reasons.

You should note that the researchers used a directional hypothesis in this study. Although they provide some rationale for this, they found no previous research to support a directional hypothesis. Under these circumstances it would have been better to have stated their hypothesis in null form.[5]

SAMPLE

You may recall that most researchers select their sample from an accessible population. In this study the accessible population consisted of all teachers from 16 rural northern Ohio counties. All teachers of moderately retarded children were selected.

---

5. You may want to review the discussion of null and directional hypotheses in Chapter 5 if you do not understand how they differ.

Random samples of the other two groups were selected. This is an excellent sampling procedure, since it produced large groups of teachers who can be expected to be highly representative of the accessible population.

However, the target population, which is the population to which we would want to generalize the research results, would probably be all teachers of moderately retarded, mildly retarded, and nonretarded children in U.S. schools. It is therefore desirable for the researchers to give us information about the characteristics of the teachers in their sample so that we can use this information to estimate how well their results might apply to other teacher groups or to the teacher population as a whole. This information was gathered in the eight questions asked in the first part of the survey and is reported in Table 1 for teachers who responded. If you were interested in the relevance of the research to your school district, you could use Table 1 to compare your teachers with the teachers who participated in the research. The more information researchers give about the characteristics of their sample, the easier it is for the reader to determine how similar the sample is to local groups with which the reader is involved. In this study it would have been useful if the authors had told us more about the 16 rural counties from which the sample was drawn.

MEASURES

The authors provide an excellent description of their principal measure, the Maslach Burnout Inventory. Both validity and reliability data are reported. It is noteworthy that reliability and validity data are given not only for the entire inventory but for the subscales as well. An error made by many researchers is to provide these data only for the entire measure even though they use subscale scores in their analysis.

The authors, however, should have provided more information on the 10-item scale used in Part II of their survey.

PROCEDURE

A major problem with questionnaire surveys is that it is very difficult to obtain a high percentage of returns. In this study, the overall percentage of returns was 46.3 percent. In some cases the persons who return a questionnaire have been found to be different from those who do not. Therefore, when there is a high percentage of nonrespondents, the reader must ask, "Would the findings of this study have been different if everyone in the sample had responded?" In this study the researchers could have taken three steps that would have increased the rate of response and helped to answer this question. First, if funds had been available, additional followups of nonrespondents could have been conducted. Research indicates that studies doing three followups after the initial mailing get on average about 20 percent more respondents than studies doing a single followup (Heberlein & Baumgartner, 1978). As the percentage of respondents becomes larger, the possibility of sampling bias is likely to become smaller.

Second, a random sample of the nonrespondents could have been contacted and administered the questionnaire either face to face or by telephone. Our experience has shown that nearly all questionnaire nonrespondents will cooperate when contacted by telephone (Borg, Worthen, & Valcarce, in press). The results of this followup could then be compared with the answers of the original respondents to estimate whether the original sample was different from the telephone followup sample.

Third, the responses to the original mailing could have been compared with the responses from the followup. It is theorized that if a sampling bias is present, persons who respond to the followup will be more like the nonrespondents than persons who responded to the initial mailing. Thus, comparing responses from the two groups can indicate if bias occurred and estimate its direction and magnitude.

RESULTS

The authors carried out an extensive analysis of their data, using appropriate statistical techniques. Their description, along with Table 2, gives a clear picture of the research results. If you have had no statistical training, you should have looked up terms such as analyses of variance, t-test, and multiple regression analysis to Chapter 7 as you read the results. Statistically significant differences were found among the three teacher groups on both dimensions of the Depersonalization subscale and the Personal Accomplishment subscale. Both favored the teachers of moderately retarded children, a result counter to the directional hypothesis stated by the researchers. This illustrates the danger of using a directional hypothesis unless there is strong evidence to support it. When you use a directional hypothesis, you are saying in effect that if any significant difference is found, it can only occur in one direction. When you say this and then the results come out in the opposite direction, it can be embarrassing.

When reviewing Table 2, you should check the statistically significant results for practical significance. To determine if a difference between two mean scores is practically significant, divide this difference by the average standard deviation. If the result is .33 or larger, it is of practical significance.[6] For example, let's determine whether the difference in Depersonalization Intensity between teachers of mildly retarded and moderately retarded children is large enough to be practically significant. Using Table 2 we first compute the difference between means ($9.92 - 6.76 = 3.16$). Then we compute the average standard deviation ($7.75 + 5.84 \div 2 = 6.80$). Finally, we divide the mean difference by the average SD ($3.16 \div 6.80 = .46$). Since this result is greater than .33, we conclude that the difference is large enough to be of practical significance.[7]

6. Some researchers use .50 as a criterion instead of .33. Obviously this criterion is arbitrary, and the researcher might be justified in setting a higher or lower criterion for practical significance depending on the nature of the specific study in question.

7. In studies where a control group is used, the control group standard deviation is used rather than the average standard deviation. In this research, however, there is no control group.

DISCUSSION

In this section the authors explore possible explanations of why the results came out as they did. This kind of discussion is very helpful to the reader in gaining insights into possible causes and into the thinking of the researchers. Reread this section carefully and try to decide why *you* believe the teachers of moderately retarded children reported lower frequencies and lower intensities of burnout.

References

BORG, W. R., & ASCIONE, F. R. (1982). Classroom management in elementary mainstreaming classrooms. *Journal of Educational Psychology, 74*(1), 85–95.

BORG, W. R., WORTHEN, B. R., & VALCARCE, B. (in press). Teacher perceptions of educational measurement. *Journal of Experimental Education.*

HEBERLEIN, T. A., & BAUMGARTNER, R. (1978). Factors affecting response rates to mailed questionnaires: A quantitative analysis of the published literature. *American Sociology Review, 43,* 447–462.

Recommended Reading

BABBIE, E. R. (1973). *Survey research methods.* Belmont, Calif.: Wadsworth.

A good source for the student who plans to conduct a survey research project. Provides detailed information on such topics as survey design, sampling, questionnaire development, interviewing, and analysis of survey research data.

BRADBURN, N. M., & SUDMAN, S. (1981). *Improving interview method and questionnaire design.* San Francisco: Jossey-Bass.

Based on the results of a research program on response effects in surveys. Variables that derive from the nature of the task, the characteristics of the respondents, and the characteristic of the interviewers were explored in a series of investigations. The studies are principally concerned with response effects related to threatening questions, that is, questions on topics about which many respondents are reluctant to talk fully and honestly. This book presents valuable evidence on how variations in question content, method of administration of questions, and interviewer behavior influence the information given by the respondent. A valuable source for students who want to develop a fuller understanding of survey research design.

FINK, A., & KOSECOFF, J. (1985). *How to conduct surveys.* Beverly Hills, Calif.: Sage.

A practical guide to the conduct of survey research. It deals with such topics as framing hypotheses, deciding on questionnaire or interview format, methods for collecting data, choosing a sample, and analyzing results. Many examples and practice exercises are provided. An excellent source for students who want to learn more about the practical aspects of survey research.

FOWLER, F. J., JR. (1984). *Survey research methods.* Beverly Hills, Calif.: Sage.

An excellent source for students who want to know more about survey research. Covers topics such as sampling, nonresponse bias, data collection, questionnaire design, interviewing, and data analysis.

HOGARTH, R. M. (1982). *Question framing and response consistency.* San Francisco: Jossey-Bass.

This small book contains chapters by several different scientists concerned with various aspects of question framing in survey research. The authors carefully integrate the finding of previous research and provide excellent reference lists for persons who want to look at this research in greater depth.

SELLTIZ, C., WRIGHTSMAN, L. S., & COOK, W. S. (1976). *Research methods in social relations* (3rd ed.). New York: Holt, Rinehart & Winston.

Contains a chapter on questionnaires and interviews that includes an interesting discussion of different types of question content. Appendix B, on questionnaire construction and interview procedure, will also be useful to the student who plans to conduct research in this area.

SUDMAN, S., & BRADBURN, N. M. (1982). *Asking questions: A practical guide to questionnaire design.* San Francisco: Jossey-Bass.

The authors have conducted extensive research in this area, which they combine with the research of others to develop a comprehensive guide to the design of questionnaires. Examples are given from actual surveys, and three complete questionnaires are included to illustrate the principles of questionnaire design. Different chapters focus upon different kinds of questions such as knowledge questions, attitude questions, and threatening questions. The final chapter provides a checklist covering all of the steps in constructing a questionnaire. Probably the best single source on questionnaire design now available.

Application Problems

Decide whether survey, direct observation, or causal-comparative research would be most appropriate for each of the following research problems and explain why:

1. An investigator wants to determine whether the amount of television viewed by young children (age four to five) is related to the amount of overt aggression they displayed in preschool and kindergarten classes.
2. An investigator wants to determine the attitudes of high school senior males toward entering occupations that are typically entered by females such as teaching in the primary grades, nursing, and secretarial work.
3. The researcher wants to study the social interactions of children in kindergarten classes to test his hypothesis that only children are less advanced socially than children having siblings.
4. Using the evaluation form given in Appendix 1, evaluate the article by Sanford and Evertson that is reprinted in this chapter.
5. Using the evaluation form given in Appendix 1, evaluate the article by Beck and Gargiulo that is reprinted in this chapter.
6. Using the evaluation form given in Appendix 1, evaluate one of the articles listed under Chapter 8 in Appendix 2.

CHAPTER 9

CORRELATIONAL RESEARCH

Overview

Correlational methodology permits the researcher to investigate the relationships among several variables in a single study. Some correlational studies explore relationships in order to get a better understanding of the complex phenomena being studied. Others employ correlation as a means of predicting future behavior.

In this chapter you will read and evaluate two correlational studies. The first is concerned with relationships between various ways teachers introduce students to new learning tasks and subsequent student engagement with these tasks. The second is concerned with the validity of different measures used to predict the future achievement of kindergarten pupils.

Objectives

1. Describe the two major kinds of correlational research and give an example of each.
2. Select a hypothetical research question and explain how it could be explored using correlational research. Could this same question be studied using causal-comparative research methodology?
3. Given the form of scores to be correlated, select the correct bivariate correlational technique.
4. Describe the study of methods of teacher presentation of classroom tasks as related to student task engagement. How do you interpret the findings?
5. Briefly describe the research by Caskey and Larson, and explain the limitations that would have to be considered if you were to apply the results of this prediction study to the placement of first-grade pupils in your school district.

The correlation coefficient is a statistical tool that can be used to compare measurements taken on two or more different variables in order to determine the degree of relationship between these variables. Correlational research is similar in many ways to causal-comparative research, and in fact correlation coefficients can usually be computed from evidence gathered in causal-comparative studies.[1] As usually conducted, however, the two types of research are somewhat different. In causal-comparative research two groups of individuals who are generally similar are selected because the two groups have present (or absent) some specific characteristic

---

1. Point-biserial and biserial correlations, which can be used when one of the variables being studied is a dichotomy, are well suited to analysis of causal-comparative data.

such as brain damage, or are high or low on some variable such as introversion-extroversion, popularity with peers, or physical strength. Having selected groups that differ on the critical independent variable, the researcher studies these groups to determine how they differ on other variables. In correlational research, instead of selecting only subjects who either have or do not have the characteristic selected as the independent variable being studied, a sample usually is selected that is likely to have scores at all levels on this variable. All members of the selected group are measured on both the independent variable being studied and other variables hypothesized to be related to the independent variable, and then correlation coefficients are computed between scores obtained by all members of the group on these variables. Therefore, causal-comparative studies are typically looking for differences while correlational studies are typically looking for relationships.

There are many bivariate correlational techniques that can be used to obtain a measure of the relationship between two variables. Which technique is used depends mainly on the form of the scores that are to be correlated. Most educational data are available in the form of continuous scores, such as scores on achievement measures. Occasionally, however, data are in the form of ranks, such as graduation ranks assigned to high school students. Some data are available in the form of a dichotomy such as students classified as passing or failing a course (artificial dichotomy) or students classified as boys or girls (true dichotomy). Finally, some data are available only in categories. For example, when students are classified as upper-class, middle-class, and lower-class socioeconomic status, they are being placed in categories. See Table 9.1 for a brief summary of the most widely used types of bivariate correlational techniques.

The following are examples of relationships that can be investigated through correlational research: (1) physical strength and peer-group popularity of sixth-grade boys; (2) algebra aptitude scores obtained in the eighth grade and subsequent measures of algebra achievement obtained in the ninth grade; (3) racial attitudes of first-grade children and the attitudes of their parents; (4) the amount that students can remember from a series of photographs viewed for one minute each, and their ability in graphic art as measured by evaluations of pencil sketches; and (5) high school grade-point average and college grade-point average for students from ghetto environments. Note that correlations can be computed based on measures of the same individuals on two or more different variables (2 and 4, above), measures of different individuals on the same variable (3, above), or measures of the same individuals on the same variable taken at different times (5, above).

Correlational studies may be classified as either "prediction studies" or "relationship studies." Relationship studies usually explore the relationships between measures of different variables obtained from the same individuals at approximately the same time. The purpose of many relationship studies is to gain a better understanding of factors that contribute to make up a more complex characteristic such as artistic ability.

For example, if we were to find that observational skills, visual acuity, small-muscle dexterity, and creative imagination were all related to artistic ability, then we would have gained some insight into the nature of this complex phenomenon. De-

Table 9.1   Bivariate correlational techniques for different forms of variables

Technique	Symbol	Variable 1	Variable 2	Remarks
Product-moment correlation	r	Continuous	Continuous	The most stable technique, i.e., smallest standard error
Rank-difference correlation (*rho*)	ρ	Ranks	Ranks	Often used instead of product-moment when number of cases is under 30
Kendall's *tau*	τ	Ranks	Ranks	Preferable to *rho* for numbers under 10
Biserial correlation	r_{bis}	Artificial dichotomy	Continuous	Sometimes exceeds 1—has a larger standard error than r—commonly used in item analysis
Widespread biserial correlation	r_{wbis}	Widespread artificial dichotomy	Continuous	Used when you are especially interested in persons at the extremes on the dichotomized variable
Point-biserial correlation	r_{pbis}	True dichotomy	Continuous	Yields a lower correlation than r_{bis}
Tetrachoric correlation	r_t	Artificial dichotomy	Artificial dichotomy	Used when both variables can be split at critical points
Phi coefficient	ϕ	True dichotomy	True dichotomy	Used in calculating inter-item correlations
Contingency coefficient	C	2 or more categories	2 or more categories	Comparable to r_t under certain conditions—closely related to chi-square
Correlation ratio, *eta*	η	Continuous	Continuous	Used to detect nonlinear relationships

Source: W. R. Borg and M. G. Gall, *Educational Research: An Introduction* (4th ed.), © 1983, p. 587. Reprinted by permission of Longman Inc., White Plains, N.Y.

scriptive studies aimed at describing the characteristics of a specific group of individuals such as successful artists, children with learning disabilities, or victims of teacher burnout often use correlations to explore relevant relationships.

Prediction studies, on the other hand, are concerned with measuring one or more variables (called predictor variables) that can be used to predict some future event (called the criterion variable). For example, the U.S. Air Force has developed a battery of tests that can be given to applicants for pilot training. Prediction studies have shown that each of these tests is related to later success in pilot training. By administering this battery of tests and by studying the correlations obtained in previous research, the researcher can predict the likelihood of any given individual successfully completing the pilot-training program.

In the public schools prediction studies are carried out to develop various kinds of aptitude measures such as reading readiness and algebra aptitude. Once an aptitude measure has been shown to relate to later performance, such as reading or algebra achievement, it can be used for counseling, class assignment, identification of children who may need special help, and similar school activities.

A major advantage of correlational research is that the investigator can explore a wide variety of different relationships in the same study. Suppose we are interested in the relationships between specific teaching behavior and the levels of pupil achievement in elementary school mathematics. A correlational study could be carried out in which observers recorded the degree to which a sample of elementary teachers used 20 different teaching strategies and techniques while teaching mathematics. At the end of the observational period (which could extend over several weeks) each teacher in the sample would have a score on each of the 20 specific behaviors that had been observed. Achievement tests would be administered to the pupils in each of these teachers' classrooms at two points in time to obtain a measure of achievement gain. Correlation coefficients could be computed between each teacher behavior and pupil achievement gain in order to estimate the degree to which each behavior contributed to either high or low pupil achievement in mathematics.

More advanced correlational techniques could be used to estimate the combination of specific teaching strategies that was most highly related to pupil achievement. In this case a multiple regression equation is developed. An individual's score on each predictor variable can be entered into this equation. The equation is then solved to give an estimate of the individual's score on the criterion variable. It is also possible to compute a multiple correlation (R). This is the correlation between the weighted combination of the predictor variables and the criterion variable.

In this chapter you will review two correlational studies. The first is a relationship study; the second is a prediction study.

Sample Relationship Study: "RELATIONSHIPS BETWEEN TEACHERS' PRESENTATIONS OF CLASSROOM TASKS AND STUDENTS' ENGAGEMENT IN THOSE TASKS"

Abstract[2]

The possibility that expectations about classroom tasks that teachers communicate to students in the process of presenting those tasks might affect student engagement

2. The abstract from the article is reprinted here in order to provide a context in which the researcher's comments can be related.

in the tasks was investigated by correlating the presence/absence of various teacher task-presentation statements with measures of subsequent student task engagement. Contrary to expectation, student engagement was generally higher when teachers moved directly into tasks than when they began with some presentation statements. Within the subset of tasks that were begun with teacher-presentation statement, those presentation statements classified as likely to have negative effects on student engagement were associated with lower student engagement, but there was no corresponding tendency for teacher-presentation statements classified as likely to have positive effects on student engagement to be associated with high rates of student engagement.

The Researcher's Comments[3]

As noted in the article, one of the motivations that led to the study was the desire to extend theory and research on teacher expectation effects from its almost exclusive emphasis on achievement expectations into other areas (in this case, teachers' expectations concerning students' affective responses to academic activities). A second motivation, alluded to but not explained in the article, was my interest in developing better theory and research on motivation in the classroom. Although a vast literature exists on the general topic of motivation, I believe that most of it is irrelevant to teachers seeking strategies for motivating their students to learn academic content and skills, and that what is relevant has only limited application, for the following reasons (Brophy, 1983; Brophy & Kher, in press).

First, most motivational research has taken place in free-choice or recreational settings, but school is established to instruct students in a set curriculum, and in order to accomplish this, it makes continuing demands on students' attention and action potential. Thus, in the school setting, motivation needs to be conceptualized and measured not in terms of what students will do when given free choice, but in terms of the quality of their engagement in academic activities—the degree to which they choose to take these activities seriously and attempt to get the intended knowledge and skill benefits from them, even though the activities are imposed on them.

Second, more attention needs to be focused on factors that cause students to value academic activities and the benefits to be derived from them. It is generally agreed that the effort that a person will invest in an activity is jointly determined by the *value* that the person places on that activity and the *expectations* the person holds concerning the difficulty level of the activity and the chances of achieving success by putting forth reasonable effort. A great deal of research has been done in recent years on the expectancy term of this equation, but not much has been done on the value term.

Third, to complement the large body of theory and research on how rewards, incentives, and other factors can affect performance on tests, assignments, or other opportunities for students to apply what they have learned, more information is needed about the motivational elements involved in the listening, reading, thinking, and other information processing that goes on when the learning is acquired in the first place. Given the highly cognitive nature of most of what is learned in school, research on student motivation to learn in the classroom needs to consider the cognitive, strategy-activation aspects of motivation, not just the affective, task-liking-and-persistence aspects.

3. This commentary was written by Dr. Jere Brophy, the senior author.

The article included here was the first in a series of three studies on classroom motiva-tion. In a subsequent publication (Brophy & Kher, in press) we report additional analyses of the data from this first study and the findings of a second, follow up study. The additional analyses revealed more reasons why the task introductions classified as neutral or positive in the first study did not have positive effects.

For example, many of the positive task introduction statements made by the teachers in the first study were specific enough to be coded into the categories shown in the table, but were too short or sketchy to have much impact on the students. Also, positive task intro-duction statements were often parts of longer statements that included negative elements as well, so that it was rare that teachers introduced activities in ways that were both unambiguously positive and sustained and specific enough to have a powerful impact on the students.

The follow-up study involved interviewing students about how they would think or feel upon hearing particular task introductory statements. This study revealed no evidence of a student tendency to discount or question the motives behind teachers' attempts to portray tasks in a positive light. However, it also revealed little student enthusiasm about academic activities and suggested the need to change or qualify some of our classifications of teacher's task introductions as positive, neutral, or negative. For example, the students reported responding positively to being told that a task would be new or challenging, but responding negatively to being told that a task would be easy (presumably because this implied to them that it would be review work that didn't involve learning anything new). Also, the students reported responding positively to time reminders that were given early enough to be helpful in planning their study time (such as reminders on Tuesday that certain assignments were due on Friday), but reacting negatively to time reminders suggest-ing that they had only a few more minutes to finish an assignment or test. Finally, rather than responding negatively to accountability statements by perceiving them as threats, students reported perceiving these as well-intended and helpful hints and thus appreciated them.

Taken together, the reanalyses and follow-up data suggested that students are potentially open to teachers' attempts to socialize motivation to learn in the classroom, but that such attempts occur relatively seldom, tend to be too brief and sketchy to have much impact when they do occur, and are often undercut by other statements suggesting that the teacher does not expect the students to enjoy academic activities. Therefore, rather than continue with research designed to document the status quo, we decided that our third study would be a field experiment in which teachers would be trained to stimulate student motivation to learn systematically when introducing and implementing classroom activities, using such strategies as modeling, interest in and enjoyment of learning, communicating the expecta-tion that students share such interest and enjoyment, projecting enthusiasm about learning in general and about particular academic activities in the classroom, inducing appreciation for the importance of activities by mentioning the value or application of the knowledge or skills that they develop, inducing curiosity or suspense by asking questions about or making reference to interesting information that a lesson will convey, inducing dissonance or cognitive conflict by asking questions about or making reference to surprising elements of the content, and elaborating on sketchy content or using well-chosen anecdotes or examples to make abstract or unfamiliar content more personally meaningful and con-cretely visualizable.

This study, presently underway, involves training seventh- and eighth-grade social stud-ies teachers to use such principles and then collecting a variety of observational, self-report, and achievement data to determine if: (1) the training was successful in enabling the teachers to implement the motivational principles systematically in their experimental class sections, and (2) if so, whether such systematic attempts to stimulate student motivation to learn had significant effects on the motivation and achievement of the students in the experimental sections (compared to students in control sections).

References

BROPHY, J. (1983). Conceptualizing student motivation. *Educational Psychologist, 18,* 200–215.

BROPHY, J., & KHER, N. (in press). Teacher socialization as a mechanism for developing student motivation to learn. In R. Feldman (ed.), *Social psychology applied to education.* Cambridge: Cambridge University Press.

RELATIONSHIPS BETWEEN TEACHERS' PRESENTATIONS OF CLASSROOM TASKS AND STUDENTS' ENGAGEMENT IN THOSE TASKS

Jere Brophy
MICHIGAN STATE UNIVERSITY

Hakim Rashid
UNIVERSITY OF SOUTH CAROLINA

Mary Rohrkemper
BRYN MAWR COLLEGE

Michael Goldberger
TEMPLE UNIVERSITY

Since publication of Rosenthal and Jacobson's (1968) *Pygmalion in the Classroom,* a great deal of educational research has documented that teachers' expectations can exert self-fulfilling prophecy effects on student achievement and has explored the processes mediating these effects by documenting differential teacher treatment of

Brophy, Jere, Rohrkemper, Mary, Rashid, Hakim, and Goldberger, Michael, "Relationships between Teachers' Presentations of Classroom Tasks and Students' Engagement in Those Tasks." *Journal of Educational Psychology,* 1982, pp. 544–552. Copyright 1982 by the American Psychological Association. Reprinted by permission of the publisher and author.

high- versus low-expectation students (Brophy & Good, 1974; Cooper, 1979). Although this work has concentrated on teachers' expectations for student achievement, Good and Brophy (1978, 1980) have pointed out that, theoretically, self-fulfilling prophecy effects may occur with respect to any student outcome about which teachers communicate consistent beliefs, attitudes, or expectations. Teachers who believe that schoolwork is inherently interesting or enjoyable, for example, may shape similar beliefs in their students if they consistently project the expectation that the students will enjoy their assignments. Similarly, teachers who see schoolwork as drudgery are likely to foster the same attitude in their students.

The same conclusion about teacher effects on student motivation follows from consideration of theory and research on the effects of adult modeling and socialization behavior on children's attitudes, beliefs, and behavior, at least if it is assumed that students find their teachers credible as sources of information and identify with them sufficiently to begin to model their attitudes and behavior. Thus, the notion that teachers' expressions of belief or attitude about academic activities should tend to develop similar beliefs or attitudes in their students can be inferred from several approaches to developmental social psychology.

It also follows that students' beliefs (especially their expectations) and attitudes about academic tasks are likely to affect their motivation concerning such tasks—whether or not they want to engage in such tasks in the first place—and the nature of their engagement (level of effort, sustained concentration, persistence, enjoyment, goal setting, etc.) if they do take up the tasks (voluntarily or involuntarily). Other things being equal (task difficulty level, time pressure factors, alternative activity options), a higher quality of student task engagement can be expected when students are working on tasks that they enjoy or believe to be interesting or worthwhile than when they are working on tasks that they dislike or believe to be boring or pointless.

Most educational psychologists would agree with this line of reasoning, but it has not played a prominent part in theory and research on student socialization or motivation. Until recently, most approaches to classroom motivation focused on individual differences between students and stressed trait concepts such as needs or values. There was little emphasis on how teachers might shape the motivation of the class as a whole. Similarly, although there has been much written about perceived and actual task difficulty level as a factor affecting student motivation, there has been relatively little attention to factors such as the perceived interest value or meaningfulness of tasks. Furthermore, when such factors are considered, they tend to be conceptualized in static terms and treated as independent variables (affecting task performance). There has been relatively little attention to the dynamic aspects of

these motivationally relevant student beliefs, expectations, and attitudes, or to the role of the teacher in shaping them.

The present study was the first of a projected series designed to consider classroom motivation with respect to not only the traditionally investigated person and incentive variables but also task variables (characteristics of tasks that affect the degree to which they are perceived as interesting, challenging, or worthwhile) and teacher presentation variables (teacher comments made while presenting tasks to students that communicate expectations about the degree to which the tasks are likely to be interesting, challenging, or worthwhile). It was not an experiment, but a naturalistic correlational study of the relationships between statements that teachers made about classroom tasks when presenting those tasks to their students (the independent variable) and the degree of student engagement subsequently observed on those same tasks (the dependent variable).

Our prediction was that student engagement would be highest on tasks presented in such a way as to engender positive student expectations or attitudes, medium on tasks introduced more neutrally or begun without any introduction at all, and lowest on tasks introduced with comments likely to engender negative student expectations or attitudes.

This seemed to be the logical place to begin a series of studies on teacher-presentation variables, even though it seemed to border on documenting the obvious. Our thought was to begin by showing orderly relationships between gross measures of teacher-presentation statements (positive, neutral, negative) and a gross measure of the quality of student task engagement, used as our measure of student motivation. Task engagement is not the only possible measure of student motivation, of course. However, it is more objective than self-report measures of such variables as liking for a task or desire to experience the task again in the future, and it is known to be related to achievement. It represents that part of motivation that deals with task concentration or effort under conditions of compulsion (or at least, strong pressure) to perform tasks, and, thus, is more relevant to conceptualizing motivation in the work setting of the classroom than measures of students' affect or behavior in free choice or play settings would be. As will be described, however, the relationships between these variables were not as straightforward as we expected.

Method

Reading and math lessons were observed (8–15 times each) in two fourth-grade, two fifth-grade, and two sixth-grade classes in a school serving a working-class population in a small midwestern city. Reading and math were taught consecutively in the mornings. Typically, each reading or math period was subdivided into two to four tasks. For example, a math period might begin with a review of the previous day's seatwork/homework assignment, followed by presentation of a new concept or skill, followed by presentation of a new assignment to be done as seatwork or completed as homework if necessary.

Prior to formal data collection, observers visited each class several times to familiarize themselves with the teachers, the students, and the daily routines, and to identify the tasks that were typically included in reading and math instruction. They also developed coding reliability, working in pairs until a criterion of 80% intercoder agreement was reached. Then they worked alone to collect the data.

Teacher-presentation data and student-engagement data were collected for each task observed. For the teacher-presentation data, the observers recorded verbatim any beliefs, attitudes, or expectations that the teachers communicated about the task (as opposed to procedural or instructional statements made in the process of teaching the task, which were not recorded). Later, these verbatim reports of teachers' presentation statements were coded for presence or absence of the 18 categories shown in the Appendix. Each category that applied was coded "present," so that multiple codes appeared whenever more than one category was included in the teacher's presentation. This categorization was done independently by two coders, who agreed on 90% of their initial classifications and later resolved disagreements by discussion.

Students' task engagement was coded twice for each task, once 5 minutes into the task, and once again 10 minutes later. Each individual student was coded as clearly engaged, probably engaged, or clearly not engaged in the task, and the percentages of the class in each of these three categories were computed later and used for analyses. In most cases, coding of student task engagement was based on observation (at a distance) of general body orientation, apparent direction of gaze, and apparent interaction with task materials rather than peers, playthings, or other nontask stimuli. Thus, our dependent measure was a rather crude index of student task engagement, probably less valid and certainly less specific than sustained individualized observations or stimulated recall interviews with each student would have been. Even so, other research (reviewed by Borg, 1980) has indicated that such general observational measures of student engagement correlate significantly with measures of achievement and also with more precise measures of student engagement. The latter correlations are high enough to justify the use of general behavioral observation as a valid, if crude, measure of student engagement.

Analyses

The data for each task observed included one or more teacher-presentation codes and (usually) six measures of student engagement. The teacher-presentation measures were in the form of "present" codes for one or more of the categories shown in the Appendix (with the rest of the categories coded "absent"). The student-engagement data, originally in the form of tallies representing the numbers of students in the class or group present at the time who were assigned to each of eight engagement categories, were combined into three percentage scores: percentage clearly engaged, percentage either clearly engaged or probably engaged, and percentage clearly off task or disruptive. These three scores were computed twice for each task, once based on the data from the first observation done 5 minutes into the task, and (usually) once again based on data from the second observation done 15 minutes into the task (unless the task did not last this long). The basic analyses for this article involved computing point biserial correlation coefficients linking presence/absence of teacher-presentation statements made prior to tasks with percentage measures of student engagement in the same tasks.

In addition to analyzing these relationships for each of the 18 teacher-presentation variables individually, we combined the data for subsets of teacher-presentation variables judged likely to engender (respectively) positive, neutral, or negative student attitudes or expectations about the tasks. There is more than one way, however, to classify teacher task-presentation statements as positive, neutral, or negative with respect to their probable effects on student motivation. We developed two classification systems, one based on what teachers implied about what the students could expect from the task itself or from the process of working on the task, and the other based on what teachers implied would be the consequences of success or failure on the task. Loosely speaking, the first classification focused on intrinsic motivation and task process, whereas the second focused on extrinsic motivation and performance outcome.

Attribution theorists would expect the first classification system to show orderly relationships to measures of student engagement, whereas reinforcement theorists would favor the second classification system. The first system, focusing on what is implied about the task itself, classifies the categories "teacher personalizes," "teacher enthusiasm," "self-actualization value," "personal reference," and "cues positive expectation" as positive task presentations likely to enhance student engagement by creating the expectation that the task will be personally meaningful or enjoyable. The categories of "apology" and "cues negative expectation" are classified as negative within this system, and the remaining categories are classified as neutral. Our prediction here was based on the hypothesis that these teacher-presentation statements would create parallel expectations or attitudes in the students, and that students would become engaged more eagerly and consistently in tasks they expected to find enjoyable or meaningful than in tasks they expected to find boring or frustrating.

Shifting focus from students' expectations about the task itself to their expectations about the consequences of success or failure on the task produces a different classification system. Here, several categories are classified as positive because they promise reward for engaging in or succeeding at the task ("recognition," "extrinsic reward," "self-actualization value," and "personal reference"). Others are classified as negative because they threaten punishment for failure ("threat/punishment," "accountability," "embarrassment"), and the remaining categories are classified as neutral because they imply neither reward nor punishment. Here, our predictions were based on the hypothesis that anticipation of rewards for task engagement or successful performance would motivate concentration and effort on the task but that such concentration and effort might be impaired by anxiety or anticipated punishment or embarrassment triggered by teachers' negative task presentations (even though, theoretically, threatening punishment should raise motivation in the sense of raising arousal level). At bottom here is the notion that performance depends not only on the level of motivation, but on its quality. Motivation that flows from factors exogenous to the task itself may interfere with ability to concentrate on a task or desire to do the task well (Kruglanski, 1978), especially if it engenders anxiety.

Results

Table 1 gives the frequencies and percentages with which each teacher used the 18 content categories in introducing tasks (note that percentage data are referenced according to the number of tasks rather than the total number of task-presentation codes made for each teacher, so that totals exceed 100% because of multiple presentation codes for some tasks). As a group, the teachers made no presentation statement at all for 49 (30%) of the 165 tasks coded. The presentation statements made for the remaining 116 tasks yielded 206 category "presence" codes, or almost 2 per task. Thus, although teachers jumped right into tasks without any introduction at all 30% of the time, the task presentations they gave

Table 1 Frequencies and percentages[a] of task-presentation codes for the six teachers (T)

Task-presentation category	Teachers and no. of tasks						Total (165 tasks)
	T_1 (50)	T_2 (16)	T_3 (30)	T_4 (26)	T_5 (22)	T_6 (21)	
1. None	13 (26)	4 (25)	10 (33)	12 (46)	9 (40)	1 (5)	49 (30)
2. Cues effort	3 (6)	1 (6)	4 (13)	7 (27)	5 (23)	4 (19)	24 (15)
3. Continuity	7 (14)	6 (38)	1 (3)	5 (19)	0 (0)	7 (33)	26 (16)
4. Recognition	3 (6)	3 (19)	1 (3)	0 (0)	0 (0)	0 (0)	7 (4)
5. Extrinsic reward	1 (2)	0 (0)	0 (0)	0 (0)	1 (5)	0 (0)	2 (1)
6. Threat/punishment	6 (12)	2 (13)	0 (0)	0 (0)	3 (14)	1 (5)	12 (7)
7. Accountability	5 (10)	3 (19)	3 (10)	1 (4)	2 (9)	4 (19)	18 (11)
8. Time reminder	8 (16)	4 (25)	1 (3)	0 (0)	0 (0)	1 (5)	14 (9)
9. Embarrassment	0 (0)	0 (0)	0 (0)	0 (0)	0 (0)	0 (0)	0 (0)
10. Apology	0 (0)	0 (0)	0 (0)	0 (0)	1 (5)	0 (0)	1 (1)
11. Cues negative expectation	11 (22)	1 (6)	1 (3)	1 (4)	5 (23)	1 (5)	20 (12)
12. Challenge/goal setting	13 (26)	1 (6)	1 (3)	1 (4)	0 (0)	1 (5)	17 (10)
13. Teacher personalizes	0 (0)	0 (0)	0 (0)	0 (0)	0 (0)	0 (0)	0 (0)
14. Teacher enthusiasm	3 (6)	0 (0)	1 (3)	0 (0)	0 (0)	0 (0)	4 (2)
15. Self-actualization value	0 (0)	0 (0)	0 (0)	0 (0)	0 (0)	0 (0)	0 (0)
16. Survival value	1 (2)	3 (19)	7 (23)	0 (0)	0 (0)	1 (5)	12 (7)
17. Personal reference-other	3 (6)	0 (0)	3 (10)	0 (0)	1 (5)	0 (0)	7 (4)
18. Cues positive expectation	14 (28)	5 (31)	9 (30)	3 (12)	1 (5)	10 (48)	42 (26)
No. of task-presentation codes	91	33	42	30	28	31	255

[a] Percentages are in parentheses, based on number of tasks observed.

the other 70% of the time were lengthy and substantial enough to include, on the average, mention of two separate considerations likely to affect student motivation.

Consideration of the data in Table 1 in the light of our classification of teacher-presentation statements as positive, neutral, or negative makes it clear that teachers (at least these six teachers) do not systematically take advantage of opportunities to present tasks in a positive light, and sometimes even present them in a negative light. Using the system based on statements about the task itself, 53 of the 206 codes were classified as positive, 132 as neutral, and 21 as negative. Using the system based on statements about consequences for success or failure at the task, 28 statements were coded as positive, 148 as neutral, and 30 as negative. Considering both classification systems simultaneously results in classification of 74 statements as positive, 81 as neutral, and 51 as negative. Teachers did try to cue positive expectations prior to about one fourth of the tasks, but otherwise made little use of opportunities to develop student motivation. In particular, none of the teachers was ever observed attempting to make students aware that they could derive personal satisfaction or self-actualization value from a task.

Student Engagement

To assess relationships between teacher-presentation codes and student-engagement rates, point biserial correlations were computed for each teacher, based on samples of tasks (Ns) varying from 16 to 50. The task-presentation codes for each task were linked with the student-engagement data for the same task, aggregated across all of the tasks observed for that classroom, and then correlated. This produced six sets of correlations for each of the 18 teacher-presentation-code categories for each classroom, because there were three engagement measures (percentage of students clearly engaged, percentage either clearly or probably engaged, and percentage clearly off task or disruptive) based on observations done 5 minutes into the task, and (usually) three more based on observations done 15 minutes into the task. All of those correlations need not be pre-

sented here, however, because much of the information they contain is redundant. That is, although there were differences in strength of relationship and level of significance, a particular task-presentation variable tended to correlate (if at all) either positively with some of the four measures of student engagement (percentage clearly engaged or either clearly engaged or probably engaged) and negatively with the either or both of the measures of off-task and disruptive behavior, or vice versa. Thus, in general, each set of coefficients (for which data were available to compute correlations) could be described as indicating a positive relationship, a negative relationship, or no relationship between the task-presentation variable and the degree of subsequent student engagement in the task.

This information is summarized in Table 2, where a plus (+) sign indicates at least one significant correlation representing a positive relationship between the task-presentation variable and student engagement on the task, and a minus (−) sign indicates at least one significant correlation representing a negative relationship between the task-presentation variable and student engagement on the task. The findings summarized in Table 2 are not at all what we expected.

The data for Category 1 (no attempt to motivate the students) showed three positive relationships and one negative relationship with student-engagement measures, of a total of six possible relationships examined. Thus, for three of the teachers, student engagement was higher when they plunged directly into the task than when they began with some kind of presentation statement.

For the other 17 categories representing positive, neutral, or negative statements about tasks, only 14 of a possible 52 relationships reached statistical significance, and 12 of these were negative relationships. That is, most relationships indicated *lower* student engagement when teachers made some statement about the task than when they did not. This includes not only statements classified as negative ("threat/punishment," "accountability," "cues negative expectation") but also statements classified as positive or neutral ("challenge/goal setting," "teacher enthusiasm," "survival value").

Table 2 Relationships between task-presentation codes and student-engagement codes across the six teachers (T)[a]

Classification based on task	Classification based on consequences	Task-presentation category	Relationship with task engagement						Total pos	Total neg
			T_1	T_2	T_3	T_4	T_5	T_6		
Neut	Neut	1. None	+	−	+	+	0	0	3	1
Neut	Neut	2. Cues effort	0	N	0	0	0	0	0	0
Neut	Neut	3. Continuity	0	0	N	0	N	0	0	0
Neut	Pos	4. Recognition	0	0	0	N	N	N	0	0
Neut	Pos	5. Extrinsic reward	0	N	N	N	0	N	0	0
Neut	Neg	6. Threat/punishment	−	0	0	0	−	−	0	3
Neut	Neg	7. Accountability	0	0	0	0	0	−	0	1
Neut	Neut	8. Time reminder	−	+	N	N	N	−	1	2
Neut	Neg	9. Embarrassment	N	N	N	N	N	N	N	N
Neut	Neut	10. Apology	0	N	N	N	0	N	0	0
Neg	Neut	11. Cues negative expectation	N	N	N	0	0	−	0	1
Neg	Neut	12. Challenge/goal setting	−	N	−	−	N	0	0	3
Pos	Neut	13. Teacher personalizes	N	N	N	N	N	N	N	N
Pos	Neut	14. Teacher enthusiasm	0	N	−	N	N	N	0	1
Pos	Pos	15. Self-actualization value	N	N	N	N	N	N	N	N
Pos	Pos	16. Survival value	0	0	0	N	0	−	0	1
Neut	Pos	17. Personal reference-other	+	N	0	N	0	N	1	0
Pos	Neut	18. Cues positive expectation	0	0	0	0	0	0	0	0

Note. Plus (+) signs indicate significant ($p < .05$) positive relationships; minus (−) signs indicate significant negative relationships; zeros (0) indicate no significant relationship; (N) indicates "no data" (correlations could not be computed because category was not used); Pos = positive; Neg = negative; Neut = neutral.

[a] Based on correlations of presence/absence codes for the task-presentation categories with percentages of students in the class who were attentive or engaged in the activity.

Table 3   Relationships between teachers' positive, neutral, or negative statements about the tasks themselves and students' subsequent task engagement[a]

Relationship to student engagement	Statement about task			
	+	Neutral	−	Total
Positive r	1	1	0	2
No significant r	9	25	4	38
Negative r	1	10	1	12
Totals	11	36	5	52

[a] $\chi^2(4) = 2.59$, $p < .05$.

Contingencies between classifications of teacher-presentation statements as positive, neutral, or negative and incidence of observed relationships to student-engagement measures (positive relationship, no relationship, or negative relationship) are given in Table 3 (for classification of teacher-presentation statements based on what they imply about the task itself) and Table 4 (for classifications of teacher-presentation statements based on mention of reward or punishment as consequences). Chi-square coefficients based on these observed contingencies were in the ex-

Table 4   Relationships between teachers' mention of reward or punishment when introducing tasks and students' subsequent task engagement[a]

Relationship to student engagement	Reward	No mention	Punishment	Total
Positive r	1	1	0	2
No significant r	10	22	6	38
Negative r	1	7	4	12
Totals	12	30	10	52

[a] $\chi^2(4) = 3.81$, $p < .05$.

pected directions but did not reach statistical significance. The data suggest that the teacher-presentation statements we have classified as negative were in fact counterproductive, but they provide no clear support for the hypothesis that the teacher-presentation statements we classified as positive would increase student engagement in tasks. Furthermore, these trends within the data for Categories 2 to 18 are overshadowed by the major finding that student task engagement was highest when teachers made no presentation statements at all.

Discussion

The findings are based on only six classrooms, and in many cases on teacher-presentation categories that occurred infrequently, so they may not be reliable or replicable. This is especially true of the categories classified as positive. Of these, only "cues positive expectation" occurred more than seven times in any one classroom, and most of the others occurred no more than three times, if at all. Thus, the general low incidence of positive task presentations may have limited their potential for correlating significantly with student engagement.

However, several other factors suggest that the data must be taken more seriously. First, the category "cues positive expectation" was used frequently and yet never correlated significantly with student engagement. Second, although there were only two significant positive relationships with student engagement, there were 14 significant negative relationships, and many of these involved teacher-presentation categories that were used infrequently. The general findings that engagement was higher when teachers moved directly into the task than when they made some presentation statement, and that relationships between presentation statements and student engagement were likely to be negative when they reached significance, held up for five of the six teachers. Therefore, the discussion will assume that these relationships reflect real trends likely to be replicated in other classrooms.

The negative correlations with student engagement for teacher-presentation categories classified as negative (likely to produce negative student expectations) were expected, of course. However, accepting these correlations requires accepting the general lack of support for the teacher-presentation categories classified as positive, and also the frequent negative correlations for teacher-presentation categories classified as neutral. What might produce this pattern of results?

One possibility is that these six teachers (or five of them at least) were particularly inept at motivating students, to the point that most of their efforts were counterproductive. A related possibility is that their students were alienated from them to the point that they reacted negatively not only to accountability pressures and threat of punishment but also to more neutral time reminders or attempts to challenge them by setting goals, and even to more positive approaches, such as emphasizing the survival value of an activity or expressing enthusiasm about it (these teacher-presentation categories all had at least one negative relationship with student engagement). We doubt these hypotheses. Even though the majority of the students were from working-class rather than middle-class families, and many represented minority groups as well, the general classroom and school atmosphere seemed positive, engagement rates were high, and there was little evidence of student alienation.

Another possibility (suggested to us by Robert Slavin) is that teachers who give more frequent and lengthy task presentations are generally more talkative in the classroom. If so, any tendency of their task-presentation statements to enhance student engagement on tasks may be undercut by their tendency to distract the students with unnecessary or intrusive comments later on. Or, more simply, there may be a trade-off between the frequency of teachers' motivation attempts and the effectiveness of these attempts. As with teacher praise (Brophy, 1981), students may learn to ignore or discount teacher motivation attempts that are too perfunctory or predictable.

The most likely explanation of these data, in our view, however, is that they reflect the effects of task variables and situational factors on both teacher-presentation statements and student-engagement rates, and not the effects of teacher-presentation statements on student-engagement rates. That is, perhaps teachers typically *attempt* to motivate students in the first place only when they have reason to believe that such an effort is needed (because the class has become difficult to control or the upcoming task is not likely to be well received by the students).

This hypothesis fits well with the research on teachers' preactive planning and interactive thinking and decision making, which indicates that teachers' thoughts tend to concentrate on the anticipated flow of instructional activities and the content presentations planned to occur in conjunction with these activities. Typically, teachers shift conscious attention from this activity flow to student responsiveness only when unanticipated problems develop (Clark & Yinger, 1979; Shavelson & Stern, 1981). Thus, there is reason to believe that teachers' *planned* motivational attempts may be stimulated by anticipated problems with activities and that their *spontaneous* motivational attempts may be stimulated by observed problems in the actual situation. If so, this would explain why student engagement was higher when teachers jumped directly into the task than when they began with a motivational attempt and would help explain why most relationships between motivational attempts and student-engagement measures were negative.

We plan to test out this possibility in a follow-up study involving interviewing students about the inferences they draw upon hearing task-presentation statements like those made by the teachers observed in this study. If teachers are in fact more likely to attempt to motivate students when they suspect trouble with a task (as described above), students will probably discover this through experience and begin to discount or even react negatively to such motivation attempts. Such sophisticated social perception (not to mention cynicism) concerning teacher behavior and its interpretation would not be expected in early elementary students, but the findings of Meyer et al. (1979), concerning student interpretation of teacher praise and blame statements, suggest that it could be expected in many of the intermediate-grade students studied here.

The notion that teachers anticipate problems with certain tasks introduces the possibility that our results were affected by variables of the tasks themselves. Future analyses will focus on task variables in an attempt to identify systematic relationships between features of tasks and rates of student engagement on those tasks. These analyses will focus not only on differences in subject matter (reading vs. mathematics) and order of tasks within the period but also on specific task attributes such as the type of media employed and the type of response demanded from the students.

A final consideration is that we may have selected too molecular a level of analysis for testing hypotheses about the effects of teachers' communications of beliefs, attitudes, or expectations on students' motivation. It may be that the task as a unit of analysis or student task engagement as a measure of student motivation are so affected by situational or context factors as to mask the effects of (genuine) trends that might be observable at a more molar level of analysis. Student task engagement, in other words, may not have been a valid or direct enough measure of student motivation to be of practical use for testing the hypotheses under study here (at least when measured with observer ratings; student task engagement measured with stimulated recall interviews might have been more useful). In any case, if a large sample of classrooms was studied in a way that allowed classification of teachers according to frequency and style (positive, neutral, or negative) of student-motivation attempts, and included more global measurement of student motivation (attendance rates, task completion rates, evidence of intrinsic interest in academic content), orderly relationships suggesting self-fulfilling-prophecy effects might be observed.

References

BORG, W. Time and school learning. In C. Denham & A. Lieberman (Eds.), *Time to learn*. Washington, D.C.: National Institute of Education, 1980.

BROPHY, J. Teacher praise: A functional analysis. *Review of Educational Research*, 1981, *51*, 5–32.

BROPHY, J., & GOOD, T. *Teacher-student relationships: Causes and consequences*. New York: Holt, Rinehart, and Winston, 1974.

CLARK, C., & YINGER, R. Teachers' thinking. In P. Peterson & H. Walberg (Eds.), *Research on teaching: Concepts, findings, and implications*. Berkeley, Calif.: McCutchan, 1979.

COOPER, H. Pygmalion grows up: A model for teacher expectation communication and performance influence. *Review of Educational Research*, 1979, *49*, 389–410.

GOOD, T., & BROPHY, J. *Looking in classrooms* (2nd ed.). New York: Harper & Row, 1978.

GOOD, T., & BROPHY, J. *Educational psychology: A realistic approach*. New York: Holt, Rinehart, & Winston, 1980.

KRUGLANSKI, A. Endogenous attribution and intrinsic motivation. In M. Lepper & D. Greene (Eds.), *The hidden costs of reward: New perspectives on the psychology of human motivation*. Hillsdale, N.J.: Erlbaum, 1978.

MEYER, W., BACHMANN, M., BIERMANN, U., HEMPELMANN, M., PLÖGER, F., & SPILLER, H. The informational value of evaluative behavior: Influences of praise and blame on perceptions of ability. *Journal of Educational Psychology*, 1979, *71*, 259–268.

ROSENTHAL, R., & JACOBSON, L. Pygmalion in the classroom: Teacher expectation and pupils' intellectual development. New York: Holt, Rinehart, & Winston, 1968.

SHAVELSON, R., & STERN, P. Research on teachers' pedagogical thoughts, judgments, decisions, and behavior. *Review of Educational Research*, 1981, *51*, 455–498.

Appendix: Categories for Coding Teachers' Task-Presentation Statements

1. None (teacher launches directly into the task with no introduction)
2. Cues effort (teacher urges students to work hard)

3. Continuity (teacher notes relationship between this task and previous work students have done)
4. Recognition (teacher promises that students who do well on the task will be recognized with symbolic rewards, hanging up of good papers in the classroom, etc.)
5. Extrinsic reward (teacher promises reward for good performance)
6. Threats/punishment (teacher threatens negative consequences for poor performance)
7. Accountability (teacher reminds students that the work will be carefully checked or that they will be tested on the material soon)
8. Time reminder (teacher reminds students that they only have limited time to get the assignment done so they had better concentrate)
9. Embarrassment (teacher tries to show the importance of the task to the students, but does this in a negative way, indicating that they are likely to be embarrassed at some time in the future if they do not learn the skills involved)
10. Apology (teacher apologizes to the students for foisting this task on them)
11. Cues negative expectation (teacher indicates directly that the students are not expected to like the task or to do well on the task)
12. Challenge/goal setting (teacher sets some goal or challenges the class to try to attain a certain standard of excellence)
13. Teacher personalizes (teacher expresses personal beliefs or attitudes directly, or tells the students about personal experiences that illustrate the importance of this task)
14. Teacher enthusiasm (teacher directly expresses his or her own liking for this type of task)
15. Self-actualization value (teacher suggests that students can develop knowledge or skill that will bring pleasure or personal satisfaction)
16. Survival value (teacher points out that students will need to learn these skills to get along in life or in our society as it is constructed presently)
17. Personal relevance—other (teacher makes some other kind of statement that tries to tie the task to the personal lives or interests of the students)
18. Cues positive expectation (teacher states directly that the students are expected to enjoy the task or to do well on it)

Critical Review

INTRODUCTION

This study expands further our knowledge related to teacher expectation and its effect upon student behavior. A look at the research in this area provides the student with a good illustration of how educational research gradually builds foundations of theory and evidence that can eventually have major implications for teaching and learning.

The original work in the area of teacher expectations, *Pygmalion in the Classroom*,[4] put forth the theory that teacher expectations of achievement for a given student lead to a self-fulfilling prophecy. That is, if a teacher consistently communicates either high or low expectations about a student's achievement, the student tends to achieve in the way the teacher expects.

4. See references section of article.

This theory has stimulated a considerable amount of controversy. There is still much we do not know about the magnitude of the effect of teacher expectations, the degree to which they may occur in areas other than achievement, and the conditions under which they are most likely to occur. It seems clear, however, that teacher expectations can have an important impact on the behavior of some students.

Thus, high but realistic expectations seem likely to stimulate better performance, at least for some students. On the other hand, low teacher expectations may have a destructive potential that teachers should be actively aware of and should guard against.

The authors of this article point out that teacher expectations are not limited to achievement and can theoretically affect any student outcomes. This research explores the possibility that teacher expectations about classroom tasks (that is, the degree to which the teacher presents the task as likely to be interesting, challenging, or worthwhile) might affect student engagement in these tasks.

The researchers predicted that student engagement would be highest on tasks presented by the teacher in such a way as to stimulate positive student expectations, medium when the teacher gave a neutral presentation or none at all, and lowest when the task was introduced with negative comments.

METHOD

Since this study was concerned with specific aspects of teacher expectations about which no previous research had been done, the authors wisely decided to conduct a correlational study using direct observation in a naturalistic setting. Correlational research is ideal when exploring a new area, since many relationships can be examined in a single study. In so doing, the researcher can often identify and define the variables that appear to be most promising and study these in subsequent experimental studies. However, there are also limitations to the correlational approach. For example, when unexpected results emerge, as was the case with this study, correlational data provide few clues to help the researcher decide what happened, or what these results mean.

By using fairly large amounts of direct observation in classrooms at three grade levels and during instruction in two different subjects, the investigators increased their chances of identifying a variety of different teacher presentation strategies. They also could estimate from these data the degree to which any findings could be generalized across different grade levels and subject areas. This is important, since recent research has demonstrated that effective teacher behavior is often specific to grade and subject taught. In other words teacher strategies that improve learning in second-grade reading may be totally ineffective for teaching fifth-grade mathematics (Fisher, Filby, & Marliave, 1978).

You will recall from Chapter 8 that when direct observation is used, observers must be trained in order to produce reliable information. Also studies that classify the behavior observed into specific low-inference categories usually produce more reliable information than studies that use broad, abstract categories or require high levels of inference on the part of the observer. This study required high levels of agreement for both the observers and the coders and focused on well-defined, low-inference behaviors.

RESULTS

Several results of the study seem worthy of attention by teachers. First, the authors note that the six teachers in this study made little effort to develop student motivation. This is illustrated clearly in Table 2 by the large number of "*N*" entries for positive task presentation approaches such as use of extrinsic rewards, recognition, and references to the self-actualization value of the learning task. If this finding emerges from other naturalistic studies of the classroom, it suggests an area where teachers and teacher educators should focus some attention, since psychological research would suggest that developing student motivation is very important to learning.

The most surprising finding was that moving directly into the learning task generally resulted in higher levels of student task engagement than teachers' use of any of the 17 kinds of introductory statements coded in this research. In fact, teacher presentation statements as a whole were associated with lower student engagement or made no difference one way or the other. You will recall that at the outset, the authors felt that the study bordered on "documenting the obvious." In other words they felt that the value of the teacher making positive remarks about the learning task was self-evident. In this case, as in many previous instances, research has shown us that the obvious is not necessarily true. Although subsequent research in which teachers are trained to present learning tasks more positively and more skillfully might still demonstrate the value of this approach, we must for the present question the value of the teacher making positive introductory statements about the learning task. At least we can conclude that the use of positive introductory statements about upcoming learning tasks *as practiced by teachers in today's classrooms* contributes little or nothing to student task involvement.

Let us now review a study in which correlational research methods were used in a prediction study.

Sample Prediction Study:
"RELATIONSHIP BETWEEN SELECTED KINDERGARTEN PREDICTORS AND FIRST AND FOURTH GRADE ACHIEVEMENT"

Abstract[5]

Kindergarten predictors, Otis-Lennon IQ, group and individual Bender scores, and teachers' ratings, were correlated with first-grade Stanford Achievement Test

5. The abstract from the article is reprinted here in order to provide a context in which the researcher's comments can be related.

scores from 152 children from three schools in the same school district, and fourth-grade Ohio Survey Test scores from 102 of the same children. Test scores from first and fourth grades were correlated as were the aptitude and achievement subtests of the Ohio Survey Test. Marked differences in predictive validity were observed; these varied from school to school and according to sex. To make predictions about academic success school districts should develop local norms, by school, and by sex.

The Researcher's Comments[6]

This study developed from an earlier project designed to assist in evaluating children enrolled in a one-half-day kindergarten program. The school district was instituting a "junior first grade" program designed to (1) eliminate having children repeat kindergarten, and (2) provide a place where an ongoing assessment of eligibility for special education services could be undertaken. Each child seen as being "at risk" for success in first grade was reviewed at a meeting attended by the superintendent, principals of the elementary schools, kindergarten teachers, and the school psychologist. The options for each child were: (1) junior first grade, (2) special education (educable mentally retarded), and (3) regular first grade. The group Bender Test results contributed to this evaluation.

Later, when it came time for me to plan for my Ph.D. dissertation, it seemed like a good idea to incorporate my group Bender experience into a pilot study, since it had been presented at a doctoral seminar as a research study. My committee was formed and the fun began (or the egg hit the fan). Eventually the school psychology member (my minor area advisor) resigned. He had at one time stated that he would accept only a correlation of .75 or higher between Bender scores and IQ and that he never had liked the Bender. Before he left the committee, he insisted on the removal of the Title I group, so a group from East Central Ohio was substituted. The suburban (non–Title I) population consisted of all the children attending kindergarten in two public schools, and the group from East Central Ohio consisted of children from three rural, small-town schools.

While trying to convince my advisor of the value of the study, I responded to his concerns about internal validity, age, sex, educational experience, parental socioeconomic status, physical condition, and other concerns by choosing to use each student as his/her own control.[7]

The results of the dissertation found the individual and group Bender scores correlating significantly ($r = .86$ $p < .0091$) with each other, suggesting that they were measuring substantially the same thing. However, to our surprise, using Fisher's Z transformation, we found the group Bender scores significantly more stable from the test to retest than the individual Bender test. The correlation between Otis-Lennon and Bender were .66 for the group Bender and .51 for the individual Bender ($p < .001$ in both cases).

Upon completing my graduate work, I moved to Tennessee and a position on the special education faculty of East Tennessee State University. In agonizingly slow steps the data from the dissertation were prepared for publication and submitted to a journal. When the

6. This commentary was written by Professor Caskey, the senior author.
7. Correlational studies collecting data from the same subjects have the advantage of subjects "acting as their own controls." In studies comparing different subjects (for example, experimental versus control groups), differences emerging from the comparisons can be due at least in part to differences in the characteristics of the two groups rather than differences brought about by the independent variable.

manuscript came back, Dr. Larson, my minor advisor, and I were discouraged, believing the decision had been made not to publish. However, the journal editor, Dr. Carol Ammons, gave us much encouragement and under her patient tutelage, we reworked the article until it was finally accepted for publication (Caskey & Larson, 1980).

When it came time to gather the achievement test scores needed for the next phase of our research, we found that the data from the Title I group were lost. The building principal who had the key to the identity of the students had resigned, and the documents had been shredded. We were able, though, to gather Title I achievement data from another principal, and these data became part of the study reported herein. The fun of doing the final phase of the research was now over, and we again embarked on the grim process of analyzing the data and preparing an article for publication. Our first hurdle was to get past the statisticians who delayed and delayed and delayed as they rotated this and that. We finally freed the data from the grasp of the statisticians and started drafting a manuscript.

After much work we came up with a "final draft" that had 15 tables and a publication cost of around $1,200.[8] Drastic surgery brought the cost down to around $950. The final cost, with the bulk of the tables no longer in the article but available on microfiche, was $450, most of which I paid personally.

With again patient (and I imagine agonizing) help from the journal editor, the article was completed. Oh, how much easier it would have been had I had a word processor, especially in the preparation of all those tables. Had we not broken the data down by sex and school, the writing would have been much easier, all correlations would have been in the predicted directions, and the findings, though less accurate, would have looked much better. One reviewer suggested that we avoid the conflicting data obtained from the Title I school by doing just that. However, it seemed to me that by pooling the data, the most significant finding would have been lost.

What I wish: (1) that we had achievement scores through the tenth grade, so that we could get really long-range insights into predictive validity of early testing, (2) that we had been able to evaluate at least two more groups of students from Title I schools, (3) that we had the achievement scores from our original Title I sample, (4) that I could get over my reflex aversion to the words "Bender test"—after scoring all those Benders, some 600+ in all, I have come to hate the very name "Bender," (5) that I could learn how to write better so as to avoid the seemingly endless rewrites of my research articles, (6) sometimes, even, that I hadn't insisted on doing my own thing and had done the dissertation, as requested, as a part of a faculty member's research grant—it would have been *so* much easier, and I would have completed the Ph.D. at least two and probably three years earlier, and (7) that I had kept the data and computer cards in a fire-proof repository—they burned in a fire that gutted our home while we were in Ohio, just before we were going to try, as one reviewer had requested, a multiple correlation and multiple regression analysis.

All in all, with all the aches and pains, the money spent for publication, the seemingly endless rewrites, I am glad I persevered. For me the 1983 article highlights an important problem faced when doing research in the field, namely that there is a great deal of variability from one school population to another, and this variability seriously restricts the degree to which we can generalize research results beyond the population sampled in the research. Thus, when different researchers obtain conflicting answers to the same ques-

8. Since professional journals typically have a small circulation, some must levy "page charges" on the authors in order to break even.

tion, it may well be that the unique results are not from a superior design, or the chicanery (fudging the data) of prior researchers, but rather, as in our study, the results may come from difficult-to-define differences beyond the control of the investigators, differences, I suspect, related to the chemistry between people (such as between teacher and students).

I have learned as a result of my first research experience: (1) not to fear "doing research," (2) that prior to the use of standardized tests in research one *must* first evaluate the tests very carefully and possibly prepare local norms. My other research all supports the necessity for the preparation of local norms and local predictive validity data, (3) that statisticians can be human, and (4) that journal editors (such as ours) can be patient, kind, and understanding beyond belief, but can also be very demanding. I believe that without the help and encouragement of Dr. Carol Ammons you would never have seen this article. The data would have been collected, reviewed, puzzled over, and forgotten.

RELATIONSHIP BETWEEN SELECTED KINDERGARTEN PREDICTORS AND FIRST AND FOURTH GRADE ACHIEVEMENT TEST SCORES

William E. Caskey, Jr.
EAST TENNESSEE STATE UNIVERSITY

Gerald L. Larson
KENT STATE UNIVERSITY

Earlier (Caskey & Larson, 1977, 1979, 1980) we reported the Koppitz/Bender test errors (Koppitz, 1964, 1975) for kindergarten children given either the standard individual or group administration of the Bender Visual-motor Gestalt Test. To ascertain the predictive validity of the Otis-Lennon IQ and the Bender errors the present longitudinal study was designed. Focus was on three areas. The first was the correlations between the kindergarten predictors (Otis-Lennon IQ, group or individual Bender errors, and teachers' ratings) and the relationships of these predictors to students' first-grade Stanford Achievement Test scores (Kelley, Madden, Gardner, & Rudman, 1964) as well as the fourth-grade scores from the Ohio Survey Test

Reprinted with permission of authors and publisher from: Caskey, W. E., Jr., & Larson, G. L. Relationship between selected kindergarten predictors and first and fourth grade achievement test scores. *Perceptual and Motor Skills*, 1983, 56, 815–822.

(Westinghouse Learning Corp., 1971). The second area was the correlations between the Stanford and Ohio test scores, while the third was the correlations between aptitude and achievement subtest scores of the Ohio Survey Test.

Method
Subjects
The subjects came from two distinct populations. One group came from a basically middle- to upper-class area (Group A) while the other students were from a basically Title I, free-lunch area (Title I group). Both were from a rural-suburban area in North East Ohio. The population was basically Caucasian, and all but one student used English as the basic language.

Procedure
During the first of May all students (116 from Group A and 63 from the Title I group) were ad-

ministered the Otis-Lennon Mental Ability Test, Primary I, Level J, 1967 Revision (Otis & Lennon, 1967), then matched pairs according to IQ were given either the individual Bender test or a group form of the Bender test (Caskey & Larson, 1977, 1980). Following the testing, with the results being unknown to them, the teachers rated each child using a Likert-type scale of one to seven as to probable success or lack of success in school. All teachers had had several years of experience in their schools.

During the latter part of the first grade the Primary I level of the Stanford test was administered to 102 Group A and 51 Title I group students, while the Ohio Survey Test was administered at the beginning of the fourth grade to 70 students in Group A and 32 students from the Title I school. Both tests were those then used by the schools and were administered by experienced and trained classroom teachers.

Using Pearson's r (Nie, Hull, Jenkins, Steinbrenner, & Bent, 1975) IQs from the Otis-Lennon, and raw scores from group Bender test, the indi-vidual Bender test, and the Kindergarten ratings were correlated with the Stanford (grade equivalents) and Ohio (percentiles) test scores. In the same manner Stanford test scores were correlated with Ohio test scores and the Ohio aptitude scores were correlated with the Ohio achievement scores.

Results and Discussion

The correlations are reported in the tables. Looking at the kindergarten IQs shows that for Group A (Tables 1 and 3) the IQs correlated positively and significantly with the Stanford and Ohio test scores in all but one instance. Tables 2 and 4, however, show a different outcome for the children from the Title I area; IQs correlated significantly with first grade Stanford test scores, for the total group and for girls, but for boys only the Arithmetic subtest. For the students from the Title I school none of the correlations between IQ and Ohio test scores were significant. In fact, all of the five correlations for boys were in the opposite (negative rather than positive) direction.

Table 1   Correlations of kindergarten predictors and Stanford Achievement Test scores: Group A

| Predictor | N | Stanford Achievement Test | | | |
		Word meaning	Paragraph meaning	Vocabulary	Arithmetic
Otis Lennon IQ					
Total	102	.47	.40	.40	.50
Boys	53	.47	.42	.58	.46
Girls	49	.48	.42	.42	.55
Bender, Group					
Total	51	−.36	−.54	−.28	−.54
Boys	24	−.07	−.29	−.28	−.40
Girls	27	−.43	−.54	−.29	−.59
Bender, Individual					
Total	51	−.38	−.18	−.32	−.22
Boys	29	−.52	−.23	−.23	−.15
Girls	22	−.17	−.18	−.37	−.32
Teachers' Ratings					
Total	102	−.52	−.61	−.44	−.56
Boys	53	−.43	−.58	−.43	−.58
Girls	49	−.62	−.66	−.45	−.55

Note. Bender errors and teachers' ratings are expected to be negative. $r \geq .28$ at $p \leq .05$.

Table 2   Correlations of kindergarten predictors and
Stanford Achievement Test scores: Title I children

Predictor	N	Word meaning	Paragraph meaning	Vocabulary	Arithmetic
			Stanford Achievement Test		
Otis Lennon IQ					
Total	50	.40	.35	.34	.57
Boys	22	−.06*	.09	.18	.58
Girls	28	.67	.57	.45	.57
Bender, Group					
Total	30	−.42	−.15	−.20	−.32
Boys	14	−.59	.07*	−.18	−.01
Girls	16	−.43	−.38	−.23	−.44
Bender, Individual					
Total	21	−.12	−.12	−.17	−.28
Boys	9	.31*	.29*	.04*	.08*
Girls	12	−.39	−.42	−.42	−.53
Teachers' Ratings					
Total	51	−.49	−.50	−.24	−.59
Boys	23	−.49	−.42	.03*	−.59
Girls	28	−.46	−.50	−.48	−.58

* Correlations for Bender errors and teachers' ratings are expected to be negative. $r \geq .32$ at $p \leq .05$.

In reviewing the scores from the two different administrations of the Bender test for Group A in Tables 1 and 3 we find that the scores from the group-test format correlated significantly with first and fourth grade test scores more often than did scores from the individual Bender format. For the Title I group scores from the individual Bender again did not show as many significant correlations as did those from the group Bender (Tables 2 and 4). It should be noted, however, that the declining number of students who were in the fourth-grade assessment pool could have been a reason for some of the nonsignificant correlations for the Bender errors at this level.

Concerning kindergarten teachers' ratings we found that for Group A the teachers did a uniformly fine job of predicting success in school as that was measured by the Stanford and Ohio test scores (Tables 1 and 3). However, for the Title I students the teachers' ratings, while correlating significantly with Stanford Achievement Test scores in 11 of the 12 combinations, did not cor-

relate significantly with the fourth-grade Ohio test scores (Tables 2 and 4).

For the students in Group A the first-grade Stanford scores correlated significantly with all fourth-grade Ohio test scores (Table 3). However, once again for the students from the Title I area the results differ; only 17 of the possible 60 combinations between the Stanford and Ohio scores were significant (Table 4).

With respect to the correlations between the aptitude sections of the Ohio test and the achievement sections (Table 5), we find that for Group A all correlations are significant, but not so for the correlations for the Title I group; there was no significant correlation between Verbal Ability and Math Achievement for girls while for boys the Math Ability scores did not correlate significantly with either Reading Achievement or Math Achievement.

In analyzing these data we were aware of the problems associated with the restricted ranges of both the Bender errors and teachers' ratings. We

Table 3   Relationship between kindergarten predictors, first-grade
SAT scores, and fourth-grade Ohio Survey Test scores: Group A

Predictor		Ohio Survey Test				
		Verbal ability	Math ability	Total ability	Read achievement	Math achievement
Kindergarten						
Otis-Lennon IQ						
Total	70	.51	.41	.47	.45	.37
Boys	36	.47	.46	.46	.49	.25
Girls	34	.53	.36	.48	.41	.47
Bender, Group						
Total	33	−.48	−.66	−.61	−.68	−.77
Boys	17	−.06	−.41	−.25	−.35	−.54
Girls	16	−.64	−.62	−.67	−.70	−.83
Bender, Individual						
Total	37	−.22	−.10	−.18	−.15	−.26
Boys	19	−.25	−.02	−.17	−.18	−.18
Girls	18	−.26	−.23	−.28	−.28	−.29
Teachers' Ratings						
Total	70	−.57	−.46	−.56	−.52	−.53
Boys	36	−.47	−.38	−.49	−.45	−.42
Girls	34	−.68	−.54	−.64	−.67	−.62
SAT Achievement						
Word Meaning						
Total		.63	.53	.63	.66	.48
Boys		.67	.51	.65	.61	.53
Girls		.52	.48	.55	.64	.38
Paragraph Meaning						
Total		.63	.57	.64	.64	.57
Boys		.54	.49	.55	.55	.48
Girls		.68	.51	.63	.60	.59
Vocabulary						
Total		.53	.48	.52	.55	.52
Boys		.37	.40	.41	.45	.49
Girls		.64	.50	.58	.66	.52
Arithmetic						
Total		.70	.66	.72	.57	.80
Boys		.72	.66	.76	.65	.78
Girls		.69	.69	.70	.53	.81

Note. $r \geq .36$ at $p \leq .05$.

suggest the significant correlations for these predictors as perhaps more meaningful than the numerical data suggest.

We were also aware of the relatively small number of students from the Title I group who were available for assessment in the fourth grade.

Since our primary concern was the predictive validity of the test scores, we believe that the results from this group clearly point to problems in assessment.

The Otis-Lennon IQ had good predictive validity for students from the middle- to upper-class

Table 4 Correlations* between kindergarten predictors, first-grade Stanford Achievement Test scores, and fourth-grade Ohio Survey Test scores for Title I children

Predictor	Verbal ability		Math ability		Total ability		Reading achievement		Math achievement	
	n	r	n	r	n	r	n	r	n	r
Kindergarten										
Otis-Lennon IQ										
Total	31	.23	31	.07	31	.16	30	.02	30	.02
Boys	11	−.75*	11	−.44*	11	−.78*	11	−.52	11	−.51
Girls	20	.14	20	.08	20	.19	19	.30	19	.30
Bender, Group										
Total	19	−.19	19	−.06	19	−.18	18	−.11	19	−.26
Boys	8	−.09	8	−.05	8	−.12	7	−.04	8	−.08
Girls	11	−.26	11	−.07	11	−.21	11	−.16	11	−.40
Bender, Individual										
Total	13	−.17	13	−.15	13	−.19	12	−.04	12	−.05
Boys	4	−.69	4	−.69	4	−.69	4	−.14	4	−.71
Girls	9	−.55	9	−.21	9	−.36	8	−.36	8	−.07
Teachers' Rating										
Total	32	−.13	32	.00	32	−.09	30	−.04	31	−.02
Boys	12	.01*	12	.27*	12	.11*	11	.14*	12	−.19
Girls	20	−.18	20	−.05	20	−.14	19	−.07	19	−.04
Stanford Achievement Test										
Word Meaning										
Total	32	.42	32	.29	32	.37	30	.53	31	.22
Boys	12	.40	12	.13	12	.35	11	.39	12	.17
Girls	20	.43	20	.35	20	.36	19	.56	19	.25
Paragraph Meaning										
Total	32	.28	32	.28	32	.36	30	.45	31	.26
Boys	12	−.17*	12	−.25*	12	−.22*	11	.39	12	.05
Girls	20	.56	20	.37	20	.49	19	.40	19	.38
Vocabulary										
Total	32	.01	32	.01	32	.04	30	.13	31	.03
Boys	12	−.22*	12	−.06*	12	−.15*	11	.27	12	−.16*
Girls	20	.16	20	.03	20	.03	19	.09	19	.04
Arithmetic										
Total	32	.13	32	.37	32	.26	30	.33	31	.28
Boys	12	−.54*	12	−.24*	12	−.56*	11	−.37*	12	−.18*
Girls	20	.35	10	.50	20	.47	19	.46	19	.45

* Correlations in opposite direction. Bender scores and Teachers' Ratings are expected to be negative. r ≥ .28 at p ≤ .05.

Table 5   Correlations* between aptitude subtests and achievement subtests of fourth-grade Ohio Survey Tests by group and by sex

	Group A		Title I	
	n	r	n	r
Reading Achievement				
Verbal Ability				
Total	70	.73	30	.65
Boys	36	.66	11	.63
Girls	34	79	19	.66
Math Ability				
Total	70	.71	30	.48
Boys	36	.62	11	.11
Girls	34	.74	19	.62
Total Ability				
Total	70	.77	30	.73
Boys	36	.71	11	.56
Girls	34	.80	19	.80
Math Achievement				
Verbal Ability				
Total	70	.75	31	.47
Boys	36	.67	12	.65
Girls	34	.80	19	.37
Math Ability				
Total	70	.81	31	.66
Boys	36	.81	12	.25
Girls	34	.80	19	.81
Total Ability				
Total	70	.80	31	.68
Boys	36	.80	12	.62
Girls	34	.85	19	.72

* $r \geq .48$ at $p \leq .05$.

area but did not do as well for students in the Title I school, particularly for boys. In fact, in the over-all comparison we find the differences in the predictive validity of all predictors, kindergarten, Stanford scores, and Ohio aptitude scores between the two groups to be, to us, astonishing. Quite frankly, at times we have wished that we had not assessed the students in the Title I area, but we did!

In light of our earlier "hunch" (Caskey & Larson, 1977) that teachers' ratings would be the least effective predictor of achievement, we stand corrected by the data. We were also surprised by the over-all larger number of significant correla-

tions for the group Bender format than for the individual Bender standard format. This suggests, to us, that for screening purposes the group Bender format which we used might be possibly more effective than the more time-consuming individual administration.

In general, the results appear to argue against the use of national norms when seeking to predict achievement in local schools. It is intriguing that even local perceptions by experienced teachers were both quite accurate and, for fourth-grade Ohio test scores for the Title I group, inaccurate. The results argue for the development and use of local norms, by school, and by sex, if tests are to be an effective base for making predictive statements concerning future academic achievement.

With one group from a predominantly Title I, free-lunch population it is tempting to speculate about research evaluating programs designed to remediate problems associated with the educational disadvantages often noted in such populations. However, the data from this study are not sufficient to make any general statements concerning this issue.

Basically the present results raise questions about research in the field. We tested children from one school district; the same researchers who used identical procedures yet found the predicted results quite variable. There are, it appears, at least two tenable positions based upon the results of this study: (1) the instruments used, kindergarten, first-grade, and fourth-grade, are imperfect and have generally low levels of predictive validity. It is logical that some attempt should be made to determine, school by school, according to sex, both concurrent and predictive validity of those instruments used to make statements concerning the academic progress, or lack of progress, of children in the school; (2) children, being human, are, at least by the present tests, quite unpredictable at times, and do not fit into neat packages. Such variability is one of the most important characteristics of humans and requires study.

Based upon these results it is quite possible to have varying results from school to school and from one part of the country to another by investigators using the same instruments and procedures with populations which are apparently similar. Caution is urged when one examines the data from one study which may differ significantly from data obtained by other researchers. It appears clear, also, that one must exercise great caution when making statements about individual children when those statements are based upon instruments which have not been demonstrated to have concurrent or predictive validity for a particular population and locality.

References

CASKEY, W. E., & LARSON, G. L. Two modes of administration of the Bender Visual-motor Gestalt test to kindergarten children. *Perceptual and Motor Skills,* 1977, *45,* 1003–1006.

CASKEY, W. E., & LARSON, G. L. Consistency of two modes of administration of the Bender Visual-motor Gestalt Test to kindergarten children in two different localities by sex. *Perceptual and Motor Skills,* 1979, *48,* 616.

CASKEY, W. E., & LARSON, G. L. Scores on group and individually administered Bender-Gestalt tests and Otis-Lennon IQs of kindergarten children. *Perceptual and Motor Skills,* 1980, *50,* 387–390.

KELLEY, T., MADDEN, R., GARDNER, E. F., & RUDMAN, H. C. *The Stanford Achievement Test.* New York: Harcourt, Brace & World, 1964.

KOPPITZ, E. M. *The Bender-Gestalt test for young children.* New York: Grune & Stratton, 1964.

KOPPITZ, E. M. *The Bender-Gestalt test for young children.* Vol. II. *Research and application 1963– 1973.* New York: Grune & Stratton, 1975.

NIE, N. H., HULL, C. H., JENKINS, J. G., STEINBRENNER, K., & BENT, D. H. *Statistical package for the social sciences.* (2nd ed.) New York: McGraw-Hill, 1975.

OTIS, A. S., & LENNON, R. T. *Otis-Lennon Mental Ability Tests.* (Rev.) New York: Harcourt, Brace & World, 1967.

Critical Review

A major use of correlational research methodology is to determine the predictive validity of assessment instruments used to assist educators in making educational decisions. Establishing the predictive validity of a test is a difficult task, since longitudinal field research must be conducted, often requiring that data be collected on a group of subjects over several years. P.L. 94-142, the Education for All Handicapped Children Act of 1975, mandated that assessment measures be validated for specific use with exceptional populations. This has stimulated many predictive validity studies, especially dealing with the prediction of pupil success in the primary grades based upon measures administered at the kindergarten or preschool level.

The article you have just read is a fairly typical example of a prediction study. Note that the authors have published three related studies over the past several years. A successful study almost always raises new questions or provides new insights, so it is not uncommon to find researchers following a single line of investigation over a long time span.

METHODS

Prediction studies use correlational research to relate predictive measures to criterion measures. In this study data on three predictors were collected: Otis-Lennon IQ, group and individual scores on the Bender Visual-motor Gestalt Test, and teacher ratings of each child's probable level of success in school. The criterion measures give us an estimate of the subjects' performance on the variable we want to predict, in this study school achievement. The predictor measures obtained at the kindergarten level were correlated with scores on the Stanford Achievement Test obtained at the end of first grade and the Ohio Survey Test administered at the beginning of fourth grade. Although the predictor and criterion tests used in this study are well known, it would have been desirable for the authors to describe briefly the specific scores obtained from each measure and summarize available reliability and validity data. Some additional data on the teacher ratings would also have been useful. For example, a readministration of the teacher ratings for a 30-pupil sample from each group after a one-month interval would have permitted an estimate of reliability for this rating.

SUBJECTS

An interesting aspect of this study is that subjects were drawn from two different populations. Predictive validity data can only be applied with confidence to subjects similar to those included in the validation study, that is, those drawn from the same broad population. By drawing samples from schools serving different socioeconomic levels, the researchers have provided the potential user with an opportunity to select the validation data that best fit her local schools. Of course, the more detail the researchers provide about the characteristics of their sample, the easier it is for the potential user to judge the relevance of the research findings to the population with which she is concerned.

Information on possible biases caused by attrition would also have been useful in giving the reader a better understanding of the data. Note that Group A dropped from 116 to 70 pupils and the Title I group from 63 to 32 pupils between kindergarten and Grade 4. Thus, complete data were obtained on 60 percent of Group A and 51 percent of the Title I group. Mean scores and standard deviations on the predictor variables comparing the lost subjects with those who were available at Grade 4 would help the reader estimate how these losses might have altered the characteristics of the sample. More detail, especially describing how the samples were selected and estimating the effects of attrition, would have strengthened this study.

RESULTS

The correlational data given in Tables 1 to 4 show that when taken singly, the predictors are not sufficiently correlated with later achievement to be very accurate in predicting individual student achievement. In order to estimate the predictive value of a correlation, you square the correlation to obtain the common variance. The common variance estimates the percentage of the criterion variance that is measured by the predictor variable. For example, you will note in Table 3 that the Group Bender Gestalt test administered in kindergarden (predictor measure) correlated $-.83$ for Group A girls with math achievement as measured by the math achievement subtest of the Ohio Survey Test administered in Grade 4. The square of $-.83$ is .69, which indicates that the Group Bender Gestalt predicts about 69 percent of the math achievement variance.

However, the predictor measures are sufficiently related to the criterion measures to make significant contributions to a multiple regression equation provided that they are not closely correlated with one another. When predictor measures are closely correlated with one another, it means they are all measuring the same aspects of the criterion measure. The ideal predictors are those that correlate highly with the criterion but are not highly related to each other.

You will recall that when scores on several predictor measures are available for a given individual, these scores can be combined in a multiple regression equation to obtain a better prediction of the subject's future performance on the criterion. It would have been helpful to potential users if the researchers had reported the correlations between the predictor measures, and prepared multiple regression equations to predict achievement of individuals in the two groups at Grades 1 and 4.

Notice that the predictive validity of the kindergarten measures is nearly always higher for girls than for boys. Many studies over the past 20 years have found that future academic performance of females is more predictable than that of males although these sex differences are usually small (Anastasi, 1982).

In reviewing the correlation coefficients in Tables 1 to 4, keep in mind that these relationships are attenuated to some degree because none of the measures that we employ are perfectly reliable. As the reliability of the measures being correlated decreases, the predictive validity coefficients also decrease. This is one reason why a brief summary of the reliability coefficients of both the predictor and criterion measures should be included in reports of predictive validity studies.

However, in spite of the omission of some information that could have been of interest to potential users of the research results, this remains a very valuable study. Its most important contribution is that it clearly illustrates the degree to which the predictive validity of measures can vary depending upon the sex and the socioeconomic level of the students in the sample. An important message given us by the researchers is (1) use predictive validity data obtained elsewhere with caution when applying these data to local schools, and (2) whenever possible, predictor measures found to be valid for other populations should be cross-validated for boys and girls in local schools before predictions are made. Good predictive validity data are very important, since predictions arising from student assessments can have an important impact on the future of students being assessed.

References

ANASTASI, A. (1982). *Psychological testing* (5th ed.). New York: Macmillan.

FISHER, C. W., FILBY, N., & MARLIAVE, R. (1978). *Executive summary of beginning teacher evaluation study*. San Francisco: Far West Laboratory for Educational Research and Development.

Recommended Reading

BORG, W. R., & GALL, M. D. (1983). *Educational research: An introduction* (4th ed.). White Plains, N.Y.: Longman.

See Chapter 14 for a nontechnical discussion of correlational research that will supplement the topics covered in this chapter.

BRUNING, JAMES L., & KINTZ, B. L. (1977). *Computational handbook of statistics* (2nd ed.). Glenview, Ill.: Scott, Foresman.

This book provides easy-to-follow computational procedures for these correlational techniques: product-moment correlation, Spearman rank-order correlation, Kendall rank-order correlation, point biserial correlation, correlation ratio, phi coefficient, contingency coefficient, partial correlation, multiple regression, and the test for difference between independent/dependent correlations.

JACKSON, DOUGLAS N., & MESSICK, SAMUEL (eds.). (1967). *Problems in human assessment.* New York: McGraw-Hill.

    Many of the articles reprinted in this book will be helpful to the student planning a prediction or selection study. Among them are Robert L. Thorndike, "The Analysis and Selection of Test Items," J. P. Guilford, "Some Lessons from Aviation Psychology," David R. Saunders, "Moderator Variables in Prediction," and Edward E. Cureton, "Validity, Reliability, and Baloney."

KERLINGER, F. N. (1973). *Foundations of behavioral research* (2nd ed.). New York: Holt, Rinehart & Winston.

    The author presents a mathematically sophisticated yet readable description of the correlational topics included in this chapter.

Application Problems

For each of the following brief research descriptions:

a. Indicate whether this would be a relationship study or a prediction study.
b. Identify a limitation that would need to be considered in applying the results.
c. Indicate the amount of common variance between the variables that were correlated.

1. A researcher wants to learn more about the nature of mathematical aptitude. He hypothesizes that verbal IQ, logical reasoning, and creativity are all related to mathematical aptitude. He selects 200 high school students who have enrolled in trigonometry, an elective mathematics course, and administers tests of mathematics aptitude (MA), verbal IQ (VIQ), logical reasoning (LR), and creativity (C) to this group. The following correlations were obtained:
       MA and VIQ = .54
       MA and logical reasoning = .40
       MA and creativity = .30

2. A researcher wants to estimate which entering college freshmen will earn the highest grades during their first year of college. He collects the following data on 500 entering freshmen: (1) high school grade point average, (2) scores on the California Test of Mental Maturity (CTMM), (3) scores on the Education Skills Test (College Edition) (EST). At the end of the year, 266 freshmen are still enrolled. The researcher computes correlations between their GPA during the first year of college and High School GPA, CTMM scores, and EST scores. He obtains the following correlations:
       First year GPA and H.S. GPA = .68
       First year GPA and CTMM = .61
       First year GPA and EST = .48

3. Using the evaluation form given in Appendix 1, evaluate the article by Brophy et al. reprinted in this chapter.

4. Using the evaluation form given in Appendix 1, evaluate the article by Caskey and Larson reprinted in this chapter.

5. Evaluate one of the articles listed under Chapter 9 in Appendix 2.

CHAPTER 10

EXPERIMENTAL, QUASI-EXPERIMENTAL, AND SINGLE-SUBJECT RESEARCH

Overview

The characteristics of experimental studies are discussed along with three experimental designs that are frequently used in educational research. The importance of internal validity is explained, and eight threats to internal validity are described. An experimental study is then presented and reviewed. Three quasi-experimental research designs are then discussed, and a quasi-experimental study is presented and reviewed. Finally, single-subject design is discussed, and a typical single-subject study is presented and reviewed.

Objectives

1. State the two essential characteristics of an experiment.
2. Describe the eight threats to internal validity, and give examples to show how each could affect the results of an educational research project.
3. Given a description of a research project, state which threats to internal validity are likely to be present.
4. Given a description of a research project, estimate the external validity for a local school situation with which you are familiar, considering population validity, personological variables, and ecological validity.
5. Describe two experimental and one preexperimental research designs.
6. Describe three quasi-experimental designs often used in educational research.
7. Describe two single-subject designs that can be used in educational research.
8. Given a description of a research project, tell what research design was used, what statistics would be appropriate, and discuss advantages and disadvantages.

Experimental Research

Most of the basic experimental designs used in education and the behavioral sciences have been adapted from the physical and biological sciences. Because of the greater difficulties in controlling experimental conditions in the behavioral sciences, experimental methods are very difficult to apply to certain kinds of educational problems. The typical experimental design in education involves the selection of a sample of subjects, random assignment of these subjects to experimental and control groups, and the exposure of the experimental group to a treatment that manipulates the independent variable. In some studies the control group is exposed to an alternate treatment while in others the treatment is withheld from the control group. Finally, an evaluation of the two groups is carried out by comparing their performance on the dependent variable, that is, the variable that you are attempting to change. Analysis of experimental research data typically involves computing the mean scores of each group on the dependent variable and then comparing the mean scores to determine whether the differences obtained are statistically significant. The statistical tools used to make these comparisons are called "inferential statistics" because they help the researcher draw inferences about the meaning of his findings. You will recall from Chapter 7 that inferential statistics can be classified as either parametric or nonparametric, depending upon what assumptions they make about the characteristics of the population from which the research subjects were drawn. Table 10.1 briefly summa-

Table 10.1   Inferential statistics often used to analyze experimental, quasi-experimental, and causal-comparative research data

Tests of statistical significance	Purpose
Parametric	
t-test, or critical ratio (z)	Used primarily to determine whether two means differ significantly from each other; also used to determine whether a single mean differs significantly from a specified population value.
Analysis of variance	Used to determine whether mean scores on one or more variables differ significantly from each other, and whether the variables interact significantly with each other.
Analysis of covariance	Used primarily in studies in which the mean scores of groups exposed to different independent variables are compared on one or more dependent variables. Similar to analysis of variance, but permits adjustments to the posttreatment mean scores of different groups on the dependent variable to compensate for initial group differences on variables related to the dependent variable.
Nonparametric	
Mann-Whitney U test	Used to determine whether two uncorrelated means differ significantly from each other.
Wilcoxon signed rank test	Used to determine whether two correlated means differ significantly from each other.
Kruskal-Wallis test	Used to determine whether three or more mean scores on a single factor differ significantly from each other.
Chi-square test	Used to determine whether two frequency distributions or sets of categorical data differ significantly from each other.

rizes the inferential statistics that are most widely used in experimental, quasi-experimental, and causal-comparative studies in education.

The two essential characteristics of an experiment are (1) there are treatments that manipulate the independent variable, and (2) the subjects who participate are randomly assigned to the treatments.

AN EXAMPLE

Let us consider an example of a simple experimental study in education. Suppose that we have developed a special program designed to improve the racial attitudes of children in racially mixed first-grade classrooms. This program would be our experimental treatment, or independent variable. Our first step in carrying out an experimental study would be to assign a group of perhaps 200 children randomly to 10 racially mixed classrooms. We would then randomly select 5 of these classrooms and include our program on racial tolerance in their curriculum. Students in the other 5 classrooms would be given the control treatment, which could either be an alternative program or no program in this area. At the end of the first grade, children in all 10 classrooms would be administered a measure of racial attitudes, the dependent variable, and statistical comparisons would be made to determine whether children in the experimental classes, who had been exposed to the special program, obtained more favorable scores than children in the control classes, who had not.

There are a great many variations on this basic experimental design. For example, in some studies pretests are administered before a program starts and posttests at the end of the experimental program, and comparisons are made between the experimental and control groups on the basis of gains rather than final performance. Also in some studies several programs may be compared in a single experiment. For example, a school district could conduct an experimental study designed to compare the effectiveness of five different first-grade reading programs. Another common variation in experimental research is for the investigator to design the research so that he is manipulating more than one independent variable. In the aforementioned study of racial tolerance, in addition to the special program that constitutes one independent variable, the investigator could assign children to classrooms in such a way that some classrooms contained 80 percent whites and 20 percent blacks; others contained half whites and half blacks; and still others 80 percent blacks and 20 percent whites. This second independent variable (usually called a moderator variable) could be called the racial composition of the classroom. In analyzing his results, the investigator could not only evaluate the overall effects of the racial tolerance program; he could also investigate the differential effects of this program in classrooms of different racial composition, in other words, how does racial composition moderate the effects of the racial tolerance program?

INTERNAL VALIDITY

When you evaluate preexperimental, experimental, and quasi-experimental studies, you must consider the degree to which weaknesses in the design can distort the results. In any experiment the results are partly due to the treatment and partly due to extraneous variables that operate during the study.

Internal validity is the degree to which the design of an experiment controls extraneous variables. Experiments are more or less internally valid depending on how well extraneous variables have been controlled by the researcher. If extraneous variables are not controlled in the experiment, we cannot know whether observed changes in the experimental group are due to the experimental treatment or to extraneous variables.

To demonstrate the importance of controlling for extraneous variables, we will consider a simple research problem that can be studied using preexperimental design. Suppose a researcher wishes to evaluate the effectiveness of a newly developed program in remedial reading. At the beginning of the school year, he selects 100 students for participation in the program; all these students meet the requirement of scoring at least two grades below the age norm on a standard test of reading achievement. After participation in the remedial program for a school year, the students are once again given a reading achievement test. Suppose the researcher finds a large, statistically significant gain (as determined by the t-test for correlated means). Can the researcher conclude that this achievement gain was caused by the experimental treatment, that is, the remedial reading program? The answer is no. The researcher cannot safely infer cause and effect unless extraneous variables have been adequately controlled. Campbell and Stanley (1963) have identified eight classes of extraneous variables that can affect internal validity. We will describe each of these threats to internal validity and discuss how each might have affected the results of aforementioned experiment.

1. History. Experimental treatments extend over a period of time, providing opportunity for other events to occur besides the experimental treatment. The students in our example participated in the remedial program over the period of a school year. Therefore, it is conceivable that other factors, such as the students' regular instruction from teachers, could have accounted for all or part of their achievement gain in reading.

2. Maturation. While the experimental treatment is in progress, biological or psychological processes within the student are likely to occur. Although Campbell and Stanley call these internal processes "maturation," they are referring to any changes internal to the subject. For example, research subjects may become older, stronger, fatigued, elated, or discouraged. All of these changes would be defined as "maturation" by Campbell and Stanley. Clearly, their definition is much broader and includes much that we do not normally think of as maturation. During the year of the remedial program described above the students were developing physically, socially, and intellectually. Possibly maturation in one of these areas, rather than the remedial program, may have enabled the students to overcome their reading deficiency.

3. Testing. In many educational experiments a pretest is administered, followed by the experimental and control treatments and then a posttest. If the two tests are similar, students may show an improvement on the posttest simply as a result of their experience with the pretest; that is, they have become "test-wise." In the case of our remedial reading example, it is unlikely that this extraneous variable would be operating. Because of the long period of time between pre- and posttesting, there is little chance that students will remember enough about the pretest to have any effect on their posttest performance. However, in many studies where the interval between pre- and post measures is short or the nature of the pretest makes it easy to remember, pretest effect is likely to occur. In this case the researcher cannot clearly determine how much of the subjects' posttest performance is due to the treatment and how much is due to exposure to the pretest.

4. Instrumentation. An apparent learning gain may be observed from pretest to posttest because the nature of the measuring instrument has changed. This often occurs in educational studies in which the researcher uses alternate forms of the same standardized test that are supposed to be equivalent but are not. Suppose in our remedial reading example the students had been administered a posttest of reading achievement that was supposed to be equivalent but was actually easier than the pretest they had taken. The gain in achievement could be attributed to the differences in the testing instruments rather than to the effect of the experimental treatment.

5. Statistical regression. Whenever a test-retest procedure is used to assess change as an effect of the experimental treatment, the possibility exists that statistical regression can account for observed gains in learning. We will not present the mathematical basis for statistical regression here (see Borg & Gall, 1983), but simply describe its effects on test scores. In our research example, a group of students was selected who fell below the 15th percentile on a test of reading achievement. If the same group of students were tested again on the same or a similar test, they would earn a higher mean score because of statistical regression, with or without an intervening experimental treatment. Furthermore, if another group of students were selected who earned very high scores on the first test, for example, above the 85th percentile, these students would earn a lower mean score when retested on a similar measure, again as a result of statistical regression. Upon retesting, regression always tends to move the average subject's score toward the mean. The researcher should be alert to the confounding effects of statistical regression whenever students have been selected for their extreme scores on a pretest and are retested later on a posttest measure that is correlated with the pretest.

The probable amount of regression can be estimated using statistical formulas and considered in the results. Whenever extreme groups are being studied, the researcher should take regression into account and interpret his results accordingly.

6. Differential selection. In quasi-experimental designs in which a control group is used, the effect of the treatment can sometimes be distorted because of differential selection of students for the experimental and control groups. Suppose in our research example students need to meet the requirements of falling below the 15th percentile in reading achievement and of volunteering to participate in the program. Further, suppose that the achievement gains of this group are compared with a control group of students who have equivalent reading deficiencies but did not volunteer for the program. If the experimental group shows greater achievement gains than the control group, the effect could be attributed to "volunteer" characteristics rather than to the experimental treatment itself. To avoid this confounding effect, the experimenter needs to select experimental and control groups that do not differ except for exposure to the experimental treatment. In other words, the same criteria should be applied to selecting subjects for both the experimental and control groups. The best way to accomplish this is to assign subjects randomly to the two groups, which is one of the basic requirements of a true experiment.

7. *Experimental mortality* (sometimes called attrition). Experimental mortality is the loss of subjects in a study during the time the study is being conducted. The reason that experimental mortality can bias research results is that the subjects who drop out of a study are usually different in important ways from the subjects who remain. You will recall that in survey research one of the most difficult problems is determining whether subjects who do not respond to a questionnaire are different from those who do and estimating how this difference, if present, is likely to distort the survey results. In experimental studies a larger number of subjects are often lost from the experimental group than from the control group. Differential attrition from these groups can distort the results when the posttreatment scores of the remaining subjects are compared. This extraneous variable might be operative in our research example if there were a systematic bias in the type of students who dropped out of the remedial program during the school year. For example, some students might leave the program because they perceived they were not making any achievement gains. If the researcher measures only the achievement gains of those students who completed the program, the effectiveness of the experimental treatment will be exaggerated. It is necessary first to measure the achievement gains of all students who entered the remedial program irrespective of whether they completed it or not; then their achievement gain should be compared to that of a suitable control group. In experimental designs, whenever there is more attrition from one group than the other, there is always the danger that this attrition has biased the results of the study.

8. *Selection-maturation interaction.* This extraneous variable is similar to differential selection, except that maturation is the specific confounding variable. Suppose that first-grade students from a single school district are selected for the remedial program previously described. The control group is drawn from the population of first-grade students in another school district. Because of different admissions policies in the two school districts, the average age of the control group is six months older than that of the experimental group. Now, suppose the research results show that the experimental group makes significantly greater achievement gains than the control group. How should we explain these results? Do they reflect the effectiveness of the experimental treatment, or do they show that reading gains in younger students are more influenced by maturational factors than in slightly older students? Because of differential assignments of students varying in maturation to the experimental and control groups, it is not clear which of these alternative explanations is correct.

When you evaluate an experimental, preexperimental, or quasi-experimental study, it is helpful to keep these eight threats to internal validity in mind and try to estimate how well the study is designed to deal with each of them. You should also keep in mind that some of these threats are important in other types of educational research. For example, experimental mortality can distort the findings of most educational studies, regardless of the design employed. You may want to think through what you have learned about descriptive, causal-comparative, and correlational research and consider how the various internal validity threats can introduce extraneous variables into each type of research.

EXTERNAL VALIDITY

External validity may be defined as the degree to which research results can be generalized to persons, settings, and times different from those of the research. Depending upon the similarity between the research conditions and the conditions found in the local schools, findings from a given study can have high external validity for use in some local settings and low external validity for others. Thus, the potential user must compare the research conditions with the local conditions to which he wants to generalize the results and make a decision as to how well the findings are likely to apply. Bracht and Glass (1968) have described specific aspects of external validity that the reviewer should consider when generalizing to the local educational setting.

   Population Validity.   You will recall from our discussion of sampling in Chapter 5 that population validity is the degree to which the results of a research can be generalized from the specific sample that was studied to the population from which this sample was drawn.

   One aspect of population validity is determined by examining evidence that shows the similarity between the *sample* used in the research, the *accessible population* from which the research sample was drawn, and the *target population* to which the research results are to be generalized. The more evidence the researcher provides to establish links between the sample, the accessible population, and the target population, the more confidence the user can have in applying the research findings to the target population.

   However, in most cases the teacher or administrator who wants to apply research findings to a problem or need in his school is interested in the similarity between the research sample and the local population rather than the target population. To establish this relationship, he should note all information the researcher has provided about the research sample such as age, sex, scholastic aptitude, racial composition, achievement, communities from which subjects were drawn, socioeconomic status, and other relevant information. He should then gather the same data for the local population to which he wants to apply the research findings. Comparing these two sets of data will give a basis for estimating the degree to which the research findings are likely to apply.

   Another type of population validity that the teacher or administrator should consider is the degree to which *personological variables* are likely to interact with the research findings. A considerable amount of accumulating evidence shows that in many cases research findings valid for subjects at one grade level, or ability level, or socioeconomic level, or in one content area may not apply to subjects who differ on these variables. For example, the Beginning Teacher Evaluation Study aimed at relating specific teacher procedures and strategies to the achievement of second- and fifth-grade pupils in mathematics and reading (Fisher et al., 1978). It was found that although some teacher strategies were significantly related to pupil achievement at both grade levels and subject areas, the majority were not. For example, academic monitoring was negatively correlated with achievement in Grade 2 reading but positively related to achievement in Grade 2 mathematics. At Grade 5, correlations between academic monitoring and achievement in both subjects were virtually zero. On the other hand, teacher use of academic feedback was positively related to achievement at both grade levels and for both subject areas.

Thus, even though a teaching procedure may have some general merit, it may vary greatly in its effectiveness at different grade levels, different subject areas, or for pupils with different characteristics.

Ecological Validity.   The third aspect of external validity that must be considered in estimating the generalizability of research finding is called ecological validity. *Ecological validity* is concerned with the extent to which the research results that were obtained under the environmental conditions that existed during the research can be generalized to other environments. When applying the research results to the local environment, the teacher or administrator must address two questions:
1. How similar is the environment in which this research was conducted to the local environment to which I want to generalize the results?
2. If major differences exist between the two environments, how are these differences likely to interact with the research results?

As a rule you can assume that the larger the difference between the research environment and the local environment to which you want to apply the research results, the less confidence you can have that the research findings will apply to the local situation.

Remember, however, that only differences that interact with the research findings will affect the generalizability of the results. Thus, the results of a study of the effect of a new first-grade reading program conducted with first-grade pupils in a small town in the South may generalize very well to other small towns, rural communities, and medium-sized cities. In other words, size of the community may have virtually nothing to do with the program's effectiveness. On the other hand, if the first-grade pupils in the research sample were in classrooms of 20 pupils and if their teachers had two part-time aides to help with reading instruction, while your classroom has 32 pupils and no aides, the research results may not apply to your classroom because of this difference in the learning environment.

Research Trade-offs.   You may have noted that the very kinds of control of the research situation that lead to high levels of internal validity tend to make the research environment different from the environment in the typical classroom and therefore reduce external validity. There is no completely satisfactory solution to this dilemma. All the researcher can do is weigh the advantages of rigorous control of extraneous variables against the advantage of doing research in natural educational environments and come to a compromise that provides acceptable levels of internal and external validity.

Let's now consider two experimental and one preexperimental design often used in educational research and discuss which threats to internal validity are typically present in each.

RESEARCH DESIGNS

Pretest-Posttest Control Group Design.   In research articles the investigator often uses symbols to describe his experimental design. R means that the subjects were randomly assigned; X is used to represent the experimental treatment; and 0 means observation, that is, either a pretest or a posttest of the dependent variable. For example, the *pretest-posttest control group design* is written:

$$R \ O \ X \ O$$
$$R \ O \ \ \ O$$

The top line represents the experimental group; the second line the control group. Translated into words these symbols mean:
1. R - the groups are randomly assigned
2. O - both groups are given the pretest
3. X - the experimental group is given the treatment, the control group gets no treatment
4. 0 - both groups are given the posttest

This is an excellent design, which Campbell and Stanley originally believed to be subject to none of the eight internal validity threats they had described. In fact, they concluded that the true experimental designs, all of which employ random assignment of subjects to X and C groups, controlled for all eight internal validity threats. Their rationale is that since initial differences between the experimental and control groups are controlled by random assignment of subjects, threats such as testing, instrumentation, and statistical regression, if they occur at all, will affect the experimental and control groups about equally. Therefore, posttreatment comparisons between the X and C groups on the dependent variable will still be valid, since extraneous variables (such as testing) will impact equally on both groups and thus tend to cancel themselves out. Similarly, extraneous events that occur during the conduct of the experiment (that is, history) are likely to affect both X and C groups in about the same way and consequently tend to cancel out when the groups are compared on the posttreatment measure of the dependent variable.

In more recent work Cook and Campbell (1979) have concluded that experimental mortality is not controlled by randomization. In many studies, even though X and C groups are initially comparable, the differences in the demands made on the subjects in the X and the C groups can lead to large differences in the number of subjects lost during the course of the experiment. Thus, posttreatment differences on the dependent variable may be due to differences in such characteristics as motivation and ability between remaining X and C group members rather than differences attributable to the experimental treatment.

Posttest-Only Control Group Design.   This design is written:

$$R \; X \; O$$
$$R \quad\;\; O$$

This indicates that subjects are randomly assigned to the experimental and control groups. Then the experimental group is given the experimental treatment, and finally both groups are given a posttest that measures the dependent variable. This design is useful in studies where differences in pretreatment performance are unlikely. It is also used when the treatment is short, since this would lead to a short interval between pre- and posttesting. The main threat to internal validity that is present in this design is experimental mortality. In a design using pre- and posttesting, if you lose subjects before the posttest, you can study their pretest scores to determine if the subjects lost are biased, that is, different from those retained. With posttest-only designs, this comparison is not possible.

One-Group Pretest-Posttest Design.   Campbell and Stanley call this design "preexperimental." Although it is a very weak design, it is often used in educational research. Consequently, it is important for you, as a user of educational research, to be familiar with its weaknesses.

The design is written $O \, X \, O,$ which indicates that a pretest is given to all subjects, they are then given the experimental treatment and then administered the posttest. There is no control group, and for this reason most of the internal validity threats are present when this design is used. The most serious threats are history, maturation, testing, and instrumentation. Since there is no control group that is subject to the extraneous variables that occur between the pre- and posttest but does not get the treatment, the effect of these variables cannot be estimated. In a control-group design the posttest performance of the experimental group is the sum of treatment effects and extraneous effects. The posttest performance of the control group reflects extraneous effects but not treatment effects. Thus, in control-group designs, we assume that the degree to which the experimental group's posttest mean score exceeds the control group's posttest mean score represents the effect of the treatment. The same rationale can be applied to maturation, testing, and instrumentation; that is, the control group controls for these effects in the same way it controls for history.

A Limitation of Experimental Research.   Most problems dealing with human behavior involve many variables that can be important to the study. One limitation in using experimental designs is that it is very difficult for the investigator to manipulate more than three or four independent variables in a single study. Nevertheless, experimental research in education still provides the most effective tool available for determining cause-and-effect relationships. In contrast, correlational research can consider simultaneously a very large number of variables, but can only help us identify *possible* cause-and-effect relationships. In exploring educational problems, researchers often use the strategy of first carrying out correlational studies in order to narrow down the number of possible variables that are important to a given problem and then conducting experiments to test the cause-and-effect relationship among those variables that have been identified in the correlational studies.

Let us now review an experimental study that has important implications for any teacher who wants to improve achievement in his classroom. First, read the abstract, then read the researcher's comments to get some insight into why he did the research, what problems he encountered, and what he has done to follow up on his research. Then read the research article itself. Finally, read the critical review of the article. This review will give you some ideas of what to look for when you read articles describing experimental research.

Sample Experimental Study: "PROGRESS SELF-MONITORING: EFFECTS ON CHILDREN'S SELF-EFFICACY AND ACHIEVEMENT"

Abstract[1]

This experiment investigated the effects of progress self-monitoring on children's achievement and percepts of self-efficacy in the context of mathematical competency development. Children lacking subtraction skills received didactic instruction in subtraction and practice opportunities. Some children (self-monitoring) monitored their own progress after each training session, whereas others (external monitoring) had their progress monitored by an adult. A third group received no monitoring. Results showed that self- and external monitoring led to significantly higher percepts of efficacy, skill, and persistence compared with no monitoring. The two progress monitoring conditions did not differ significantly on these measures. The utility of self-monitoring procedures in actual classrooms is discussed.

The Researcher's Comments

Background

I conducted this study as part of my research program to explore the influences on students' self-efficacy during cognitive skill learning. This study is based on the idea that conveying information to students about how well they are learning should enhance their *self-efficacy*, or beliefs about their capabilities. In turn, higher self-efficacy ought to lead to greater

---

1. The abstract from the article is reprinted here in order to provide a context in which the researcher's comments can be related.

learning. This study explored the role of explicit progress monitoring. Other studies in my research program have investigated the effects of instructional procedures involving modeling, goal setting, and rewards.

The procedures in this study were quite straightforward: Children counted the number of pages they completed during each training session or observed an adult proctor count their pages. A page count is, of course, a rather rough index of progress; however, in this context it signified learning, because the subjects were students who were deficient in subtraction despite classroom instruction. This point is important, because if students have already learned a skill, the number of pages completed does not signify learning but rather speed of performance. In the present context, it was important to convey information to students about how well they were learning, not about how fast they could work.

Experiences

This study was well received in the schools in which it was conducted, because it was concerned with teaching low achievers skills that they had failed to learn. Initially, I showed participating teachers the skill test and asked them to nominate students who probably could not correctly solve more than one-quarter of the problems and therefore might benefit from the program. Because this study was concerned with the development of self-efficacy and skills, including students who were proficient in subtraction would have served no purpose. If you look at the pretest skill means (Table 1), you will see that the average achievement was below 4.5 problems correct (that is, 25 percent of 18 problems).

Conducting research in elementary schools has advantages and disadvantages compared with a more formal laboratory setting. An important advantage is that we can examine learning where it typically occurs. Thus, our results are likely to be generalizable to other schools. At the same time, procedures often are not implemented exactly as planned. For example, students are absent one or more days, fire drills occur, and there seem to be innumerable minor disruptions (for example, students misbehave, announcements are made over the public address system, and so on).

To minimize potential disruptions, I decided not to conduct the experimental sessions in the children's regular classes. With the help of the teachers, we finally decided to use the school cafeteria when it was not in use for lunch. This setting worked well. Several children could participate in training at once; they could be spread out to discourage conversing with one another; and the proctor could remain nearby but out of sight. Although there still were a few minor distractions (such as students walking down the hallway next to the cafeteria), the experimental procedures could be properly implemented.

Aftermath

The results of this study, along with those of the other studies in my research program, provided support for the idea that instructional procedures do more than simply teach. They also convey information to students about their level of knowledge and skill. In the present study, students who did not receive monitoring completed as much work during the training sessions as did the subjects in the two monitoring conditions; yet the latter students judged their capabilities higher and solved more problems correctly on the posttest.

This study is not the first piece of educational research to show that minor variations in instructional procedures result in different student outcomes, or that performance feedback is important in learning. The contribution of this study, I believe, is that it suggests a possible mechanism for why these effects occur; namely, the information provided to students about how well they are learning. Students who believe that they are capable of learning are apt to feel more competent for continuing to improve their skills.

Implications

I think that the major educational implication of this study is that practitioners need to consider what kind of information about level of competence they convey to students when they present instruction and provide feedback. We know that there are different ways to teach skills. In planning lessons, teachers need to consider how their teaching and students' activities might affect students' beliefs about themselves. There is much educational research showing that students' confidence in their abilities bears a positive relationship to school learning.

Many students can determine on their own how well they are learning; for example, they may notice that they are "catching on" more rapidly than they used to. Gauging one's own progress may be more apparent in higher ability students and those in the upper grades. Young children, however, have short time frames of reference and may not have developed the ability to relate their present performance to their prior accomplishments. Students who have difficulty learning may have the same problem. For these students, explicit progress feedback may be quite important.

The procedures used in this study are easy to implement in the classroom. Many teachers provide students with progress feedback by monitoring their work, displaying charts, providing verbal feedback ("You're doing much better"), and giving awards or recognition for improvement. It is important to keep in mind that if we want to build students' confidence in their abilities, the feedback needs to indicate improvement. Especially with students who have encountered some difficulties learning subject matter in school, such feedback may have to be explicit and delivered frequently.

PROGRESS SELF-MONITORING: EFFECTS ON CHILDREN'S SELF-EFFICACY AND ACHIEVEMENT

Dale H. Schunk
UNIVERSITY OF HOUSTON

There is growing interest in the role of self-regulation as a means of initiating and maintaining behavioral change (2, 12). The self-regulation process consists of three distinct components:

Schunk, Dale H., "Progress Self-Monitoring: Effects on Children's Self-efficacy and Achievement." *Journal of Educational Research*, 1982, pp. 89–93. Copyright 1982, Heldref Publications, Washington, D.C. Reprinted by permission.

self-monitoring, self-evaluation, and self-reinforcement (10, 11). Self-monitoring refers to deliberate attention to some aspect of one's behavior, and is often accompanied by recording its frequency or intensity. During self-evaluation, persons compare their level of attainment against some desired performance standard. Depending on the outcome of the evaluation, some form of self-reinforcement may then be administered. Feelings of self-satisfaction and perceptions of competence result when attainments match standards, whereas a perceived negative discrepancy between attainments and desired performance level should motivate individuals to strive toward improvement.

The purpose of the present study was to determine how self-monitoring of instructional progress in the context of children's arithmetic competency development affects achievement and percepts of self-efficacy. The conceptual focus was Bandura's theory of self-efficacy (1, 3). According to this theory, psychological procedures change behavior in part by strengthening perceived self-efficacy. Self-efficacy is concerned with judgments of how well one can organize and execute courses of action required in situations that may contain novel, unpredictable, and stressful elements. Percepts of efficacy can affect choice of activities, effort expended, and perseverance in the face of difficulties. Efficacy information is conveyed through enactive attainments, socially comparative vicarious measures, social persuasion, and inferences from physiological arousal.

Self-monitoring was originally employed in the larger context of therapeutic programs to determine the baseline rate of behaviors targeted for alteration. However, research using a variety of behaviors and different subject populations has demonstrated that self-monitoring in the absence of over self-imposed standards or reinforcement contingencies promotes behavioral change (5, 9, 13, 14, 17, 18). In one study (19), students periodically monitored their performances during mathematics sessions and recorded whether or not they were working on the appropriate instructional materials. Self-monitoring alone significantly increased students' time on task and mathematical achievement.

Where explicit performance standards and reinforcement contingencies do not exist, the effectiveness of self-monitoring may depend on the extent to which covert self-evaluation occurs (10, 19). In the self-efficacy analysis (1, 3), self-monitoring of instructional progress should promote and validate percepts of efficacy, as well as boost achievement. As children observe their progress while engaged in a cognitive learning task they experience a heightened sense of efficacy. Explicit monitoring to include recording of one's performance attainments provides a reliable guide to progress and helps validate percepts of efficacy. A strong sense of efficacy for being able to perform cognitive tasks should sustain subsequent task involvement and promote achievement.

In the present study, children who had failed to master subtraction operations in their regular classrooms received didactic instruction and opportunities to solve subtraction problems over several sessions. One group of children (self-monitoring) reviewed their work at the end of each training session and recorded the number of pages they completed. To investigate the effects of monitoring procedures more generally, a second group (external monitoring) had their work reviewed at the end of each session by an adult proctor who recorded the number of pages completed. To control for the effects of providing instruction, a third group (no monitoring) received the competency development program but no monitoring. Children were not provided with explicit performance standards, nor were overt reinforcement contingencies in effect.

If self-monitoring derives its effectiveness largely from covert self-evaluative processes (10, 19), then the monitoring agent may be less important than the monitoring itself since self-evaluation could conceivably occur as a result of monitoring by others. Self- and external monitoring were therefore expected to prove equally effective in promoting children's achievement and percepts of efficacy. In the absence of monitoring, however, children are on their own to gauge their progress. Since they might not do this, perceived efficacy may not be validated. These children were therefore expected to feel less efficacious and achieve less than those receiving either form of progress monitoring.

Method
Subjects
Subjects were 30 predominantly middle-class children ranging in age from 8 years, 6 months to 9 years, 5 months (mean age = 8.8 years). The 15

males and 15 females were drawn from two elementary schools. Since this study focused on processes whereby skills and percepts of efficacy could be cultivated when they were initially lacking, teachers were initially shown the subtraction skill test and nominated children who they felt could not solve correctly more than 25% of the problems. Children were individually administered the pretraining assessment by one of two female adult testers.

Procedure
Pretraining Assessment

Self-efficacy judgments. Children's percepts of self-efficacy for correctly solving subtraction problems were measured following procedures of previous research (4, 20, 21). The efficacy scale ranged from 10 to 100 in 10-unit intervals from high uncertainty through intermediate values to complete certitude, where the higher the scale value, the stronger the perceived efficacy. Initially, children were given practice by judging their certainty of being able to jump progressively longer distances ranging from a few inches to several yards. This practice familiarized children with the scale's direction and general meaning of the values.

Children then were shown briefly 18 sample pairs of subtraction problems, which allowed assessment of difficulty but not actual solutions. For each pair, children privately judged their certainty of being able to solve correctly the type of problem depicted by circling an efficacy value. Each problem pair corresponded in form and operations required to one problem on the skill test, but they were not identical. Children were judging their capability to solve types of problems and not whether they could solve any particular problem. Self-efficacy was scored as the number of judgments in the upper-half (certainty side) of the efficacy scale.

Subtraction skill test. Immediately following the efficacy assessment, children received the subtraction skill test consisting of 18 problems ranging from two to six columns. Each problem tapped one of the following operations: no borrowing, borrowing once, borrowing from a one,

borrowing twice, and borrowing caused by a zero. These problems were similar in form and operations required to some of the problems children would subsequently solve during training. The tester presented problems to children one at a time. Children were instructed to examine each problem and to place the page on a completed stack when they were through solving the problem or chose not to work on it any longer. They were given no performance feedback. The measure of skill was the number of problems that children solved correctly. The tester also recorded the time children spent with each problem. These persistence times were summed across problems and averaged.

Training Procedures
Following pretesting, children were randomly assigned within sex and school to one of three conditions ($N = 10$): self-monitoring, external monitoring, no monitoring. On three consecutive school days, children received 30-minute training sessions, during which they worked individually on an instructional packet consisting of six sets of material. Each set covered a different subtraction operation and they were ordered in terms of least-to-most difficult (6) as follows: no borrowing, borrowing once in 2-column problems, borrowing once in 3-column problems, borrowing once caused by a zero, borrowing twice, and borrowing from a one. The format of each set was identical. The first page contained written explanation of the subtraction operation and two step-by-step worked examples. The next six pages each contained several problems to solve.

Children were brought individually by an adult proctor and were seated at desks spread over a large area to preclude visual and auditory contact with others. Initially, the proctor placed the entire packet in front of the child. The proctor then showed the children the first explanatory page and informed them that whenever they arrived at a similar page they were to bring it to the proctor. The proctor then read the narrative on this page while pointing to the exemplified operations. If children asked for further assistance, the proctor simply reread the relevant instructions but did not supplement them. The proctor stressed the importance of careful work and then retired to an out-of-sight location. Children solved problems alone. The proctor returned at the end of the session and gave the appropriate monitoring instructions but did not score the children's papers. Children marked their places in the packet by drawing a line and resumed there the following day.

Monitoring Conditions

Self-monitoring. The proctor instructed these children at the end of each session to count the number of pages they completed during the period and to record that number on the progress sheet which was a separate page filed at the end of the child's training packet. It contained the child's name and space to record the number of pages completed each session. The proctor departed immediately after giving these instructions; children recorded their progress privately. Children departed once they recorded their pages, after which the proctor returned and checked whether the children had done so. All children did for each session. In two instances, children erroneously counted one page short, but the proctor did not correct these errors.

External monitoring. This condition was similar to self-monitoring except that the proctor counted and recorded the child's pages at the end of each

session while the child observed: The proctor did this matter-of-factly and without any accompanying verbal reinforcement.

No monitoring. Children in this condition received the same instructional material and practice opportunities as subjects in the preceding conditions but no monitoring. At the end of each session, the proctor simply informed children that the period was over.

Posttraining Assessment

The posttest was administered individually by an adult tester the day after the third training session. It was similar to the pretest except that a parallel form of the skill test was employed to eliminate possible familiarity with the problems. In a separate assessment (4) using children similar to the present sample, these forms were highly correlated, $r = .87$. For any given child, the same tester administered both pre- and postassessments and was blind to the child's experimental condition.

Results

Means and standard deviations by experimental condition are presented in Table 1. Preliminary analyses of variance revealed no significant differences due to tester, school, or sex of child on any

Table 1   Means and standard deviations

Measure	Phase	Experimental condition					
		Self-monitoring		External monitoring		No monitoring	
		$\overline{X}$	SD	$\overline{X}$	SD	$\overline{X}$	SD
Self-efficacy[1]	Pretest	5.1	1.8	4.8	2.0	5.0	2.1
	Posttest	15.6	2.3	14.9	2.6	7.2	4.7
Skill[2]	Pretest	2.5	1.7	2.7	1.4	2.4	1.5
	Posttest	13.3	2.9	12.1	3.3	5.8	3.4
Persistence[3]	Pretest	15.7	8.3	17.2	10.1	14.8	6.9
	Posttest	30.6	10.7	33.7	12.1	18.6	10.0
Progress[4]	—	29.3	4.6	27.5	4.7	26.1	3.2

Note: $N = 30$; $n = 10$.
[1] Number of efficacious judgments on 18 problems.
[2] Number of accurate solutions on 18 problems.
[3] Average number of seconds per problem.
[4] Number of pages completed out of 36 during training.

pre- or posttest measure nor any significant inter-actions; the data were pooled across these vari-ables. There were no significant between-condi-tion differences on any pretest measure. Analysis of covariance procedures were applied to each posttest measure using the appropriate pretest measure as the covariate. Significant results were further analyzed using the Newman-Keuls multi-ple comparison test (16). Since the use of analysis of covariance necessitated demonstration of slope homogeneity across treatment groups (15), tests of slope differences for each measure were made by comparing a linear model that allowed separate slopes for the three treatment groups against one that had only one slope parameter for estimating the pre-posttest relationship pooled across treat-ments. These analyses found the assumption of slope homogeneity across treatments to be tena-ble.

For the measure of subtraction self-efficacy, analysis of covariance yielded a significant treat-ment effect, $F(2,26) = 7.60$, $p < .01$. Post-hoc comparisons revealed that the two monitoring conditions did not differ significantly from one another but each made significantly ($p < .01$) more efficacious judgments than the no monitor-ing condition.

A significant treatment effect was also obtained on the skill measure, $F(2,26) = 7.14$, $p < .01$. Children who received monitoring procedures ex-hibited significantly ($p < .01$) higher subtraction skill than did no monitoring subjects. The two monitoring conditions did not differ significantly.

Analysis of covariance yielded a similar treat-ment effect on the persistence measure, $F(2,26) = 6.85$, $p < .01$. Children who received monitoring subsequently persisted on test problems signifi-cantly longer ($p < .01$) than did children whose training progress was not monitored, e.g., the monitoring groups did not offer.

No hypothesis was advanced concerning the effects of monitoring on instructional progress. To investigate this possibility, an analysis of variance was applied to the number of pages of problems the children completed during the training ses-sions. This result was nonsignificant. The same finding was obtained using the number of training problems that children solved correctly.

Discussion

The present study demonstrates that progress monitoring in the context of competency develop-ment is highly effective in promoting percepts of efficacy and achievement. Further, it was the monitoring process itself, and not the monitoring agent, that was important. These beneficial out-comes were obtained even though experimental conditions did not differ on measures of instruc-tional progress.

These results may be explained as follows. As children observe their progress during training, they develop a heightened sense of efficacy (3). Subsequent monitoring directs children's atten-tion to the work they completed and provides an objective indicant of progress, which helps to val-idate perceived efficacy. In a subsequent test situ-ation in which children decide how long to spend on problems, a heightened sense of efficacy sus-tains task involvement and results in greater achievement. Conversely, when children's per-formances are not monitored they are on their own to assess their progress. Even though skills develop, children may be unsure of their capabili-ties. During testing, lower percepts of effi-cacy lead to less persistence and lower achieve-ment.

Data analyses revealed no differences in any measure due to monitoring agent. In many class-room situations, self-monitoring would seem pref-erable to external monitoring. Once teachers had instructed students on how to monitor their pro-gress, self-monitoring would allow teachers to de-vote more time to other matters. Self-monitoring also allows students to gain capability information on their own. This should help foster a more gen-eral sense of responsibility for mastering cognitive learning, which is an important developmental task accomplished chiefly in school (3).

The present self-monitoring procedure included elements of reviewing and recording. Future re-search might examine whether recording pro-motes achievement outcomes beyond the effects due to reviewing. From a developmental perspec-tive, recording of progress may be highly impor-tant for young children who tend to have short time frames of reference and who may not always be cognizant of what they have accomplished. As children develop, they become better able to keep prior progress information in mind.

This study supports the theoretical idea that judgments of self-efficacy are not mere reflections of past performance (3). This idea has been supported by previous research in the area of achievement behavior (4, 20, 21). Although experimental conditions did not differ in instructional progress, subjects who received monitoring later judged efficacy significantly higher.

This is not surprising since judgments of personal capabilities derived from one's performance vary depending on the weight placed on personal and situational factors that affect how one performs (3). In forming efficacy judgments, persons weigh the relative contribution of ability and nonability factors, such as perceived task difficulty, effort expended, amount of external aid received, situational circumstances under which the performance occurs, temporal pattern of successes and failures, and evaluative standards against which performances are appraised.

The self-monitoring process bears a striking resemblance to the procedures involved in goal setting. Goal setting represents a form of self-motivation in which persons compare present performances to internal standards (2, 22). The anticipated satisfaction of attaining a goal leads to sustained involvement until performances match standards. Goal-setting procedures can be easily integrated with regular classroom instruction (7, 8). A system in which students pursue attainable goals and periodically monitor their progress toward those goals should prove highly effective in cultivating skills and validating a sense of efficacy for applying them.

References

1. Bandura, A. Self-efficacy: Toward a unifying theory of behavioral change. *Psychological Review*, 1977, *84*, 191–215.

2. Bandura, A. *Social learning theory*. Englewood Cliffs, N.J.: Prentice-Hall, 1977.

3. Bandura, A. Self-referent thought: A developmental analysis of self-efficacy. In J. H. Flavell & L. Ross (Eds.), *Social cognitive development: Frontiers and possible futures*. Cambridge: Cambridge University Press, 1981.

4. Bandura, A., & Schunk, D. H. Cultivating competence, self-efficacy, and intrinsic interest through proximal self-motivation. *Journal of Personality and Social Psychology*, 1981, *41*, 586–598.

5. Broden, M., Hall, R. V., & Mitts, B. The effect of self-recording on the classroom behavior of two eighth-grade students. *Journal of Applied Behavior Analysis*. 1971, *4*, 191–199.

6. Friend, J., & Burton, R. *Teachers' guide: Diagnostic testing in arithmetic: Subtraction*. Palo Alto: Xerox Palo Alto Research Center, 1981.

7. Gaa, J. P. Effects of individual goal-setting conferences on achievement, attitudes, and goal-setting behavior. *Journal of Experimental Education*, 1973, *42*, 22–28.

8. Gaa, J. P. The effects of individual goal-setting conferences on academic achievement and modification of locus of control orientation. *Psychology in the Schools*, 1979, *16*, 591–597.

9. Gottman, J. M., & McFall, R. M. Self-monitoring effects in a program for potential high school dropouts: A time-series analysis. *Journal of Consulting Psychology*, 1972, *39*, 273–281.

10. Kanfer, F. H. Self-regulation: Research, issues, and speculations. In C. Neuringer & J. L. Michael (Eds.), *Behavior modification in clinical psychology*. New York: Appleton-Century-Crofts, 1970.

11. Kanfer, F. H. The maintenance of behavior by self-generated stimuli and reinforcement. In A. Jacobs & L. B. Sachs (Eds.), *The psychology of private events*. New York: Academic Press, 1971.

12. Kanfer, F. H. Self-management methods. In F. H. Kanfer & A. P. Goldstein (Eds.), *Helping people change: A textbook of methods* (2nd ed.). Elmsford, N.Y.: Pergamon Press, 1980.

13. Kazdin, A. E. Reactive self-monitoring: The effects of response desirability, goal setting, and feedback. *Journal of Consulting and Clinical Psychology*, 1974, *42*, 704–714.

14. Kazdin, A. E. Self-monitoring and behavior change. In M. J. Mahoney & C. E. Thoresen (Eds.), *Self-control: Power to the person*. Monterey: Brooks/Cole, 1974.

15. Kerlinger, F. N., & Pedhazur, E. J. *Multiple regression in behavioral research*. New York: Holt, Rinehart & Winston, 1973.

16. Kirk, R. E. *Experimental design: Procedures for the behavioral sciences*. Belmont, Calif.: Brooks/Cole, 1968.

17. Lipinski, D. P, Black, J. L., Nelson, R. O., & Ciminero, A. R. Influence of motivational variables on the reactivity and reliability of self-recording. *Journal of Consulting and Clinical Psychology*, 1975, *43*, 637–646.

18. Nelson, R. O., Lipinski, D. P., & Black, J. L. The effects of expectancy on the reactivity of self-recording. *Behavior Therapy*, 1975, *6*, 337–349.

19. Sagotsky, G., Patterson, C. J., & Lepper, M. R. Training children's self-control: A field experiment in

self-monitoring and goal-setting in the classroom. *Journal of Experimental Child Psychology*, 1978, *25*, 242–253.

20. Schunk, D. H. Modeling and attributional effects on children's achievement: A self-efficacy analysis. *Journal of Educational Psychology*, 1981, *73*, 93–105.

21. Schunk, D. H. Effects of effort attributional feedback on children's perceived self-efficacy and achievement. *Journal of Educational Psychology*, in press.

22. Schunk, D. H., & Gaa, J. P. Goal-setting influence on learning and self-evaluation. *Journal of Classroom Interaction*, 1981, *16*, 38–44.

Critical Review

INTRODUCTION

This study compares the effectiveness of self-monitoring, external monitoring, and no monitoring upon achievement in subtraction and children's perceptions of self-efficacy. The study is introduced in the context of Bandura's theory of self-efficacy. Most research in education is not clearly linked to theory. However, research that tests a theory often contributes both to our understanding of teaching and learning, and to classroom practice. Thus, most researchers consider theory-based research to be preferable.

METHOD

More information on the characteristics of the subjects chosen would be desirable, since such information helps the reader to judge the relevance of the research to his own students. Also, a larger sample would have been desirable. The main problem involved in using small samples is that a large difference between groups will be needed to reach statistical significance. This increases the probability of making a "Type 2 Error," which leads us to conclude that the treatment had no effect, when in fact a real effect did occur and would have reached statistical significance if a larger sample had been used. In practical terms, when a Type 2 Error is made, the result can be that we will abandon an effective strategy that if continued would lead to improvement in the dependent variable. A "Type 1 Error" leads us to conclude a treatment effect when there was none.

In many educational studies the researcher faces the choice of collecting a large amount of data on a small sample or a small amount of data on a large sample, since the total time available to conduct the study is limited. Under these conditions it is generally better to follow the first option, since research that studies a small sample in depth is usually more productive. This is the course that Schunk followed, probably because all measures were administered to the children on an individual basis, thus requiring a considerable amount of time to collect data on each child.

In this study, because of the very strong effects of the two monitoring treatments, the results were significant in spite of the small size of the sample.

Data on four dependent variables were collected in this study: children's perceptions of self-efficacy in solving subtraction problems, children's skill in solving subtraction problems, children's persistence in trying to solve subtraction problems, and children's progress in studying subtraction. Little validity or reliability data was given. Some discussion of the construct validity of the self-efficacy measure should have been provided. Validity of the skill measure is not needed, since solving subtraction problems clearly measures subtraction skills. Alternate-form reliability of this measure was reported to be .87 for a similar group of subjects. Persistence was measured by recording the time children spent on each problem and computing an average. Since time measures can be taken very accurately, reliability data on this measure are not needed. However, since children correctly solved many more problems on the posttest and since once a problem is solved, there is no reason to persist further, the posttest data may underestimate the level of persistence. Perhaps the mean time devoted to problems not solved on the pre- and posttests would have been a more valid measure of persistence.

You will recall that experimental research requires (1) random assignment of subjects to treatments, and (2) manipulation of the independent variable. In this study both of these requirements were met. The three experimental conditions manipulated only the monitoring variable. Self-monitoring required the child to count and record the number of pages of instructional material he completed for each of the three training sessions. For the external monitoring group the proctor counted and recorded the pages completed while the child observed. In the no-monitoring condition, children worked on the same material but no page counting or recording occurred.

As the author points out in his introduction, the self-regulation process consists of self-monitoring, self-evaluation, and self-reinforcement. Although this study focused on self-monitoring, some self-evaluation and self-reinforcement could also have taken place. For example, upon counting the pages completed in a lesson, the child could have evaluated his progress and concluded that he was doing a good job of learning subtraction skills. Such incidental outcomes are very difficult to control in field research.

In any case the results of this study are very impressive and suggest that even a moderate amount of monitoring, whether conducted by the student or the teacher, can have an important impact on achievement, as well as on favorable student self-perceptions and persistence.

Since both kinds of monitoring were effective, teachers may want to use a mix of the two approaches, depending upon the learning task. In reviewing the results of this research, consider the following questions:

1. What other kinds of monitoring could have been used in this study? For example, would counting and recording the number of correct training problems make this monitoring procedure more powerful?

2. Can monitoring, evaluation, and reinforcement ever be completely separated?

3. What could you do to develop a treatment that would attempt to maximize the effects of self-monitoring, self-evaluation, and self-reinforcement on achievement and efficacy? Be as specific as you can in spelling out such a treatment.

Quasi-experimental Research

Many educational studies employ what is called quasi-experimental design. The main difference between a true experiment and a quasi experiment is that in a true experiment it is possible to assign subjects randomly to the different treatments or experimental conditions, whereas in quasi-experimental research random assignment, for one reason or another, is not possible. For example, in many studies conducted in the public schools, the classes are already formed before the researcher comes onto the scene. In this case it is usually necessary to work with these intact groups. If the researcher plans ahead, it is sometimes possible to have students randomly assigned to several different classes as part of the school's regular scheduling procedure. However, this is the exception rather than the rule. Another difference often found between the two types of research is that true experimental designs always have a control group, while some quasi-experimental designs do not.

Carefully designed quasi-experimental studies in education can provide valuable information, but this information must be accepted with less confidence than we would have if the study had employed true experimental design. Let us briefly review three of the most widely used quasi-experimental designs.

RESEARCH DESIGNS

Posttest-Only Design with Nonequivalent Groups.   This design is similar to the posttest-only control-group design except in the way that subjects are assigned to groups. Assignment of subjects to the experimental and control groups is random in the posttest-only control-group design but not in the nonequivalent group design.

The steps involved in applying the posttest-only design with nonequivalent groups are as follows: (1) two groups of subjects are selected from the same population, (2) one group of subjects is administered the experimental treatment and is then posttested, and (3) another group of subjects is given the posttest only. These steps are represented by the following diagram:

$$\frac{X \qquad O}{O}$$

where X represents the experimental treatment, O represents posttest measurement of the dependent variable, and the broken line indicates that the experimental and control groups are not formed randomly.

The main threat to internal validity in this design is differential selection. That is, posttest differences between groups can be attributed to characteristics of the groups as well as to the experimental treatment. For example, suppose teachers in one school are given an experimental treatment and posttest, and teachers in another school are given only the posttest. If differences on the posttest are found, it can be argued that they are due to differences between teachers in the two schools rather than to the effect of the experimental treatment. In this situation where random assignment cannot be used, it is preferable to use the nonequivalent control-group design discussed next.

Another possible source of internal invalidity in this design is experimental mortality. To illustrate this problem Campbell and Stanley (1963) discuss a hypothetical experiment comparing first- and fourth-year college women. This experiment can be considered a posttest-only design with nonequivalent groups, since the fourth-year women have received the experimental treatment (a college education) but the first-year women have not, and the two groups have not been formed randomly.[2] Now suppose it were found that the first-year women received significantly higher ratings of beauty than fourth-year women. Would we conclude from these results that college education has a "debeautifying" effect on women? The finding can be explained more plausibly in terms of differential mortality. Although the first-year women are an intact group, by the fourth year many women have dropped out of college during the course of the treatment. We could argue, then, that the differences between groups are caused by the more beautiful women leaving college to be married, or for other reasons. Thus, the findings are explained more plausibly in terms of mortality in the experimental group rather than in terms of effects of the experimental treatment.

The posttest-only nonequivalent group design is a relatively weak quasi-experimental design, and when you review studies that employ this design, its weaknesses should be kept in mind.

Pre-Post Design with Nonequivalent Groups. This is probably the most widely used quasi-experimental design in educational research. It is similar to the posttest-only design with nonequivalent groups except that both groups are given a pretest, which can be used to determine whether the two groups were initially equivalent on the pretest variable even though they have not been formed by random assignment.

Thus, differential selection is less of a threat in this design than in the posttest-only design with nonequivalent groups. However, although this design gives evidence of group comparability on our pretreatment measure of the dependent variable, we have no evidence that the groups are initially comparable on other variables that could influence the results of the study. This is because some systematic bias of which we are unaware might lead subjects high on variable X to be placed on one classroom, while those low in that variable would be placed in another classroom.

For example, suppose we are using this design to compare the effectiveness of two methods of teaching Spanish. Students in third-period Spanish are taught with Method A while those in the sixth-period class are taught with Method B. Both classes are given a foreign language aptitude test and obtain very similar mean scores. However, the basketball team practices sixth period, so boys who want to be on the basketball team must take Spanish third period. Since basketball practice runs for two hours every afternoon, these students have less time to study and are more tired in the evenings than students taking sixth-period Spanish. As a result the sixth-period students make higher grades on the posttest on Spanish achievement. We might erroneously conclude that Method B is more effective when the achievement difference in fact is due to study time and fatigue. On the other hand, random

---

2. This could also be classified as a causal-comparative design.

assignment of subjects to groups gives us a basis for expecting the groups to be moderately comparable on all relevant variables, since we know that no systematic bias or unknown variable is operating to determine the group to which any given subject is assigned.

This design is represented by the following diagram:

$$O \quad X \quad O$$
$$\overline{}$$
$$O \qquad\quad O$$

where X represents the experimental treatment, O represents pretest or posttest measurement of the dependent variable, and the broken line indicates that the experimental and control groups are not formed randomly.

To illustrate the steps involved in setting up this design further, suppose that the researcher has available for his experiment six classrooms in each of two schools. Because of administrative considerations, he must assign all the classrooms in School A to the experimental group and all those in School B to the control group. The first step in the nonequivalent control-group design is to administer a pretest to each student in all the participating classrooms. Next, one set of six classrooms is assigned to the experimental treatment group, and the other set is assigned to the control group. At this point mean scores on the pretest can be computed for each group to determine if the groups are initially comparable on the dependent or pretest variable. Third, the treatment is applied to the experimental group. Finally, after the treatment has been completed, all students in both groups are administered the posttest.

Let us now consider a common situation in educational research that makes use of this quasi-experimental design necessary. Suppose a researcher is interested in testing the effect of a new educational strategy or curriculum product in the public schools. This strategy or product is such that it must be administered to an entire classroom or not at all. For example, the researcher might be interested in whether a series of instructional films in social studies has an effect on student achievement. To answer this question, suppose he sets up two groups: an experimental group that receives the treatment variable (the instructional films) in addition to conventional instruction in social studies, and a control group that receives only the conventional instruction. Now, it is hard to imagine how the researcher can assign students randomly to these two conditions, unless he can wait until the next term and assign pupils at random to different social studies sections before the new term begins. Once the term has started, the teacher cannot easily arrange to have half the students in his classroom view the films and the other half not view them. Although the researcher might ask to have the control students leave the classroom while the films are being shown, this procedure would probably not be approved by the principal, since it would have a disruptive effect on the teacher's classroom. In addition, the researcher would need to arrange a special learning situation to occupy the time of the control students while they were out of the classroom. Faced with these difficulties, the researcher had best assign all the students in a given classroom to either the experimental or the control group. Of course, this procedure constitutes nonrandom assignment, since each student does not have an equal chance of being placed in either the experimental or control group.

Remember, that the difficulty with nonrandom assignment is that the experimental and control groups may differ in some characteristics, thus confounding the interpretation of the research results. Suppose the researcher was able to recruit six teachers in two schools to participate in the study. The classrooms of three of the teachers are chosen to view the instructional films; the other three classrooms are to serve as the control group. Assuming 30 students per classroom, there will be 90 students in each group. It may be that the experimental and control classrooms differ in some vital respect. Suppose that teachers in the experimental group are drawn from one school and control teachers are drawn from another school. Under these circumstances, differences in the mean achievement gain of the two groups might be attributed to characteristics of the schools rather than to the experimental treatment. For example, the teachers in the experimental group may work in an urban school, whereas the control teachers work in a rural school, or the principal of one school may place more emphasis on achievement than the principal of the other, or one school may serve a neighborhood having a higher socioeconomic status than the other. In summary, any number of extraneous variables having nothing to do with the instructional films could affect social studies achievement in the two schools.

When using this design, the researcher should report as much descriptive data as possible about his experimental and control groups such as the location of the participating schools, experience level of teachers, socioeconomic level of the schools, average achievement scores of pupils in the different schools. This kind of information can help the reviewer decide how comparable the groups are who have participated in the study. In many quasi-experimental studies the investigator draws his experimental and control subjects from closely comparable groups and in this case his results can be given nearly as much weight as if he had used a true experimental design.

Time-Series Design.   In the time-series design a single group of subjects is measured at periodic intervals. The experimental treatment is administered between two of these time intervals. This design can be represented as follows:

$$O\ O\ O\ X\ O\ O\ O$$

This indicates that three observations (or pretests) were made, then the treatment (X) was introduced, and then three additional observations (or posttests) were made. The effect of the experimental treatment, if any, is indicated by a discrepancy in the measurements before and after its introduction. For example, a researcher might count the mean attendance of college students at six consecutive lectures in several different courses. Suppose the attendance at the first three lectures is 100, 115, and 104 (out of the mean total enrollment of 175 students). At the end of the third class period, all enrolled students are informed that the professor will conduct a question-and-answer session during the fourth class meeting. Attendance for this class increases to a mean of 160 students. For the fifth and sixth class sessions the professor again conducts question-and-answer, and the attendance is maintained at 152 and 154 students, respectively. These hypothetical results suggest quite strongly that the use of a question-and-answer session leads to increased student attendance.

The time-series design is similar to the one-group pretest-posttest design. Both designs involve the study of a single group, and both designs involve measurement before and after the experimental treatment. The use of additional measurements preceding and following the experimental treatment makes the time-series design more powerful. These additional measurements enable the researcher to rule out maturation and testing effects as sources of influence on shifts from pretest to posttest.

Let us now review a quasi-experimental study that employs a variation of the pre-post design with nonequivalent groups. In this study the dependent variable is achievement. However, since achievement measures would have been inappropriate at the pretreatment level, data were collected on several measures that have been found to be correlated with achievement. The study is especially important to teachers because it is concerned with the effects of one of the Follow Through programs that have been designed to improve the achievement of low-income children. The study is also of interest because it is longitudinal, following the same children over a period of five years. First read the authors' comments, then the article, and finally the critical review.

Sample Quasi-experimental Study:
"A FOLLOW-UP OF FOLLOW THROUGH: THE LATER EFFECTS OF THE DIRECT INSTRUCTION MODEL ON CHILDREN IN FIFTH AND SIXTH GRADES"

Abstract[3]

The later effects of the Direct Instruction Follow Through Program were assessed at five diverse sites. Low-income fifth and sixth graders who had completed the full three years of this first- through third-grade program were tested on the Metropolitan Achievement Test (Intermediate Level) and the Wide Range Achievement Test (WRAT). Results were contrasted with those of children in local comparison groups using analysis of covariance procedures. Results indicated consistently strong, significant effects in WRAT reading scores (decoding), consistent effects in math prob-

---

3. The abstract from the article is reprinted here in order to provide a context in which the researcher's comments can be related.

lem-solving and spelling, and moderate effects in most other academic domains. Students appeared to retain the knowledge and problem-solving skills they had mastered in the primary grades. However, without a continuing program, most students demonstrated losses when compared to the standardization sample of the achievement tests. Implications for improved instruction in the intermediate grades were discussed.

The Researcher's Comments[4]

Background

The question addressed in this study is one that constantly comes up in discussions of educational interventions, particularly "compensatory" programs such as Head Start, Follow Through, or innovative special education models. It comes up in conversations among teachers, among politicians, among academics. Namely, do the effects of a specialized program of intervention last? That is, two or three years after the programs end, do students demonstrate any enduring effects?

Of course, everyone hopes that their model will produce lasting effects, yet rarely do evaluations address this issue. In the typical approach, students are assessed and tested at the conclusion of the program, the results of the evaluation are reported, and the reader is left to wonder what might have happened afterward.

It is rare that a project has the resources to conduct a follow-up study. Fortunately, we did. The logistics involved in testing more than 1000 students in six states were not easy. But the fact that Follow Through remained in existence for over 15 years allowed us to have the evaluation staff and resources to conduct the study. In addition, Wes Becker, the senior author, had established fine rapport with certain districts, which facilitated the selection of local comparison groups. Interestingly, he had much more success with rural districts such as Uvalde, Texas, and the moderate-sized cities such as Dayton, than with the large cities.

Issues Addressed in the Study

Before the study was conducted, there was a good deal of evidence to suggest that the highly structured Direct Instruction Follow Through Program had significant positive effects on all aspects of academic achievement for the low-income students in the 20 communities that participated. The results of an independent evaluation conducted by Abt Associates for the U.S. Office of Education (Stebbins, 1976; Stebbins et al., 1977) showed that, by and large, students who participated in the program from the first through the third performed at a much higher level than students in traditional classrooms. In addition, the work of Jane Stallings (1975) indicated that students in the Direct Instruction classrooms spent significantly more time actively engaged in reading and math activities. The Abt evaluation also suggested that the self-concept of these students was a bit higher than their peers, although some controversy exists about the measures used (House et al., 1978).

Critics of structured programs often argue that their effects will dissipate once the structure is removed. For this reason alone, this study is important. Before conducting the analyses, we expected to find effects, though perhaps modest in many areas. The reason

---

4. This commentary was written by Dr. Russell Gersten.

was simple. Follow Through was conducted in some of the poorest, most disorganized districts in the country. Once the program ended (i.e., in the third grade), students were placed in regular classrooms. Sometimes, the quality of the teaching was less than optimal. In Follow Through, special curricula were used that (1) attempted to teach strategies to students, (2) focused on mastery of each step in the learning process, and (3) focused on active student involvement. Neither the teaching nor the texts the students encountered in Grades 4, 5, and 6 had any of these features.

Nonetheless, we felt that what students had learned well—primarily oral language skills, the ability to read with comprehension, and basic math concepts—would still contribute appreciably to their performance in the upper elementary grades.

In fact, that is what the results of the study showed. Many of the effects are modest but consistent. The area of greatest strength is oral reading. Math problem solving and science also show reasonably strong effects. However, students did not make the gains expected in areas such as math computation and reading comprehension. This confirmed our belief that the programs in the intermediate grades need to be dramatically improved. When we reviewed the results over five communities, only 2 of the 180 effects were negative. Thus, there was clear evidence that something had happened.

Implications of the Study

It is interesting to compare these results with those of a more recent meta-analysis of the effects of Head Start. The Head Start findings, in general, show no enduring effects. The reasons for the difference may be that an intensive three- or four-year program, like Direct Instruction Follow Through, may be necessary to secure a lasting effect, whereas the one year of preschool is probably inadequate. Furthermore, Direct Instruction focused on building academic skills rather than the more generic "readiness" skills often emphasized in Head Start. As we said in our conclusions, these results can serve as a source of optimism or pessimism—optimism in the sense that intensive early intervention can lead to lasting positive effects, pessimism in that the Follow Through graduates, though continuing to achieve at a higher level than their low-income peers in traditional programs, did fall behind middle-class students once the intervention ended.

Reactions to the Article

This last finding was emphasized by several individuals after the article was published. They took it to show that Direct Instruction, like all other interventions, is flawed (Doyle, 1983). What Doyle and others failed to take into account was that, in our views, the students declined in Grades 4, 5, and 6 when compared to middle-class students primarily because the quality of education they received in Grades 4, 5, and 6 was significantly weaker than most middle-class students received. Over the years, as I've traveled to most of these communities from which the data came, I've become more convinced of this. The need to upgrade both the texts used and the fashion of teaching does not stop in third grade. Fortunately, many districts have since embarked on school improvement efforts, some of which have markedly improved the quality of instruction. There is now a large national movement to upgrade basal texts. However, in our view, the move to upgrade the quality of teaching in the elementary grades has only begun. Serious use of instructional principles such as those used in Follow Through—such as teaching to mastery, teaching of strategies, use of phonics, large amount of interactive teaching—is still erratic.

Subsequent Research

My own research has gone off in two very different directions. The first is a literal out-growth of this study. In 1980 the time had come to look at the high school careers of these students, and I directed a study that examined the issue. The preliminary findings (Gersten, Carnine, & Keating, 1984) are, in some ways, more optimistic than those reported here. In many communities, we saw significant reduction in dropout rate and few retentions. In two communities (New York City and Cherokee, North Carolina), students were still reading at grade level in the ninth grade. But there was more to the study than the numbers. I spent six months in 1982 and three months in 1983 at the sites, working out the details of the study, riding the subway lines, and seeing every vocational high school in Brooklyn and Manhattan. I drove through swampy country roads in South Carolina to high schools located in cow pastures. It was impossible to miss seeing how low teachers' expectations are for these low-income adolescents. Sometimes this was reflected in apathy, sometimes in sarcasm and overt hostility. On the one hand, it was gratifying to observe Follow Through's impact on adolescents from one of the poorest sections in New York City, long known for its low achievement. Many were reading at a higher level and few dropped out. Likewise, in one of the poorest counties in the country, with one of the highest illiteracy rates, it was gratifying to see that Follow Through has improved the graduation rate. On the other hand, even with Follow Through and the high reading scores, the dropout rate is still 40 percent for the New York students.

The other side of my work has been examination of exactly what were—and are—the components that lead to the success of the Direct Instruction Follow Through Program. This has included research on curriculum design (Darch, Carnine, & Gersten, 1984), teaching procedures (Gersten, Carnine, & Williams, 1982), and a project that attempts to look at the day-to-day realities of in-service training and supervision in inner-city schools. I still see the major hope for school improvement as lying with knowledgeable, caring, in-service work for teachers who work with "at-risk" students. Current research findings now identify certain particularly effective practices. The major task at this time is conveying this information to the field in a concrete, meaningful way.

References

DARCH, C., CARNINE, D., & GERSTEN, R. (1984). Explicit instruction in mathematical problem-solving. *Journal of Educational Research, 77*(6), 350–359.

DOYLE, W. (1983). Academic work. *Review of Educational Research, 53*(2), 159–199.

GERSTEN, R., CARNINE, D., & KEATING, T. (1984). *The lasting impact of the Direct Instruction Follow Through Program: Preliminary findings of a longitudinal study of 1500 students.* Paper presented at American Educational Research Association, New Orleans, La.

GERSTEN, R., CARNINE, D., & WILLIAMS, P. (1982). Measuring implementation of a structured educational model in an urban setting: An observational approach. *Educational Evaluation and Policy Analysis, 4,* 67–79.

HOUSE, E. R., GLASS, G. V., MCLEAN, L. D., & WALKER, D. E. (1978). No simple answers: Critique of the "Follow Through" evaluation. *Harvard Educational Review, 48,* 128–160.

STALLINGS, J. (1975). Implementation and child effects of teaching practices in Follow Through classrooms. *Monographs of the Society for Research in Child Development, 40.*

STEBBINS, L. (ed.). (1976). *Education as experimentation: A planned variation model* (Vol. IIIA). Cambridge, Mass.: Abt Associates.

STEBBINS, L., ST. PIERRE, R. G., PROPER, E. L., ANDERSON, R. B., & CERVA, T. R. (1977). *Education as experimentation: A planned variation model* (Vols. IVA–D). Cambridge, Mass.: Abt Associates.

A FOLLOW-UP OF FOLLOW THROUGH: THE LATER EFFECTS OF THE DIRECT INSTRUCTION MODEL ON CHILDREN IN FIFTH AND SIXTH GRADES

Wesley C. Becker and Russell Gersten
UNIVERSITY OF OREGON

Project Follow Through evaluated a variety of educational approaches to teaching low-income children in various communities from kindergarten (or first grade) through third grade. The originators of Follow Through believed that gains made by students in Head Start could be enhanced and solidified in a comprehensive, systematic 3- or 4-year program. One of the approaches found to be most effective in the longitudinal evaluation conducted by Abt Associates and Stanford Research Institute under the auspices of the U.S. Office of Education (USOE) was the Direct Instruction Model (Bereiter & Kurland, 1981–82; Kennedy, 1978; Stebbins et al., 1977).

The present study investigated the later effects of Direct Instruction Follow Through; that is, what happened to fifth- and sixth-grade graduates of the Direct Instruction Follow Through program. These children were tested on all subtests of the Intermediate Form of the Metropolitan Achievement Test (Durost, Bixler, Wrightstone, Prescott, & Balow, 1970) and the Reading subtest of the

Becker, Wesley C., Gersten, Russell, "A Follow-up of Follow Through: The Later Effects of the Direct Instruction Model on Children in Fifth and Sixth Grades." *American Educational Research Journal,* 1982, pp. 75–92. Copyright 1982, American Educational Research Association, Washington, D.C. Reprinted by permission.

Wide Range Achievement Test (Jastak & Jastak, 1965). Results were compared to children in local comparison groups with similar demographic characteristics using analysis of covariance (ANCOVA) with multiple covariates. In addition, the longitudinal progress of the samples for the 3 years of the program and the 3 years after the program was compared to the norm samples of the Metropolitan and Wide Range Achievement Tests.

Background

The Direct Instruction Model represents a highly structured approach to early-childhood education with an emphasis on high levels of academic-engaged time through small-group instruction in reading, oral language, and arithmetic. The Distar® curriculum materials used in this approach are designed to explicitly teach general principles and problem-solving strategies. Teachers and paraprofessional aides are trained to teach these programs in a fast-paced, dynamic fashion with high frequencies of unison group responses and systematic corrections of student errors.

In some communities, Follow Through began in kindergarten and lasted 4 years; in others, Follow Through began in first grade and lasted 3 years. For a variety of logistical reasons (primarily having to do with difficulties in obtaining cooperation in larger northern cities) this follow-up study deals only with the 3-year programs. (See Becker & Englemann [1978] for further details.)

Results of the national evaluation (Stebbins et al., 1977) indicated a high proportion of significant positive effects for both 3- and 4-year Direct Instruction sites. When third-grade students completing the Direct Instruction Follow Through program in the 3-year sites were compared to a pooled national comparison group, they performed significantly higher in 60 percent of the instances for total reading, 80 percent for total math, 100 percent in language, and 50 percent in spelling.

The absolute level of performance on standardized achievement tests was typically higher for students in the 4-year programs than the 3-year programs, particularly in reading. Because of this fact, the results reported here represent a low estimate of what might have been achieved. Figure 1 presents mean scores on all subtests of the Wide Range Achievement Test (WRAT) Level I, and 1970 Metropolitan Achievement Test (MAT), Elementary Level, for all low-income students in the 3-year program. These data were collected for four groups of children in eight communities. The WRAT scores, on the left, are presented in the form of a norm-referenced comparison (Horst, Tallmadge, & Wood, 1975; Tallmadge, 1977). The mean standard scores at the beginning of the program (entry into first grade) and end of the program (end of third grade) are converted to percentiles in order to assess growth against the norm sample of the WRAT. The right half of Figure 1 presents MAT scores. Again, the mean standard scores at the end of third grade are converted to a percentile. No pretest level of the MAT was available. The performance of Direct Instruction Follow Through students is contrasted with typical third-grade performance of low-income, minority students in math and reading, according to USOE reports (Ozenne et al., 1974; 1976). Note that MAT math and language scores are within a few percentile points of the national median, and all scores are significantly above the typical level of low-income, minority students. The large discrepancy between decoding skills (word reading as assessed by the WRAT) and reading comprehen-

sion scores (as assessed by MAT reading) is probably due primarily to low-income children's problems with the large, virtually uncontrolled reading vocabulary required on third-grade achievement tests (which reflects the content of fourth-grade textbooks) (Becker, 1977). Schools expect vocabulary development to occur at home, yet Becker makes a clear case that is not happening in many low-income homes. Note that no corresponding discrepancy appears in Math, where the MAT tests computation, high-order problem solving, conceptual skills, and the WRAT tests only computation.

It seemed important to examine the later effects of the Direct Instruction Follow Through program to see if the students maintained and built on the gains they made during the first 3 years of elementary school, and to determine in which academic domains these gains were maintained. To do so we compared Follow Through graduates with children in local comparison groups. It also seemed worthwhile to trace the longitudinal progress of the Follow Through children through their entire 6 years in elementary school, and contrast their scores with the standardized sample of the achievement tests.

Method

A quasi-experimental design (Cook & Campbell, 1979) was used. In each of five Direct Instruction Follow Through sites, roughly equivalent comparison groups were located by the school district. Demographic information was collected on income level, sex, primary home language, and mother's education. These variables were used as potential covariates in the analyses. Despite the problems in using analysis of covariance (Campbell & Boruch, 1975; Elashoff, 1969; House, Glass, McLean, & Walker, 1978), it was the only feasible option for a follow-up study. As Cook and Campbell (1979) state, when one is using a quasi-experimental design and imperfect data analysis techniques, it is crucial to replicate. In this case, replications were conducted (a) across five communities, (b) across two grade levels, and (c) across two cohorts of children.

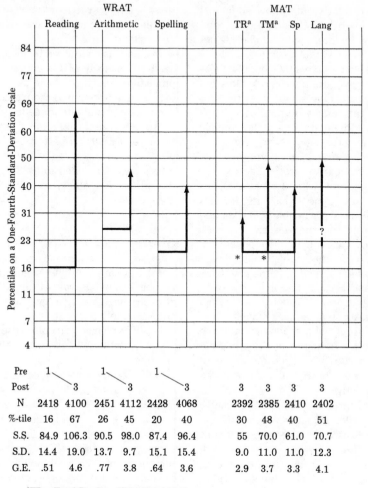

Figure 1 Norm-Referenced Gains on the WRAT and End-of-Third-Grade Scores on MAT Low-Income, Direct Instruction Follow Through Students (3-Year Program)

Subjects, Sites, and Testing

In the spring of 1975, fifth- and sixth-grade students who had previously completed the Follow Through program were tested on all subtests of the MAT (Durost et al., 1970), Intermediate Level, and Levels I and II of the reading subtest of the WRAT (Jastak & Jastak, 1965). The same battery

was given to children in the local comparison group who had undergone traditional education in the community.

The only selective factors operating in choosing sites were the availability of a local comparison group and district cooperation. All 15 sites affiliated with the model were invited to participate provided (a) the district would allow additional testing of fifth- and sixth-graders, and (b) a comparison group of children with similar demographic characteristics could be found. Eight of the 15 sites agreed to participate. Generally, these were rural sites in the South and moderate-sized cities in the Midwest. One small, rural site was eliminated from the final analyses because the sample size was too small ($N = 6$) to produce reliable results. In another site, a Native American reservation in North Carolina, it was impossible to find a reasonable comparison group. Because five of the six remaining sites were 3-year programs, analyses were limited to the 3-year sites. (Results for the one 4-year site are available in Becker and Englemann [1978] and Becker and Gersten [1979]. They show basically similar patterns to the sample analyzed in the large study.)

The five sites which agreed to participate were Dayton, Ohio, and East St. Louis, Illinois (with urban black populations); Tupelo, Mississippi (with a rural, black population); Smithville, Tennessee (with a rural white population); and Uvalde, Texas (with a primarily Hispanic population). In 1976, the study was replicated in four of the five sites. (Dayton did not participate in the 1976 replication study.)

These five sites appear to offer a representative sample of the 15 sites affiliated with the Direct Instruction Model. The wide range of populations typical of Follow Through is represented. Two of the sites deemed most effective in the national evaluation of Follow Through (Stebbins, 1976; Stebbins et al., 1977)—Williamsburg County, SC, and New York, NY—were not able to participate, whereas Tupelo, MS, a site with inconsistent, often nonsignificant results in the national evaluation was able to participate.

The 1975 study involved 624 Follow Through graduates and 567 non-Follow-Through students; the 1976 study included 473 Follow Through graduates and 403 non-Follow-Through children. Table 1 presents fifth-grade sample sizes and demographic information for each site. (See Becker & Englemann, 1978; Becker & Gersten, 1979 for sixth-grade demographics, which are quite similar.) Low-income students were sought in each case. As it turned out, there were a few students in

most samples who were not from low-income families, so income level was used as a potential covariate.

Testing was conducted by local staff after training by University of Oregon supervisors on the procedures specified in the publishers' test manuals. Actual testing was monitored by supervisors to ensure that standard procedures were followed. In Tupelo, Mississippi, the California Achievement Test results (collected by the local district) were used in place of the MAT and the reading scores were converted to MAT equivalents using the Anchor Test Study (Loret, Seder, Bianchini & Vale, 1974).

Strategies for Data Analysis

Analysis of covariance using ethnicity, income, home language, mother's education, sex, and number of siblings was performed on each subtest at each site. One strategy that was considered, and ultimately rejected, was pooling together all Follow Through and all comparison (non–Follow-Through) children in all five sites (see Goodrich & St. Pierre, 1979). Despite the immense gain in sample size and statistical power, this option was deemed inappropriate because subjects in both Follow Through and comparison groups came from at least four highly distinct populations (urban black, rural black, rural Anglo, and Hispanic), and it seemed highly unlikely that the assumptions of ANCOVA would be met. Thus, separate ANCOVAs were performed on each site for each subtest for each year.

The remaining problem was one of meaningfully synthesizing and collating the results of the multitudinous analyses. Using the site as a unit of analysis was rejected because there were too few sites to give adequate power to any test. Three analytic strategies were adopted for synthesizing the results.

In the first analysis, the results of each ANCOVA were classified as (a) significant ($p < .05$, two-tail), (b) suggestive of a trend ($.05 < p .15$), or (c) nonsignificant. For each subtest, the number of sites falling into each category was tabulated. Because sample sizes tended to be small (ranging from 25 to 117, but averaging around 50), it

Table 1 Comparison of Follow Through (FT) and non—Follow-Through (NFT) groups on selected demographic variables for the fifth grade

Site	Sample size		Mother's ed. scale[a]		Proportion low income		Proportion non-white	
	FT	NFT	FT	NFT	FT	NFT	FT	NFT
E. St. Louis, IL								
1975	43	45	4.35	3.68	.93	1.00	1.00	1.00
1976	45	44	4.76	. . .	1.00	. . .	1.00	. . .
Smithville, TN								
1975	47	51	3.30	3.70	.87	.54	.17	.00
1976	71	38	3.43	3.40	.86	.86	.00	.05
Uvalde, TX								
1975	117	86	2.86	2.34	.87	.95	1.00	.95
1976	103	74	2.77	2.35	.98	.98	.98	.80
Dayton, OH[b]								
1975	104	87	4.75	5.00	.85	.71	1.00	.91
Tupelo, MS								
1975	46	35	3.22	3.50	.95	.97	.93	.53
1976	56	42	4.11	4.15	.87	.95	.95	.64

Note. Leaders indicate missing data.
[a] 5 = High school graduates.
[b] Did not participate in 1976 study.

seemed appropriate to record those sites in which $.05 < p < .15$. The researchers reasoned that, if, for a particular subtest (e.g., math problem solving), only 1 out of 6 comparisons was positive at $.05 < p < .15$, this would rightfully be considered a chance finding. If, on the other hand, 8 of the 10 comparisons were found to be "suggestive" at the .15 level, this would be evidence of a replicable phenomenon.

The second procedure used was the meta-analysis technique advocated by Gage (1977) (after Jones and Fiske, 1953). For each site-level ANCOVA the exact p values (both significant and nonsignificant) are converted to chi-square ratios (with two degrees of freedom). Total chi-square values were then tested for significance with $2(n − 1)$ degrees of freedom (where n = number of studies in the meta-analysis). This technique is one of the only meta-analytic techniques to offer statistical significance levels for the comparisons.

Finally, the average magnitude of effect in pooled standard deviation units for each subtest at each grade level was calculated (Glass, 1976; Pil-

lemer & Light, 1980; Smith & Glass, 1977). (In this case, the standard deviation was computed by pooling the comparison sample. This seemed the most reasonable procedure since the larger sample size gives more stability to the estimate and the sample of F-T graduates is not a treatment group in Glass' sense.) The method gives an estimate of the treatment effect that is not biased by the differential sample sizes at the various sites.

Results

Table 2, which summarizes the data from the first method of analysis, indicates the number of site level ANCOVA comparisons in both the 1975 and 1976 studies falling into each of the three categories outlined in the previous section. Table 3 presents the results of the Gage (1977) and Jones and Fiske (1953) meta-analysis procedures; chi-square values are shown for grades five and six, and then for the total number of comparisons. Table 4, which presents results of the third method of analysis, shows the mean magnitude of

Table 2 Significance levels (two-tailed test) for fifth- and sixth-grade
Follow Through/non–Follow-Through comparisons with covariance adjustment

| | WRAT reading | | Metropolitan Achievement Test | | | | | | | | | | Summary of effects |
	Level I	Level II	Word know	Rdg.	TOTAL RDG	Comp.	Con-cepts	Prob. solv.	TOTAL MATH	Sci.	Lang.	Spelling	
				Reading				Math					
a) 1975 study													
Favoring FT ($p < .05$)	7	7	3	2	2	2	3	3	3	2	2	1	37
FT ($.15 > p > .05$)	0	0	0	1	1	2	0	1	0	0	0	4	9
ns ($p > .15$)	1	1	7	7	7	4	5	4	5	6	6	3	56
Favoring NFT	0	0	0	0	0	0	0	0	0	0	0	0	0
Total	8	8	10	10	10	8	8	8	8	8	8	8	102
b) 1976 study													
Favoring FT ($p < .05$)	5	4	0	1	1	0	2	0	0	1	3	2	19
FT ($.15 > p > .05$)	0	2	1	0	1	1	0	3	0	1	0	2	11
ns ($p > .15$)	2	2	7	7	6	1	4	3	5	4	3	2	46
Favoring NFT ($.15 > p > .05$)	0	0	0	0	0	1	0	0	1	0	0	0	2
Total	7	8	8	8	8	3	6	6	6	6	6	6	78

Table 3   Pooled results from 1975 and 1976 follow up studies in seven Follow Through sites, chi-square ratios calculated by Jones & Fiske (1953) meta-analysis procedures

Subtest	Grade 5			Grade 6			Combined		
	Chi-square	df	p	Chi-square	df	p	Chi-square	df	p
a) Metropolitan Achievement Test (Intermediate) (1970)									
Word knowledge	33.8	18	<.05	26.7	18	ns	60.5	36	<.01
Reading	30.3	18	<.05	20.3	18	ns	50.6	36	ns
Total reading	36.2	18	<.05	22.7	18	ns	58.9	36	<.01
Language	22.7	14	ns	24.8	15	<.05	47.5	28	<.05
Spelling	29.1	14	<.05	27.2	14	<.05	56.3	28	<.005
Math computation	16.3	14	ns	25.5	14	<.05	41.8	28	<.05
Math concepts	21.1	14	ns	33.3	14	<.05	54.3	28	<.01
Math problem solving	33.2	14	<.05	28.0	14	<.05	61.2	28	<.005
Total math	16.8	14	ns	24.8	14	<.05	41.6	28	<.05
Science	26.6	14	<.05	22.4	14	ns	49.0	28	<.01
b) WRAT Reading (Decoding)									
Level I	80.0	14	<.005	54.0	16	<.005	134.1	30	<.005
Level II	73.3	16	<.005	61.1	16	<.005	134.4	32	<.005

effect in pooled SD units (Glass, 1976) for each subtest.

The strongest, most consistent finding is for reading decoding, as assessed by both Level I and Level II of WRAT reading: $\chi^2_{(30)} = 134.1$, $p < .005$ for Level I; $\chi^2_{(32)} = 134.4$, $p < .005$ for Level II. The mean magnitudes of effect (in Table 4) range from .38 to .56 pooled standard deviation units, well over the conventional criteria set for educational significance of .25 or .33 pooled standard deviation units (Horst, Tallmadge, & Wood, 1975; Stebbins et al., 1977). This test measures children's ability to accurately read isolated words. The consistency is demonstrated across sites, grade levels, and levels of the test. The teaching of decoding (or word attack skills) is one of the strongest early outcomes of the Direct Instruction Model; mean end-of-third-grade performance corresponds to the 67th percentile on the WRAT for entering-first-grade students. It appears that these skills are maintained 2–3 years after the program ends.

A strong, consistent effect is also found on MAT spelling (Table 3), with significant effects for both grades five ($p < .05$) and six ($p < .05$) and the combined sample ($p < .005$). It is possible that the enduring effect in spelling is related to the phonic and word-attack skills the students mastered in the early grades.

The other strong, consistent effect is in math problem solving. Table 2 shows that in each year, half of the site level ANCOVAs significantly favor Follow Through at either the .05 or .15 level, and no comparisons significantly favor the comparison children. The chi-square analyses (Table 3) are also significant at the .05 level for both Grade 5, Grade 6, and at the .005 level for the combined sample. Mean magnitude of effects (Table 4) are .27 for Grade 5 and .18 for Grade 6. Note that the math problem-solving effects are consistently stronger than math computation. At first, this would seem unusual for a program with a heavy emphasis on acquisition of basic skills. Yet the finding is consistent with the emphasis in the Dis-

Table 4   Mean magnitude of effects in pooled standard deviation units between Follow Through and non–Follow-Through samples pooled from 1975 and 1976 studies.

Test	5th Grade	6th Grade
WRAT Level II	.50	.51
WRAT Level I	.56	.38
MAT Word Knowledge	.19	.23
MAT Reading	.16	.14
MAT Total Reading	.20	.19
MAT Math Computation	.09	.13
MAT Math Concepts	.18	.24
MAT Math Problem Solving	.27	.18
MAT Total Math	.18	.26
MAT Science	.20	.26
MAT Language	.21	.20
MAT Spelling	.24	.17

tar arithmetic programs on teaching general-case problem-solving strategies, including basic algebraic principles.

More variable effects are found for the word knowledge, math concepts, science, and language subtests, as well as for the composite scores for total reading and total math. For example, for word knowledge and science, the chi-square analysis (Table 3) indicate significant effects for the combined ($p < .01$) and the fifth grade ($p < .05$) samples, but not for the sixth grade. Yet the magnitude of effects (Table 4) is actually somewhat higher for Grade 6. Site level analyses (Becker & Englemann, 1978; Becker & Gersten, 1979) do not shed any great light on these patterns, other than indicating that the largest site, Uvalde, seemed to have consistent effects in science and word knowledge.

Overall, there is reasonable evidence of significant later effects. Of the total of 180 comparisons in Table 2, 56 favor the Follow Through sample at the .05 level; none favor the comparison group. If one uses the more liberal .15 significance level to explore potential trends (Carver, 1978), 76 effects (42%) favor Follow Through, and only 2 (less than 1%) favor the comparison groups. The tests with the strongest effects are WRAT reading, MAT spelling, and MAT math problem solving. Meta-analysis techniques revealed a similar pattern.

Table 5   Unadjusted percentiles for Follow Through and non–Follow-Through in 1975 study

	WRAT Reading[a]		Total reading		Total math		Spelling		Science	
	FT	NFT	FT	NFT	FT	NFT	FT	NFT	FT	NFT
Grade 5										
E. St. Louis	. . .	. . .	17	17	16	18	41	39	11	14
Smithville	63	39	34	34	49	56	39	39	36	36
Uvalde	45	23	16	17	24	21	37	37	22	19
Dayton	61	27	20	16	19	12	34	27	20	13
Tupelo	42	27	18	18	. . .	. . .				
Grade 6										
E. St. Louis	. . .	. . .	32	18	33	21	53	43	20	12
Smithville	73	25	36	21	52	28	59	39	42	26
Uvalde	32	18	15	15	22	17	39	28	21	17
Dayton	50	27	22	22	19	17	13	25	23	21
Tupelo	44	13	36	28	. . .	. . .	. . .	. . .	. . .	. . .

* Level I for Grade 5, Level II for Grade 6.

The mean magnitude of effect (Table 4) is well above .33 pooled SD units for all levels of WRAT Reading and in the .17 to .26 range for most MAT subtests. The two tests with consistently low magnitudes of effect are math computation and reading (comprehension). Using the Jones and Fiske (1953) statistical tests for the combined sample, there is evidence of significant, enduring effects in all domains except MAT Reading (a test of reading comprehension). There are no consistent patterns indicating that one particular site or one particular grade level displayed more lasting effects. Thus, the effects appear to be due to the model.

To round out the picture, Table 5 presents the *unadjusted* percentiles for WRAT reading and total reading, total math, spelling, and science for each site in the 1975 study. These percentiles are converted from the unadjusted mean standard scores. Table 6 presents the mean magnitude of effects for *adjusted* scores on a site level basis for the children who were in fifth grade in 1975 and sixth grade in 1976. Table 6 shows reasonably high consistency across grade levels when the same children are followed.

Longitudinal Tracebacks: Gains and Losses of Follow-Through Children Against the National Norm Sample

Table 7 traces the growth of the Follow Through children against the norm sample of the WRAT for the children during the 3 years of the Follow Through program, followed by their decline during the intermediate grades. East St. Louis is omitted because data were unavailable. Entry (pretest) scores were unavailable from Tupelo and Dayton; however, on the basis of similar Follow Through children tested at entry in these communities in later years, one can estimate the entry scores at approximately the 14th percentile for Dayton and the 9th percentile for Tupelo (Becker & Engelmann, 1978).

Note in Table 7 that the major growth in reading decoding occurs during the first 2 years of school, when a major program emphasis is on word-attack skills. The level is basically maintained in grade three. By grades five and six, there are appreciable drops in Smithville and Tupelo. Although the Follow Through students signifi-

Table 6   Mean magnitude of effects in pooled standard deviation units A within-cohort follow-up of 1975 5th graders as 6th graders in 1976

Site Date	Uvalde		Smithville		E. St. Louis		Tupelo	
	1975 → 1976		1975 → 1976		1975 → 1976		1975 → 1976	
N =	117	108	46	38	43	37	56	55
Test:								
WRAT reading level II	.47	.41	.61	.53	. . .	−.15	.78	.46
WRAT reading level I	.47	.52	.52	.48	. . .	−.15	.63	. . .
MAT word knowledge	.03	.19	.06	.02	.00	−.03	.38	.18
MAT reading	.21	.20	.25	.02	−.12	−.20	.20	.01
MAT total reading	.11	.20	.15	.02	.01	−.11	.28	.09
MAT language	.13	.39	.09	.03	.03	−.06	. . .	. . .
MAT spelling	.01	.25	.36	.37	.13	−.06	. . .	. . .
MAT math computation	.11	.04	.09	.15	.05	−.30	. . .	. . .
MAT math concepts	.10	.31	.09	−.08	.21	−.30	. . .	. . .
MAT math problem-solving	.33	.23	.20	−.28	.02	−.22	. . .	. . .
MAT total math	.10	.16	.15	−.08	.01	−.33	. . .	. . .
MAT science	.15	.36	.23	−.04	−.15	. . .	. . .	. . .

Note. Leaders indicate missing data.

Table 7   Longitudinal analysis of WRAT reading at entry and at the end of grades 1, 2, 3, 5, 6

Site	WRAT Reading (Level I)					
	Pre-grade 1 (fall, 1970)	Grade 1 (1971)	Grade 2 (1972)	Grade 3 (1973)	Grade 5[a] (1975)	Grade 6[b] (1976)
Uvalde, TX						
Percentile	9th	43rd	64th	55th	45th	42nd
Mean Standard Score[c]	79.7	97.4	105.5	102.0	98	97
N	81	110	110	110	117	108
Smithville, TN						
Percentile	20th	66th	74th	75th	63rd	39th
Mean SS	87.6	106.0	109.4	110.1	105	96
N	40	46	43	46	46	38
Tupelo, MS						
Percentile	. . .	39th	57th	55th	42nd	34th
Mean SS	. . .	96.0	102.5	102.1	97	94
N	. . .	24	25	25	56	55
Dayton, OH						
Percentile	. . .	52	73	67	61	. . .
Mean SS	. . .	100.7	108.8	106.7	104	. . .
N	. . .	97	104	102	93	. . .

Note. Leaders indicate missing data.
[a] Estimate based on raw score for Level I.
[b] Estimate based on raw score for Level II.
[c] Mean = 100, SD = 15.

cantly outperform non–Follow-Through students at all sites on the WRAT, they are "losing" a bit when compared to the norm sample.

This decline is even more dramatic on the Metropolitan Achievement Test (Table 8). The MAT is a well-normed, comprehensive test of reading, math, and language, including both basic skills and higher order, cognitive operations (Bereiter & Kurland, 1981–82; Wolf, 1978). To conserve space, Table 8 presents only percentile equivalents for the composite scores—total reading, total math, and spelling. (The mean scale scores, standard deviations, and sample sizes, and detailed site level analyses are available in Becker and Engelmann [1978] and Becker and Gersten [1979].)

By the end of the third grade, with 3 years of Direct Instruction Follow Through, all sites were within a few percentile points of the national median in total math and within one-fourth standard deviation in spelling. In total reading, Smithville students are at the national median, the Dayton

sample within one-fourth of a standard deviation unit, and Tupelo and Uvalde one-half standard deviation below. Yet 2 years after the program had ended, all samples made appreciable, significant drops against the national norm group in both math and reading. In the case of Smithville, there are even further drops during sixth grade. Though in many domains Follow Through graduates outperform the control students in Grades 5 and 6 (Table 2–5), low-income Follow Through students are losing against the national normal sample. The same phenomenon occurs for other low-income students in the intermediate grades (National Center for Educational Statistics, 1978). The losses are much smaller in MAT Spelling and WRAT Reading (decoding) than MAT Reading and Language.

Conclusions

There are two basic findings in this study. The first is that there is evidence that, in most domains

Table 8   Longitudinal analysis of Metropolitan Achievement Test: Same children followed from grades 3 to 6

	Grade 3 (1973)	Grade 5 (1975)	Grade 6 (1976)
a) Total reading percentiles[a,b]			
Site			
Uvalde, TX	31st	16th	16th
Smithville, TN	52nd	34th	26th
Tupelo, MS	28th	18th[c]	17th[c]
Dayton, OH	40th	20th	. . .
b) Total math percentiles[a]			
Site			
Uvalde, TX	53rd	24th	19th
Smithville, TN	78th	49th	36th
Dayton, OH	55th	19th	. . .
c) Spelling percentiles[a]			
Site			
Uvalde, TX	40th	37th	35th
Smithville, TN	62nd	39th	39th
Dayton, OH	40th	34th	. . .

Note. Leaders indicate unavailable data.
[a] Percentiles converted from mean standard score for the sample.
[b] Third grade tested on Elementary Form, Grades 5 and 6 on Intermediate Form.
[c] CAT scores converted by Anchor Study tables.

assessed by standardized achievement tests, low-income graduates of a 3-year Direct Instruction Follow Through program perform better than comparable children in their communities who did not attend the program. These enduring effects are strongest and most consistent in WRAT reading (decoding), math problem solving and spelling. There are lesser effects in MAT science, math concepts, math computation, and word knowledge. The fact that this study was conducted at five quite diverse sites across two grade levels and replicated in 1976 adds confidence to the results. Because none of the outcomes signifi-

cantly favored the comparison groups at the .05 level, and 31 percent favored Follow Through, it is extremely unlikely that these results are due to chance. These results are from the second and third cohorts of Follow Through children, when the program was not fully developed. Also, only sites with a 3-year (rather than 4-year) program participated. For both these reasons, the results cited here, in all likelihood, represent a low estimate of program effectiveness. For example, a quasi-experimental follow-up study by Gersten, Gutkin, and Meyer (Note 1) demonstrated that low-income fifth graders from the 4-year program in New York City were significantly outperforming comparison group children, and were well *above* national median levels in reading on the Comprehensive Test of Basic Skills (CTBS). Also, Weber and Fuhrmann (Note 2) reported significant later effects in reading and math on the California Achievement Test for *ninth graders* who had completed the program; Follow Through graduates were .24 standard deviation units (or .8 grade equivalent units) ahead of comparable students in the district.

The second finding is less optimistic. When compared to the national norm sample, these children invariably lose ground in the 3 years after they leave Follow Through.

Two reasonable conclusions can be formed from these findings. The first is that if students learn skills and problem solving strategies well, they do not lose this knowledge. Follow Through graduates often perform significantly higher than other low-income fifth and sixth graders in their communities, especially in the areas of reading decoding, math concepts, math problem solving, and science.

The second conclusion is that without effective instruction which continues to build on these skills in the intermediate grades, the children are likely to lose ground against their middle-income peers. They are failing to master new computational skills (such as long division and complex multiplication), and are failing to develop their vocabularies and reading comprehension abilities at the rate of middle- and higher-income students. Limited English-speaking students appear to lose the most. In order for these children to become fully literate adults, it appears that they need high-quality instructional programs in the intermediate grades (and probably beyond). Key areas for program development are instruction in reading comprehension (Jenkins, Stein, & Osborn, 1981; Perfetti & Lesgold, 1977; Resnick, 1981); vocabulary development (Becker, 1977); independent study skills (Adams, 1980; Chall, 1979; Durkin, 1978–1979); mathematical problem solving (Silbert, Carnine & Stein, 1981); expressive writing (Frederiksen, Whiteman & Dominic, 1981); and independent reading for information and pleasure (Brown & Smiley, 1977).

An ever-increasing body of knowledge has accrued from correlational and experimental studies of effective classroom practices in the elementary grades (Brophy & Evertson, 1976; Fischer et al., 1980; Gersten, Carnine & Williams, in press; Good & Grouws, 1979; Stevens & Rosenshine, 1981). These studies isolate teaching practices that are consistently effective, and that have always been central to the Direct Instruction Follow Through Model, such as high student success rate, clarity of tasks, amount of guided practice, and systematic use of correction procedures. There is now a need to implement and evaluate instructional programs in the intermediate grades that systematically utilize principles of direct instruction, which include mastery learning, high levels of feedback, and incremental steps to develop independent reading, writing, and critical thinking.

Reference Notes

1. Gersten, R., Gutkin, J., & Meyer, L. *Evaluation of P.S. 137 (New York City) Follow Through.* Final report submitted to Joint Dissemination Review Panel, Department of Education, Washington, D.C., 1981.

2. Weber, B., & Fuhrmann, M. *A study of District A's former Follow Through students' retention of basic skills after six years out of the program.* Paper prepared for District A, April 1978.

References

ADAMS, A., CARNINE, D., & GERSTEN, R. Instructional strategies for studying content area texts in the intermediate grades. *Reading Research Quarterly,* in press.

BECKER, W. C. Teaching reading and language to the disadvantaged—What we have learned from field research. *Harvard Educational Review,* 1977, *47,* 518–543.

BECKER, W. C., & ENGELMANN, S. *Analysis of achievement data on six cohorts of low-income children from 20 school districts in the University of Oregon Direct Instruction Follow Through Model.* (Follow Through Project, Technical Report #78-1). Eugene, Ore.: University of Oregon, 1978.

BECKER, W. C., & GERSTEN, R. M. *Follow-up study of fifth and sixth graders: The 1976 replication study.* (Follow Through Project, Technical Report #78-1). Eugene, Ore.: University of Oregon, 1979.

BEREITER, C., & KURLAND, M. A constructive look at Follow Through results. *Interchange,* 1981–82, *12,* 1–22.

BROPHY, J., & EVERTSON, C. *Learning from teaching: A developmental perspective.* Boston: Allyn & Bacon, 1976.

BROWN, A. L., & SMILEY, S. S. Rating the importance of structural units of prose passages: A problem of meta-cognitive development. *Child Development,* 1977, *48,* 1–8.

CAMPBELL, D. T., & BORUCH, R. F. Making the case of randomized assignments to treatments by considering the alternatives: Six ways in which quasi-experimental evaluations in compensatory education tend to underestimate effects. In C. A. Bennett & A. A. Lumsdaine (Eds.), *Evaluation and experiment: Some critical issues in assessing social programs.* New York: Academic Press, 1975.

CARVER, R. P. The case against statistical significance testing. *Harvard Educational Review,* 1978, *48,* 378–399.

CHALL, J. S. The great debate: Ten years later, with a modest proposal for reading stages. In L. B. Resnick & P. A. Weaver (Eds.), *Theory and practice of early reading* (Vol. 1). Hillsdale, N.J.: Lawrence Erlbaum, 1979.

COOK, T., & CAMPBELL, D. T. *Quasi-experimentation: Design and analysis issues for field settings.* Chicago: Rand McNally, 1979.

DURKIN, D. What classroom observations reveal about reading comprehension instruction. *Reading Research Quarterly,* 1978–1979, *15,* 481–533.

DUROST, W. N., BIXLER, H. H., WRIGHTSTONE, J. W., PRESCOTT, G. A., & BALOW, I. H. *Metropolitan Achievement Tests*. New York: Harcourt Brace Jovanovich, 1970.

ELASHOFF, J. D. Analysis of covariance: A delicate instrument. *American Educational Research Journal*, 1969, 6, 383–401.

FISCHER, C. W., BERLINER, D. C., FILBY, N. N., MARLIAVE, R., CAHEN, L. S., & DISHAW, M. M. Teaching behaviors, academic learning time and student achievement: An overview. In C. Denham & A. Lieberman (Eds.), *Time to learn*. Washington, D.C.: USOE/NIE Printing, 1980.

FREDERIKSEN, C. H., WHITEMAN, M., & DOMINIC, J. (Eds.). *Writing: The nature, development, and teaching of written communication*. Hillsdale, N.J.: Lawrence Erlbaum, 1981.

GAGE, N. *The scientific basis of the art of teaching*. New York: Columbia Teachers College Press, 1977.

GERSTEN, R., CARNINE, D., & WILLIAMS, P. Measuring implementation of a structured educational model in an urban setting: An observational approach. *Educational Evaluation and Policy Analysis*, in press.

GLASS, G. V. Primary, secondary, and meta-analysis of research. *Educational Researcher*, 1976, 5, 3–8.

GOOD, T. L., & GROUWS, D. A. The Missouri Mathematics Effectiveness Project: An experimental study in fourth-grade classrooms. *Journal of Educational Psychology*, 1979, 71, 355–362.

GOODRICH, R., & ST. PIERRE, R. *Opportunities for studying later effects of Follow Through*. Cambridge, Mass.: Abt Associates, 1979.

HORST, D. P., TALLMADGE, G. K., & WOOD, C. T. *A practical guide to measuring project impact on student achievement*. Monograph No. 1 on Evaluation in Education. Washington, D.C.: U.S. Government Printing Office, 1975.

HOUSE, E. R., GLASS, G. V., MCLEAN, L. D., & WALKER, D. E. No simple answer: Critique of the "Follow Through" evaluation. *Harvard Educational Review*, 1978, 48, 128–160.

JASTAK, J., & JASTAK, S. *Wide Range Achievement Test*. Wilmington, Del.: Jastak Associates, 1965.

JENKINS, J. R., STEIN, M., & OSBORN, J. What next after decoding: A look into instruction and research in reading comprehension. *Exceptional Education Quarterly*, 1981, 2, 27–40.

JONES, L., & FISKE, D. W. Models for testing the significance of combined results. *Psychological Bulletin*, 1953, 50, 375–381.

KENNEDY, M. Findings from the Follow Through planned variation study. *Educational Researcher*, 1978, 7, 3–11.

LORET, P. G., SEDER, A., BIANCHINI, J. C., & VALE, C. A. *Anchor test study: Equivalence and norms tables for selected reading achievement tests (grades 4, 5, 6)*. (Office of Education Report No. 74-305). Washington, D.C.: U.S. Government Printing Office, 1974.

NATIONAL CENTER FOR EDUCATIONAL STATISTICS. *The condition of education*. Washington, D.C.: U.S. Government Printing Office, 1978.

OZENNE, D., et al. United States Office of Education. *Annual evaluation report on programs administered by the U.S. Office of Education, FY 1973*. Washington, D.C.: Capital Publications, Educational Resources Division, 1974.

OZENNE, D., et al. United States Office of Education. *Annual evaluation report on programs administered by the U.S. Office of Education, FY 1975*. Washington, D.C.: Capital Publications, Educational Resources Division, 1976.

PERFETTI, C. A., & LESGOLD, A. M. Coding and comprehension in skilled reading and implications for reading instruction. In L. B. Resnick & P. A. Weaver (Eds.), *Theory and practice of early reading* (Vol. 1). Hillsdale, N.J.: Lawrence Erlbaum Associates, 1977.

PILLEMER, D. G., & LIGHT, R. J. Synthesizing outcomes: How to use research evidence from many studies. *Harvard Educational Review*, 1980, 50, 176–197.

RESNICK, L. B. Instructional psychology. In M. R. Rosensweig & L. W. Porter (Eds.), *Annual Review of Psychology*, Palo Alto, Calif.: Annual Reviews, 1981.

SILBERT, J., CARNINE, D., & STEIN, M. *Direct instruction arithmetic*. Columbus, Oh.: Charles E. Merrill, 1981.

SMITH, M. L., & GLASS, G. V. Meta-analysis of psychotherapy outcome studies. *American Psychologist*, 1977, 32, 752–760.

STEBBINS, L. (Ed.). *Education as experimentation: A planned variation model* (Vol. IIIA). Cambridge, Mass.: Abt Associates, 1976.

STEBBINS, L., ST. PIERRE, R. G., PROPER, E. L., ANDERSON, R. B., &

CERVA, T. R. *Education as experimentation: A planned variation model* (Vols. IV A-D). Cambridge, Mass.: Abt Associates, 1977.

STEVENS, R., & ROSENSHINE, B. Advances in research on teaching. *Exceptional Education Quarterly*, 1981, *2*, 1–10.

TALLMADGE, G. K. *JDRP ideabook*. Washington, D.C.: USOE/NIE Printing, 1977.

WOLF, R. Review of Metropolitan Achievement Test. In O. K. Buros (Ed.), *The sixth mental measurements yearbook*. Highland Park, N.J.: Gryphon Press, 1978.

Critical Review

INTRODUCTION

This study addresses one of the most important questions of our day—the long-term effects of one of the programs developed under Project Follow Through. Head Start and Follow Through represent the largest national efforts ever launched to improve the achievement of children from low-income families, at a cost of many millions of dollars.

METHOD

The research is classified as quasi-experimental because subjects in the comparison groups, that is, those who were in or not in the Follow Through Programs, were not assigned randomly.[5] You will recall that when subjects cannot be assigned randomly, it is important for the researcher to supply data on relevant variables to show the degree to which the groups are comparable. Differences in achievement in studies of this sort can be due either to the Follow Through Program (independent variable) or to differences in the characteristics of subjects in the two groups.

You will recall that when different criteria are used to select students for the experimental and control groups, we have differential selection, one of the internal validity threats described earlier in the chapter. Since comparison groups in this study were drawn from different schools than Follow Through groups, other internal validity threats also may have been operating, such as history and regression. In studying compensatory programs, selecting comparison groups is especially difficult because specific criteria were applied to determine which schools were eligible for the program in the first place. Thus, schools selected for the program were definitely different from those not selected. Under these circumstances, the more evidence the researchers provide that the children in the two groups are comparable, the more confidence we can have that any achievement differences found are due to the Follow Through Program. In this study, the investigators collected data on ethnicity, income level, sex, primary home language, number of siblings, and mother's education. Since all of these variables have been found to relate to student achievement, comparability of the groups on these variables provides reasonably strong evidence of overall comparability between the Follow Through and the comparison groups.

Replication is also very important in establishing the generalizability of the finding

---

5. This could also be classified as a causal-comparative study.

of quasi-experimental studies. As the authors point out, the fact that this study was replicated in five different communities and at two different grade levels is probably the most compelling evidence that the findings are valid.

MEASURES

Widely used standardized achievement measures were used in the study. The reliability and overall content validity of such measures is typically high, although content validity can vary from school to school because of differences in curriculum, textbooks, and other instructional materials.

RESULTS

Analysis of covariance (ANCOVA) was the principal analysis tool used in this study. This is the best choice, since it permitted making adjustments to the final achievement means to account for initial differences between the Follow Through and the comparison groups on characteristics such as ethnicity and income described earlier. Using all of these variables as covariates would adjust for much of their effect on achievement. This, in turn means that we can place more confidence in the comparability of the two groups on the adjusted final achievement means than would have been the case if covariance analysis had not been used.

The authors also chose to analyze the data separately for each of the five sites in which the study was conducted. If they had pooled data from all sites, the chances of getting significant results would have been much greater because of the very large N. However, this would have been a poor analysis decision for several reasons. First, as the authors point out, the students from the different sites represented different populations, and combining the samples would have violated the assumptions of ANCOVA. Second, by pooling the samples, the advantages of replication would have been lost. One significant finding in a given direction with a large sample is far less impressive than five significant findings in independent studies involving smaller samples.

Finally, pooling the data could have hidden much important information and could have produced misleading results. For example, if highly significant results had been found at two sites and nonsignificant results had emerged from the other three sites, pooling the data could have produced an overall significant result that would have hidden the fact that Follow Through had failed in three of the five sites.

Once the findings from replications have been obtained, this information can be combined to measure overall patterns. The authors used two such methods.[6] The chi-square method as described by Gage (1978, Chap. 1) gives an estimate of overall *statistical significance,* while the Glass meta-analysis method gives an estimate of *practical significance.*

Tables 2 and 3 give a good overall picture of statistical significance. You will recall that the difference between group means is divided by the standard deviation to give an estimate of practical significance. This ratio is similar to the effect size computed

6. The meta-analysis procedure developed by Glass and his associates is described in Chapter 5.

as part of Glass's meta-analysis procedure. Using .33 or larger as a criterion for practical significance, you will note in Table 4 that achievement differences on the WRAT reached this criterion while those on the MAT did not.

A study of Tables 5 to 8 gives some valuable insights into the performance of the Follow Through and non–Follow Through students at the various sites. An additional table giving the adjusted posttreatment achievement means for the Follow Through and non–Follow Through groups at each site would have further aided interpretation of the replication data. Clearly, the effects of Follow Through varied considerably from site to site. Marked grade level and subject area differences also occurred. Thus, the more evidence we have to help understand these differences and the reasons for them, the more useful the study would be in helping us plan future compensatory programs.

Single-Subject Research[7]

For about the past 30 years, psychologists and educators have relied primarily on research designs that have compared the effects of various treatments on groups of subjects to gain information about how behavior changes. These group designs consequently have become highly sophisticated in an attempt to answer the many different questions that researchers ask. Their use has often required more than a fundamental understanding of statistical methods, and it has been necessary to have a number of subjects available in order to conduct a study.

Group research methods can be very useful in helping researchers investigate important educational problems provided the researchers have fairly well-developed skills with statistics and access to large number of subjects. Since these prerequisites are often not available, fortunately there are research methods available to the researcher who does not enjoy the benefits of statistical knowledge and a large subject pool.

Single-subject designs are especially appropriate for the study of many teaching problems, since teachers find it increasingly necessary to work with individual students. Using single-subject designs, the teacher can diagnose a student's problem, devise a strategy to solve the problem, and rigorously test the effectiveness of this strategy.

Counseling is another area in which single-subject design can be very useful since counselors are often interested in evaluating the effects of a specific counseling strategy upon a given client. In order to help you see the usefulness of these designs in actual practice, they will be discussed here from the viewpoint of the counseling process. Keep in mind that whatever is said about these designs' application to counseling also applies to the teaching process, and, for that matter, to any process that involves measureable changes in behavior.

7. This section was written by Dr. John T. Zweig, Department of Psychology, Salisbury State College, Salisbury, Md. Dr. Zweig wishes to acknowledge the assistance of Dr. N. Kenneth LaFleur, University of Virginia, in preparing parts of this discussion of single-subject research.

As a general rule, single-subject research methods allow the study of one individual as he progresses through counseling. Since clients are both treated and studied one at a time, it is not necessary to form groups of clients who have the same concern in order to conduct research. In fact, no matter how unique the client's concern, a single-case design will permit an investigation.

Since counselors (except group counselors) are concerned with helping persons on an individual basis, the ability to study one individual at a time offers a convenience. Likewise, single-subject designs allow the counselor to function simultaneously as both counselor and researcher, whereas the use of group designs often has relegated these functions to different people. For a more detailed description of the advantages of single-subject methods, see Dukes (1965) and Lazarus and Davison (1971).

A-B LOGIC

Basic to all single-case designs is A-B logic, which can be described as follows: Whenever environmental conditions are constant and a certain behavior is observed to occur at a consistent, stable rate under such conditions, we have *Condition A*. If one of the environmental conditions changes and a concomitant change is observed in the behavior, we have *Condition B*. The logic comes in when we make the inference that the change in environmental conditions had something to do with the change in the behavior. This inference is predicated on the assumption that the behavior would have continued at its stable rate as long as Condition A remained in effect. While this inference seems to make sense, it is easy to see that it would be very difficult indeed for a counselor to "hold constant" all of the variables that might influence the client's behavior. If the counselor, through some miraculous power, could hold all variables constant during Condition A, the logical inference could then be made with confidence. This is not the case, and before an inference can be made, a more convincing demonstration of causation must be made.

A-B logic alone is not sufficient to convince counselors that their treatment, not some random, uncontrolled variable, produced changes in client behavior. However, even the most skeptical counselor will consider the possibility that the treatment may have caused the change. Thus, A-B logic is a starting point for demonstrating the mechanisms of change.

Consider a hypothetical example. A client seldom studied and reported difficulty in school. The counselor learned that evenings were the only times during which the client could study, due to an otherwise busy schedule. The counselor also learned that the client usually watched television after supper until bedtime. The counselor asked the client to keep a daily record of his study time. After several weeks, the client's record showed that he had averaged less than 15 minutes of study per night. At this point, the counselor made her services contingent on the client studying at least five hours during the week prior to the counseling session. The client was asked to continue recording his study behavior. The client returned the next week, having studied a total of six hours.

It seemed probable to the counselor that the treatment may have caused the increase in study time. However, it was April, and the client's first week of treatment also happened to be the first week of network reruns. Was it the treatment or the reruns that caused the decrease in television viewing and increase in study time?[8]

THE REVERSAL OR ABAB DESIGN

The counselor in the above example saw the A-B logic in operation. She was not sure about the cause of change. So she decided to find out for sure. When the client returned for the next session, the counselor said that it would no longer be necessary for the client to study 5 hours per week to "earn" his next counseling session. In other words, the counselor withdrew her treatment procedure, thus reinstating Condition A. In the next counseling session, the client reported a reduced study performance of only 1 1/2 hours for the previous week. The counselor then reinstated the 5-hour requirement (Condition B) and found that the client again increased to over 5 hours per week. Figure 10.1 shows the pattern of study time per day during the six weeks of the study. Note the large differences between the two baseline conditions (A_1 and A_2) and the two treatment conditions (B_1 and B_2). This graph is typical of the type used by researchers to report the results of single subject studies. The differences obtained in such studies are usually sufficiently clear that no statistical treatment is needed.

8. Note that a potentially controlling variable, television reruns, seems apparent here. In most cases it will be more difficult to identify influential variables.

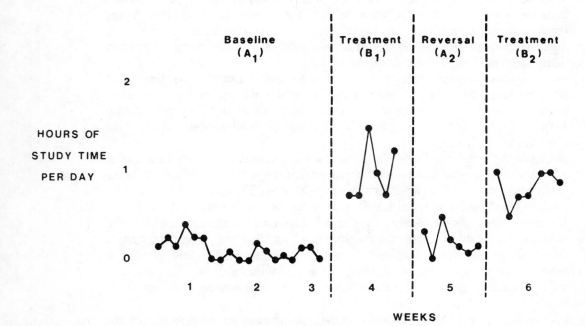

Figure 10.1 Study Time and Treatment: A Typical ABAB Design

The counselor was now convinced that the reruns had little to do with the client's behavior, and that the treatment procedure was effective in producing the change the client wanted. With only A-B logic, the counselor was unable to distinguish the effects of the treatment variable from the effects of an uncontrolled variable (television reruns). Reinstating Condition A (reversal) caused a second variation in the treatment variable while the uncontrolled variable remained constant. The concomitant change of client behavior with the onset of the reversal period was convincing evidence that the counselor had gained control over the client's behavior. The subsequent increase in study time with the reinstatement of the treatment Condition B was further evidence that the variable which influenced study time, that is, the amount of time spent watching television, had been identified and controlled through implementation of the treatment conditions.

This design is usually called the reversal, or ABAB, design (Baer, Wolf, & Risley, 1968); it is also referred to as a withdrawal design (Leitenberg, 1973), intrasubject replication design (Sidman, 1960), and equivalent time-samples design (Campbell & Stanley, 1973). This design provides a very conservative test of control and gains an advantage over the A-B design by returning to Condition A or *baseline* conditions. The purpose of this reversal of conditions is to demonstrate that the client's behavior is not changing by chance but is under the control of the treatment.

In this example, the counselor was interested in dealing with the behavior of a single client. This would be called an action research project, since it is not designed to produce knowledge that can be generalized to other clients. (We will discuss action research in Chapter 11.) A major criticism of single-subject research is that it is weak in external validity. That is, research results based upon a single subject cannot be generalized to other similar subjects with any confidence. The solution to this weakness is *replication,* that is, repeating the study with other clients. Let us suppose that the counselor had five clients who did little studying and were failing in school. If she applied the same treatment to each of these students individually and all five made major gains in study time, then she could generalize her method to other students having the same difficulty with some confidence. A finding that occurs consistently with all five individuals is much stronger from a scientific standpoint than a finding that only occurs once.

Caution should be exercised in selecting the reversal design for use. As Kazdin (1973) has indicated, not all behaviors can be reversed. For example, goals for counseling may include learning various academic or social skills such as table manners, how to take multiple-choice tests, or how to use vocational information materials. Such skills are often very much like learning to ride a bicycle: You may get rusty without practice, but once you learn how, you never forget. It is important to note that when a behavior does not reverse, control is not demonstrated. Since the reversal of conditions eliminates other, nontreatment explanations for a change in behavior, the failure of a behavior to reverse is tantamount to a failure to eliminate rival hypotheses, such as the television reruns used in our example.

If the client's behavioral goal includes a behavior that would appear nonreversible (resistent to extinction), or if the counselor is not sure, other designs are available.

MULTIPLE-BASELINE DESIGNS

There are three basic multiple-baseline designs, all of which employ A-B logic: (1) across behaviors, (2) across situations, and (3) across individuals.

Multiple-Baseline across Behaviors.   In the across-behaviors design, baseline measurements are taken on two or more behaviors of one subject. After baselines are stable, a treatment condition is applied to one of the behaviors. The treatment is continued until a noticeable change occurs in that behavior. Then, the treatment condition is applied to the second behavior, until a change is observed, and so on.

One important consideration in deciding whether or not to use the across-behaviors design is the discreteness of the behaviors to be observed. If the occurrence of either of the two behaviors is relatively dependent upon the occurrence of the other, treatment of one behavior may cause a change in both. If this occurs, explanations that could account for change other than the treatment remain possible. Thus, this design is used most effectively when discrete, independent behaviors of one individual are observed.

Let's consider an example of this design. Suppose you want to train a teacher in the use of three behaviors designed to provide reinforcement for correct pupil responses during a recitation lesson. The three behaviors to be learned are: (1) teacher smiles and nods to pupil who gives a correct response; (2) teacher gives responding pupil a token that can be exchanged for extra free time; and (3) teacher praises responding pupil. Here are the steps you would take in conducting this study:

1. You would first collect baseline data on the number of times the teacher emitted each behavior during five half-hour recitation lessons (i.e., one a day for one week) and record on Figure 10.2.

2. Then you would train the teacher to use Behavior 1.

3. Over the subsequent five days you would record the number of times the teacher used each of the three reinforcement behaviors during half-hour recitation lessons. If your training has been effective, the teacher will increase her use of Behavior 1 but not change materially on Behaviors 2 or 3 (see Figure 10.2).

4. You would then train the teacher to use Behavior 2.

5. Again you would record the teacher's use of all three behaviors during five half-hour recitation lessons and record on Figure 10.2. At this point, Behaviors 1 and 2 should be higher than baseline, but Behavior 3 should stay about the same.

6. You would then train the teacher to use Behavior 3.

7. You would again record the teacher's use of all three behaviors during five half-hour recitation lessons and record on Figure 10.2. At this point, if the training has been effective, all three behaviors should occur more frequently than was the case during the baseline condition.

Inspection of Figure 10.2 indicates that the training in all three behaviors was effective. However, notice that Behavior 1 gradually decreased near the end of the

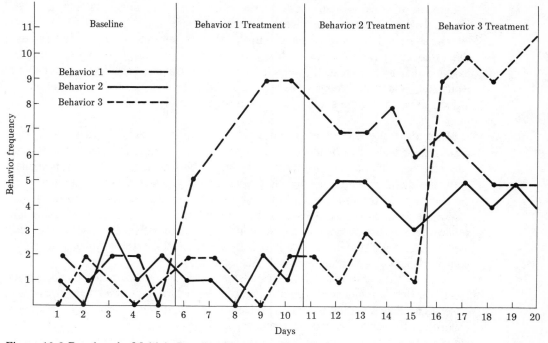

Figure 10.2 Results of a Multiple-Baseline Study across Behaviors

study. This could indicate that your training program for this behavior should be more powerful, or follow-up instruction may be needed to achieve more permanent results.

Notice that the frequencies of teacher use of Behavior 2 never reaches the levels of Behaviors 1 and 3. This could indicate that (1) more training is needed in Behavior 2, (2) tokens are used less frequently, since they take up more class time, or (3) teachers sense that pupils respond better to smiles and praise. Of course, other interpretations, that is, alternate hypotheses, could also be used to explain the results obtained. In many cases, the researcher will conduct additional research designed to test the alternate hypotheses. As the alternate hypotheses are supported or rejected in subsequent studies, the researcher learns more and more about the phenomena he is studying.

Multiple-Baseline across Situations.   In this design, one behavior of one individual is observed and recorded in two or more situations. After baseline rates stabilize, the treatment condition is applied in one situation, but not in the other situation. After a change has been demonstrated for the behavior in the first situation, the behavior is treated in both situations.

Like the multiple-baseline design across behaviors, this design is limited to the extent that the behavior in different situations is correlated. For example, if a client learns assertive behavior in dealing with a used-car salesman, the client may also use the same assertive behavior with a grocery store cashier. The use of multiple-baseline design to assess the effects of assertive training across these situations would not yield fruitful results. Since most of the behaviors we study in education do, in fact, generalize across situations, the design is rarely used.

Multiple-Baseline across Individuals.   In the multiple-baseline design across individuals, two or more clients with the same behavioral goal are selected. After the baseline rates of behavior are stable for both clients, a treatment is applied with one client. When a change has been noted in the frequency, intensity, or duration of the treated client's behavior (whichever measure is of interest), the treatment is applied in the case of the second client. This design is essentially replication and can be used in conjunction with the other two multiple-baseline designs. You should remember that in order to improve the external validity of single-subject designs, replication is usually necessary.

A major consideration for using this design is that the employment of a successful treatment for one individual often influences the behavior of other individuals who observe it. This situation may be a problem when treatment is provided for several children in the same classroom, members of the same family, or employees in the same work location.

The multiple-baseline designs use several baselines to demonstrate the continuing stability of the behavior whenever stimulus conditions are constant. By altering one variable in one baseline and observing a change in behavior, a causal inference is permitted. The continued stability of the second baseline constitutes a further demonstration of treatment control. By comparison with the multiple-baseline designs, the reversal design is a more stringent measure of treatment effects. After demonstrating that the behavior changes with the onset of the treatment condition, the reversal phase demonstrates active control of the behavior by removing the contingencies that are hypothesized to have caused the change. Reinstatement of the contingencies provides further convincing evidence of control, and permits a strong causal inference about the treatment.

In counseling situations where it may not always be desirable to withdraw a successful treatment from a client, multiple-baseline designs are advantageous. This is generally true when anxiety levels are reduced as a function of treatment. The use of multiple-baseline designs will give counselors the advantages of not having to withhold treatment from a distressed client and allowing the study of treatment-induced behaviors that are not reversible or that have a high resistance to extinction.

SUMMARY

Single-subject research designs enable teachers and counselors to assess the effects of an instructional strategy or treatment on the behavior of individual subjects. In all of these designs, two conditions must occur contiguously in order to permit causal inferences. First, conditions under which the problem behavior naturally occurs must be held constant or left free to continue undisturbed in their natural state. Second, one variable, usually a form of treatment, must be introduced or manipulated while other conditions remain constant. The concomitant change in behavior observed with the onset of treatment provides the basis for a causal inference. These causal inferences are strengthened through the withdrawal and reinstatement of contingencies in the reversal design and through the use of additional baselines that are sequentially manipulated in the multiple-baseline designs. While the reversal design is a more conservative test of causation, the multiple-baseline designs have the advantages of permitting the assessment of nonreversible behaviors and eliminating the necessity to withhold treatment from a distressed client.

Sample Single-Subject Study: "A PARENT-ADMINISTERED PROGRAM TO REDUCE CHILDREN'S TELEVISION VIEWING"

Abstract[9]

A parent-administered program to reduce television viewing of primary school-aged children was tested on two boys and three girls from three different families who were heavy viewers of television. Children were given 20 unearned tokens each week by their parents, which they could exchange for up to 10 hours of viewing time. The child earned a gold token for viewing in accordance with the rules for 4 consecutive weeks, which was exchanged for a reward. Parents were given instructions to follow the program independently. Data on hours of television viewing, homework, and reading were recorded each day by one or both parents. A multiple-baseline analysis of the effects of the TV reduction program indicated that children reduced their baseline television viewing by more than half once the program was implemented, and continued to maintain these changes six months and one year after the program was discontinued. Reading time increased for all children whereas effects on homework varied across children. The results support the effectiveness of a parent-administered program for nonbehavior problem children who watch excessive amounts of television.

The Researcher's Comments[10]

Descriptors

Television, homework, reading, parents, children.

---

9. The abstract from the article is reprinted here in order to provide a context in which the researcher's comments can be related.
10. This commentary was written by Dr. David A. Wolfe, the senior author.

Background

This study resulted from a local newspaper story describing the Canadian government's interest in children's television viewing. In 1981, several guidelines were published by a Senate subcommittee on children, youth, and families that expressed the urgent need for television programs and educational material that would curtail excessive television viewing among some children who were being described as "addicted" to TV. A local group of concerned parents had joined together to develop some ideas for reducing children's TV viewing, and their efforts produced the "Jason Method," a copyrighted, parent-administered package that allowed parents and children to monitor their TV viewing more carefully.

After reading an article in the local newspaper about this new method for monitoring children's amount of TV viewing, researchers from the Department of Psychology at the University of Western Ontario contacted the group and designed an investigation that would explore the effectiveness of the method. Because the Jason Method was developed in accordance with behavior modification principles (i.e., self-monitoring one's TV viewing), an evaluation study was designed that involved a small number of subjects who could be followed over an extended period of time.

Experiences

Conducting a study to control children's television viewing proved to be problematic from a number of angles. First of all, despite widespread parental and governmental concern about children's excessive TV viewing, few definitions of "excessive" viewing existed. We attempted to establish some criteria for including children in the study, but found that there is a wide variability in terms of what any particular family might consider to be "excessive." Two hours of viewing per day is considered excessive by some parents, although this amount is below the norm for school-aged children (which exceeds an average of three hours per day). Conversely, some parents are willing to tolerate six hours per day (over 40 hours per week) in order to reduce conflict with the child, avoid arguments, and so on. Therefore, we chose to establish a "baseline viewing rate" for each subject in the study, and measure changes in viewing in reference to pretreatment baseline. This baseline averaged 21 hours per week for the five children in the study (and ranged from a low average of 15 hours to a high average of over 35 hours per week across the subjects).

A second challenge to conducting the study was encountered during our attempt to obtain participants. We advertised the program in schools, on television, in the newspaper, and through the radio; yet, few parents contacted us for further information. This was likely due to the unfamiliarity with the issue, as well as parental uncertainty about becoming involved in modifying their child's TV viewing per se (rather than modifying, for example, homework completion or compliance). One of the authors of the study made a personal appeal to several school counselors and to members of a neighborhood club, which lead to increased referrals to the program.

Because this study used a multiple-baseline, small-N methodology, several research advantages may be noted. This approach enabled the researchers to become more familiar with each family, to provide individual training and assistance when needed (especially regarding data collection), and to provide a more personal intervention plan than a group design might have allowed. This was especially advantageous in recognition of the highly variable nature of the referred problem, as noted above.

Implications and Future Issues

One of the most important issues to arise from our investigation concerns the usefulness of this "reinforcement/self-monitoring method" for modifying children's TV viewing. That is, many children whose parents are concerned about their viewing choices and time could perhaps modify this behavior readily without the use of a structured program. For example, setting clear limits and viewing rules, teaching the child to be discriminating in choice of programs, and praising the child for responsible viewing would clearly be the method of choice for parents who have not attempted to monitor their child's viewing. On the other hand, a small minority of children may require highly structured and systematic forms of intervention to reduce television viewing in instances where their social activities, school performance, and behavior (such as aggression, sex-role stereotyping) are significantly affected. In the latter case, a program that involves the parents and children in a therapeutic procedure whereby TV viewing is made contingent on the display of particular behavior (such as homework, peer activities, reading) would perhaps be of more significance than the present self-monitoring approach.

In addition, it may be stressed from the findings of this study that we should pay particular attention to the factors that might influence a given child's TV viewing, beyond the more obvious entertainment reasons. For example, several of the children in our study watched excessive amounts of television and were seldom required to learn alternative forms of entertainment or education. That is, the television may be a "stabilizing force" in some families that serves the function of reducing demands on the parents, siblings, target child, or others. If we were to alter these viewing patterns, other aspects of the family system's "balance" might be negatively affected (that is, the child may demand more time from his/her parents, more sports equipment and money, more books, and more attention for his/her school work, and so on). In the present study, we attempted to measure changes in two other aspects of the child's daily behavior, schoolwork and reading, which indicated that one or both of these desired activities may be positively affected by decreasing TV viewing time; however, we made no attempt to measure "negative" changes (such as mood, routine, attention-seeking) that might occur in some families, other than through general interview questions asked of each parent. Other researchers and interested practitioners may wish to keep in mind the importance of assessing the child's excessive TV viewing within the context of the current family environment, which may have important implications for the choice and timing of the present form of intervention.

A PARENT-ADMINISTERED PROGRAM TO REDUCE CHILDREN'S TELEVISION VIEWING

David A. Wolfe, Maria G. Mendes, and David Factor
UNIVERSITY OF WESTERN ONTARIO AND THISTLETOWN REGIONAL CENTRE FOR CHILDREN AND ADOLESCENTS

Wolfe, David A., Mendes, Maria G., and Factor, David, "A Parent-Administered Program to Reduce Children's Television Viewing." *Journal of Applied Behavior Analysis*, 1984, Volume 17, pp. 267–272. Copyright 1984 by the Society for the Experimental Analysis of Behavior, Inc. Reprinted by permission.

Children in North America watch, on the average, 24.5 hours of television per week (Comstock, Chaffee, Katzman, McCombs, & Roberts, 1978). Literature regarding the effects of heavy viewing (greater than 15 hours/week) of currently available television fare has indicated that children may be affected in many ways (Murray, 1980), although the extent of television's direct influence on child development is still unknown (Rubinstein, 1983). Studies commissioned by the National Institute of Mental Health to investigate the effects of television on children's behavior led the agency to conclude that violence on television may promote aggressive behavior by children and stereotyping of social behavior (Rubinstein, 1983). Furthermore, Morgan (1980) and Hornik (1978) have shown that children who watch greater amounts of television perform more poorly on reading tests and homework completion, suggesting an inverse relationship between heavy viewing and school achievement. These findings on the relationship between TV viewing and undesirable behaviors among some children have led to increased concerns over the quality and quantity of children's viewing, and increased emphasis on teaching children critical television viewing skills (Murray, 1980; Singer, 1983).

Evidence accumulated over the past 15 years has clear implications for behavioral scientists and practitioners. Researchers stress that, in general, children spend more time watching television than they spend in school and, possibly, in direct communication with their parents (Singer, 1983). Given the possible dangers as well as benefits of television viewing by children, excessive television viewing seems to be an issue that is best defined by the parents of the child. Although television viewing per se is not likely to be a primary factor in child behavior and learning problems, parents may wish to limit the amount or type of viewing by their child as a precautionary measure to reduce academic problems or social avoidance behavior. In particular, a young child who has been free to watch television as often as he or she wishes may fail to decrease viewing time as academic demands increase at an older age.

We evaluated a method for assisting parents who wish to decrease their child's excessive television viewing and possibly to increase desired alternative behavior as a substitute. Children were given unearned tokens permitting them up to 10 hours of television viewing per week. By budgeting their tokens and in turn their TV viewing, the children could decrease their baseline rate of TV

viewing. In addition, children could earn rewards at monthly intervals for complying with the program. Measures of reading and homework time were recorded covertly by the parents to evaluate the positive benefits of the program on other desirable activities.

Method
Participants
Participants were solicited through a newspaper article, a television advertisement, and contact with a local Parent Teacher Association group. Five children from three families participated in the study. Heidi, age 8 and Mark, age 11 from Family 1; John, age 11 from Family 2; and Carrie, age 10 and Mary, age 12 from Family 3. All children resided with both natural parents.

The three families were from working class neighborhoods and were rated 4 on a 9-point scale of socioeconomic status (1 = low, 9 = high) based on father's and mother's occupation(s). We screened children for absence of excessive behavior problems by interviewing the parents and completing the Achenbach Child Behavior Profile (CBP; Achenbach, 1979). None of the children or family members was receiving any form of mental health services, and the children's CBP scores were within the normal range on this instrument. Two children (John and Carrie) were performing below average at school and had previously received special tutoring.

Parents considered their children to be heavy television viewers and indicated that their own previous attempts (e.g., reminders, criticisms) to reduce television viewing had been unsuccessful. All three families indicated that they were eager to modify their child's television viewing due to concerns about the child spending too much time in the house and being "addicted" to television. None of the families had any specific rules for TV viewing, and parents complained that their children preferred TV viewing over most other activities at home.

Measures
The major dependent variable was number of hours of television viewing by each of the five

children per week, as recorded by the parents. Two supplementary activities were also monitored by the parents; homework time and reading time. The total number of hours for each activity was derived from event recording procedures in which the child's continuous involvement in an activity for a quarter hour comprised an event. The parents were requested to record the data according to operational definitions provided. A typed form with this information was reviewed with the parents and left with them for future reference:

Recording Procedure for Television Viewing

(a) Record child's television viewing in the TV guide throughout the day. After the child has gone to bed, calculate the total number of quarter-hour segments viewed and record this information on the data sheet provided. For example, if your child watched a half-hour show in the afternoon and an hour after supper, his total number for the day would be 6. (b) If your child turns the television on but watches it for a period of less than 10 minutes do not count this time. (c) If your child is playing together with a friend or sibling and the television is on, determine which behavior is primary. If it is television, count the time; otherwise, do not count it.

Recording Procedure for Homework

(a) Homework involves work specifically assigned by the teacher for your child to do, e.g., math, English, or reading a story. (b) Record homework time in quarter-hour segments throughout the day and record the total segments on the data sheet at the end of the day. (c) If your child is doing homework while watching television, count the time and mark the time under both categories. (d) You may ask the child once each day about homework assignments, but try not to alter your regular methods of discussing or supervising homework. If you are uncertain whether the child has been working on schoolwork, do not count the time.

Recording Procedure of Reading

(a) This category includes extracurricular reading, e.g., comic books, magazines, or books, for his or her own interest. (b) Reading books for school

book reports should come under this heading, as well as books for read-a-thons. (c) Count reading in quarter-hour segments and record the total each day.

During baseline the children were not told that their TV, reading, and schoolwork were being recorded or that their TV viewing was going to be decreased. During the program phase, the children were aware that their parents were recording their TV viewing time and number of tokens spent. When the tokens were discontinued, follow-up recordings were conducted periodically without the child's awareness. Television viewing outside the home was not recorded. The mother was the principal data collector in all three families.

To obtain reliability estimates of the parent recordings, both parents were asked to keep independent recordings during the times they were at home together. Observer agreement was assessed on 18% of the total number of recording days. As mentioned previously, each quarter hour of TV viewing, homework, or reading was considered a unit. Interparent agreement was calculated by dividing the smaller number of units recorded for the day by the larger number of units recorded. Across all sessions, agreement for TV viewing ranged from 66% to 99% with an average agreement of 87%. Average agreement for homework was 82% (range 65% to 92%) and reading was 71% (range 52% to 86%).

Procedure

A multiple-baseline design across families was used in this study. Prior to baseline, parents reviewed data recording procedures and had practiced recording for several days. Once reliable and correct procedures were evident, baseline data were collected for a minimum of 7 weeks prior to implementing the treatment program. An envelope containing 21 large, colored tokens and an instruction sheet was given to the parents at the beginning of the treatment phase (one kit per child). The program was explained to the parents as a simple method of teaching their children how to manage their own TV time. This program has been copyrighted by a Parent Teacher Association group. (Used by permission of Jason-Roth Products, Ingersoll, Ontario.)

Each child received 20 tokens each week. Each token was worth a half hour of TV time and the child was allowed to choose any child-oriented show (e.g., cartoons, family program, science, or history) with the 15 white tokens and any other type of show (within reason) with the five red tokens. The determination of TV show content as well as viewing times was left up to the discretion of the parents. The remaining gold token could be earned by the child for viewing in accordance with the rules for 4 consecutive weeks, and was exchanged for a reward. The child was not permitted to watch television on another child's token or when parents were watching TV, unless the child used a token. Any show that the parent preferred the child to watch was not deducted from the child's tokens.

At the beginning of the program, parents were simply told to explain the full program to the child and to continue with their usual television habits. We did not suggest any negative contingencies in the event of the child's failure to follow the program rules. Parents were given full responsibility to engage the program on their own with minimal contact with us.

All families completed baseline and intervention phases of the study during the school year. The program (i.e., tokens) was withdrawn completely after 3 months of reduced viewing, and parents in Families 1 and 2 continued to record TV viewing, homework, and reading times on the last week of each month during follow-up over 3 summer months and 4 school months. More than a year after the program was withdrawn, these families again recorded data for 1 week in August and 1 week in September. Family 3, however, was unable to provide follow-up data because they moved at the close of the school year.

Results

Figure 1 shows the children's hours of television viewing, homework, and reading each week across baseline, treatment, and follow-up. The number of hours of TV viewing per week for all children during baseline averaged 21 hours, and

except for the holiday season (indicated by week and month at the base of the graph), their viewing seldom fell below 15 hours per week. With the initiation of the TV reduction program there was an immediate decrease in television viewing to 10 or fewer hours per week. The children remained within the 10-hour limit throughout the 3 months in which the program was in effect (except Heidi, who watched 11 hours on two occasions). All children were given a reward (e.g., trip to the zoo, amusement parks) each month for fulfilling their goal. When the tokens were sequentially withdrawn from each family, follow-up data indicated that the two children in Family 1 continued to remain below 10 hours per week throughout summer and once school began. John (in Family 2) increased his viewing slightly once the program was withdrawn, yet averaged 6 hours less per week than in baseline. Satisfactory maintenance of TV reduction was evidenced by parent recordings during the 13th and 14th months following program withdrawal.

Figure 1 also shows that two children (Mark and Mary) moderately increased their homework time when the program began, whereas the remaining three children showed little change in homework hours. The data on reading in Figure 1 indicate that all five children moderately increased the amount of time engaged in reading activities when the TV package was in effect.

Discussion

The reduction of children's excessive television viewing in this study supports the effectiveness of a parent-administered program with children between the ages of 8 and 12 years. Children's television viewing was reduced with a minimum of difficulty or effort encountered by the parents because the program was structured in an enjoyable fashion that provided rewards for compliance. Parents reported that the children enjoyed the game and often saved tokens for special occasions (e.g., friends visiting to watch a movie) or for "peak periods" (e.g., Saturday mornings). In addition, parents reported that children in Family 1 showed an increased interest in family activities. The child in Family 2 increased his reading

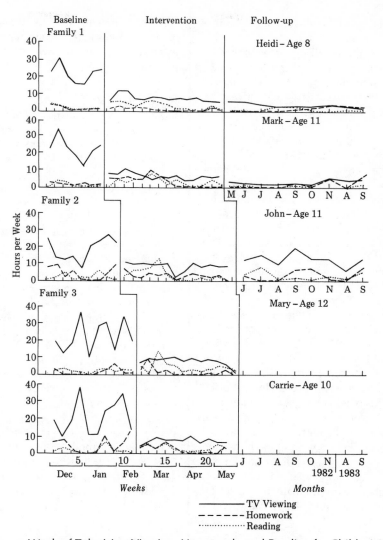

Figure 1 Hours per Week of Television Viewing, Homework, and Reading for Children in Families 1, 2, and 3 during Baseline, Intervention, and Follow-up

and he showed very few outbursts of temper as a result of restricted television viewing, as had commonly occurred on previous attempts by parents to restrict viewing.

Positive benefits from this TV reduction program were evident in the reading time data, which increased over baseline levels for each child. This suggests that the children substituted appropriate recreational activities when TV time was reduced. Homework data were less clear, possibly as a function of variability of homework assigned by teachers (which was not measured). However, no family had expressed particular concern about the child's homework completion but rather were interested in the child developing more varied interests.

Because our study relied on parent-collected data and implementation, recording errors or systematic bias could have been introduced that were not detected. One suggestion for advancing the assessment methodology involves the development of an electronic recording device for home use that would record the time of day and duration of viewing while the set is on. Such a device could be activated by each family member's key or code to record the person(s) viewing, and would eliminate the need for parent recording. Alternatively, researchers could improve the data gathering method presented here by providing parents with a simple-to-use interval recording device that the parent could activate when the child was watching TV, and conducting periodic telephone probes to determine whether the child was watching at that moment.

Limiting or modifying children's television viewing appears to be an appropriate concern for many parents (Eron, 1982; Singer, 1983), and researchers should investigate alternative educational strategies. For some families, simple rules and consequences may be sufficient to control TV viewing, whereas other parents and children may require more assistance and structure. Behavioral methods to increase alternative child behaviors, derived from extensive research in the home and classroom, may offer significant educational and prosocial advantages for the child and parent. Teaching the child to discriminate and select TV programs, offering the child alternative activities and entertainment, and establishing viewing standards and limits in the family appear to be logical extensions of this study which warrant investigation.

References

ACHENBACH, T. M. (1979). The Child Behavior Profile: An empirically based system for assessing children's behavioral problems and competencies. *International Journal of Mental Health, 7*, 24–42.

COMSTOCK, G., CHAFFEE, S., KATZMAN, N., MCCOMBS, M., & ROBERTS, D. (1978). *Television and human behavior.* New York: Columbia University Press.

ERON, L. D. (1982). Parent-child interaction, television violence, and aggression of children. *American Psychologist, 37*, 197–211.

HORNIK, R. (1978). Television access and the slowing of cognitive growth. *American Educational Research Journal, 15*, 1–15.

MORGAN, M. (1980). Television viewing and reading: Does more equal better? *Journal of Communication, 30*, 159–165.

MURRAY, J. P. (1980). *Television and youth: 25 years of research and controversy.* Boys Town, Nebraska: The Boys Town Center for the Study of Youth Development.

RUBINSTEIN, E. A. (1983). Television and behavior: Research conclusions of the 1982 NIMH report of their policy implications. *American Psychologist, 38*, 820–825.

SINGER, D. G. (1983). A time to reexamine the role of television in our lives. *American Psychologist, 38*, 815–816.

Critical Review

INTRODUCTION

The effects of television viewing on children are a major concern of many parents as well as teachers and clinical psychologists. This study evaluates a parent-administered program to reduce television viewing. *Independent* evaluation of educational programs such as this one is an important contribution that educational research makes to the teaching profession. When the persons who develop a program also carry out the evaluation, there is always the danger of bias, since the developers have a stake in the program. Such evaluations need not be biased but the possibility of bias is present and should be kept in mind by the reader.

Unfortunately, many of the audio-visual materials, instructional programs, and curricula being marketed to the public schools have undergone no systematic evaluation. In considering the adoption of new educational materials, school personnel should examine the available evaluation data very carefully before making decisions.

METHOD

Subjects.   A major problem in single-subject research design is the degree to which results can be generalized to the population from which the subjects were drawn. The reader has two bases for estimating the degree to which program results can be generalized. One is the description of the research subjects. The more similar these subjects are to individuals in the reader's own school, the safer it is to generalize the results to the local population. The other basis is replication. Single-subject research findings that agree across several replications (that is, different subjects) can be accepted with far more confidence than findings based upon a single individual. In this study, the children selected had no excessive behavior problems, were in later childhood (aged 8 to 12), and were from lower-middle-class complete families. These characteristics, and the fact that replications were carried out, should be kept in mind when interpreting the research results.

Measures.   Data in all three student behavior categories, that is, time devoted to television viewing, homework, and reading, were collected by the mothers.[11] Even though time records of this sort are quite objective, a brief training session for the parent-observers would have been desirable. The average interparent agreement coefficients for the three child behaviors were satisfactory for research purposes. However, reliability was lower than is usually obtained for low-inference behaviors when observers are trained.

This study uses a multiple-baseline design across subjects. This form of multiple-baseline design is more generalizable than other single-subject designs, since each subject constitutes a replication. As mentioned earlier, replication is an important means of determining the generalizability of single subject research findings.

An important question in most educational research is: How long will the effects of this research upon the subjects persist? When some form of reinforcement is employed, such as the gold tokens used in this study, it is always important to determine whether the behavioral changes brought about in the study will persist after the reinforcement is withdrawn. In this study, although the token system was withdrawn after three months, parents continued to record times for TV viewing, homework, and reading one week per month during the subsequent months. During this time the parental attention involved in these time recordings could have been a form of reinforcement that helped maintain the lower levels of TV viewing and bring about the small increases in reading and homework time reflected in Figure 1.

It should be noted that homework and reading time were not reinforced during the

---

11. Fathers also observed in some cases to provide reliability data.

intervention phase of this study. Only reduction of TV viewing to the amount permitted by the program resulted in the child receiving the gold tokens.

This study could have been conducted as a multiple-baseline study across behaviors. To implement this design, reduced television viewing would have been reinforced during the first three months, increased reading would have been reinforced during the second three months, and increased homework time during the last three months.

RESULTS

Figure 1 shows clearly that levels of TV viewing dropped drastically for all five children during the intervention phase of the study. These results were maintained during the follow-up phase (seven months) when parents continued to record the child's performance but did not award tokens. The final data were collected a year after the end of the intervention and five months after the last parent recording of the child's behavior. It may be seen that the low level of TV viewing had persisted. Thus, the program appears to have been effective in bringing about fairly permanent reductions in the TV viewing of the three children who were available for the entire study.

References

BAER, D. M., WOLF, M. M., & RISLEY, T. R. (1968). Some current dimensions of applied behavior analysis. *Journal of Applied Behavior Analysis, 1,* 91–97.

BORG, W. R., & GALL, M. D. (1983). *Educational research: An introduction* (4th ed.). White Plains, N.Y.: Longman.

BRACHT, G. H., & GLASS, G. V. (1968). The external validity of experiments. *American Educational Research Journal, 5,* 437–474.

CAMPBELL, D. T., & STANLEY, J. D. (1963). Experimental and quasi-experimental designs for research on teaching. In N. L. Gage (Ed.), *Handbook of research on teaching.* Chicago: Rand McNally.

COOK, T. D., & CAMPBELL, D. T. (1979). *Quasi-experimentation design and analysis issues for field settings.* Chicago: Rand McNally.

DUKES, W. F. (1965). N = 1. *Psychological Bulletin, 64,* 74–79.

FISHER, C. W., et al. (1978). *Teaching and learning in the elementary school: A summary of the beginning teacher evaluation study.* San Francisco: Far West Laboratory for Educational Research and Development.

GAGE, N. L. (1978). *The scientific basis of the art of teaching.* New York: Teachers College Press.

KAZDIN, A. E. (1973). Methodological and assessment considerations in evaluating reinforcement programs in applied settings. *Journal of Applied Behavior Analysis, 6,* 517–531.

LAZARUS, A. A., & DAVISON, G. C. (1971). Clinical innovation in research and practice. In A. E. Bergin & S. L. Garfield (Eds.), *Handbook of psychotherapy and behavior change: An empirical analysis.* New York: Wiley.

LEITENBERG, H. (1973). The use of single-case methodology in psychotherapy research. *Journal of Abnormal Psychology, 82*(1), 87–101.

SIDMAN, M. (1960). *Tactics of scientific research.* New York: Basic Books.

Recommended Reading

BORG, W. R., & GALL, M. D. (1983). *Educational research: An introduction* (4th ed.). White Plains, N.Y.: Longman.

Chapters 15 and 16 cover experimental, quasi-experimental, and single-subject research designs in a nontechnical manner, although giving more details than this chapter.

CAMPBELL, D. T., & STANLEY, J. C. (1963). *Experimental and quasi-experimental designs for research.* Chicago: Rand McNally.

This monograph, although now more than 20 years old, is still a valuable reference for the student who wants to learn more about research design than the brief introduction given in this text. Many research designs are described and analyzed in terms of internal and external validity.

COOK, T. D., & CAMPBELL, D. T. (1979). *Quasi-experimentation design and analysis issues for field settings.* Chicago: Rand McNally.

This rather difficult book contains useful information on internal and external validity, causal inference, and specific quasi-experimental designs. Useful if you want to carry out quasi-experimental research but of limited value to the educational practitioner.

DAYTON, C. M. (1970). *The design of educational experiments.* New York: McGraw-Hill.

This text provides a comprehensive survey of experimental designs. One of its helpful features is the use of examples from the research literature in education to illustrate each type of design. There is a separate chapter on the application of analysis of covariance to different experimental designs.

KAZDIN, A. E., & TUMA, A. H. (1982). *Single case research designs.* San Francisco: Jossey-Bass.

Discusses the rationale, procedures, and applications of single-subject research designs in both basic and applied research.

RICHEY, H. W. (1976). Avoidable failures of experimental procedure. *Journal of Experimental Education, 45*(2), 10–13.

The author provides down-to-earth advice about conducting experiments in this article. The advice is based on a personal experience in which an experiment failed. Most of the reasons given for the failure are described in other sources, but the author's presentation is especially convincing. Recommendations to other investigators are given, including the suggestion that an investigator imagine himself (or herself) a subject in the experiment and then intuit how he or she would react to each experimental procedure.

ROSENTHAL, R., & ROSNOW, R. L. (eds.) (1969). *Artifact in behavioral research.* New York: Academic Press.

This collection of papers is organized around the theme of biases and errors that can distort the results of experimental research. The topics include the subject's awareness of and compliance with the experimenter's intent, the nature of the volunteer subject, pretest sensitization, the effects of researchers' expectancies about the outcomes of their experiments, and subject apprehension about being evaluated in an experiment.

Application Problems

For each of the brief research descriptions:
a. Indicate what kind of research design the researcher is using.
b. Indicate the major threats to internal validity.
c. Explain how each threat is likely to affect the results.

1. A researcher has developed a remedial spelling program for college freshmen. He administers a spelling test to all students in 20 freshman English classes and identifies 200 students who score less than 50 percent on the test. He then asks these students to volunteer for the 10-hour spelling program. A total of 120 volunteer and he randomly assigns 60 of these to the experimental group and 60 to the control group. He teaches the program one hour per week for 10 weeks to the experimental group. At the end of 10 weeks, 28 students have completed the program. He administers another spelling test to the 28 and to the 58 remaining in the control group. The mean posttest score for the experimental group is 80. The mean for the control group is 66. This difference is significant at the .01 level.

2. Two second-grade teachers in Adams School have self-contained classrooms. However, they work together in teaching reading. During the reading period Mrs. Jones takes all the below-average children from both classes (19 children) while Mrs. Smith takes the rest (25 children). They decide to evaluate the new "Let's Read" series. Mrs. Jones agrees to continue to use the "Reading Is Fun" series. They administer the ABC Reading Test to all their students at the start of the school year. The 19 children in Mrs. Jones's reading class obtain a mean grade placement score of .8 while Mrs. Smith's children obtain a mean score of 1.5. Near the end of the school year in May all children are tested with another form of the ABC Reading Test. Mrs. Jones's group obtains a mean score of 1.5 while Mrs. Smith's group mean is 1.9. The national average on this test for second grade pupils tested in May is 1.7. Since Mrs. Jones's pupils gained .7 years (1.5 − .8) while Mrs. Smith's pupils only gained .3 years, the teachers concluded that the "Let's Read" series was more effective.

3. The four sixth-grade teachers at Washington Elementary School have decided to adopt a new program to teach the metric system. They administer a metric system achievement test in September in all four classes (105 pupils) to see what their pupils already know. The mean score for the four classes is 56.2 out of a possible score of 100. They then teach the metric program during the school year. In May when the program has been completed, they again test their pupils, who obtain a mean score of 78.3 on the metric achievement test. They conclude that the program has brought about significant gains on the metric system.

4. Using the evaluation form given in Appendix 1, evaluate the article by Schunk that is reprinted in this chapter.

5. Using the evaluation form given in Appendix 1, evaluate the article by Becker and Gersten that is reprinted in this chapter.

6. Using the evaluation form given in Appendix 1, evaluate the article by Wolfe, Mendes, and Factor that is reprinted in this chapter.

7. Evaluate one of the articles listed under Chapter 10 in Appendix 2.

CHAPTER **11**

ACTION RESEARCH

Overview

Action research is called for when the research literature does not provide the teacher or administrator with a sufficient basis for making an important educational decision. In this chapter action research is compared with regular educational research, and an article reporting an action research project is provided. The steps to take in conducting action research are then described, including defining the problem, selecting a research design, sample, measures, and analysis procedures. Several sample analysis procedures are described in detail and examples are given.

Objectives

1. Briefly review the terms *independent variable, dependent variable,* and *moderator variable,* and give an example of an action research project in which these three types of variable are included.
2. Given a description of an action research project, identify the type of research design, the dependent variable, and the independent variable.
3. Given a local educational problem, plan an action research project. This plan will include development of a hypothesis and selection of a research design, measures, sample, and analysis procedure.
4. Describe five simple research designs that can be used in action research.
5. Referring to the steps in this chapter and given a set of appropriate scores, the learner will be able to compute the mean, median, standard deviation, independent means t-test, Mann-Whitney U-test, sign test, Wilcoxon T, chi-square, Spearman rank correlation, and KR-21 reliability coefficient.

Why Do Action Research?

In some cases a search of the previous research literature does not produce enough information to form the basis for making an important decision related to your local school or district. Research evidence cannot provide firm answers to many school problems simply because there are many areas where sufficient research has not been done. Even when the reviewer locates a number of studies that relate to his problem, differences between the local school and the schools studied in the research may cast some doubts on the applicability of the research results. Under these conditions, it is often desirable for the local practitioner to carry out a small-scale action research project to supplement information obtained by reviewing previous research.

The main goals of educational research are the testing of theory and the advancement of scientific knowledge. The researcher is concerned with obtaining results that can be applied beyond the limits of his sample (that is, to broad populations) and must therefore design his research to reach as high a level of external validity as circumstances permit.

In contrast, the goal of action research is to gather evidence that can help the teacher or administrator make decisions related to the local schools. In effect, action research is the application of the scientific method to the solution of day-to-day school problems. The practicing educator is not interested in generalizing his results beyond the local school district, and in many cases is concerned only with a single school or classroom. Therefore, although action research uses the same methods as regular educational research, many of the rigorous criteria applied to regular research can be relaxed in doing action research. For example, selecting a sample is much easier in action research, since the investigator is usually interested in generalizing only to a small accessible population such as all third-grade classes in his own school. Similarly, since the action researcher is much more interested in practical significance than statistical significance, simple nonparametric statistical tests are usually sufficient to analyze his results.

Although action research is less rigorous and easier to do than regular educational research, this method coupled with review of previous research provides the best approach we now know for making educational decisions. Many important decisions made in the public schools—decisions that involve large sums of money and critically affect the futures of thousands of students—are made on the basis of either personal experience or expert opinion. Let us briefly review these approaches to decision making, first discussed in Chapter 1.

Both personal experience and expert opinion have led to many blunders in education. The opinions of authorities should be critically evaluated and checked for supporting evidence before being accepted. Uncritical application of Freudian concepts to elementary school education led to amazing blunders in some of the "progressive schools" of the 1920s. Uncritical acceptance of the sales pitch of producers of multimedia learning materials by today's educators may well lead to another educational fiasco because these programs, though promising, are often untested and are far from the level of perfection suggested by the sales representatives. A tragic feature of the uncritical acceptance of authority opinion is that it is usually followed by disillusionment and reaction. Thus, many of the useful concepts given to us by such men as John Dewey and Sigmund Freud are rejected by educators after the fad of blind acceptance has passed.

Reliance upon personal experience is equally faulty as a means for arriving at solutions to our educational problems. Personal experience almost always constitutes insufficient evidence upon which to make decisions, even if the individual could remember and objectively evaluate that experience. We know from psychological research that the individual tends to remember evidence that supports his opinion and to forget or distort evidence that does not. Personal experience often leads the individual to draw conclusions or assume relationships that are false. Yet, personal experience still plays a major role in decision making in the public schools.

The goal of this chapter is to give you the basic tools needed to plan and conduct action research in your classroom, school, or district.

Defining Your Problem

The first step in carrying out an action research project is to describe your problem as specifically as you can. Precisely what information do you need to help with the decision you make? It is often useful to state hypotheses that your action research project will test, following the suggestions and criteria given in Chapter 5.

In developing your hypotheses, you should identify and define your independent, moderator, and dependent variables. You will recall that the independent variable is the variable you manipulate in the treatment that you apply to your subjects while the dependent variable is the characteristic or behavior of your subjects that you are trying to change with the treatment. For example, suppose your problem were to select from between two reading programs the one that was most effective in improving reading achievement of first-grade pupils in your school.

You could state as your null hypothesis: "There will be no difference in the reading achievement of first-grade pupils who are trained with Reading Program A as opposed to Reading Program B." In this case, the independent variable would be the two reading programs you plan to compare. The dependent variable would be reading achievement. But suppose that your previous experience suggests that Program A may be more effective with pupils who score high on a reading readiness test while pupils who are low or average on that test seem to achieve more when taught with Program B. In this case your null hypothesis might be: "There will be no difference in the achievement of first grade pupils at high, average, or low levels of reading readiness who are given Reading Program A as compared with those who are given Reading Program B." In this case, reading readiness is a moderator variable since the effects of the treatment are expected to be different at different levels of reading readiness. In other words, treatment effects are *moderated* by reading readiness.

Moderator variables describe the characteristics of the subjects or the conditions under which the independent variable is hypothesized to influence the dependent variable. We have learned that the results of educational research, that is, the influence of the independent variable on the dependent variable may differ considerably for subjects with different characteristics such as different age or grade levels, different ability levels, or different socioeconomic levels. For that matter there are probably a great many variables that influence or moderate to some extent the effect of the independent variable on the dependent variable in a typical educational research project. It is often possible to introduce one or more moderator variables into an action research project in order to get better insights into the way the independent variable affects the dependent variable and to help estimate the conditions under which that effect is greatest.

In the aforementioned example, when we include reading readiness as a moderator variable, our results may show that one program is more effective for students at the low readiness level, the other program is more effective for students with high readiness, and the two programs are equally effective for pupils of average readiness. It is usually not desirable to introduce more than one or two moderator variables into an action research project because each new variable introduced makes the study more complex. However, if the one or two variables that appear to be most likely to moderate the results can be explored, the study is likely to produce much more useful results. If you have identified more than two moderator variables you want to manipulate, you can carry out a series of parallel small-scale experiments, manipulating different moderator variables in each experiment, while using the same independent and dependent variables. In educational studies in which students are the subjects, almost any student characteristic can be used as a moderator variable. Some moderator variables frequently used in educational research include sex, age or grade level, scholastic aptitude, reading achievement, self-concept, interests, and socioeconomic status. In some action research projects teachers rather than students are the subjects, while in others teacher characteristics can moderate the treatment effects on students. For example, suppose you wanted to study the effects of our two reading programs on achievement in the classrooms of first-year versus experienced teachers. In this case our main concern is the effects of the two programs on student achievement, but we suspect that one program may be easier for first-year teachers to master, and thus we introduce teacher experience as a moderator variable.

Let us look at one more action research problem statement to illustrate further the relationships among independent, moderator, and dependent variables. The objective of this study is to determine whether praise of the pupil or praise of his work is more effective in improving the attitude toward school of white, Hispanic, and black sixth-grade pupils. The *independent variable* is the type of praise, that is, in one treatment the teachers would use personal praise while in the other treatment teachers would praise the pupil's work. The *dependent variable* would be pupil attitude toward school, and the *moderator variable* would be student race.

Simple Research Designs

Most action research projects are aimed at determining the effectiveness of new curriculums, instructional materials such as visual aids, alternative teaching methods, or different ways of organizing the classroom. The new materials or practices being considered for adoption are usually compared with what the school is already doing. Therefore, although all the approaches illustrated in Chapters 8 through 10 can be used in action research projects, the simple experimental and quasi-experimental designs are often the most appropriate. In the following pages we will briefly review a few simple research designs and discuss their advantages and disadvantages in action research.

SINGLE-GROUP PRE-POST DESIGN

In this design a single group of subjects, such as the pupils in a single classroom, are given a pretest on the dependent variable, and then they are exposed to the experimental treatment and then retested on the dependent variable. The pre- and posttest scores are then compared to determine if a significant change has taken place. The data can be analyzed by using any of several simple statistical techniques such as the sign test, the Wilcoxon matched-pairs signed-ranks test, or the t-test for correlated means.

This design is especially helpful for studies a teacher wants to carry out in a single classroom. Its main weakness is that since no control group is used, it is subject to most of the threats to internal validity. That is, it is not possible to determine how much of the difference between the pre- and posttest scores on the dependent variable is due to the treatment and how much is due to extraneous variables.

For example, single-group design would be a poor choice for evaluating a new program intended to improve the manual dexterity of children in a preschool program, because at this age level dexterity increases rather rapidly due to maturation. Thus, your program could be worthless, and you would probably still find a significant gain in manual dexterity if the time between the pre- and posttests were long enough for maturation to occur. Single-group design is most useful for studying stable dependent variables, that is, characteristics or behavior patterns that are likely to stay about the same unless considerable effort is made to change them. For example, racial attitudes have generally been found to be quite stable in adults. When fairly stable dependent variables are studied, there is less chance that pre-post differences have been caused by extraneous variables.

For example, suppose a fifth-grade teacher in an inner-city school has found it impossible to keep her students in their seats during classwork. Pupils are constantly getting up and wandering about the classroom and consequently are learning nothing from the lesson. Reprimands and threats have had no effect, so the teacher decides to set up an action research project and evaluate a new approach. She starts by having a parent volunteer observe in the classroom for one week. The observer checks the class at five-minute intervals and counts the number of pupils out of their seats. The teacher finds that during the week before observation the mean number of pupils out of their seats is 16.36 out of a class of 26. This mean is fairly stable from day to day.

The teacher then introduces the experimental treatment. She places an alarm clock on her desk, setting it to go off at random times throughout the day. Whenever the alarm goes off the teacher gives a token to each student who is in his or her seat. At the end of each week the children can exchange the tokens for small rewards such as pencils, small toys, and so on that have been donated by local merchants, or they can save the tokens in order to get larger rewards, such as movie tickets, later.

After three months the parent observer again records out-of-seat behavior at five-minute intervals for one week. The mean number of pupils out of their seats is 3.72. A comparison of the pre- and posttreatment mean scores of out-of-seat behavior, using the correlated means t-test, shows a statistically significant improvement. This improvement is clearly large enough to be of practical significance. The teacher reports her findings at the annual district conference, and 26 other teachers having the same problem adopt her method. The district grants $100 per classroom to teachers who adopt this method, so that they can buy rewards for their pupils.

CONTROL-GROUP DESIGNS

A later action research project comparing the 26 elementary classrooms using the alarm clock system to 63 similar classrooms not using this approach shows significant achievement differences on the standard achievement battery used in the district favoring the classes that have used the alarm clock approach.

Posttest-only Design with Nonequivalent Groups.   This second action research project has used a control group design, in this case the posttest-only design with nonequivalent groups. In this design, comparable subjects (or in this case classrooms) are assigned to the experimental or control groups. The experimental group is given the experimental treatment, and the control group is either given an alternate treatment or no treatment. In this example the teachers in the experimental group had already decided to adopt the alarm clock procedure. Thus, the research employs a quasi-experimental design. If it had been possible to assign classrooms *randomly* to the experimental and control groups, a true experimental study using the posttest-only control-group design would be carried out. At the end of the treatment both groups would be measured on the dependent variable, which in this example is achievement. Scores of the two groups are then compared using a simple statistical tool such as the *t*-test for independent means, the chi-square test or the Mann-Whitney *U*-test to determine if the two groups differ significantly on achievement.

Pre-Post Design with Nonequivalent Groups.   This design is similar to the first two designs we have discussed. Subjects are assigned to the experimental or control groups. Then, all subjects are administered a pretest that measures the dependent variable. In most action research projects it is not possible to assign subjects randomly to treatments, and therefore quasi-experimental designs are used. In cases where random assignment is possible the parallel experimental design, the pretest-posttest control-group design, would be used.

Once subjects have been assigned to groups, the experimental group is given the experimental treatment, and the control group is given an alternate treatment or no treatment. Finally, all subjects are given the posttreatment measure of the dependent variable. The results are then analyzed. The groups are first compared on their pretest scores, using the Mann Whitney *U*-test or the *t*-test. If not significantly different on the pretest, the groups are compared on the posttest, using the same statistical technique. If the groups are significantly different on the pretest, analysis of covariance (ANCOVA) is usually used to compare the posttest scores, making adjustments for pretest differences (see Chapter 7). When ANCOVA is used, the pretest need not be the same measure as the posttest although the pretest must measure a variable related to the dependent variable. For example, using ANCOVA in a study of two methods of teaching algebra, the pretest could be an algebra aptitude test while the posttest could be an algebra achievement test. The amount of adjustment made to the posttest means using ANCOVA is determined by the size of the pretest differences between groups and the correlation between the pretest and the posttest. This is a rather complex procedure, and if you carry out an action research project that requires ANCOVA, you should seek help in doing your analysis.

One of these three designs, that is, the single-group pre-post design, the posttest-only design with nonequivalent groups, or the pre-post design with nonequivalent groups, can be used for most action research projects. When random assignment of subjects is possible, the parallel experimental designs would be used.

A common variation of the control-group designs occurs when you wish to employ more than two groups or evaluate more than two curriculums or instructional programs. For example, suppose that in searching for a new first-grade reading program you locate four programs that you want to evaluate. In this case, first-grade classrooms could be randomly assigned to each program. If it appeared likely that the classrooms selected would differ initially in reading achievement, then a pre-post control group design would be used. On the other hand if the groups were closely comparable, a posttest-only control-group design could be used. In selecting the measure of the dependent variable, in this case reading achievement, it would be important to check the available measures carefully and to select a measure that was equally appropriate for all reading programs (see content validity, Chapter 6). This is important in any study but is most difficult when several programs are being compared, since the content of each program should be compared with the test content. At the end of the school year, after your groups had completed the various programs you were evaluating, you would administer the reading achievement test you had selected in all classrooms. The mean achievement scores could then be arranged in order of magnitude and a simple statistical tool such as the independent means t-test could be used to compare any pair of means for statistical significance. In comparing the four different programs you might discover, for example, that Program A was significantly more effective than Programs B, C, and D, which in turn were not significantly different from one another.

RANDOM VERSUS NONRANDOM ASSIGNMENT

An important consideration in planning an action research project in which a control-group design will be used is to determine how subjects or classrooms will be assigned to the experimental and control groups. If you are able to assign subjects or classrooms to your treatments randomly, you are using an experimental design. If you cannot assign your subjects or classrooms randomly, you are using a quasi-experimental design. Random assignment is preferable because it removes the danger of systematic errors. Thus, we can accept the results that we obtain from experimental research with more confidence than results obtained from quasi-experimental research. Often, if you plan your project to start in the fall, students can be randomly assigned to classes during the regular scheduling process. For example, if there are to be 10 ninth-grade algebra sections in your school in the fall, you can assign students randomly to these sections during the summer when your scheduling occurs. Similarly, if you plan to compare 2 third-grade mathematics programs, you can randomly assign your eight third-grade teachers, four to each program, and can randomly assign children to the eight classrooms if you plan sufficiently in advance of the start of the academic year.

Random assignment should be used whenever possible. However, there are many occasions in which it is not possible to assign students or classrooms to your treatments at random. In this case try to assign subjects to treatments in such a way as to avoid systematic errors. Obviously, if you assign all of your strongest students to Treatment A and all your weakest to Treatment B, your results will tell you nothing about the relative merits of the treatments. All you will find out is that strong students usually do better than weak students—hardly a surprising discovery. In some small-scale action research projects where random assignment is not possible, you can match students in pairs on the dependent variable or on a variable closely related to the dependent variable. For example, in studies of achievement pupils are often matched for scholastic aptitude (IQ), which is correlated with achievement. Matching presents some problems. For instance, if you pair only students who have very similar scores on the matching variable (for example, ± 5 IQ points) you will find some students who cannot be matched. These are usually the very bright and very dull, and eliminating them changes the characteristics of your group. Another matching method that does not lose subjects is to rank the students in each group on the matching variable and then match the two students who rank number 1, the two who rank number 2, and so on. The weakness of this method is that if the groups are somewhat different to start with, this method does nothing to make them more comparable. In action research studies where matching seems necessary, perhaps the best rule is to use the first method when the two groups have somewhat different means on the matching variable and the second method when the means are similar. When matching is used in control-group design, the groups can be compared on the dependent variable (that is, the posttest) using any one of several simple statistical tests. Among these are the correlated means t-test, the Wilcoxon matched-pairs signed-ranks test, and the sign test.

CORRELATIONAL STUDIES

In some action research projects you are interested in the relationship between two variables, or in using one measure to predict future performance on another measure. Suppose, for example, that for your new first-grade class you set up a three-day orientation session immediately before the start of the school year. The purpose of the session is to help children adjust to the school situation, which you believe should improve their achievement during the first grade. At the end of the session, you rank the children who participated to indicate the degree to which each child adjusted to the school situation during orientation. Then, at the end of the first grade you administer an achievement test battery to your pupils. You now have two scores for each pupil, the orientation rank and the achievement score. You could determine the relationship between these two sets of scores using a simple correlation technique such as the Spearman rank difference correlation.

Let's consider another example. As a third-grade teacher you have observed that pupils who are below grade level in reading also seem to have difficulty in articulation, often mispronouncing words or selecting the wrong word when talking. You wonder whether these two variables are really related. Thus you decide to carry out an action research project that hopefully will give you a better understanding of reading problems in your class. You check the *Ninth Mental Measurements Yearbook* and find there are several articulation measures. You select the Arizona Articulation Proficiency Scale and administer this scale and the reading subtest from the California Achievement Tests to pupils in your class. To determine the relationship between the two scores the product moment correlation could be computed, or the test scores could be changed to ranks by ranking the highest score number one and so on. The relationship between the two sets of ranks could then be computed using the Spearman rank difference correlation procedure, which is somewhat simpler.

SINGLE-SUBJECT DESIGN

Single-subject design is well suited for many action research projects that are carried out in the classroom. Single-subject designs are especially useful when you have a child in your class who needs special help and you want to determine the effectiveness of one or more approaches in bringing about desired changes. More than one child can be involved in a single-subject study, but in this case the data for each child are studied separately rather than being combined as is done in group research. Let's review one of the types of single-subject design that we discussed in Chapter 10 and see how it can be used in action research.

ABAB Design. In this design you observe the child and keep a record of his performance on the dependent variable, that is, the behavior you want to change. This record, taken over a period of time provides a *baseline* (A). You then apply your experimental treatment, (B), the approach you have chosen to change the dependent variable. During or after the treatment (depending on what the treatment is) you continue to observe and record the child's behavior in the dependent variable. Performance during baseline and treatment are recorded on a chart, called a frequency polygon, to see if the behavior changed after the experimental treatment was introduced. The treatment is then stopped to see if the child's behavior will return to the baseline condition (A). Then the treatment is reinstated (B), and the child's behavior is again recorded. If the behavior improves under the first B condition, then returns toward the baseline during the second A condition, and finally improves again under the second B condition, we have strong evidence that the treatment caused the change in the dependent variable.

Assume, for example, that you are a preschool teacher, and one child in your class, Billy F., frequently hits the other children. You decide to see if rewarding the child for each minute that he does not hit another child will reduce his hitting behavior. For one week you observe the child an hour per day during a free play period and chart the number of times he hits other children (see Figure 11.1). Note that his baseline ranges from 10 to 15 hits per hour over the five days. Then, during the next five days you give him an M&M candy for each minute when he does not hit anyone. Note on Figure 11.1 that his hitting behavior drops, going from eight at the start of

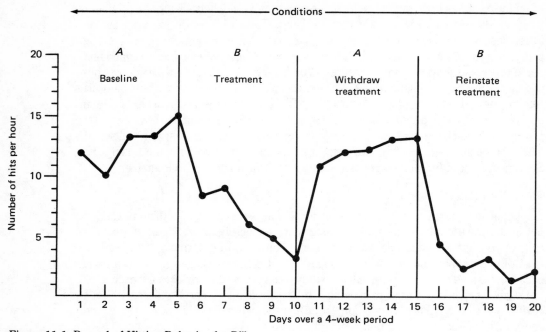

Figure 11.1 Record of Hitting Behavior for Billy

the week down to three on Friday. You then stop giving him the M&M's during the third week (A) and find that his hitting behavior increases, ranging from 11 to 13. Finally, you reinstate the reward (B) and find that his hitting behavior again drops markedly. The results of your four-week project demonstrate clearly that the reward brings about a marked reduction of hitting during both "B" periods. You can't spend an hour a day handing out M&M's to this child indefinitely, but there are approaches you can use that will take much less of your time. For example, you can gradually lengthen the periods between rewards. Or, you can not only lengthen this time but also give the rewards at an irregular interval, so that the child cannot predict when he is due to receive one. Also, you can try gradually substituting verbal praise for the rewards and if this works, gradually lengthen the period between praise statements. By the end of the term there is a good possibility that the hitting behavior will be permanently reduced.

You may wonder why the teacher went through two A-B cycles. The main reason is that this greatly increases confidence that the treatment was really the cause of the improved behavior. If you had used an A-B design instead of ABAB, differences during the B period might have been due to some extraneous variable such as a change in the home atmosphere. The chances of extraneous variables causing differences in an ABAB design are much more remote.

Most researchers who use single-subject designs do not carry out any statistical analysis. If the treatment is powerful enough to show clear differences on a frequency polygon such as Figure 11.1, tests of statistical significance are not needed.

There are other kinds of single-subject design that you can learn about by reading one of the references at the end of this chapter (also see Chapter 10). However, the ABAB design is probably the most useful in action research.

The Sample

Since the person doing action research usually plans to generalize the results to a limited local population, such as all students taking algebra at Roosevelt Junior High School, sampling is not as difficult or as critical as is the case when the researcher wants to generalize results to a broad population. However, it is still important when selecting your sample to choose students who appear to be representative of the population to which you plan to generalize. For example, in evaluating a new eighth-grade general mathematics textbook for adoption by your school district, you should draw classes from all schools in your district that teach eighth-grade students. If these classes cannot be selected at random, you should avoid any obvious sources of systematic error or bias such as selecting the most experienced teachers to use the new text and using teachers who are left to form the control group. Teacher ability and experience are important factors in the success or failure of any instructional program, so biased assignment of teachers to the experimental and control treatments can greatly distort the results of your study. For this reason, it is usually desirable to have at least two teachers involved in each treatment. If you have three teachers in your experimental group and one gets very large student achievement gains with a new program and the other two do no better than the control teachers, then in all probability the differences are due to teaching ability and have nothing to do with the new program you are evaluating. If you only have one teacher in each treatment, it is impossible to estimate the degree to which any differences found are due to teacher differences as opposed to differences in your treatments.

Describing the Treatment

In many action research projects the teacher wants to evaluate a new teaching method or set of materials that he has developed himself. For example, over a period of years Bill Jones has developed a method of teaching reading that seems to work very well with bilingual first graders who are very weak in English. Other first-grade teachers in his school urge him to organize the program so they too can use it. Bill decides to carry out an action research project to see if his method is really better. He asks three other teachers to use the program next fall. They agree, and work together for a day just before start of the school year. Bill gives them ditto copies of his material and tells them how he teaches. Forty bilingual children with poor English enter in the fall and are randomly assigned to eight first-grade classrooms. Bill and the three teachers he has worked with teach four classes (experimental) while the other four first-grade teachers in the school teach the four control classes. At the end of the school year the 40 bilingual children are all given a reading achievement test. The 20 children in the experimental classes have a mean achievement score of 33.75, while the 20 children in the four control classrooms have a mean score of 30.07. This difference is not statistically significant nor is it large enough to have any practical significance. What went wrong? Bill goes back and checks the mean scores for each teacher's bilingual pupils. He finds that his pupils had a mean of 44.05, while the other three experimental teachers had means of 28.60, 31.35, and 31.00. Means for the control classrooms were 32.06, 29.31, 27.08, and 31.83. From these means we can see that either Bill is a much better teacher or the other experimental teachers were not using Bill's methods. The latter proved to be the case. When the three experimental teachers observed Bill's class, they found he was doing many things that he had not told them about, and he used his materials in ways he had not described or explained. Therefore, these teachers had not really given Bill's method a fair test. Not adequately describing an innovation or new program to be used as an experimental treatment is a common and serious problem in many action research projects. If you develop a new approach that produces desirable results, you have an obligation to your colleagues in teaching to describe that approach in detail and to provide the help and materials other teachers will need to learn to use your innovation. Action research can provide the field-test evidence needed to demonstrate that your idea really works.

Selecting Measures

The references described in Chapter 6 are the most useful for locating measures that you can use in an action research project. However, the way you use these sources to locate a measure for an action research project is different from the procedure used to evaluate a measure used in someone else's research. The first step in selecting a measure is to define as specifically as you can the variables you want to measure. You may need more than one measure. For example, in a descriptive study comparing black and white sixth-grade children in skills and attitudes you believe are important to school success, you may want to administer several measures to your subjects in order to get scores on all of the variables you have identified. Or, in an experimental study using a pre-post control-group design, you may need an aptitude test for your premeasure and an achievement test for your postmeasure.

After you have defined the variables you want to measure, you should go through the Score Index of the *Ninth Mental Measurements Yearbook*. This comprises about 50 pages at the end of Volume 2. It provides an alphabetical list of all of the variables for which scores may be obtained for all of the tests included in this reference. Therefore, you need only look up the variables you have previously defined in order to locate tests that provide scores on these variables. You can then study the information provided on each test in the Tests and Reviews section.

Let's see how we would use the *Ninth Mental Measurements Yearbook* to locate a measure of student attitudes toward mathematics that could be administered to sixth graders. We can start by looking for "attitude toward math" in the Score Index.

There is one entry, 1263. When we check 1263 in the Tests and Reviews section, we find the Test of Mathematical Abilities, which produces six scores, one on attitude toward math. The test covers the correct grade range, and a critical review is also provided to help you judge the test and decide whether it will meet your needs. If no suitable tests are found through the Score Index, it is advisable to check your topic in the Classified Subject Index. Since attitude measures are classified under "Personality" in this index, this section would be checked. A laborious check turns up the Estes Attitude Scales, which measure attitudes toward several school subjects including mathematics. The test is appropriate for sixth-grade pupils and a critical review is provided. It would also be advisable to check Mathematics in the Classified Subject Index, and this turns up another possible test, the Mathematics Attitude Inventory 664. Unfortunately a check of this test in the Test and Reviews section reveals that although dealing with our topic, it is designed for grades 7 to 12.

The above exercise illustrates the fact that if you want to find tests that meet your needs, you have to do a considerable amount of searching through the various indexes of the *Ninth Mental Measurements Yearbook*. Cross-referencing among the various indexes is obviously poor. It would be desirable to order specimen sets for these two measures, which usually contain a copy of the test, scoring key, and test manual and are very useful in making your final selection from among available tests. There are also references listed in the *Yearbook* for most measures, and checking those that appear relevant can help you decide which measure to use in your action research project.

Tests in Print III (Mitchell, 1983) uses somewhat less rigorous criteria for including a test than the *Ninth MMYB* and provides brief information on 2672 published tests. If you are seeking tests in a given subject category, the Classified Subject Index is a fairly good place to start looking. This index is reasonably satisfactory for most topics but is too broad in some cases. For example, if you were looking for self-concept measures, you would have to search through the titles of 576 tests that are lumped into the broad topic of personality.

A far better source for locating tests on a given topic are the *ETS Test Collection Bibliographies*. Instead of trying to classify all tests into a few very broad categories, these bibliographies are classified into over 200 specific topics. One entire bibliography is devoted to Attitudes toward Mathematics. This bibliography covers virtually all measures available on this topic, both published and unpublished, and is far superior to the *Ninth MMYB* or *Tests in Print III* for locating measures in a given subject area.

Another excellent source of information on tests to use in action research projects is *Tests and Measurements in Child Development: Handbooks I and II*. These volumes have subject indexes that are helpful, but it is necessary to check the descriptions of the measures to find measures you need. For example, there are no measures in *Handbook II* listed in the index under attitudes toward mathematics. Under "School, attitude toward," several measures are listed, and on checking these, we find that three of them measure attitude toward mathematics. The best strategy for using these handbooks to locate measures of a given variable is first to look up the variable in the Subject Index and then check the table of contents to locate the category in which tests of your variable would be listed. In *Handbook II* the measures are organized into eleven major categories. One of these, "Attitudes and Interests," would be the place to look for measures of attitude toward mathematics.

Now that we have briefly reviewed the steps necessary to plan and carry out an action research project, let's review a typical project and see how the action researcher has applied these procedures. First read the researcher's comments, then the article, and finally a critical review of the study.

Sample Action Research:
"SELF-REINFORCEMENT AND DESCRIPTIVE PRAISE IN MAINTAINING TOKEN ECONOMY READING PERFORMANCE"

Abstract[1]

The effectiveness of two variables, self-reinforcement and descriptive praise, in maintaining reading problem solution was measured following removal of tokens. A 2(self-reinforcement) × 2(descriptive praise) × 3(phase) factorial design was used. A significant three-way interaction indicated that while self-reinforcement and descriptive praise were most effective when tokens were used, only the combination group maintained reading increases when tokens were removed. The unique role of the interaction of these variables was discussed.

The Researcher's Comments[2]

Background

Working as classroom management consultants, Gary Novak and I became aware of the need for motivating students to become actively engaged in the learning process in the classroom. Token economies have proven to be effective tools that can be used to achieve such a goal. However, a simplified, replicable procedure for changing the stimulus control from the material reinforcers of the token system to the stimulus control of naturally occurring reinforcers has not been clearly demonstrated.

Classroom teachers need to use proven techniques as a part of a sequential approach to moving students from being controlled by a material system to reinforcers that are a spontaneous result of academic achievement. My feeling is that this process should be as much a part of the curriculum as helping students develop in reading from simple decoding to inferential comprehension.

In contingency management research I found that most studies that involve working from the stimulus control of token reinforcers to the stimulus control of naturally occurring

---

1. The abstract from the article is reprinted here in order to provide a context in which the researcher's comments can be related.
2. This commentary was written by J. Mark Hammond, now affiliated with Turlock School District.

reinforcers (such as teacher and parental praise, improved grades, sense of accomplishment, and the intrinsic value of improved academic skill) are done with single-subject designs. In these single-subject designs, "shaping procedures" are used in that the contingencies are continuously modified as the subject's level of performance improves and as he accepts the changes in the contingencies. The value of this kind of research is severely limited for the classroom teacher with 25 to 30 students.

The need for developing students' motivation beyond the stimulus control of a material reinforcement system has been clearly established in educational research. As it presently stands, for the elementary teachers who use token reinforcement, the school year begins and ends with the motivation of their students being subject to the stimulus control of material reinforcement. The reason is primarily lack of identification and development of the scope and sequence of teaching strategies needed to motivate students adequately by naturally occurring reinforcers. The purpose of this research was to evaluate the effectiveness of two techniques that may be used as a part of a sequential development of motivation that can be implemented with a standard-sized class.

Implementation

This research was conducted as a master's thesis. The key to the success of this project was the careful implementation of the various treatment procedures by the teacher, Carolyn Trimble. The most problematic extraneous variable to be controlled was the contamination of the various groups by a treatment procedure that was not prescribed for it. This could have happened very easily because the treatment procedures were implemented at the same time in the same classroom. Trimble's careful implementation of the procedures as prescribed prevented this contamination from occurring. Trimble commented on the ease with which these techniques could be used with an entire class and their effectiveness in positively shaping students' motivation. Experience with this research has led me to conclude that a teacher can successfully shape the motivation of his or her students so that they are engaged in the learning process for the sake of praise, sense of accomplishment, and even the joy of learning.

SELF-REINFORCEMENT AND DESCRIPTIVE PRAISE IN MAINTAINING TOKEN ECONOMY READING PERFORMANCE

Gary Novak
CALIFORNIA STATE COLLEGE, STANISLAUS

J. Mark Hammond
CERES UNIFIED SCHOOL DISTRICT

Novak, Gary, and Hammond, J. Mark, "Self-reinforcement and Descriptive Praise in Maintaining Token Economy Reading Performance." *Journal of Educational Research*, 1983, pp. 186–189. Copyright 1983, Heldref Publications, Washington, D.C. Reprinted by permission.

With the demonstrated effectiveness of token economies in initially modifying classroom behaviors (O'Leary & Drabman, 1971; O'Leary & O'Leary, 1976), the question of response maintenance following the withdrawal of the token system has become a critical issue. The available evidence suggests that effective maintenance of modified behavior should not be expected when the treatment procedures have been abruptly withdrawn (Walker & Buckley, 1972; Walker, Hops, & Johnson, 1975; Walker, Mattson, & Buckley, 1971). Though studies have reported response maintenance that was not specifically programmed (e.g., Bennett & Maley, 1973; Kazdin, 1973), removal of specialized contingencies usually results in a return of performance to levels at or near baseline (Kazdin & Bootzin, 1972; Kazdin & Craighead, 1973). As a result, some type of programming must be specifically designed to maintain behavior change in the classroom. Two procedures that may be used to prolong changes in behavior established through tokens are self-reinforcement and description of natural contingencies.

In self-reinforcement procedures, students are taught to observe, record their behavior, and assign tokens to themselves based on criteria established by and taught to them by their teacher. Reliability of observation and token dispensing is established by an initial training period during which the teacher monitors self-reinforcement (O'Leary & O'Leary, 1976). Bolstad and Johnson (1972) compared the use of self-reinforcement with teacher-imposed reinforcement for controlling disruptive behaviors. They found self-reinforcement superior to external reinforcement in both treatment and generalization (i.e., maintenance) phases.

Another approach to maintaining behavior change is to teach the student the naturally occurring reinforcing contingencies of the academic behavior. This is accomplished by accompanying the dispensing of tokens with verbal praise by the teacher. This praise suggests what the ultimate reinforcers are for the behavior. Consequently, when the tokens are withdrawn, the student has learned that these behaviors result in good grades, teacher approval, parental approval, etc. Haber (1973) demonstrated that increasing the subjects' awareness of contingencies operating in a novel situation led to faster generalization of the behavior in a different setting.

The present study made a direct comparison of self-reinforcement and contingency description in maintaining reading problem solution of fourth grade children.

Method

The study was conducted in a fourth grade classroom with one teacher. The entire class of 28 students was designated as subjects. The children represented a predominantly middle to lower-middle socioeconomic, Caucasian neighborhood in a city of approximately 14,000 population in an agricultural area of central California.

Setting and Design

The study was conducted entirely within a single classroom setting. The standard size classroom contained tables and chairs that could be rearranged to permit individual, small-group, and large-group activities at different times of the day.

Reading was taught primarily during one morning period (from 9:20 a.m. to 10:30 a.m.), although it occurred at other times of the day (e.g., during silent reading and afternoon learning centers) as well. This study used the curriculum program that was already being used in the classroom. The treatment procedures were instituted in conjunction with this program.

Informal observations revealed an emphasis on individualized instruction and a number of positive behavioral contingencies that were applied with regularity. Reinforcing consequences for being quiet, completing assignments, cooperating, etc., were unsystematically awarded at various times during the day.

The study employed a between-subjects repeated measures design to assess the effects of the reinforcement methods. All groups were subjected to an ABA manipulation. The baseline period A (13 days) was characterized by the normal classroom procedures used by the teacher prior to the start of the study. The formal treatment procedures were instituted under Condition B (13 days). Under Condition B all groups received token reinforcement. The three experimental groups received token reinforcement plus one of the three experimental conditions (token system alone, self-administration of reinforcement, descriptions of natural consequences, or a combination of self-administration of reinforcement and descriptions of natural consequences). After 13 days of treatment, all treatment procedures were removed, thus reverting back to reinforcement Condition A. This phase of the study, called follow-up, also ran 13 days in duration. Subjects were randomly assigned to the four groups by lottery.

Procedure

Prior to experimental treatment, the class was asked to name some possible classroom reinforcers, and a list of 15 items was obtained. Then each student was asked to rank order the 15 items according to desirability. Based on the results of this survey and the discretion of the teacher and experimenter, these items were given point values. Under baseline conditions the students worked independently during reading time. Some children worked with the S.R.A. reading laboratory and some children worked with Distar Work Books. Both activities required a similar amount of effort to complete the problems (comprehension questions) associated with them.

Contingencies were applied (treatment Condition B) during the morning reading period to all four groups at the identical rate of one token per question completed. At all other periods of the school day, the reinforcement conditions were similar to Condition A (baseline).

The tokens took the form of the teacher's initials on a token card. The initials were written on the card contingent on appropriate problem completion. Back-up reinforcers included special privileges and teacher recognition.

Each of the four groups was randomly assigned to one of the following treatment conditions:

Self-administration of Reinforcement

This group received tokens in the manner described for approximately 4 days. They were told that they were to administer the tokens (write initials on their card) to themselves the same way that the teacher had been doing it. The performance criterion was fully explained to them. At the same time, the teacher recorded the response rate of assignment completion. These records were compared with each student's records to check the student's accuracy of self-administra-

tion of reinforcement. If the agreement between the student's recordings and teacher's were to fall below 80%, points were to be taken away from the student. The students responded well to self-administration of reinforcement and their accuracy was consistently above 80%. The checking of the students' accuracy of self-administration of reinforcement was done for 4 days. For the final 5 days of Condition B (treatment) this group was left to administer tokens to themselves for problem completion without being checked for accuracy. The group was pulled out of the classroom to meet with the experimenter for approximately 10 minutes on the 13th day. The experimenter discussed with this group the performance criterion for receiving tokens, and the manner that is suggested for recording the occurrence of criterion performance.

Description of Natural Consequences

This group received a descriptive statement regarding its behavior and a possible natural consequence when the token was presented, contingent on the occurrence of a completed problem (as defined previously). Examples of possible descriptions of natural reinforcers used were as follows: "You're working hard. You can go to learning centers first today," and "You sure had a lot correct. You should get a good grade in reading this term." The group that was to have descriptions of natural reinforcers presented to it was pulled out of the classroom to meet with the experimenter for approximately 15 minutes on the 13th day. The experimenter discussed with this group the natural consequences of increased reading problem completion.

Combination

This group received a descriptive statement regarding its behavior and a possible natural consequence in the same manner as the group described in the preceding. This group also received tokens and was instructed regarding how to self-administer tokens in the same manner as the first group described. Because the teacher was not dispensing tokens for the final 9 days of the treatment phase, she randomly praised each child in this group and briefly described the natural consequence of her or his behavior. The combination

Table 1   Means of reading problem completion by groups

		Phase		
Group	N	Baseline	Treatment	Follow-up
Token only	7	2.03	9.16	5.87
Self-administration of reinforcement	7	2.55	12.23	5.71
Description of natural consequences	7	3.20	13.01	5.92
Combination	7	1.58	9.21	7.74

group was pulled out of the classroom to meet with the experimenter for approximately 10 minutes on the 13th day. The experimenter discussed with this group the performance criterion for receiving tokens and the manner that is suggested for recording the occurrence of criterion performance. The experimenter also discussed with this group the natural consequences of increased reading problem completion.

Token Reinforcement

This group received tokens for problem completion. This group was also pulled out of the classroom to meet with the experimenter on the 13th day. The experimenter discussed with this group the number of tokens the members had been earning. Such statements as, "That looks good" or

"Good work" were applied with the administration of tokens to this group.

Follow-up

During the last 13 days of the study the teacher followed the same classroom procedures as described in baseline.

Results

Table 1 shows the means and standard deviations for reading problem completion. These means are depicted in Figure 1. A 2(self-reinforcement) × 2(natural contingencies) × 3(phase) analysis of variance was performed.

All four groups showed increased problem completion during treatment and a decline in follow-up. This main effect for phase was significant

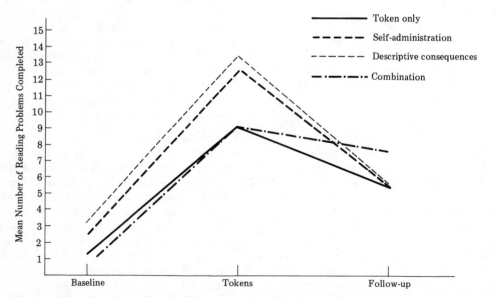

Figure 1   Mean Number of Reading Problems Completed by Groups during Baseline, Treatment, and Follow-up

at the .0001 level. The main effects for self-reinforcement, $F(1,27) = .001$, $p < .05$, and natural contingencies, , $F(1,27) = .716$, $p < .05$, were nonsignificant. Likewise the two-way interactions were also not significant. However, the self-reinforcement × natural contingencies × phase interaction was significant, $F(2,56) = 11.689$, $p < .005$. Inspection of Figure 1 reveals this significant interaction to be due to decreases in follow-up that occurred for all treatment groups except the combination group, which remained at essentially its treatment level.

Discussion

The results indicated that all four token systems produced problem-solving levels above baseline. However, important differences between groups did exist. Three of the groups showed subsequent decreases as the systems were removed in the follow-up phase. Although all groups displayed more problems solved in follow-up compared to baseline, the two groups showing the greatest improvement during treatment also declined the most during follow-up. As a result, they were indistinguishable during follow-up from the token-only group, which had a modest treatment increase but declined less sharply in follow-up. Most importantly, while the combination group had only the third largest treatment gain, these gains remained intact when the tokens were withdrawn.

These last findings are most relevant for the long-term effectiveness of token economy programs on academic performance. The study suggests that by teaching the child rules about (1) how reinforcement is earned, and (2) the type of natural contingencies available in the classroom, the effectiveness of token economies can be maintained after the tokens themselves are no longer used. It appears that both of these rules, applied at the time of token use, are central to the maintenance issue.

References

BENNETT, P. S., & MALEY, R. F. Modification of interactive behaviors in chronic mental patients. *Journal of Applied Behavior Analysis,* 1973, 6, 609–620.

BOLSTAD, O. D., & JOHNSON, S. W. Self-regulation in the modification of disruptive behavior. *Journal of Applied Behavior Analysis,* 1972, 5, 443–454.

HABER, L. C. Response generalization as a function of contingency awareness (Doctoral dissertation, University of Tennessee, 1973). *Dissertation Abstracts International,* 1973, 33, 2865B–459B. (University Microfilms No. 73-2450)

KAZDIN, A. E. Role of instructions and reinforcement in behavior changes in token reinforcement programs. *Journal of Educational Psychology,* 1973, 64, 63–71.

KAZDIN, A. E., & BOOTZIN, R. R. The token economy: An evaluative overview. *Journal of Applied Behavior Analysis,* 1972, 5, 343–372.

KAZDIN, A. E., & CRAIGHEAD, W. E. Behavior modification in special education. In J. L. Mann & D. A. Sabatino (Eds.), *The first review of special education* (Vol. 2). Philadelphia: Buttonwood Farms, 1973.

O'LEARY, K. D., & DRABMAN, R. Token reinforcement programs in the classroom: A review. *Psychological Bulletin,* 1971, 75, 379–398.

O'LEARY, S. G., & O'LEARY, K. D. Behavior modification in the school. In H. Leitenberg (Ed.), *Handbook of behavior modification and behavior therapy.* Englewood Cliffs, N.J.: Prentice Hall, 1976.

WALKER, H. M., & BUCKLEY, N. K. Programming generalization and maintenance of treatment effects across time and across settings. *Journal of Applied Behavior Analysis,* 1972, 5, 209–224.

WALKER, H. M., HOPS, H., & JOHNSON, W. M. Generalization and maintenance of classroom treatment effects. *Behavior Therapy,* 1975, 6, 188–200.

WALKER, H. M., MATTSON, R. H., & BUCKLEY, N. K. The functional analysis of behavior within an experimental class setting. In W. C. Becker (Ed.), *An empirical basis for change in education.* Chicago: Science Research Associates, 1971.

Critical Review

INTRODUCTION

The usual purpose of action research is either to improve the educational process in the local schools or to provide evidence that will aid in local decision making. Action research studies therefore are rarely published except in school district newsletters and other such sources.

The Novak and Hammond study can be considered an action research project because it was conducted in a single classroom by the classroom teacher and Hammond, who also worked in the district. On the other hand, the study could be regarded as a regular experimental study because (1) children were randomly assigned to the reading groups, (2) each group received an experimental treatment, (3) the study was concerned with a problem that is not limited to the local schools, but has national implications, and (4) the research design controlled many of the threats to internal validity, and therefore the results could be generalized to other similar classrooms.

As the authors point out, token reinforcement systems, although effective, are very difficult for classroom teachers to carry out over a long period of time. Thus, unless the token reinforcement can be combined with other forms of reinforcement or can be phased out and less time-consuming reinforcement procedures substituted, any desirable behavior changes achieved by the research subjects are not likely to be maintained.

PROCEDURES

Let's now look at some of the characteristics of the study and discuss how these would affect the control of extraneous variables and the generalizability of the results. You may want to review the sections of Chapter 10 dealing with internal and external validity before continuing.

1. The study was conducted in a regular classroom and adapted to the regular curriculum. This is desirable in action research, since it provides a natural setting. It also increases external validity, since results can easily be applied to similar fourth-grade classrooms in the school district because they would typically be using the same curriculum in a similar classroom environment.

2. Pupils were randomly assigned to the four treatment groups, thus making this an experimental study. In many action research studies on reading achievement, intact reading groups are used. This is much less satisfactory than using random assignment, since in most classrooms reading groups are organized according to reading level, so that all slow pupils are in one group and all advanced pupils are in another. This leads to the internal validity threat of "differential selection." When this threat is present, it is difficult to determine how much of the performance gains during the treatment phase can be attributed to the treatments and how much to ability or to past achievement differences among the groups.

3. The baseline data obtained in this study illustrate, however, that random assignment does not ensure that groups will be comparable when we are working with small samples. Although *systematic biases* as described above will not occur, large *chance differences* can occur when random assignment is used with small samples; they apparently did occur in this study. Mean baseline scores on the dependent variable, that is, reading comprehension problems completed, varied from 1.58 to

3.20 (Table 1). Thus, the baseline performance of the "Descriptive Consequences" group was about twice as high as that of the "Combination" group, indicating that the internal validity threat of "differential selection" was operating to some degree despite random assignment.

Although no solution to the problem of initial group difference is entirely satisfactory, probably the best solution in this study would have been to use analysis of covariance (ANCOVA) instead of analysis of variance (ANOVA) to analyze the results. You will recall that ANCOVA makes adjustments to the final mean scores on the dependent variable that partially compensate for the initial group differences. Thus, these adjusted mean scores are an estimate of what the posttest means *would have been* if the groups had been initially comparable on the pretest.

4. The dependent variable in this study was the number of reading comprehension questions (problems) completed by the student. Some children were using the SRA books and others, the DISTAR books. Different comprehension questions were associated with these two sets of books. Thus, although the authors state that these problems required "a similar amount of effort," we must assume that the internal validity threat of "instrumentation" was operating. To reduce this threat, the authors could have analyzed the results separately for SRA and DISTAR students, but this was precluded by the small sample. Another option would have been to demonstrate that the two sets of comprehension questions were closely comparable. Providing objective evidence of comparability of two measures based on two different reading series would be very difficult and beyond the scope of this study.

5. Remember, however, that the classroom teacher who participated in the project surely knew a great deal about the 28 children—how well they were reading at the outset of the study, and how the treatments affected not only the four groups but the individual children as well.

Therefore, although differential selection and instrumentation introduce serious extraneous variables, the results were still meaningful for the teacher, who could probably estimate the effects of these internal validity threats and allow for them. This illustrates the fact that action research can be a useful decision-making tool for the teacher who does it or is fully knowledgeable about the local situation even in cases where flaws in internal validity diminish the value of the findings outside of the local situation.

RESULTS

Although essentially an action research project, some of the findings could be of value to other teachers working with similar fourth-grade classrooms. Most noteworthy of these is the superior follow-up performance of the "Combination" group. As a group these seven children were the poorest in reading comprehension at the outset of the study. Their gains were about the same as the other groups during the treatment phase. However, they exceeded all other groups during the followup because of much smaller losses in their performance on the reading comprehension problems. The implication of these results for the elementary teacher seems to be that a variety

Table 11.1   Scores of 26 pupils on a measure of attitude toward reading

Group A			Group B		
Name	Score	Square	Name	Score	Square
1. Ana	28	784	1. Allen	32	
2. Bill	28	784	2. Betty	27	
3. Clara	36	1296	3. Carl	23	
4. Doug	23	529	4. Debra	30	
5. Edie	21	441	5. Ed	22	
6. Fred	20	400	6. Flo	19	
7. Gloria	18	324	7. George	18	
8. Herb	31	961	8. Helen	13	
9. Ida	22	484	9. Juan	14	
10. Jim	13	169	10. Jill	11	
11. Kathy	27	729	11. Karl	14	
12. Len	19	361	12. Lil	17	
13. Mary	20	400	13. Mike	16	
TOTAL	306	7662	TOTAL		

of reinforcement strategies that are easy to use and that can be implemented naturally in the classroom, such as teacher praise and self-reinforcement, can have an important impact on pupil achievement. Other research has shown that natural rates of reinforcement in the typical classroom are distressingly low (White, 1975).

Easy Analysis Procedures

In carrying out an action research project it is usually desirable to analyze your results in order to help estimate statistical significance, reliability of your measures, and practical significance. In this section you will learn six simple procedures that will be sufficient to analyze most action research projects.

CENTRAL TENDENCY

For some projects, a simple comparison of means is sufficient to give you an estimate of the practical significance of your findings. Suppose you want to determine whether using comic books for supplemental reading assignments in your fourth-grade class leads to better reading attitudes than using regular children's books that are at the correct reading level. You randomly divide your class into two groups of 13 by drawing names out of a hat. For three months, you assign comic books to Group A and regular supplemental books to Group B. All children are then given the Dulin-Chester Reading Attitude Scale, Form I that you located in *Tests and Measurements in Child Development, Handbook II*. See Table 11.1 for the scores your pupils obtain.

To compute the median score for each group, you would check off the highest score, then the next score, and so on until you reached the seventh score. The median is the middle score, so with 13 scores the middle score would be the seventh score, since there are 6 scores higher and 6 lower. Check off the scores in Group A and Group B with your pencil and find the median for each group. You should have gotten a median of 22 for Group A and 18 for Group B. An easy way to determine the median is to put the test papers in numerical order for each group and find the middle paper. If the number of pupils in your group is even, you find the two middle scores, add them and divide the two to compute the median. The two medians indicate that Group A has a more favorable attitude toward reading.

However, the mean is a more stable measure of central tendency and is preferable, especially for small groups where changing one score can sometimes make a considerable change in the median. To compute the mean for each group, you simply add up the scores for the group and divide by the number of pupils (N) in the group. The total for Group A is 306 (written ΣX in statistical formulas), which divided by 13 gives a mean score of 23.54.[3] Dividing the Group B total of 256 by 13 gives a mean score of 19.69. In research articles the mean is usually written as M or $\bar{X}$.

Thus, Group A is about four points higher than Group B for both the mean and the median.

VARIABILITY

It is difficult to estimate how important the four-point difference is when using only the mean and/or median. If the scores vary a great deal from pupil to pupil, a four-point difference may be insignificant. On the other hand, if the variability in scores is small, a four-point difference may be very significant. Thus, we need a way to estimate the variability of the scores in order to judge the importance of the difference between means. The best measure of the variability and the one that is used in most educational research is called the *standard deviation* (see Chapter 7). Let's compute the standard deviation for Group A step-by-step.

Step 1: Square each of the 13 Group A scores. For example, $28^2 = 784$. You can quickly compute the squares using a desk calculator, or you can look them up in a table of squares and square roots. We have written each square in the column provided in Table 11.1. You may want to follow these same steps for Group B.

Step 2: Add up the 13 squares for Group A. This gives you a total of 7662. In statistical formulas this sum is written ΣX^2.

Step 3: Divide 7662 (ΣX^2) by the number of pupils (N) in Group A, that is, 13. This gives us 589.38.

Step 4: Now square the mean (M) of 23.54 that we computed earlier for Group A. The square of 23.54 is 554.13, which is usually written as M^2 or $\bar{X}^2$.

Step 5: Subtract the result of 554.13 (M^2) found in Step 4 from the result of 589.38 (i.e., $\Sigma X^2/N$) found in Step 3. The result is 35.25.

---

3. The Greek capital letter sigma, Σ, is used in statistical formulas to indicate "the sum of." Capital X is usually used to represent test scores. Thus, ΣX means the sum of the test scores, while ΣX^2 means sum of the squares of the test scores.

Step 6: Compute the square root of 35.25. Most hand calculators have a square root key that will give you the square root of 5.94. This square root is the standard deviation for Group A.[4] You may also want to compute the standard deviation for Group B or for the entire class. If you have computed the standard deviation for Group B, you should have obtained 6.43.

You will recall that a common rule of thumb is that the difference between the means being compared (such as Group A versus Group B) should be one-third of a standard deviation or larger to be of practical significance. This difference in our example is $23.54 - 19.69$, or 3.85. When we divide this difference by the larger, that is, $3.85 \div 6.43$, we obtain .60. Since this is larger than .33, we can conclude that the pupils in Group A probably have a more favorable attitude toward reading than pupils in Group B, and this difference is large enough to be of practical significance. Therefore, the teacher doing this action research project would probably use more comic books for supplemental reading in her class.[5]

THE INDEPENDENT MEANS T-TEST

For most decision making related to actions the teacher takes in her own classroom, the comparison of the mean difference with the standard deviation such as we did in the above example will be sufficient analysis. However, if you wish to compute the statistical significance of this difference, there are several statistical techniques available. We will now use the information we have obtained from the above example to illustrate how you would compute the independent means t-test.

First let's summarize the information we have for Groups A and B in Table 11.1:

	Group A	Group B
Number of pupils (N)	13	13
Sum of scores (ΣX)	306	256
Mean (M)	23.54	19.69
Sum of squares of scores (ΣX^2)	7662	5578
Standard Deviation Squared (S^2)	35.25	41.38
Standard Deviation (S)	5.94	6.43

In the following steps, we will use symbols given above to save space.

Step 1: Divide S^2 for Group A by N, that is, $35.25 \div 13 = 2.71$.
Divide S^2 for Group B by N, that is, $41.38 \div 13 = 3.18$.

---

4. The formula you have applied in carrying out these steps is

$$s = \sqrt{\frac{\Sigma X^2}{N} - M^2}$$

5. The data used in this and subsequent examples are fictitious and were created to provide simple illustrations of the procedure.

Step 2:   Add 2.71 to 3.18 to obtain the sum 5.89.

Step 3:   Compute or look up the square root of 5.89 which is 2.43. This is called the standard error of the difference between means (S_D).[6]

Step 4:   Divide the difference between the Group A and Group B means (23.54 − 19.69 = 3.85) by the S_D of 2.43, that is, 3.85 ÷ 2.43 = 1.58. this is called "*t*" or the "*t* ratio" or "*t*-value."[7]

Step 5:   Subtract two from the total number of pupils in both groups, (26 − 2 = 24) which gives the degrees of freedom (*df*).

Step 6:   Look up the "*t*-table" in any elementary statistics text until you come to 24, which is the *df* for our example.[8] Reading across, we find that we need a *t* of 1.71 to be statistically significant at the .10 or 10 percent level. A *t* of 2.06 is needed at the .05 or 5 percent level, 2.49 at the .02 level, and 2.80 at the .01 level. Since our *t* is smaller than any of these values, the difference between the reading attitude mean scores of Group A and Group B is not significantly different.

Note that a simple comparison of mean difference and standard deviation led us to conclude that our difference was of practical significance but our *t*-test has indicated that the difference was not statistically significant. This disagreement arises because the number of subjects is very critical in tests of statistical significance. Therefore, in studies made in a single classroom, large differences may be found that do not reach statistical significance. In our example, if the action research project had been conducted in two classrooms, the same difference between Group A and B means of 3.85 would have been statistically significant at the .05 level, and if three classrooms (78 pupils) had been studied, the difference would have been statistically significant at the .01 level. Thus, if your action research project is to be used to help make a decision that will affect several classrooms (such as a district or school decision), it is desirable to involve several classrooms in the research. Results from a larger study can be accepted with more confidence. Also, involving several teachers reduces the chance that the results obtained are due to one nontypical teacher rather than the treatment.

THE MANN-WHITNEY U-TEST

This is another statistical test that can be used to determine whether two independent groups are significantly different on the dependent variable. This test could be used to analyze the data in Tables 11.1 or 11.2. However, it is especially useful when we have very small samples or when subjects have been ranked on the dependent

6. The formula you have used for S_D is: $S_D = \sqrt{\dfrac{S_A^2}{N_A} + \dfrac{S_B^2}{N_B}}$

7. The formula you have used is: $t = \dfrac{M_A - M_B}{S_D}$.

8. Nearly all introductory statistics textbooks contain the tables you will need for this chapter. If you plan to do action research, you should buy one of these texts, or check one out of your library and copy tables you need. A good source is McCall (1980).

variable. This technique requires rank scores but can be used with regular test scores if the scores are placed in numerical order and ranked in order of increasing size. In this case the lowest score is given a rank of one, next-lowest, two, and so on. Once the scores are ranked, follow the steps described in the example.

Suppose you teach first grade in a small rural school. The school has only one classroom per grade. The kindergarten class is usually only about half as big as the other grades, since many parents do not send their children to kindergarten. The school district has suggested that kindergarten be dropped to save money. Some parents argue that kindergarten helps children do better in first-grade reading. There are 15 children in your class: 8 went to kindergarten, and 7 did not. You give all 15 a reading test. On each test paper you write E (experimental) for children who went to kindergarten and C (control) for those who did not. You then place the papers in numerical order and write a rank on each test paper giving the lowest paper a rank of one and so on, with the highest paper ranked 15. The ranks and group classification (that is, C or E) are shown in Table 11.2. Notice there are 7 pupils (N_1) in Group C and 8 pupils (N_2) in Group E. The smaller group is always labeled N_1 and the larger N_2. Let's briefly review these initial steps:

Step 1: Label each test paper either E, for experimental group, or C, for control group. If neither group is really experimental, call the group that you expect to get higher scores the E group. See how many pupils are in the smaller group. In our example the control group is smaller, and $N_1 = 7$. The experimental group has eight pupils, so $N_2 = 8$.

Step 2: Put the papers in numerical order based on the test scores.

Step 3: Give the paper with the lowest score a rank of one, next-lowest a rank of two, and so on. The highest score will have the highest rank.

Step 4: Make up a list like Table 11.2, that is, list rank (in order) in Row A and indicate for each paper whether subject is in the experimental (E) or control (C) group in Row B.

Step 5: Our next step is to count the number of E scores that are lower than each C score and write this number below the C score. The first C score is the lowest, so there are no E scores below it. Thus you write "0" under this score. The next C score (rank 3) has one E score below it, so write "1" under the C score. The next C score (rank 4) also has one E score below it, so again enter "1." Go ahead and work out the rest of numbers in Row C and see if your numbers agree with those given in Table 11.2.

Step 6: Add up the numbers in Row C. The total, which is called U, is 16.

Table 11.2   Reading ranks of 15 first-grade pupils

Row															
A. Rank:	1	2	3	4	5	6	7	8	9	10	11	12	13	14	15
B. Group:	C	E	C	C	E	C	E	C	E	C	E	C	E	E	E
C. U Score:	0		1	1		2		3		4		5			

Step 7: Look in the table for Mann-Whitney U in your statistics text where N_2 is 8 (N_2 value is given at top center of each table).

Step 8: Now read across the N_1 row at the top of the table until you come to 7, which is number of cases in our smaller group.

Step 9: Go down the 7 column until you are opposite the U value of 16. The U values are given in the left column.

Step 10: At the point where the 7 column and the 16 row intersect you will find the number .095. This means that the difference between the reading scores of the kindergarten children and the children who did not attend kindergarten is significant at about the .10 level (that is, .095 is slightly lower than .10). As we have discussed earlier, the significance levels used in most education research studies are the .10, .05, and .01.

Step 11: Since U is statistically significant at the .10 level, you can conclude that kindergarten *may* lead to better first-grade reading achievement. We can't be sure of this conclusion, however, because the children were not assigned randomly to kindergarten. We don't know why some parents sent their children to kindergarten and some did not. Therefore, our conclusion must be tentative.

THE SIGN TEST

In action research projects that use the single-group pre-post research design our analysis problem is to determine whether the scores made by the students on the pretest are significantly different from the scores made on the posttest. The simplest statistical test we have to compare the scores of a group of subjects on the same test given before and after the treatment is the sign test. This statistic can also be used to compare related samples, such as samples that have been matched on some variable such as IQ.

Suppose you are the teacher of a racially mixed sixth-grade class containing 16 white and 3 black pupils. You give your pupils a test of racial attitudes, then carry out a three-month program designed to increase racial tolerance, and then readminister the same racial attitudes test. The scores on the pre- and posttests for each pupil are given in Table 11.3. You would take the following steps to use the sign test to determine if the posttest scores were significantly more favorable (that is, higher) than the pretest scores.

Step 1: Using Table 11.3 compare the pre- and posttest scores for each pupil. If the posttest score is higher, enter a plus in the "+ or −" column; if the pretest score is higher, enter a minus; and if the scores are the same, enter a zero.

Step 2: Count the number (N) of pupils whose pre- and posttest scores are different. Of the 19 students only one, Ann, had the same pre- and posttest scores. Thus, $N = 18$.

Step 3: Count the number of plus signs and minus signs. In this example there are 13 plus signs and 5 minus signs. Designate the number of fewer signs (in this example, the number of minus signs) as x. In this example, $x = 5$.

Table 11.3   Pretest and posttest racial attitude scores for 19 sixth-grade pupils

Pupils name	Pretest score	Posttest score	Use for sign test + or −	Use for Wilcoxon T d	Use for Wilcoxon T rd
Ed	60	54	−	6	8.5
Doris	42	46	+	4	6.5
Uris	51	70	+	19	16
Connie	58	65	+	7	10
Art	54	50	−	4	6.5
Ted	47	48	+	1	2
Inez	41	43	+	2	4
Otto	40	63	+	23	17
Nellie	59	51	−	8	11.5
Ann	53	53	0	0	omit
Larry	58	70	+	12	14
Russ	57	58	+	1	2
Elwin	52	61	+	9	13
Steve	56	55	−	1	2
Ellen	48	72	+	24	18
Amy	43	49	+	6	8.5
Rose	45	53	+	8	11.5
Cheryl	59	72	+	13	15
Hal	47	44	−	3	5

Step 4:   Now, look in the sign test table in your statistics text. Read down the *x* column headed 5 until you are opposite 18 in the *N* column. The number at the intersection of the *x* column for 5 and the *N* row for 18 is .048. This is the probability that the posttest scores are higher than the pretest scores. In other words, since .048 is smaller than .05, the difference between pre- and posttests is significant at the .05 or 5 percent level.

WILCOXON MATCHED-PAIRS SIGNED-RANKS TEST

This statistical test, also known as the Wilcoxon *T,* can be used in pre-post comparisons or comparisons of matched pairs of individuals. These are also the applications for which the sign test is used. The sign test is concerned only with the *direction* of differences between pairs of scores (that is, plus or minus). The Wilcoxon *T* considers both *direction* and *magnitude* of differences and therefore is a more power statistical test than the sign test. Using the data in Table 11.3, let us now go through the steps needed to compute the Wilcoxon *T*. It will help you learn if you carry out each step and check the figures given in Table 11.3.

Step 1:   In Table 11.3, column *d,* enter the difference between each person's pre- and posttest scores. Do not enter a plus or minus sign.

Step 2:   Now rank the differences given in column *d* and enter the rank of the difference in the *rd* (rank of *d*) column. Omit cases where the difference is zero. In our example only one pupil, Ann, has a d of zero. The smallest differences (d column) is given the lowest rank. When more than one pupil has the same score in the d column, the average of the ranks that would be assigned to these pupils if their difference scores have been slightly different is given to all who are tied. For example, three students have 1 in the d column. Add the ranks they would have been given, that is, $1 + 2 + 3$ and divide by the number who are tied, that is, 3, to get the average rank. That is, $1 + 2 + 3 = 6 \div 3 = 2$. Thus, Ted, Russ, and Steve are all given rank of 2 in the rd column. Whether the differences in the d column are plus or minus is not considered in this step. Since we have used ranks 1, 2, and 3, the next-lowest entry in the d column, Inez, will receive a rank of 4. Hal, with the next-lowest d entry of 3, will receive a rank of 5. Two pupils, Doris and Art, have d entries of 4. Thus we take the average of the next two ranks $(6 + 7)$ and give both this average of 6.5. Go ahead and check the rest of the ranks we have entered in the rd column. It is easy to make a mistake in computing these ranks, so you must work carefully. One check is that all 18 ranks must be used, since there are 18 pupils. Remember, Ann was omitted because her pre- and posttest scores were the same.

Step 3: Now check the $+$ or $-$ column and determine which sign occurs less frequently. We already did this for the sign test and know that there are fewer minus signs (5).

Step 4: Now, circle the five ranks in the rd column that have minus entries in the $+$ or $-$ column. These are Ed, Art, Nellie, Steve, and Hal.

Step 5: Add up the rd values that you have circled for these five pupils. You should have gotten $8.5 + 6.5 + 11.5 + 2 + 5$, or a total of 33.5. This is the value of T, that is, $T = 33.5$.

Step 6: The number of pairs of scores N is 18, the same as for the sign test, since in both instances Ann was omitted.

Step 7: Look in your statistics text for the Wilcoxon Test Table to determine the significance level of our T of 33.5 with an N of 18. Notice that as the value of T gets smaller, the results become more significant. For example, for an N of 18, if T is less than 28, the difference is significant at the .01 level. If T is larger than 28 but not over 33, it is significant at the .02 level, while if T is larger than 33 but not over 40, it is significant at the .05 level. Since the T in our example (33.5) is above 33 but less than 40, it is statistically significant at the .05 level.

CHI-SQUARE CONTINGENCY TABLE

Some measures that are of interest to the action researcher produce categorical information rather than ranks or scores on tests. For example, many studies in recent years have compared the performance of students from different racial groups. Race is categorical in that each pupil fits into a racial category. Other categories that are often used in educational research include sex (M and F), type of community (rural, suburban, urban, inner-city, and so on), and socioeconomic status (upper, middle, and working classes). Also, data from test scores or ranks can be converted into categories if doing so is likely to help the action researcher to understand the variables being studied better.

The chi-square contingency table can be used to analyze categorical data. Two or more groups can be compared. Let us suppose, for example, that you want to compare the degree to which white and black ninth-grade students participate in extracurricular activities in a racially mixed junior high school. There are 19 major extracurricular activities, and you record the number of activities in which each child participates. You collect the data and then tally the number of black and white students who participate in 1 to 5 activities, 6 to 10 activities, and 11 to 15. You can then record the results of your tally in a table such as the following:

Number of activities	White students	Black students
1–5	33	27
6–10	56	51
11–15	61	22

There are several ways you could have divided the number of activities into categories. We could have divided the range of 15 (that is, 1 to 15 inclusive) into five equal categories instead of three. Another approach would have been to make the categories of such size that they represented the top, middle, and lower third of the 250 students in terms of numbers of activities. To do this we would tally the activities for all 250 students, place the students in numerical order, and then count how many black and white pupils were in the top one-third ($N = 83$), the middle one-third ($N = 84$), and the lower one-third ($N = 83$). This would have resulted in a table such as the following:

	Number of activities		
	Top 1/3	Middle 1/3	Bottom 1/3
White	56	54	40
Black	27	30	43

Either of these tables can be used to determine if the frequencies of extracurricular activities are significantly different for black and white students.

Let's put the first table into cells and see what steps we would take to compute chi-square (χ^2).

Step 1:   Make up a table such as Figure 11.2, Part 1, and enter the frequencies from your tally.

Step 2:   Add the number of students in each row and each column and the overall total and enter as shown in Figure 11.2, Part 2. Note that there are 250 students in the study, 150 white and 100 black.

Part I

Number of Students Engaged in:

	1–5 Act	6–10 Act	11–15 Act
White Students	33	56	61
Black Students	27	51	22

Part II

	1–5 Act	6–10 Act	11–15 Act	Totals
White Students	33	56	61	150
Black Students	27	51	22	100
Totals		107	83	250

Part III

	Row 1 (1–5 Act)	Row 2 (6–10 Act)	Row 3 (11–15 Act)	Totals
Column 1 (White)	33 (36)	56 (64.2)	61 (49.8)	150
Column 2 (Black)	27 (24)	51 (42.8)	22 (33.2)	100
Totals	60	107	83	250

Figure 11.2 Computing Chi-square to Compare Two Groups

Step 3: Note that in Part 3 of Figure 11.2 we have labeled the rows and columns in the table. Each cell is in a row and a column. For example, white students in the lower one-third in extracurricular activities (33) are in row 1 and column 1. We now compute independence values for each cell. The independence value is the value (that is, numbers of students) that would be in each cell if there were no difference in the distributions of extracurricular activities between black and white students; that is, if exactly the same proportion of black and white students were in each of the three extracurricular activity categories. To compute the independence value for each cell, you multiply the total number of subjects for the row the cell is in by the total for the column the cell is in and divide the result by the overall total number of subjects. For example, white students involved in 1 to 5 extracurricular activities are in column 1 and row 1. To get the independence value for this cell, you multiply the column 1 total of 150 by the row 1 total of 60 and divide by the overall total of 250, giving a result of 36. Computations of independence values for the six cells are given below:[9]

Cell	Independence Value
Col. 1–Row 1:	$\dfrac{150 \times 60}{250} = 36$
Col. 1–Row 2:	$\dfrac{150 \times 107}{250} = 64.2$
Col. 1–Row 3:	$\dfrac{150 \times 83}{250} = 49.8$
Col. 2–Row 1:	$\dfrac{100 \times 60}{250} = 24$
Col. 2–Row 2:	$\dfrac{100 \times 107}{250} = 42.8$
Col. 2–Row 3:	$\dfrac{100 \times 83}{250} = 33.2$

Note that the independence value for each cell is entered in parentheses in Figure 11.2, Part 3.

Step 4:   The next step is to calculate the chi-square value for each cell. To do this we first compute the difference between the actual number of students in a given cell and independence value for that cell.[10] For the cell in column 1– Row 1, there are 33 students and the independence value is 36, giving a difference of 3. Next, we square this difference (that is, $3^2 = 9$), and finally we divide the squared difference by the independence value ($9 \div 36 = .25$) to get the chi-square value of .25. Computations of the chi-square values for the six cells are given below:

$$\text{Col. 1–Row 1:} \quad \frac{(36.0 - 33.0)^2}{36} = \frac{3.0^2}{36} = \frac{9.00}{36} = .25$$

$$\text{Col. 1–Row 2:} \quad \frac{(64.2 - 56.0)^2}{64.2} = \frac{8.2^2}{64.2} = \frac{67.24}{64.2} = 1.05$$

9. There are some short cuts for computing independence values but unless you must compute several chi-squares it is probably safer to follow the procedure given.
10. Subtract the smaller value from the larger.

$$\text{Col. 1–Row 3:} \quad \frac{(61.0 - 49.8)^2}{49.8} = \frac{11.2^2}{49.8} = \frac{125.44}{49.8} = 2.25$$

$$\text{Col. 2–Row 1:} \quad \frac{(27.0 - 24.0)^2}{24} = \frac{8.2^2}{24} = \frac{9.00}{24} = .38$$

$$\text{Col. 2–Row 2:} \quad \frac{(51.0 - 42.8)^2}{42.8} = \frac{8.2^2}{42.8} = \frac{67.24}{42.8} = 1.57$$

$$\text{Col. 2–Row 3:} \quad \frac{(33.2 - 22.0)^2}{33.2} = \frac{11.2^2}{33.2} = \frac{125.44}{33.2} = 3.78$$

Step 5: Add up the chi-square values for the six cells (.25 + 1.05 + 2.52 + .38 + 1.57 + 3.78 = 9.55)

Step 6: Compute the number of degrees of freedom (*df*). This equals the number of rows minus one multiplied by the number of columns minus one. For our example this is $(3 - 1) \times (2 - 1)$ or $2 \times 1 = 2$.

Step 7: Look in your statistics text for the chi-square table, locate 2 in the *df* column, and read across the row opposite *df* 2 until you find the level of significance of the chi-square value you obtained. For example, if the chi-square were less than 4.605, it would not be significant. A chi-square between 4.605 and 5.990 would be significant at the .10 level, between 5.991 and 7.823 significant at .05 level, and between 7.824 and 9.209 significant at .02 level. A chi-square of 9.210 or larger would be significant at the .01 level. Thus, the chi-square of 9.55 obtained in our example is significant at the .01 level. This means that there is a significant difference between black and white students in their patterns of participation in extracurricular activities. The size of the chi-square values in each cell tells us where the differences between the two groups are greatest. Thus, we see that the greatest difference is that there was a smaller proportion of black students who were involved in 11 to 15 activities. There were proportionately more black students in the 6 to 10 activity and 1 to 5 activity categories, but these differences were smaller, which means they contributed less to the overall difference between the two groups.

RANK CORRELATION (USUALLY WRITTEN rho OR ρ)

Correlation is a statistical procedure used to measure the relationship between two sets of scores that have been obtained from the same group of subjects or from different subjects on the same measure. There are many different kinds of correlation that can be used with different kinds of scores.[11] Most of these are easy to compute. The Spearman rank correlation is especially well suited to action research, since it is very easy to compute and works well with small numbers of subjects.

Suppose that you are a junior high school Spanish teacher who has found the students in your recent classes to be so different in interest and aptitude that it is

---

11. See Chapter 9 for a brief nontechnical description of the different types of correlation.

almost impossible to use the same teaching methods and materials for all of them. However, it has taken five or six weeks to assign children correctly into small groups, and little learning took place before this was done.

You have decided that you need some way of predicting during the first week how well students assigned to your class will achieve. If you can estimate the students' aptitude, it will be possible to assign each to a small group within your class where you can use teaching methods and curriculum more likely to meet each group's needs. You are unable to find a satisfactory test of Spanish-language aptitude, so you develop an oral test and administer it individually to your 15 students during the first two days of class. Then, based on your oral test, you rank your students on aptitude with the best student getting a rank of one. At the end of the year you administer a Spanish achievement test to your class. You now want to determine the *predictive validity* of your oral aptitude test by determining the correlation between the aptitude test ranks and the achievement test scores. Here are the steps you would take to compute this correlation, using rho:

Step 1: List your 15 students in rank order on your aptitude test. See Table 11.4, column 1.

Step 2: List each student's Spanish achievement test score in column 2.

Step 3: Find the highest achievement test score in column 2 (Ana), and enter a rank of 1 in column 3. Now find the next highest, Karl, and give him a rank of 2. Continue until each student has an achievement rank in column 3. Note that Ned and Rose both have the same achievement scores. To

Table 11.4   Spanish aptitude ranks and achievement scores of 15 ninth-grade students

Name	Col. 1 Rank on oral test	Col. 2 Ach. test score	Col. 3 Rank on ach. test	Col. 4 D	Col. 5 D^2
Randy	1	82	3.0	2.0	4.00
Ana	2	87	1.0	1.0	1.00
Ned	3	73	5.5	2.5	6.25
Karl	4	83	2.0	2.0	4.00
Cheryl	5	79	4.0	1.0	1.00
Oscar	6	70	7.0	1.0	1.00
Rose	7	73	5.5	1.5	2.25
Ralph	8	65	9.0	1.0	1.00
Elvis	9	60	10.0	1.0	1.00
Lori	10	69	8.0	2.0	4.00
Art	11	53	12.0	1.0	1.00
Ted	12	51	13.0	1.0	1.00
Ima	13	47	14.0	1.0	1.00
Olive	14	57	11.0	3.0	9.0
Nick	15	42	15.0	0.0	0.00
					37.50

compute their ranks add the two ranks they would receive if their scores were different but adjacent, divide by two, and give both the average rank. In this case, they would have received the ranks of 5 and 6. Add 5 and 6 and divide by 2 to get 5.5, and give both Ned and Rose this rank. Since we have used ranks 5 and 6, Oscar, whose achievement score is next highest, will be given a rank of 7. The general rule for computing ranks for persons who are tied is to add all ranks the tied persons would receive if their scores were adjacent, divide by the number of persons tied to get the average rank, and then give all tied persons the average rank.

Step 4:   Compare each person's ranks in column 1 and column 3. Subtract the lower rank from the higher and enter the difference between ranks in column 4. For example, Randy's ranks are 1 and 3 and the difference is $3 - 1 = 2$.

Step 5:   Square each of the differences in column 4 and enter the squares in column 5.

Step 6:   Add up the squares in column 5. This sum is called ΣD^2.

Step 7:   Multiply the sum of column 5 (ΣD^2) by six, that is, $37.50 \times 6.0 = 225$.

Step 8:   The number of pupils (15), is N. The square of N (or N^2) is 225. Subtract one from N^2 to get ($N^2 - 1$), which is 224.

Step 9:   Multiply N by ($N^2 - 1$), in this case $15 \times 224 = 3360$.

Step 10: Divide the result of Step 7 by the result of Step 9, in this case, $225 \div 3360 = .07$.

Step 11: Subtract .07 from 1.00 to get .93. This is the Spearman rank correlation between the teacher's Spanish oral aptitude ranking of her 15 students and their later scores on the Spanish achievement test. As you learned in Chapter 9, a correlation of .93 indicates a very close relationship between the two measures. The results also mean that the oral aptitude measure has a *predictive validity* of .93, and the teacher can use this test at the beginning of the year to organize her class into small groups for instruction. In most cases, the correlation between an aptitude and achievement measure in an action research project of this kind would range from .70 to .85. These correlations are still sufficiently high to be helpful in making many educational decisions.[12]

TEST RELIABILITY

In action research projects, teachers often make up achievement measures in cases where no standard test is available that covers the specific content that the teacher wants to test. To a lesser degree, teachers may make up other measures such as attitude scales when a satisfactory test cannot be found. As you learned in Chapter 6, reliability is an important characteristic of tests. When a teacher develops a new test or alters an old test to meet local needs, it is desirable to determine test reliability.

---

12. The formula you have used to compute the rank difference correlation is: rho $= \rho = 1 - \dfrac{6 \times \Sigma D^2}{N(N^2 - 1)}$

Table 11.5   Test scores of 19 students
on a test on the binary number system

	Column 1	Column 2
Student	X	X^2
1. Rolo	26	676
2. Elaine	18	324
3. Linda	16	256
4. Inez	19	361
5. Art	12	144
6. Bert	20	400
7. Ingrid	24	576
8. Larry	15	225
9. Ima	16	256
10. Ted	14	196
11. Yetta	15	225
12. Ivan	23	529
13. Sam	10	100
14. Sally	13	169
15. Izar	16	256
16. Maud	22	484
17. Paul	17	289
18. Lou	13	169
19. Eva	14	196
Total	323	5831

The easiest method of computing reliability uses the Kuder-Richardson Formula 21 (KR-21). Using an example, let's go through the procedure you would follow to compute reliability using this formula.

Suppose that a high school mathematics teacher has decided to evaluate a new program he has developed to teach the binary number system and its relationship to digital computers. He develops a 30-item test to measure achievement on his program and administers it to the 19 students in his class.

Here are the steps you would take to compute the KR-21 reliability of his test from the test scores in Table 11.5.

Step 1:   List students' names and enter their test scores in column 1. Remember that X is used in statistics to represent test scores.

Step 2:   Using the procedure described earlier in this chapter under Central Tendency, compute the mean (M) for these 19 scores. The mean for these scores is $323 \div 19 = 17.00$.

Step 3:   Using the procedure described earlier in this chapter under Variability, compute the standard deviation. You should obtain a standard deviation (s) of 4.23 and s^2 of 17.89.

Step 4:   We now have all of the information we need to compute KR-21:

Number of Pupils (N)   = 19
Number of Test Items (n)   = 30
Mean (M)   = 17.00
Standard Deviation (s)   = 4.23
Square of Standard Deviation (s^2) = 17.89

In the following steps we will use the above symbols to save space.

Step 5: Multiply n by s^2: $30 \times 17.89 = 536.7$
Step 6: Multiply M by $(n - M)$: $17 \times (30 - 17) = 17 \times 13 = 221.$
Step 7: Subtract the Step 6 result from the Step 5 result: $536.7 - 221 = 315.7$
Step 8: Multiply s^2 by $(n - 1)$: $17.89 \times 29 = 518.81$
Step 9: Divide the result of Step 7 by the result of Step 8: $315.7 \div 518.81 = .61$. This is the reliability coefficient of the teacher-made test on the binary number system. This reliability coefficient would be sufficient if the mean score for the entire group were being studied in an action research project. But the reliability is too low if the individual student scores are to used for some purpose such as assigning grades. For individual grading or diagnosis, the teacher should analyze the items, add more items, and recheck the reliability of the revised test.[13]

Conclusion

You now have the basic tools you need to use educational research literature and action research as an aid to solving problems and making decisions in education. Since this book has been written to give you only the minimum skills needed to interpret research evidence, you will occasionally find studies that use methods that you have not learned about. The recommended readings we have included will help you supplement what you have learned from this book.

Once you have developed some expertise in locating and evaluating studies that are relevant to your problems, we believe you will find educational research interesting and, on occasion, exciting. There are thousands of dedicated researchers who are trying to learn more about the educational process and to improve virtually every aspect of education. As is true in all science, only a few educational studies make major contributions while a great many contribute little or nothing. This does not mean that educational research is worthless—it simply illustrates the fact that new knowledge is difficult to find and many efforts to seek it will fail. Thus, you should not be discouraged when you find that many of the research reports you read do not help very much with your problem. If you persist, you will find promising new approaches to many of the educational problems that confront you.

---

13. The formula for KR-21 reliability is: $r = \dfrac{ns^2 - M(n - M)}{s^2(N - 1)}$

Also keep in mind during your initial attempts to use educational research that you must usually contribute some creative thinking of your own to the ideas you find. Research findings are rarely spelled out in terms that make them easy to apply to local school problems. But often a bit of thinking on your part will reveal ways to apply these findings that the researcher never dreamed of.

Finally, remember that the scientific method that is used in educational research and that you can apply in action research is the most effective way to discover new knowledge and solve problems that people have ever developed. Make this method work for you and you will be a better educator.

References

MCCALL, R. B. (1980). *Fundamental statistics for psychology* (3rd ed.). New York: Harcourt Brace Jovanovich.

MITCHELL, J. V. (1983). *Tests in print III*. Lincoln, Neb.: Buros Institute of Mental Measurements.

WHITE, M. A. (1975). Natural rates of teacher approval and disapproval in the classroom. *Journal of Applied Behavior Analysis, 3*(4), 7–12.

Recommended Reading

MCCALL, R. B. (1980). *Fundamental statistics for psychology* (3rd ed.). New York: Harcourt Brace Jovanovich.

This text covers in detail all of the procedures described in this chapter except the sign test and methods of computing test reliability. Explanations are thorough and frequent examples are given.

SCHUTTE, J. G. (1977). *Everything you always wanted to know about elementary statistics (but were afraid to ask)*. Englewood Cliffs, N.J.: Prentice-Hall.

This brief and readable elementary text is written in question-and-answer fashion. A good choice for the student with a weak background in mathematics.

SHARP, V. F. (1979). *Statistics for the social sciences*. Boston: Little, Brown.

A carefully written elementary text that covers most of the statistical procedures described in this chapter.

Application Problems

Problems 1, 2, and 3 are brief descriptions of action research projects. For each, list:

a. type of research design,
b. dependent variable,
c. independent variable, and
d. an analysis procedure that could be used.

1. Mrs. Jones, a sixth-grade teacher, wants to determine whether a new activity-based social studies program results in better achievement in social studies than the current program,

which centers around reading and discussing a textbook. At the start of the year, the four sixth-grade teachers draw lots to see who will teach the new program. Mrs. Jones and Mrs. Smith will teach the new program, while Miss Brown and Mr. White will teach the current program. Form A of the Stanford Achievement Test, Social Studies Subtest, is administered in all four classes in September; Form B of the same test is administered the following May.

2. Mr. Adams teaches a regular fourth-grade class in the Wilson Elementary School. He has two emotionally handicapped boys in his class who frequently make loud remarks or yell answers during recitation when they are not called on. This disturbs the class. He records this behavior for a week and finds that Frank interrupted class 30 times on Monday and 27, 33, 31, and 39 times the other four days. Fred interrupted 39, 34, 36, 30, and 43 times during the same period. He calls the boys in and tells them that next week they will have to stay after school one minute each day for each interruption. During the following week Frank interrupts 21, 15, 12, 7, and 9 times; Fred interrupts 26, 20, 11, 7, and 10 times. The teacher talks to the boys on Friday and tells them that since they have improved, they will not have to stay after school next week. Interruptions the following week are 20, 27, 33, 36, and 38 for Frank, and 23, 30, 34, 37, and 41 for Fred. Mr. Adams again meets with the boys on Friday and reinstates the after-school rule for the following week. Interruptions are 20, 14, 10, 8, and 6 for Frank, and 21, 16, 11, 9, and 8 for Fred.

3. Mr. Fisk teaches two sections of ninth-grade introductory Spanish at Hoover Junior High in a small town in South Dakota. The school has just set up a language laboratory with 10 tape recorders plus practice tapes. Mr. Fisk wants to compare the achievement of students who work in the language lab each Friday for two hours with those who attend a conversation section during the same time. He randomly divides each of his classes, and on Friday half go to the lab and half to the conversation section. All students get the same instruction on Monday through Thursday. At the end of the school year all students are given a comprehensive final on Spanish.

4. In a study similar to that done by Mr. Fisk in problem 3, Mr. Henry carries out the same project in his small 12th-grade Russian class. He randomly divides his 13 students into six who go to language lab and seven who attend the conversation section. Their scores on the final examination are as follows:

Language lab (E)		Conversation (C)	
Art	96	Ana	87
Betty	80	Bill	76
Carl	83	Clara	91
Donna	77	Don	64
Edward	99	Ellen	82
Flo	69	Fred	61
		George	70

    a. Compute the mean score for each group.

    b. Determine if the two groups are significantly different, using the Mann-Whitney U-test.

APPLICATION PROBLEMS: SAMPLE ANSWERS

Chapter 2

1. **a.** There are 128 books in the 1984–1985 subject index under Classroom Management, 48 under Discipline of Children, and 63 under School Discipline. Among recent books that appear most relevant are:

    (1) J. C. Carson and P. Carson. (1984). *Any teacher can: Practical strategies for effective classroom management.* New York: C. C. Thomas.

    (2) C. M. Charles. (1984). *Building classroom discipline.* White Plains, N.Y.: Longman.

    (3) T. L. Good and J. E. Brophy. (1984). *Looking in classrooms.* New York: Harper & Row.

    b. D. L. Duke (Ed.). (1979). *Classroom management: The seventy-eighth yearbook of the National Society for the study of education,* Part II. Chicago: University of Chicago Press.

    (1) Chapter 2: Walter Doyle, "Making Managerial Decisions in Classrooms."

    (2) Chapter 6: Jere E. Brophy and Joyce G. Putnam, "Classroom Management in the Elementary Grades."

    c. Articles from Vol. 49 of the *Review of Educational Research* that appear relevant to our problem include:

    (1) In Vol. 49, No. 2: Michael Pressley, "Increasing Children's Self-Control Through Cognitive Interventions," pages 319–370.

    (2) In Vol. 49, No. 3: Richard Borth, "Home-based Reinforcement of School Behavior; A Review and Analysis," pages 436–458.

    (3) In Vol. 49, No. 4: John A. Bates, "Extrinsic Reward and Intrinsic Motivation: A Review with Implications for the Classroom," pages 557–576. (This article provides good background information but is not as relevant to our problem as the others.)

    d. For each of these preliminary sources, check the subject index for "Classroom Management and Discipline."

Chapter 3

COMPUTER SEARCH RECORD FORM

_____   _____   ____ ____

Your Name   Person Requesting Search

Purpose of Search: *To review information on the use of individualized instruction for children with learning disabilities to help develop a program at our school.*

Problem Definition: *What information is available on the use of individualized instruction with elementary school children who have learning disabilities?*

Secondary Sources Reviewed: *Gearheart, B. (1981) Learning Disabilities: Educational Strategies, 3rd Ed. Mosby; Hallahan, D.P. et al (1985) Introduction to Learning Disabilities, 2nd Ed. Prentice-Hall*

Data Base to be Searched: *Psychological Abstracts*

ERIC Descriptors or Psychological Index Terms:

1. *Individualized Instruction*   990
2. *Learning Disabilities*   3728
3. *Elementary School Students*   12948
4. *Teaching Methods*   1897
5. *Programmed Instruction*   885
6. *Tutoring*   238
7. *Learning Disorders*   752
8. *Handicapped*   2518

9. *Minimally Brain Damaged* 58
10. _____
11. _____
12. _____
13. _____
14. _____
15. _____
16. _____

Search 1: *1 and 2, and 3*

Search 2: *(1 or 6) and (2 or 7) and 3*

Search 3: *(1 or 4 or 5 or 6) and (2 or 7 or 8 or 9) and 3*

Search 4:

Search 5:

Search 6:

Application Problem 2: Sample Answer

Chapter 4

1. **a.** J. Newfield and V. B. McElyea. (1983). Achievement and attitudinal differences among students in regular, remedial, and advanced classes. *Journal of Experimental Education, 52* (1), 47–56.
    b. B. B. Burkhalter and J. P. Wright. (1984). Handwriting performance with and without transparent overlays. *Journal of Experimental Education, 52* (2), 132–135.
2. **a.** C. L. Weeden. (1985). The effects of a treatment program on the self-concept of seventh and eighth grade students (University of Mississippi, 1984). Abstract in *DAI, 45*(10), sec. A, 3101A.
    b. You could have located this study in two ways. The preferable approach would have been to look up key words from the problem statement in Keyword Title Index at the back of the issue. The study is listed under "Self-Concept."

    Another approach would have been to check "Education Psychology" in the Table of Contents. You would have found that abstracts related to the topic started on page 3092A. You would have found Weeden's dissertation abstracted on page 3101A. A related dissertation by H. C. Herbert, "The Effects of a Course in Intrapersonal Relationships on the Academic Self-Concept of High Risk College Freshmen," might also be useful but is less relevant than Weeden's work and also failed to produce significant changes in self-concept.

Chapter 5

1. When we apply the first three questions regarding possible bias to this introduction, we find the following:
    a. Phraseology favoring one side of question:
        (1) The title
        (2) "We felt this approach had many advantages . . ."
        (3) Biased purpose statement
    b. Emotional or intemperate language:
        (1) "Timeworn lecture approach that students find so dull"
    c. Researcher stake in a particular point of view:
        (1) The author recommended the team teaching approach and thus has a stake in its success.
2. Null hypotheses:
    a. There will be no difference in achievement of social studies concepts for students of teachers who use a high frequency of thought questions and students of teachers who use a high frequency of fact questions.
    b. There is no relationship between the cognitive level of teacher questions and student achievement in social studies concepts.
    c. Teacher's use of higher order questions as opposed to fact questions will have no effect on student achievement.
    Directional hypothesis:
    a. Teacher use of thought questions will lead to greater student achievement in social studies concepts than teacher use of fact questions.
3. It is doubtful if this can be considered to be a hypothesis, but it appears to serve this purpose in the article. Although relationships are implied, they are not clearly stated, nor are they stated in terms that are testable.

4.   **a.** To select random sample of 1000 students:

    (1) Number all sixth-grade students on the district roster.

    (2) Starting at a random point and using a table of five-digit random numbers, select 1000 numbers.

    (3) Select the 1000 pupils whose numbers on the roster match those selected from the table of random numbers.

  b. To select a systematic sample of 1000

    (1) Divide the population number (19,206) by the desired sample size (1000), giving 19.2.

    (2) Randomly select a number from 1 to 19. (This could be done either by taking the first two digits from numbers randomly selected from the table of random numbers until you get one from 1 to 19, or by drawing a number from slips placed in a hat.)

    (3) Suppose we draw the number 8 in Step 2. We would then take the 8th name on the district roster and every 19th name thereafter.

    (4) This would give us 1010 names. We could either use all 1010 or randomly discard 10 to give us 1000.

  c. To select a sample of 1000 stratified for socioeconomic status:

    (1) Compute the percentage of students in schools at different socioeconomic levels as follows:

        Upper middle class, 3520/19206 = 18.33%
        Lower middle class, 4968/19206 = 25.87%
        Working class, 6211/19206 = 32.34%
        Welfare, 4507/19206 = 23.47%

    (2) Multiply these percentages by 1000 and round off to the nearest whole number to find out how many students will be selected from each type of school.

    (3) Divide the district roster for sixth-grade pupils into four rosters, one for each type of school.

    (4) From each roster select the number of pupils determined in Step 2. This will give us 1000 pupils. The number of pupils representing each socioeconomic level will be proportional to the number representing that level in the population.

  d. To select a cluster sample of about 1000 pupils:

    (1) We will consider each classroom as a cluster. Since there is an average of 24 pupils per classroom, we will need to select 42 classrooms to get approximately 1000 pupils.

    (2) Number all classrooms on the district roster from 1 to 800.

    (3) Using a table of random numbers, select 42 numbers, discarding any numbers over 800.

    (4) Select all students in these 42 classrooms, approximately 1000 pupils.

5. The accessible population was the 19,206 pupils in the large school district involved. Since the researcher was interested only in her own district and planned to apply the findings only in this district, the accessible population and the target population are the same. To the degree that this large school district is similar to other large school districts the results could be generalized. We might be able to generalize the results further to all sixth-grade pupils in American public schools, but this could not be done with very much confidence since many students are in districts that differ greatly from those in the district studied. If you wanted to apply the findings to your district, it would be necessary for you to gather as much information as you could on the similarities and differences between your district and the district studied. This information would then have to be weighed to decide how differences in the districts could affect the applicability of the research results.

Chapter 6

1. **a.** N   This item could be threatening to teacher who had not completed the teacher training program or felt that they had attended a poor college, but the item would probably threaten very few teachers.

   b. L   Clearly a leading question. A nonbiased question would be: "How much of your teacher training applied directly to classroom teaching?"

   c. T   This question would be threatening to teachers who cannot maintain order, since it is an admission that they are failing in part of their job. It is doubtful that valid information in areas such as this can be obtained from a questionnaire. Direct observation or interviews are preferable.

2. Yes. The researcher should not conduct these interviews, since he knows which teachers completed his program. He also has a stake in the success of the program. Thus, there is serious danger of bias. Another person who knows nothing about the program and who does not know which teachers took the program should be trained to conduct the interviews.

3. Observer B's scores will probably be more reliable than Observer A's. While Observer A bases his rating on an overall impression of the teacher's performance, Observer B actually classifies and tallies each question. Thus, Observer A must use a much higher level of inference than Observer B. The *Eighth Mental Measurements Yearbook* is a good source for locating standardized achievement tests, but it is somewhat out of date.

4. **a.** (1) The most complete and up-to-date source for *locating* tests would be the *ETS Test Collection Bibliography* entitled *Social Studies—Grades 4–6*.

   (2) The *Mental Measurements Yearbook Data Base (MMYD)* would also be an excellent source for both locating and evaluating available tests.

   b. (1) The *MMYD* would be the best source for evaluative data.

   (2) The *Ninth Mental Measurements Yearbook* would be as good as *MMYD* except for very recent tests (that is, since 1985).

   (3) Usually, *Test Critiques* would be the next best source, but this source is very weak on standardized achievement measures.

   (4) The test manuals and technical reports provided by the publisher are usually a good source of information on standardized achievement tests.

   c. Content validity.

   d. By comparing the specific content of the test with the content of the curriculum and textbook used in your district. The test that best fits your social studies curriculum and textbook would have the highest content validity. If the test developers provided content validity data in the test manual *for the textbook used in your district,* this would also be helpful.

5. **a.** (1) 138—College Placement Test in Greek Reading, page 222.

   (2) 1078—Computer Operator Aptitude Battery, page 1691, or 1079—Computer Programmer Aptitude Battery, page 1694.

   b. (1) Preferred Student Characteristics Scale, page 1017.

   (2) Maryland Parent Attitude Survey, page 807.

Chapter 7

1. The independent means *t*-test was not the correct statistical procedure. The teacher should have used the correlated means *t*-test, since the same children were being compared on their pre- and posttreatment attitude scale scores. If two groups of children had been used, and if one had been given the treatment (multiracial teams) and one had not, then a comparison of the posttreatment means on the attitude scale would have been made using the independent means *t*-test.

   Using the independent means *t*-test when the correlated means *t*-test should be used is a common error in educational research. However, the error is not serious, since it simply results in the researcher slightly underestimating the significance of her findings.

2. The teacher should have used the point biserial correlation instead of the biserial correlation because sex is a true dichotomy. The point biserial correlation is used to relate a true dichotomy, such as sex, to a continuous variable. The biserial correlation is used to relate an artificial dichotomy, such as pass-fail in a course, to a continuous variable.

3. Since the researcher had administered a pretest and since the three groups were significantly different on the pretest, ANOVA was not the appropriate tool to use. Instead, analysis of covariance, ANCOVA, should have been used. In this case the pretest would have been used as a covariate to adjust the postttest means to compensate for the pretest differences. If the groups had not been significantly different on the pretest, either ANOVA or ANCOVA could have been used. If no pretest had been given, then ANOVA would have been used. However, in this case the results would have been misleading because the initial differences in reading readiness would have been ignored.

Chapter 8

1. Causal-comparative research, which would include direct observation, would probably be most appropriate since it would be very difficult to manipulate TV viewing for children over any significant period of time as would be necessary in an experimental study. Also, the amount of TV viewing permitted is probably consistent over time in most families. Thus, the researcher would collect data on the amount of TV viewed by each child over a period of a month or more and would classify the children in his sample into two or more groups based on amount of viewing. The next step, measuring the amount of overt aggression, would probably best be done by direct observation, that is, observers would tally the instances of overt aggression displayed by each child over a period of a week or more. Then, the amount of overt aggression displayed by the different groups would be compared.

2. This is clearly a descriptive study and would probably be conducted by administering a questionnaire or an attitude scale to a large sample of male high school seniors.

3. This study, like Problem 1, could best be done using causal comparative research coupled with direct observation. Children would first be classified into two groups: only children, and those with siblings. Then social interactions could best be measured by direct observation of their behavior in kindergarten.

Chapter 9

1. a. This is a relationship study aimed at learning more about the nature of mathematical ability. If a mathematical ability test were being used to determine which students would do best on an advanced mathematics course, it would be a prediction study.

b. A serious limitation is that the researcher selected students from an advanced mathematics course. Since this is an elective course, we can expect that most students who take it will be above average in mathematics aptitude. This would restrict the range of aptitude and tend to reduce the correlations.

c. Common variance is determined by squaring the correlation. The correlation between MA and VIQ was given as 0.54. The common variance would be $.54^2$ or .29. This means that 29 percent of the variance measured by these two tests is common, or put another way, verbal IQ accounts for 29 percent of the variance in mathematics aptitude. Logical reasoning accounts for 16 percent of the variance in mathematical aptitude (i.e., $.40^2$); while creativity accounts for 9 percent (i.e., $.30^2$).

2.   a. This is a prediction study. The goal is to determine how well high school GPA and the two tests predict first-year GPA in college.

b. The main limitation is that the correlations were limited to the 266 freshmen who successfully completed their first year. It would be better to include all freshmen who earned at least one quarter's grades even if they subsequently dropped out.

c. First year GPA and HS GPA, $.68^2 = .46$ or 46%
First year GPA and CTMM, $.61^2 = .37$ or 37%
First year GPA and EST, $.48^2 = .23$ or 23%

Chapter 10

1.   a. Experimental design, specifically the pretest-posttest control group design, was used.

b. Experimental mortality is the major threat to internal validity. Only 2 cases were lost from the control group as compared with 32 from the experimental group.

c. Since the most-motivated experimental students probably completed the spelling program, while the less-motivated dropped out, the higher mean for the experimental group was probably a combination of learning and motivation. Thus, we cannot be sure how much of the spelling difference (if any) was caused by the spelling program.

2.   a. This is a quasi-experimental design, since pupils were not randomly assigned to the two reading programs. Specifically, the teachers used the nonequivalent control group design.

b. The major threats to internal validity are: (1) *differential selection,* since Mrs. Jones's class was made up of below average readers and Mrs. Smith's class contained average and above average readers, and (2) *statistical regression,* since there is a tendency for scores to regress toward the test mean; regression would tend to increase the average score for Mrs. Jones's group and decrease average score for Mrs. Smith's group.

c. Differential selection would make the results very difficult to interpret because we would be trying to compare the performance of two groups that are not very comparable. Suppose one of the reading series was much better suited for above average readers than the other. If Mrs. Smith used this series, the results would probably be very good, since the series would be well suited to her children. But if Mrs. Jones used this series, the results would probably be poor, since the series would not be suited to below average readers. Therefore, the results could be due primarily to which teacher used which series and may tell us nothing about the overall effectiveness of the two series.

d. Statistical regression would tend to increase the apparent gain for Mrs. Jones's pupils, since they were initially below average and decrease the apparent gain for

Mrs. Smith's pupils. Unless a statistical correction is made for regression, the results could be misinterpreted.

3.   a. The teachers have used a preexperimental design, specifically the one-group pre-test-posttest design.

   b. This design, since it does not employ a control group, is subject to several threats to internal validity. In this particular study, the most serious threat is probably history.

   c. Since much attention is currently being given the metric system, it is possible that the pupils at Washington School learned about the metric system outside the school program. For example, most TV weather reporters give temperature in both Fahrenheit and Celsius, road signs may give speed limits in both miles and kilometers per hour, and the weight of many grocery items is given in both ounces and grams. Since there is no control group to help estimate out-of-school learning, it would be impossible for the teachers to determine how much of the gain in metric achievement is due to their metric program and how much is due to out-of-school experience.

Chapter 11

1.   a. Pre-post design with nonequivalent groups (quasi-experimental, since students were not randomly assigned to the four classrooms).

   b. The dependent variable is social studies achievement as measured by Form B.

   c. The independent variable is type of social studies program, that is, new activity-based program versus the current program.

   d. ANCOVA would be best choice. However, if groups earn comparable mean scores on Form A, the t-test for independent means could be used.

2.   a. ABAB single-subject design.

   b. Dependent variable—number of interruptions.

   c. Independent variable—after-school time versus no after-school time for each interruption.

   d. A computation of weekly means and a graphing of daily interruptions for each boy is usually sufficient for this kind of research.

3.   a. Posttest-only control-group design (this is an experimental study, since students were randomly assigned to the Friday sessions).

   b. Dependent variable—Spanish achievement as measured by the final examination.

   c. Independent variable—Language lab versus conversation section.

   d. Independent means t-test or ANOVA would be the preferred analysis procedures.

4.   a. The mean for the language lab group is $504 \div 6 = 84.00$. The mean for the conversation group is $531 \div 7 = 75.86$.

   b. The following steps should be taken to compute the Mann-Whitney U-test:

   (1) List all scores in numerical order as follows and label each case either E for language lab or C for conversation section. Fred has the lowest score, 61, so we rank him 1 and enter a C, since he took the conversation section.

	Fred	Don	Flo	Geo.	Bill	Donna	Betty	Ellen	Carl	Ana	Clara	Art	Ed
Score	61	64	69	70	76	77	80	82	83	87	91	96	99
Rank	1	2	3	4	5	6	7	8	9	10	11	12	13
E or C	C	C	E	C	C	E	E	C	E	C	C	E	E
U-Score	0	0		1	1			3		4	4		

(2) Now count the number of E scores that are lower than each C score and write this number below each C score. These are already written into the above table.

(3) Add up these numbers to get U equal to $1 + 1 + 3 + 4 + 4 = 13 = U$.

(4) Look up the table for the Mann-Whitney test in your statistics book. $N_2 = 7$ and $N_1 = 6$ in our problem. Find the table with $n_2 = 7$ at the top. Go down the $N_1 = 6$ column until you are opposite U of 13. The probability is .147, and since this is higher than .10, we conclude that the scores on the Russian final examinations are not significantly different for students who took the language lab and those who took the conversation section.

APPENDIX 1

FORMS

MANUAL SEARCH RECORD FORM

_____   _____   _____   _____
Your Name   Person Requesting Search   Starting Date   Due Date

Purpose of Search:
_____

Preliminary Problem Definition:
_____
_____
_____
_____

Secondary Sources Reviewed:
_____

Preliminary Source Selected:
_____

Instructions: Start with current year and work back. Enter a check mark
after you have checked a key word and made up necessary
bibliography cards. Enter an "N" if you find no relevant
references for a given key word.

Key Words, Index Terms of Descriptors (in alphabetical order)	Dates or Volume				
	19___	19___	19___	19___	19___

COMPUTER SEARCH RECORD FORM

_____   _____
          Your Name   Person Requesting Search

Purpose of Search: _____

Problem Definition: _____

Secondary Sources Reviewed: _____

Data Base to be Searched: _____

ERIC Descriptors or Psychological Index Terms:

1. _____   9. _____

2. _____   10. _____

3. _____   11. _____

4. _____   12. _____

5. _____   13. _____

6. _____   14. _____

7. _____   15. _____

8. _____   16. _____

Search 1: _____

Search 2: _____

Search 3: _____

Search 4: _____

Search 5: _____

Search 6: _____

RESEARCH REPORT EVALUATION FORM
A Checklist for the Educational Research User

INTRODUCTION

The Problem

1. Do the author's language or affiliations suggest possible bias? (check one)
   Yes ＿＿   No ＿＿   ? ＿＿

2. Is the problem stated in a way that you understand?   Yes ＿＿   No ＿＿

3. How closely is the problem addressed in this research related to the problem or question about which you are seeking information?

   Very closely related ＿＿   Somewhat related ＿＿   Not related ＿＿

   Remarks: ＿＿＿＿＿＿＿＿＿＿＿＿＿＿＿＿＿＿＿＿＿＿＿＿＿＿＿

   ＿＿＿＿＿＿＿＿＿＿＿＿＿＿＿＿＿＿＿＿＿＿＿＿＿＿＿＿＿＿＿＿

   ＿＿＿＿＿＿＿＿＿＿＿＿＿＿＿＿＿＿＿＿＿＿＿＿＿＿＿＿＿＿＿＿

Review of Previous Research

1. Are recent sources cited?   Yes ＿＿   No ＿＿

2. Does previous research cited agree or disagree with investigator's findings?
   Agree ＿＿   Disagree ＿＿

3. Are you aware of any important studies that disagree with the author's view that have been overlooked?   Yes ＿＿   No ＿＿

4. Are any of the studies cited related to your problem or question?
   Yes＿＿   No＿＿   If yes, copy the bibliographical data for related studies onto three-by-five-inch index cards and review these when time permits.

   Remarks: ＿＿＿＿＿＿＿＿＿＿＿＿＿＿＿＿＿＿＿＿＿＿＿＿＿＿＿

   ＿＿＿＿＿＿＿＿＿＿＿＿＿＿＿＿＿＿＿＿＿＿＿＿＿＿＿＿＿＿＿＿

   ＿＿＿＿＿＿＿＿＿＿＿＿＿＿＿＿＿＿＿＿＿＿＿＿＿＿＿＿＿＿＿＿

Objectives and/or Hypotheses

1. Are objectives and/or hypotheses stated briefly and clearly?
   Yes ＿＿   No ＿＿

2. Are hypotheses in directional ＿＿ or null ＿＿ form? If directional, does researcher provide justification?   Yes ＿＿   No ＿＿

3. Do hypotheses state an expected relationship or difference?
   Yes ＿＿   No ＿＿

4. Are hypotheses supported by theory and/or previous research?
   Yes ＿＿   No ＿＿

5. Can hypotheses in this research be tested?   Yes ＿＿   No ＿＿

Remarks: _____

_____

_____

PROCEDURES

1. What specific characteristics of the sample are given (e.g., age, grade level, location, socioeconomic status, sex, etc.). _____

_____

_____

2. How are the subjects in this study similar to or different from the students in your school or district with respect to these characteristics? _____

_____

_____

3. Estimate how any differences might affect application of the results to your problem or question. _____

_____

_____

4. Check the phrase that best describes how the sample was selected:

_____ a. Random sample from a national population (e.g., all 11th-grade students in American public secondary schools).

_____ b. Random sample from a local or regional population (e.g., all science teachers in California high schools).

_____ c. Nonrandom sample from a national population (e.g., 6th-grade pupils from 30 schools who volunteered to participate).

_____ d. Nonrandom sample from a local or regional population (e.g., all students taking Introductory Psychology at Stanford University).

_____ e. Other; describe: _____

_____

_____

Measures

Check each measure used and enter the following information:

Col 1. Name of measure: _____

Col 2. Indicate age or grade level that measure is appropriate. If none given, write "N."

Col 3. Is it a published measure (P) or an experimental measure (X); i.e., developed by another investigator for use in research?

Col 4. Reliability coefficient. If more than one is given, write in all. If none is given, write "N."
Col 5. Validity evidence:
  a. Evidence is described (enter validity coefficients if given).
  b. Author says measure is valid but gives no evidence.
  c. References that purport to give evidence are cited.
  d. Validity is not mentioned.
Col 6. Is this measure worth reviewing for possible use in your school or district? Indicate *yes* or *no*.

Name of measure	Level	Pub.?	Rel.	Val.	Poss. use?

Remarks: _____

_____

_____

RESULTS

1. Summarize results that are reported as statistically significant and give significance level: _____

_____

_____

2. Which of the above results are sufficiently large to be of practical significance? Indicate these with an asterisk.

3. Your evaluation of the results: _____

_____

_____

APPENDIX 2

SAMPLE ARTICLES

The following articles have been selected to provide additional examples of various research designs, measurement procedures, and analysis procedures. All articles included are exemplary, although all have limitations that the student should watch for. The articles report findings that will be of interest to most teachers, school administrators, and graduate students in education.

CHAPTER 5

BANGERT, R. L., KULIK, J. A., & KULIK, C. C. (1983). Individualized systems of instruction in secondary schools. *Review of Educational Research, 53,* 143–158.

GRAUE, M. E., WEINSTEIN, T., & WALBERG, H. J. (1983). School-based home instruction and learning: A quantitative analysis. *Journal of Educational Research, 76,* 351–360.

CHAPTER 8

CRONNELL, B. (1985). Language influences in the English writing of third- and sixth-grade Mexican-American students. *Journal of Educational Research, 78,* 168–173.

NAFPAKTITIS, M., MAYER, G. R., & BUTTERWORTH, T. (1985). Natural rates of teacher approval and disapproval and their relation to student behavior in intermediate classrooms. *Journal of Educational Psychology, 77,* 362–367.

REEVES, C. K., & KAZELSKIS, R. (1985). Concerns of preservice and inservice teachers. *Journal of Educational Research, 78,* 267–271.

RIDLEY-JOHNSON, R., COOPER, H., & CHANCE, J. (1983). The relation of children's television viewing to school achievement and I.Q. *Journal of Educational Research, 76,* 294–297.

SASSENRATH, J., CROCE, M., & PENALOZA, M. (1984). Private and public school students: Longitudinal achievement differences. *American Educational Research Journal, 21,* 557–563.

VELDMAN, D. J., & WORSHAM, M. (1983). Types of student classroom behavior. *Journal of Educational Research, 76,* 204–209.

YAGER, R. E., & YAGER, S. O. (1985). Changes in perceptions of science for third, seventh, and eleventh grade students. *Journal of Research in Science Teaching, 22,* 347–358.

CHAPTER 9

BUTLER, S. R., MARSH, H. W., SHEPPARD, M. J., & SHEPPARD, J. L. (1985). Seven-year longitudinal study of the early prediction of reading achievement. *Journal of Educational Psychology, 77,* 349–361.

HANNA, G. S., & SONNENSCHEIN, J. L. (1985). Relative validity of the Orleans-Hanna Algebra Prognosis Test in the prediction of girls' and boys' grades in first-year algebra. *Educational and Psychological Measurement, 45,* 361–367.

SMITH, L. R. (1985). Presentational behaviors and student achievement in mathematics. *Journal of Educational Research, 78,* 292–298.

HALPIN, G., HARRIS, K., & HALPIN, G. (1985). Teacher stress as related to locus of control, sex, and age. *Journal of Experimental Education, 53,* 136–140.

KAISER, C. F., & BERNDT, D. J. (1985). Predictors of loneliness in the gifted adolescent. *The Gifted Child Quarterly, 29,* 74–77.

NICHTA, L. J., JR., FEDERICI, L., & SCHUERGER, J. (1982). The Screening Test of Academic Readiness (STAR) as a predictor of third-grade achievement. *Psychology in the Schools, 19,* 190–193.

TSAI, SHIOW-LING, & WALBERG, H. J. (1983). Mathematics achievement and attitude productivity in junior high school. *Journal of Educational Research, 76,* 267–272.

CHAPTER 10

FIELDING, G. D., KAMEENUI, E., & GERSTEN, R. (1983). A comparison of an inquiry and a direct instruction approach to teaching legal concepts and applications to secondary school students. *Journal of Educational Research, 76,* 287–293.

GIMMESTAD, B. J., & DE CHIARA, E. (1982). Dramatic plays: A vehicle for prejudice reduction in the elementary school. *Journal of Educational Research, 76,* 45–49.

KUNTZ, S. W., & LYCZAK, R. (1983). Sustained effects of Title I over the summer months. *Journal of Educational Research, 76,* 148–152.

MURPHY, H. A., HUTCHISON, J. M., & BAILEY, J. S. (1983). Behavioral school psychology goes outdoors: The effect of organized games on playground aggression. *Journal of Applied Behavior Analysis, 16,* 29–35.

SAIGH, P. A., & UMAR, A. M. (1983). The effects of a good behavior game on the disruptive behavior of Sudanese elementary school students. *Journal of Applied Behavior Analysis, 16,* 339–344.

SMITH, L. R. (1985). Teacher clarifying behaviors: Effects on student achievement and perceptions. *Journal of Experimental Education, 53,* 162–169.

TAYLOR, V. L., CORNWELL, D. D., & RILEY, M. T. (1984). Home-based contingency management programs that teachers can use. *Psychology in the Schools, 21,* 368–374.

WARNER, R. E. (1984). Enhancing teacher affective sensitivity by a videotape program. *Journal of Educational Research, 77,* 366–368.

INDEX